306.342
THR

D1584002

Knowing Capitalism

University of the
West of England
BRISTOL

BOLLAND
LIBRARY

14854/8
LL

Theory, Culture & Society

Theory, Culture & Society caters for the resurgence of interest in culture within contemporary social science and the humanities. Building on the heritage of classical social theory, the book series examines ways in which this tradition has been reshaped by a new generation of theorists. It also publishes theoretically informed analyses of everyday life, popular culture, and new intellectual movements.

EDITOR: Mike Featherstone, *Nottingham Trent University*

SERIES EDITORIAL BOARD
Roy Boyne, *University of Durham*
Mike Hepworth, *University of Aberdeen*
Scott Lash, *Goldsmiths College, University of London*
Roland Robertson, *University of Aberdeen*
Bryan S. Turner, *University of Cambridge*

THE TCS CENTRE
The *Theory, Culture & Society* book series, the journals *Theory, Culture & Society* and *Body & Society*, and related conference, seminar and postgraduate programmes operate from the TCS Centre at Nottingham Trent University. For further details of the TCS Centre's activities please contact:

Centre Administrator
The TCS Centre, Room 175
Faculty of Humanities
Nottingham Trent University
Clifton Lane, Nottingham, NG11 8NS, UK
e-mail: tcs@ntu.ac.uk
web: http://tcs.ntu.ac.uk

Recent volumes include:

Critique of Information
Scott Lash

Liberal Democracy 3.0
Stephen P. Turner

French Social Theory
Mike Gane

The Body and Social Theory, 2nd Edition
Chris Shilling

Knowing Capitalism

Nigel Thrift

U.W.E.

28 FEB 2005

BE

Library Services

SAGE Publications
London • Thousand Oaks • New Delhi

© Nigel Thrift 2005

First published 2005

Apart from any fair dealing for the purposes of research or private study, or criticism or review, as permitted under the Copyright, Designs and Patents Act, 1988, this publication may be reproduced, stored or transmitted in any form, or by any means, only with the prior permission in writing of the publishers, or in the case of reprographic reproduction, in accordance with the terms of licenses issued by the Copyright Licensing Agency. Inquiries concerning reproduction outside those terms should be sent to the publishers.

 SAGE Publications Ltd
1 Oliver's Yard
55 City Road
London EC1Y 1SP

SAGE Publications Inc
2455 Teller Road
Thousand Oaks, California 91320

SAGE Publications India Pvt Ltd
B-42 Panchsheel Enclave
Post Box 4109

British Library Cataloguing in Publication data

A catalogue record for this book is available from the British Library

ISBN 1 4129 0058 1
ISBN 1 4129 0059 X

Library of Congress Control Number 2004111069

Printed in India at Gopsons Paper Ltd, Noida

Contents

Preface and Acknowledgements

This book has gathered itself only slowly. I have tried to say something new about contemporary capitalism but this takes time, and in that time many elements of capitalism have changed: some of the key players in what I call the cultural circuit of capitalism have gone to the wall, business publishing is in crisis, the new economy has come and gone, financial boom has been followed by financial bust, and so on. This collection of writings spans nearly a decade and thus some references, some phenomena may already seem outdated: but this is also one of my main points. To analyse contemporary capitalism requires an ability to follow only a little way behind change: too far behind and what is written becomes merely academic; too close and the academic starts to take on the hyperbolic view of the future which is a part of how contemporary capitalism reproduces itself. I am sure that I have not always succeeded in this task of nearly analysis but, on the other hand, I am also sure that the task is a necessary one.

This book is therefore, on the one hand, a history and geography of the nearly present, battered this way and that by the power of events. But it is also, on the other hand, an attempt to show how that very uncertainty is increasingly being taken up and worked with by capitalism in ways which are productive of new kinds of aggregation and ordering which have most decidedly not been present before and which need pointing to, since on them are being built new means of reproducing an order which many would argue has life-denying characteristics.

However, I should also make clear that the criticisms that I have of capitalism are not those of many critics. I do not believe that capitalism is part of a neoliberal imperium or even a new kind of sovereignty. For all its undoubted powers, its strivings are far too tentative and incomplete for that. Neither do I believe that it is possible to have a grand programme for ridding the world of the beast. I think such programmes are born, as Hans Blumenberg (1985) would put it, out of a misguided desire to answer questions put by the great systems of Christian theology using the tools of modern reason – tools which were not made for that job and are badly bent out of shape when they are used to attempt it. In other words I accept as valid much more limited forms of critique: forms of critique which accept that the relations and practices on which capitalism rests are not all bad; forms of critique which are able to honour the 'local' as not just an instance of 'global' struggles; forms of critique that do not believe that the vanguard is always the place to be; forms of critique that understand their own situatedness and so live up to Foucault's dictum, 'a critique is not a matter of saying that things are not right as they are. It is a matter of pointing out on what kinds of assumptions, what kinds of familiar, unchallenged, unconsidered modes of thought the practices that we accept rest' (1998, p. 155). That is why this book has so many references to the power of creativity and intuition. For – as I will attempt to show – while these may be watchwords of contemporary capitalism, they are also the qualities that must be fostered in order to overcome many of contemporary capitalism's depredations.

I hope it is also clear that I do not therefore believe that it is necessary to be mealy-mouthed about some of capitalism's iniquities and cruelties, whether petty or great. But I will not, in the manner of some more declarative commentators, make too easy points which have as a consequence only the salving of the liberal conscience.

This book is the product of joint action in the spirit of generosity that I would dearly love to amplify. Many people have made an input to it, through either co-authorship, general wise counsel, or making comments on the individual chapters. In particular, I want to mention the help of Ash Amin, Andrew Barry, Mick Billig, Steve Brown, Michel Callon, Howard Caygill, Stephen Collier, Bob Cooper, Shaun French, Steve Fuller, Michael Gardiner, Paul Glennie, James Griesemer, Paul Heelas, Kevin Hetherington, John Hughes, Patrick Keiller, Scott Lash, Bruno Latour, John Law, Andrew Leyshon, Orvar Löfgren, Celia Lury, Gregor McLennan, Doreen Massey, Danny Miller, Rolland Munro, Kris Olds, Aihwa Ong, Tom Osborne, Alan Radley, Annelise Riles, Nikolas Rose, Saskia Sassen, Gregory Seigworth, Judith Squires, David Stark, Marilyn Strathern, Lucy Suchman, John Urry, Sarah Whatmore, and Steve Woolgar.

The author and publishers would like to thank the following for permission to use copyright material:

Taylor & Francis Journals for paragraphs in Chapter 1 from: 'Chasing capitalism' by Nigel Thrift , New Political Economy, vol. 6 no. 2: 375-380 (2001).

Routledge, Chapter 2: Thrift, N. J. (1997a) 'The rise of soft capitalism', Cultural Values, vol. 1 (1997): 29-57 and Thrift, N.J. (1997b) 'The rise of soft capitalism', in A. Herod, G. O. Tuathail, and S. Roberts (eds), Unruly World: Globalisation, Governance and Geography.

SAGE Publications, Chapter 3: Thrift, N. (1999) 'The place of complexity', in Theory, Culture and Society, vol. 16, no. 3. 31-70.

Berg Publishers, Chapter 4: Thrift, N. (1999) 'Virtual capitalism: some proposals', in J. Carrier and D. Miller (eds), Virtualism: The New Political Economy. pp.161-186.

Blackwell Publishing, Chapter 5: Thrift, N.J. and Olds, K. (2004) 'Cultures on the brink: re-engineering the soul of capitalism - on a global scale', in Ong, A. and Collins, S. (eds), Global Anthropology: Technology, Governmentalities, Ethics.

Taylor & Francis Journals, Chapter 6: 'It's the finance, not the romance' by Nigel J. Thrift, Economy and Society, vol. 30: 412-432 (2001).

Blackwell Publishing, Chapter 7: Thrift, N. (2000) 'Performing cultures in the new economy', *Annals of the Association of American Geographers*, vol. 87: 674-692.

Blackwell Publishing, Chapter 8: Thrift, N. and French, S. (2002) 'The automatic production of space', *Transactions of the Institute of British Geographers*, NS27, 309-335.

Arnold Journals, Chapter 9: Thrift, N. (2003b) 'Closer to the machine? Intelligent environments, new forms of possession and the rise of the supertoy', *Cultural Geographies*, 10 (4): 389-407.

Taylor & Francis Journals, Chapter 10: 'Electric animals' by Nigel J. Thrift, *Cultural Studies*, vol. 18: 461-482 (2004).

Pion Ltd, Chapter 11: 'Remembering the technological unconscious before grounding knowledge of position' scheduled for publication in *Environment and Planning D: Society and Space*, 2004, vol. 22, issue 1: 175-190.

1

Adventures of Capitalism

Business art is the step that comes after Art ... Being good in business is the most fascinating kind of art. (Andy Warhol, cited in Taylor, 2001, p. 233)

There are no bad ideas. (Rasiel, 1999, p. 97)

Alas, it is fast, it is digital: still one is bored. (Ciborra, 2002, p. 172)

Introduction

This is a book about what happened when capitalism began to consider its own practices on a continuous basis. This is a book about what happened when capitalism began to use its fear of uncertainty as a resource. This is a book about what happened when capitalism began to circulate new ideas of the world as if they were its own. This is a book about what happened when capitalism began to intervene in, and make a business out of, thinking the everyday. This is a book about capitalism at (serious) play.

I can hear the complaints now. Surely, capitalism is a system of oppression whose only purpose is to grind out mass commodities? And surely its Dionysian side is just one more symptom of its wrong-headedness?

But it is precisely these kinds of automatic responses that I want to take issue with in this book. For quite a few people, capitalism is not just hard graft. It is also fun. People get stuff from it – and not just more commodities. Capitalism has a kind of crazy vitality. It doesn't just line its pockets. It also appeals to gut feelings. It gets involved in all kinds of extravagant symbioses. It adds into the world as well as subtracts.[1]

And it follows that I do not want to see capitalism as a kind of metaphysical entity, a grid of power relations rather like interconnected ley lines which lie under the social landscape and dictate much of what it is about. I take seriously the idea that capitalism is 'instantiated' in particular practices and that it is therefore better thought of as rather like a Foucauldian diagram, an impulse without determinate goals, a functioning which stamps particular forms of conduct on human multiplicity through 'distributing in space, laying out and serializing in time, composing in space–time, and so on' (Deleuze, 1986, p. 35). An unstable and fluid affair which constantly evolves, the diagram is 'almost blind and mute, even though it makes others see and speak' (1986, p. 35).

So what, more specifically, is my theoretical stance to capitalism? I take capitalism to be a series of relations of relation instituted over time through different organizations of time–space. These relations are rolled out as the world in three ways. One is via the kind of stance to the world adapted at each moment by actors of all kinds which assumes that that is how the world is. This stance is mainly pre-reflexive, written into the body and other spatial layouts through repetition. But since all repetitions include openings too, nothing can be permanently fixed. If every performance repeats itself, then every repetition also consists of an interval in which risk and excess can potentially disrupt the unproblematic bridges between events that is our anticipation of how the world is (Butler, 1991). The second is through the interventions of objects, from delivery schedules to barcodes to office lay-outs to charts to spreadsheets, that assume the world is actively mediated in particular ways and directs bodies and other objects along those ways. Then, the third way is as organizational templates that, instituted as practices, roll over particular ways of doing people and things, lighting up and sustaining particular territories, from subject positions to corporate cultures.

Such a stance in turn depends on a series of assumptions. One is that the world does not consist of unities or totalities. The unified field is a dream. Every system is overcoded and proliferates in only relatively stable and rel-atively predictable ways. There are all kinds of gaps and hesitations, excesses and remainders, which arise from the fact that all kinds of things other than capitalism are constantly going on which constitute lines of interference which can never totally be tuned out. Opacity, division and wildness result. Second, the world always comes loaded with ethical content. It certainly contains multiple spaces of oppression and lockdown, but it also contains little spaces of joy and generosity which cannot be locked out. There can never be a pure morality of law derived from a supersensible realm (Connolly, 1999). This is a world that is hybrid and must negotiate. Third, the world is still enchanted (Thrift, 1997a). I have no truck with accounts of capitalism that insist that capitalism has disenchanted the world. The world of capitalism is best seen, I think, as one closer to the imaginary of the medieval world of dark superstitions and religious bliss than we fondly choose to believe (Miyazaki, 2003). I just do not accept that history has rolled as far forward as the theorists of modernity would like to tell us. I am not at all convinced that the managers of capitalist firms – jointly or sever-ally – know what they are doing for quite a lot of the time. And I am sure that commodities retain their ability to animate us in ways which are not just extensions of commodification, and which can still catch us up in minor pleasures and inspirations that reflect affective-cum-ethical concerns (Bennett, 2001) as well as slavish compliance.

Which brings me to the four methodological rules that I insist on when analysing contemporary capitalism. One is that it is important to deploy what I have called elsewhere a 'backward gaze'. That means thinking rather as a historian from the future might, looking back at our present time and seeing vast numbers of unresolved issues, differences of interpretation and general confusions, exactly as historians see the past now. This is in contrast to many social theorists who too often let their historical imagination atro-phy in order that they can make large claims about 'modernity', which are meant to set the seal on history, to wrap everything up.

Another is that I take it that most historical events have a good deal of contingency built into them. Capitalism could have (and has) gone in a number of different ways and many of the ways that it has proceeded on are the cumulative result of 'small' events that, at the time, no doubt, seemed to have little significance:

> to follow the complex course of descent of accidents is to maintain passing events in their proper dispersion; it is to identify the minute deviations – or conversely, the complete reversals – the errors, the false appraisals, and the faulty calculations that gave birth to these things that continue to exist and have value for us. (Foucault, 1970, p. 146)

This is hardly news – after all, many economists now recognize (albeit partially) this phenomenon in their emphasis on increasing returns to scale, path dependence, and the like – but it is important because it has seemingly suggested to many corporate strategists that the spoils go to those able to take advantage of events as they unfold, able to be prepared for surprise, able to become skilled at harnessing the 'power of now' (Ranadive, 1999).

Thus, and this is a further rule, capitalism is performative: it is always engaged in experiment, as the project is perpetually unfinished. Capitalism is therefore a highly adaptive and constantly mutating formation; it is a set of poised systems (DeLanda, 2002). The whole point of capitalism, then, is precisely its ability to change its practices constantly, and those who run corporations must be able to surf the right side of the constant change that results, or risk being washed up on the reefs of irrelevance – and thrown into bankruptcy. (It is always worth remembering just how few capitalist firms survive over the long term; surely Schumpeter was right to argue that capitalism is a flawed leviathan arising out of creative destruction.)

But, there is one more rule: always look for the routine, even boring, as well as the sexy. It is all too easy to get carried away and depict capitalism as a kind of big dipper, all thrills and spills. But capitalism can be performative only because of the many means of producing stable repetition which are now available to it and which constitute its routine base (Miyazaki and Riles, 2004).[2] Chief amongst these means of producing the everyday life of capitalism – apart from the sheer unremitting hard work of so many labour forces – are two apparatuses which are particularly crucial. One is the whole apparatus of installation, maintenance and repair.[3] The other is the apparatus of order and delivery. For some reason, perhaps to do with their extreme everydayness, these apparatuses are constantly ignored in the literature and yet it could be argued that they constitute the bedrock of modern capitalism. As importantly, they have recently gone through their own revolution, born out of the progressive application of logistical knowledges of various kinds by large, specialized firms which now constitute a vital component of the knowledge economy.

To summarize, I regard capitalism as a set of networks which, though they may link in many ways, form not a total system but rather a project that is permanently 'under construction'.[4] Capitalist firms may be able to mobilize power and enrol allies but they are as uncertain about the future as we all are because the future unfolds as a virtuality – it is continually creating temporary actualizations out of new questions – not a known quantity, or at least a distinct possibility. So capitalist firms may sit on the bridge of the world, able at their best attempts to steer it in certain directions, but they still cannot know what is around the corner, whether it be an emerging energy crisis, a financial downturn, a set of protests that threaten a brand's image, or something more mundane like a cashflow crisis. This essentially performative notion of capitalism, conceiving of it as a continually renewed set of responses to new drivers, means that I see capitalism, to repeat, as a constantly mutating entity, made up of fields or networks which are only ever partly in its control. No matter how many assets are engaged, it must constantly face the pressure of unexpected events.

Such a Latourian-cum-Deleuzean notion of political economy as composed of a series of modulations is not without its ironies, of course. For it increasingly resembles capitalism's description of itself. As Boltanski and Chiapello (1999) have noted, there are clear homologies between the current Anglo-Saxon ideologies of capitalism and the writings of Derrida, Deleuze and Serres. They both set out a new moral plan based, in part, on the affective and the ludic, they both produce new figures of immanence (for example, the network[5]), and they both attempt to produce new practices which are resolutely inauthentic. What is clear is that we have reached a point in which the kind of divides that kept capitalists and anti-capitalists apart are not easily separated linguistically and, in some cases, even practically. Part of the reason for this is because the language of economics has become common linguistic currency, making it increasingly difficult to conceive of the world in any terms except those of a calculus of supply and demand. Then, it is a fact that capitalists and anti-capitalists alike often share many of the same tropes, of speed, flow, network, and so on. They both want to dance change and create community. An emphasis on pure Nietzschean action, in particular, is one that can be found equally in currency markets and on anti-road protests (Barry, 2001). Then, finally, capitalist firms have taken on some of the language and practices of the opposition, moving from an emphasis on an overall strategy to something more closely approximating de Certeau's tactical interventions, as in how they enact decisions (cf. Weick, 2001), how they create innovative 'communities' (Wenger, 1999; Wenger et al., 2002), and how they market commodities (as in recent attempts to engineer 'smart mobs' and the rise of 'viral' or 'buzz' marketing: e.g. Rheingold, 2002; Barabasi, 2002; Buchanan, 2002). In other words, capitalist firms are increasingly utilizing the weapons of the weak – contextual fleeting practices – to make themselves strong (Wenger, 1999; Clippinger, 1999).

Elements of a new political economy

One of the chief aims of this book is to rework certain elements of political economy for these uncertain times. Not all elements, note. But some. This is not a book which is trying to wrap up what is going on in some enormous theoretical infrastructure, not least because I think there are good theoretical reasons for suggesting that this kind of slab thinking is trying to complete an impossible task. But I do think it is possible to shine some light on the current situation, particularly by listening hard.6 Straightaway, however, I want to argue against taking three particular routes as the be-all and end-all of a contemporary political economy, not because I think they are unimportant, but because I do not think that they lie at the heart of what is new about contemporary capitalism. One is to lay an undue emphasis on money and finance. Even in continental Europe, the 'financialization' of the economy is now a fact of life, as are its effects – rampant speculation, asset price bubbles, and so on. Though an event like the 'new economy' was in large part an asset price bubble, driven by the demands of new and extreme kinds of financial 'discipline' (such as shareholder value), aided by the advent of new kinds of financial instrument, fuelled by the spread of pension funds, mutual funds, and middle class financial literacy, and buttressed by all-too-familiar forms of greed and avarice, it constituted, I believe, not a new development but rather a more extreme version of past developments. The second is to lay an undue emphasis on information technology. Though one could hardly argue against the view that the rise of information technology (and especially software) is an important development which is a necessary background to much of what is going on in contemporary capitalist economies – as I will show below – I believe that it should be seen as having differential effects on numerous circuits of practice, rather than as having a uniquely determining effect of its own. In other words, information technology is both more and less important than it is often depicted to be. The third is to argue that there has been a major shift in the regulation of the rules of possession. It is surely the case that new prescriptive and normative frameworks have been coming on apace arising out of new legal orthodoxies, the proliferation of global actors and the assembly of different kinds of commodity. In turn, it may be that these frameworks presage new bundles of rights of ownership and even new commodity forms (for example, in the realm of bioscience). But I am not convinced that, so far at least, this process has been more than an incremental evolution of past practice, impressive though that evolution undoubtedly is (cf. Dezalay and Garth, 2002b).

What is most interesting about contemporary capitalism is how these juggernauts of finance and information technology and regulation have interwoven with new developments to produce new possibilities for profit. It is to these new developments that I now want to turn.

So how has contemporary capitalism produced the goods? I want to suggest an account which I will amplify in this book, which concentrates on three particular arenas: the discursive power of what I call the 'cultural circuit' of capitalism, the changing form of the commodity, and the pivotal role of space and time as not merely metrics but resources.

So one development I will consider in detail is the extraordinary discursive apparatus which has been perhaps the chief creation of the capitalism of the post-1960s period, and which I call the 'cultural circuit' of capitalism – business schools, management consultants, management gurus and the media. This has produced a process of continual critique of capitalism, a feedback loop which is intended to keep capitalism surfing along the edge of its own contradictions. The development of this circuit is, I am sure, of pivotal importance for at least four reasons. To begin with, it has made capitalism into a theoretical enterprise in which various essentially virtual notions (network, the knowledge economy, the new economy, community of practice) are able to take on flesh as, increasingly, the world is made in these notions' likeness through the power of consulting solutions – what Miller (1998) and others call the rise of 'virtualism'. Then, there is the emphasis that the cultural circuit has placed on the body. Much of modern capitalism is concerned, in a touchy-feely replay of Taylorism, with producing new kinds of managerial and worker bodies that are constantly attentive, constantly attuned to the vagaries of the event, through an emphasis on the ludic and affective. Again, there is the important fact that the cultural circuit itself constitutes a new and vibrant set of markets for capitalism. Its thirst for information technology, expertise, and all kinds of infrastructure is self-reinforcing. Then, last, the cultural circuit can be seen as a means of vacuuming up all those knowledges which have evaded capitalism until now: for example, knowledges which are transmitted through gossip and small talk which often prove surprisingly important are able to be captured and made into opportunities for profit via artefacts like new kinds of office space and tightly knit teams.

Another way of interpreting the rise of this cultural circuit is as the latest permutation of a knowledge economy which has been growing since at least the latter part of the eighteenth century (Mokyr, 2001). In particular, Mokyr (2001) identifies the main boost to early industrialization as arising out of the conglomeration of a vast array of social networks which conveyed not just theoretical or what he calls propositional knowledge but also all manner of 'useful knowledge' of practice and technique, what he calls prescriptive knowledge. The combination of these networks and various technological advances (in transport, metrology, visualization, and the like) radically reduced costs of access to information, most especially to 'how to' prescriptive knowledge, producing a 'knowledge revolution'. What the cultural circuit represents is the latest phase of this process, the dissemination of what had hitherto been high-flying management theories on a mass scale in the guise of all manner of small-scale 'how to' practices through a new conglomeration of social networks, in a mass sharing of management expertise (e.g. Ackerman et al., 2003). A good proportion of these management theories were directly or indirectly concerned with creativity and innovation, and one way of looking at the knowledge revolution inspired by the cultural circuit of capital is as the routinization of innovation, or even the bureaucratization of innovation, as what had been exceptional practices carried out by only a few firms or consultancies (such as project organization) became routine means of attempting to manage change fruitfully, organize continuous innovation, and, in general, raise productivity.[7] It is, of course, debatable whether any of these goals were actually reached but, in a sense, it is also irrelevant: these practices had become a key part of the everyday life of so many firms that they had sunk into the corporate background. And, of course, they also had the useful rhetorical by-product of defining what knowledge was useful, so completing the circle.

A second development I want to point to that the new political economy must take note of is new forms of the commodity and commodity relation. I would argue that consumption in the West has been boosted to such an extent that it has begun to produce new commodity forms bound up with new kinds of relation. Most particularly, these forms are intimately bound up with the increasing mediatization of everyday life, as the various media become ubiquitous, ambient presences in our lives (Bolter and Grusin, 1999; McCarthy, 2001), always present, always on.[8] In turn, the self-evident world of things has become something more complex, more evanescent (Attfield, 2000; Molotch, 2003). This new world registers itself in several ways. To begin with, there is the ubiquity of the brand, those small ideographs which, though they exist right on the edge of perception, are able to contain so much (Lury, 1999; Thrift, 2000a). Then there is the refashioning of the bounds of the commodity. Thus, for example, commodities may increasingly be delivered as time-limited rights to streams of content (Rifkin, 2000). Again, commodities are becoming increasingly animated. This does not mean simply that consumer objects have become more interactive – though through the auspices of Internet and wireless technologies, consumers and producers now increasingly interact jointly to produce commodities, and, increasingly, commodities become objects that are being continuously developed (as in the case of, for example, various forms of software). Rather, more and more consumer objects are becoming part of an animate surface that is capable of conducting 'thought'; thought is increasingly packaged in things. And, as a parting shot, commodities are increasingly carefully designed to produce strong affective cues that will amplify their effectivity by lodging them firmly in the phenomenal register. Indeed, the growth of an 'experience economy', whose concern is to construct rich experiences that will make their inventors rich, by working at the intersection between performance and reliable repetition, looks set fair to become one of the key elements of future capitalist economies (Pine and Gilmore, 1999). These changes in the form of the commodity also point to the increasingly active role that the consumer is often expected to take. Consumers are expected to make more and more extravagant investments in the act of consumption itself, through collecting, subscribing, experiencing and, in general, participating in all manner of collective acts of sensemaking.

Another way of considering the new commodity form is as the application of knowledges that were originally generated in the 1940s and 1950s around systems theory and allied developments (cf. Hayles, 1999; Mirowski, 2002). These knowledges allowed minimal representations of commodities to be constructed for the first time around a few simple concepts like equilibrium, entropy, open and closed systems, metasystems, homeostasis and feedback (Beer, 1972; Simon, 1981; Wilden, 1968). Gradually, as gathering expertise (and especially developments like the reworking of homeostasis into autopoiesis and the new outgrowths of systems theory like complexity theory which emphasize non-linearity) combined with all manner of new organizational technologies (from market research to databanks to novel metrologies) and new means of representation (such as novel advertising techniques and especially branding), so it became possible to operationalize these representations in the small interstices of space and time, thereby producing a new field concerned with the management of impressions through the efficient use of expression (Lury, 1999; Manovich, 2001; Rasch and Wolfe, 2000), a field of what might be called the elementary forms of capitalist life.[9] In particular, the idea that affect and sensation could be the object of systematic intervention has been made possible through the design of new 'quasi-corporeal' spatiotemporal orders that arise directly out of events being able to be recast as super-empirical entities that in turn allow abstract maps of transformation to be generated which will catalyse movement. As Massumi puts it:

> The activity of the actor is less to imitate a character in a script than to mimic in the flesh the incorporeality of the event. Blank mimicry is supplemented seeing (acting injected with real passion and yielding real change) and seeming supplemental (the attainment of real passion and real change through the staging of the body in suspended animation). The rig, the order word, the question–response, induction, possession, ventriloquism, the development of an emotionally charged ideal of unity and the quest to reach that ideal – all these are technologies for making seeming being, for making a life of acting, for making something unified of supplementarity, something central of liminality, for filling the fractal rim to make a (w)hole. (2002, p. 64)

Then, third, the new political economy is being constructed through new spatial forms that are not just incidental to some supposed overlaying capitalist dynamic but are what capitalism is. I emphatically do not mean by this to suggest the kind of scalar geographies so beloved of many writers of late for reasons I quite fail to understand.[10] I mean something more complex and less able to be so neatly packaged. To begin with, I would point to the means by which transnational corporations are altering their spatial dynamics so that they can make best use of loop forms (Manovich, 2001), from new forms of merchant subcontracting, which mean that capitalism can often forgo many production risks, through the new kinds of logistical networks that make it possible to shrink inventory and produce event-driven firms, to the new logistical software which is able to represent and track all the movements and communications within a firm (Amin and Cohendet, 2003).

Then, there is the appearance of new spaces of production, machines for living like Swindon and Milton Keynes in the UK, which in future years will, I am sure, be looked back on as frontier towns, experiments in producing new decentralized landscapes. The 'big sheds' and massed ranks of housing which typify such spaces, often incorporating important architectural innovations, and the obeisance to total mobility that they stand for, are indexes of a new class sensibility which is not as easily dismissed as its old-fashioned critics might like. And, as one more take on spatiality, there are the myriad spaces of consumption that now criss-cross the landscape, many of them carefully designed – from their architecture to their musical background (de Nora, 2000) – to produce the hard sell in new, more seductive ways. Geographers and anthropologists have spent a large amount of time considering these spaces (e.g. Miller et al., 1998) and they are now being joined by writers from other disciplines.

Another way of considering these changes returns us in part to Massumi. It is the increasing ability that capitalist firms have to micro-engineer space and time. This ability manifests itself in two ways. One is signified by the recent rash of books and papers on the history of topics like cinematic space and time (e.g. Crary, 1999; Doane, 2002; Bruno, 2002) – only one of many indicators of the ways in which our time is resurrecting topics which find a particular resonance now. For what we can see in these works is precisely a prehistory of the invention of new concepts, percepts and affects which might sway populations in new ways and which have now become second nature to us. What is interesting about the present conjunction is the way in which a new battery of concepts, percepts and affects is now being invented which are boosting old reactions and adding a layer of new ones. In particular, these concepts, percepts and affects rely on the mobilization of very small spaces and times to produce a naturalized world which consists of an increasingly tight-knit grid of all kinds of theories of these spaces and times put into practice through instruments like software, toys, robotics and surfaces, ranging from theories of cognition, through theories of embodied knowledge, to more general theories gleaned from biology and ethology. The other way is through the micro-ordering of the apparatuses of installation, maintenance and repair, and order and delivery. One of the key sets of knowledges of the modern world is now logistical and, increasingly, this set of knowledges has become concerned with an analytics of space and time which will allow more and more objects to be sent and received as efficiently as possible, with obvious but still crucial effects such as driving down inventory, engineering faster production and consumption, producing new kinds of spatial arrangement, instituting continuous tracking and making so-called 'planful opportunism' routine. If I had to summarize what developments like these meant, it would be that something like a Spinozan world of geometrical order is being created in which the basic phenomenological correlates of the world (including affect) are founded on the universal rules and laws of nature; through the medium of artefacts like software, the world is being naturalized and an active and self-causing Spinozan universe is being brought into existence. Perhaps this will bring us the peace of mind which Spinoza sought – but I doubt it!

Each of these three developments needs to be seen in one other way: as a form of mass moral engineering. They are means of governing bodies and other objects for the sake of profit: through forging new practices of managing labour, many of which are designed to be internalized by both managers and workers, through the design of new commodity systems which have much greater affective potency and so a greater pull, and through the design of micro spaces and times which are intended to form a productive grid. These new means of *vitalization* could be described as a shift in governmentality, a theoretical infrastructure I deploy in a number of chapters in this book, although I have become increasingly sceptical of this terminology of late, most especially because it seems to me to be unable to easily deal with shifts in the nature of materiality.

What seems certain to me is that we need a politics which can measure up to these new developments – and that we currently do not have one. This is the task I have set myself in recent years under the guise of 'non-representational theory' (Thrift, 1996a). In particular, non-representational theory is concerned with attempting to hone existing practices and invent new ones that can provide performative counters to the prevailing notions of what constitutes knowledge and creativity, how the world is being commodified in new ways, and the increasingly fine macerations of space and time that both allow these developments to take place and spur them on. In finding new ways of forging responsible communities and ethical stances that can deal with these novel conditions, my project chimes with a number of others, for example Connolly's (2002) 'neuropolitics' and Massumi's (2002) various repotentializations of potential (see Thrift, 2003a; 2003c; 2004d). Each of these projects is necessarily modest in scope and hesitant in form, but they seem to me to provide at least the beginnings of a means of fighting back against some of the more insidious manifestations of attempts to capitalize the world down to the last millisecond and millimetre. Given space constraints, another book will take this political effort on.

Closing remarks

New and interesting forms of resistance to capitalism have been produced of late, many of them based upon a resistance to corporate power (Klein, 1999). Various groupings have been able to produce a kind of deconstructive acting-up which is able to use new technologies to its advantage (Barry, 2001). These new pragmatics have echoed through the Davos corporate establishment, producing insecurities which, in turn, are producing new (sometimes positive and sometimes worrying) developments, from a renewed emphasis on corporate ethics to a general interest – through the widespread application of information technology like radiofrequency identifiers (RFIDs) – in hyper-surveillance of the population. When these pragmatics are combined with more conventional means of representation (such as trade unions), they suggest that the lack of alternative imagined futures to capitalism that writers like Harvey (2000) have argued now exists may be less of a problem than might be thought. Indeed, I would argue that the world is replete with all manner of political interventions into capitalism which, though they may not amount to a 'democratic phoenix' (Norris, 2002), are full of promise and constitute a modern version of Bloch's (1986) politics of hope. Whenever I write this someone always tries to paint me as a Panglossian prater, not willing to do their bit in the great battle against neoliberalism, but once one sets aside the idea of politics as just about determinate political programmes with set goals, this seems to me a less telling criticism.

Adding to this weight of pragmatic imaginations making their way into the world is the large amount of work in the social sciences and humanities which is looking for ways out of the current world of greed and inequality. Indeed, what I find inspiring about the current conjuncture is precisely the interdisciplinary (or perhaps transdisciplinary) push by those who recognize that to understand contemporary capitalism we need to mobilize many heritages, many viewpoints, in order to build however temporary a vantage point before the machine moves on (Appadurai, 2000). Like Clough (2000), I believe that this means cultivating a different kind of academic positionality which we might call, following Simmel, 'the glance' – an attempt to produce writing which can function as critical direct action through its *close attention to the present*. Such quick-response writing to the quick responses of capitalism, located somewhere between academia and journalism, is currently starved of outlets and yet it seems to me that if we want to keep up with capitalism's ceaseless experimentation – and its constant creation of new trajectories of inequality (Williams, 2001) – we will need to cultivate this art more than any other. Otherwise, we will become disconnected from the very entity we wish to critique. The chapters in this book, though often foiled by circumstance,[11] were attempts to do precisely this.

The book is split into two parts. The first part charts the rise of an agency which I call 'soft' capitalism, signifying both this new formation's adaptive characteristics and its supposedly caring, sharing ethos. This form of capitalism has chiefly been conjured into existence by the discursive apparatus of the cultural circuit of capital which, through the continuous production of propositional and prescriptive knowledge, has the power to make its theories and descriptions of the world come alive in new built form, new machines and new bodies. I argue that this form of capitalism has become a remarkably powerful formation in a remarkably short time and is now a permanent feature of capitalism.

Not surprisingly, however, in the current economic slowdown, the cultural circuit is experiencing rough times. For example, business publishing has experienced a downturn in lockstep with the more general economic downturn: business books slipped from 5.8 per cent of total American book sales in 1999 to 4.2 per cent in 2001, as the celebratory tone of the 1990s was replaced by the more muted tone of the early part of the first decade of the millennium (*The Economist*, 14 November 2002).[12] The downturn has also been felt in the realm of business ideas. Many writers have expressed concern that firms in the 1990s suffered from 'initiative overload' and 'ideas indigestion' as they frantically tried to implement the next management fad (Abrahamson, 2004; London, 2003b). In turn this state of affairs has led to widespread cynicism about – or at least much greater care over – which consulting solutions to implement (Argyris, 2000), and to a general lack of management ideas which look like they might be the contenders for the next big idea. Certainly, business bestsellers at the moment tend to the pragmatic rather than the idealistic. A general and fairly obvious model can be suggested from this experience: business ideas sell better in booms, and the stronger the boom the faster the turnover. In recessions, business ideas are more difficult to sell and solutions tend to be more mundane. What such a model also suggests is that the cultural circuit of capital will be back in force when the global economy recovers.

The second part of the book then considers one particular outcome of this cultural apparatus, namely the so-called 'new economy' of the 1990s. I chart the rise (and fall) of this formation. I want to argue against the current tendency of those on both the left and the right to write the new economy off as nothing but a chimera, either because it did not produce large increases in productivity,[13] or because it was mainly media-driven hype (Gadrey, 2003), or because it was an enormous financial scam, a 'dot.con' (Cassidy, 2002) – or some combination of all three of these. I think more was going on than just some kind of crooked mood music.[14] In particular, I would argue that the new economy represented the first concerted global discursive operation of the cultural circuit of capital which involved attempts to describe itself to the world (as the 'knowledge economy'), to persuade itself that this was what the world was like, and to extend this description to the rest of the economy, and indeed to the world at large.[15] But perhaps the new economy's lasting legacy will prove to be the boost it gave to the unfolding of a digital environment that has increasingly begun to constitute a kind of 'second nature' which, through the metaphorical practices of computer code, is being used to understand and rework 'first nature' (Doyle, 1997). The result, I believe, is the beginnings of a radically new environment which will automatically refuse distinctions like 'nature' and 'culture' or 'human' and 'environment' or 'human' and 'non-human' as all sorts of 'non-organic life' (DeLanda, 2002) spread. Lest the reader automatically picks up an apocalyptic tone, one of my purposes in the second part of the book is to underline the extreme mundanity of this reworking of materiality: for me the future is likely to come in with a whimper, not a bang. I illustrate what I have in mind through a series of cuts: through software, new kinds of software-rich toy, the informational biotics of robotics, and all the new means of addressing the world that have allowed quite new kinds of time–space to arrive.

How to summarize this work? In the end, I have come to see it as 'the revenge of the 1940s and 1950s' so brilliantly laid out by Mirowski (2002). For it was then, or so I believe, that the bulk of the developments I document in this book were first laid down as working templates as a result of allied developments in the economy, science and the military (see Mitchell, 2002). These were the heady days of the invention of cybernetics and systems theory and of the first attempts to produce stripped-down versions of the world that could transgress what had been considered discrete ontological domains ('organic' versus 'mechanical', 'natural' versus 'cultural', and so on), that could be calculated, and that could be continually modulated. These were the days when many of the first management experiments were made which were attempts to humanize the workforce and allow it to use its creative powers – experiments that have now been converted into a full-blown technology of the body moving. These were the days when the potential of new forms of computer writing that came to be called 'software' first began to be understood (Campbell-Kelly, 2003; Ferry, 2003). These were the days when many key logistical techniques were invented. And so on. The question now is whether another renaissance can take place 50 years later which can be something lighter and less encompassing.

The chapters

The 10 chapters that follow all cleave to the idea of capitalism as a continual struggle to release new forms of representation that can capture how the world is, new forms of subject that can populate the world, new forms of commodity that can hold the world in their grip, and new forms of surface that can define how space and time should turn up in that world. The first part of the book is chiefly concerned with what I call the 'cultural circuit of capital' and its attempts to produce new styles of fast thought. The second chapter therefore outlines in some detail the genesis and evolution of this tightly interlocked set of institutions, responsible for strewing the world with knowledge of business and for making that knowledge of business into a business. In particular, it considers how the circulation of ideas seemingly garnered from almost any disciplinary nook and cranny became a normal part of the business of business. This aspect is taken up again in the third chapter. I consider the way in which ideas circulate in and through business and other arenas (like New Age activities) and become contagious things, concentrating on the suite of ideas known as complexity theory which proved a vibrant source for management thinking on organization in the 1990s (see also Maasen and Weingart, 2000). Since those days other near-academe ideas have also made their way on to the stage: I am thinking here of ideas like communities of practice (see Wenger, 1999; Wenger et al., 2002) and, more recently again, ideas centred around Watts's (1999; 2003) resurrection of Milgram's small-world ideas (see Barabasi, 2002; Buchanan, 2002). Complexity theory is making something of a comeback too, but reconstituted as a slightly more modest affair based on ideas like emergence (cf. Taylor, 2001; Urry, 2003).16 These ideas are repackaged and instrumentalized,17 and one of the most fascinating sets of relevant research questions must surely be concerned with their exact efficacy: how much of their content is left to be injected into practice? Are they just a thin veil of legitimation? And, what precisely is an idea anyway?

The next two chapters look at the hesitant but seemingly insuperable progress of the cultural circuit and its ideas out from its heartland in the United States into the world, concentrating especially on the Asia–Pacific region. The fourth chapter considers this progress in general. Its concern is to show how business ideas increasingly seem to know no borders because the institutions of the cultural circuit are being set up across the world. But it is also concerned to speculate about the degree to which local content is being injected into the circuit, producing ideas on, as just one example, brands, which are gaining larger exposure. The fifth chapter (co-written with Kris Olds) looks at the latest episode of this saga, the attempt to produce a major hub of business and other knowledge in Singapore which, in turn, would make Singapore into the chief node of the cultural circuit in the Asia–Pacific region. Singapore has become something of an experiment in government through management theory, for example by taking in the persons and ideas of management gurus like Michael Porter.[18] This economic-cum-geopolitical story continues to move ahead: since the chapter was finished other major world higher education institutions have continued to move into the island state in line with a target of 150,000 foreign students being in residence there in 10 years' time. For example, in 2003 it was announced that Duke University has agreed to co-operate on setting up a new medical school with the National University of Singapore, starting in 2006; and one report in the *Straits Times* suggested that Singapore would soon get a fourth university which would likely be an established foreign university (see Thrift, 2002, for a cogitation on the wider significance of these moves).

The second part of the book is concerned with one particular episode in the history of capitalism, the so-called 'new economy'. This phenomenon of the 1990s makes much more sense when it is placed within the discursive loop of the cultural circuit of capital, as I do in the sixth chapter. Then we are able to see how the discursive fuel that the cultural circuit supplied fanned the financial flames, producing a mutually confirming account. However, as I outline in the following chapter, what is also interesting about the new economy were the parallel attempts to fashion a new kind of self-discovering subject able to survive in this world. We will live with these attempts for some time to come, since many of the practices which became general in the 1990s and which are documented in this chapter have continued to maintain a hold – albeit in muted form – on business subjects, from managers to workers, and have also made their way out into wider arenas (and most notably the educational system), thereby changing our selves as they produce all manner of new communities.[19]

One interpretation of the new economy is that it was a flash in the pan, a rhetorical sleight of hand, but I think not. I believe the new economy is much better understood as a bringing forward of vast amounts of capital which in turn allowed (in amongst the hucksterism and ripoffs) some quite fundamental new products to be hastened into existence, a process that Brenner (2003) brilliantly labels 'stock market Keynesianism'. Thus, in the final four chapters I move my focus to the boost the commodity received from this influx of capital and the changing phenomenology that has begun to result as these new experiments with matter gain a grip.

So the eighth chapter (co-written with Shaun French) considers what happens when software appears in such profusion that it starts to become a key horizon of experience, a writing machine (Hayles, 2002) that is increasingly writing the world into existence through a progression based on a shuffling between loops which are all active simultaneously, which are constantly changing their character in response to new events, and which can communicate with each other in a kind of continuously diffracting spatial montage (Manovich, 2001) – the ultimate 'do' loop, if you like.[20] I take this change to be important for both its current and its likely future effects. There is a short but already famous piece of writing on the web which tries to envisage what programming languages would say if they 'could speak, really speak, not just crunch bytes and stream bits' (Burningbird, 2002). Called 'The parable of the languages', it envisages a time and space where the 200 odd extant programming languages can come together, loosen up, and speak of their problems. What is clear is that they all feel resentful about their lowly status. As C++ puts it:

> Without me entire industries would fail, banks would close, ships would sink, trains would crash. Why, I virtually run the world. Yet the only time I'm noticed is when a memory leak is found or an exception occurs, and then I'm cursed, and sworn at, and ruthlessly debugged with nary a thought for my sensibilities.

At the end of the story, the programming languages round on the markup language XML, rather than forming a united front. Quite clearly this story is a piece of whimsy, but it has a serious side too. For it brings to the fore the whole question of the nature of computer code: what it is, what it does, and whether it has any kind of agency. In this chapter, I want to examine that question in a little more depth by making a series of cuts into the enigmatic presence of code, understood both as a process of writing production (on which see Newman, 1998) and as a process of production of a writing world.

The two subsequent chapters then consider the case of how commodities have gradually moved to being a testbed for a new kind of world in which thinking (including affect) is partially relocated. As they have been loaded up with software, so commodities are increasingly able to be designed with powers to interact and adapt to their environment, powers that allow them to take on a much more active role in the world and become new kinds of cohabitee. Local machine intelligence certainly has the potential to become a persistent feature of everyday life (cf. Shneiderman, 2002). The first hesitant steps towards such a vision are now being taken and, as I endeavour to show in the ninth chapter, some of the most important testbeds turn out to be humble children's toys. Here, in the world of childhood, new ethologies are being formed that will begin to question what 'life itself' might mean – ethologies that are both grand and utterly mundane.

The tenth chapter takes the story of local machine intelligence on by concentrating on the more general case of robotics and the theoretical infrastructures that support it. As software plasters the everyday world with a new and active surface, so the character of the everyday world is being changed. This change is based on theoretical models of the world which are written into software and which have as one of their key roots particular notions of biology. How can one understand this new kind of everyday life in which theoretical models drawn from biology come back to haunt the surfaces that define us as they are incorporated in all manner of increasingly 'lively' devices? Obviously a series of characterizations could be made, but in this chapter I propose that one of the best of these may turn out to be that of the companion animal. Everyday life is chock full of these animals, yet they too are hardly ever remarked upon in the literature: their strange familiarity is so obvious that they are deemed to be unworthy of notice. But, as software makes the world increasingly lively, perhaps we should start to think of its agency, especially as it is incarnated in the rapidly proliferating number of independently mobile objects, as calling forth similar kinds of relationship of dominance and affection – and a pressing ethical task.

The final chapter rounds the book off by considering all the new spaces and times that are currently being brought into existence through the motif of the 'technological unconscious'. I use this term to signify the basic forms of positioning and juxtapositioning which make up the basic 'atomic structure' of the sendings and receivings of contemporary Euro-American life. Because of the potential vastness of the topic, the chapter concentrates on just one form of this positioning and juxtapositioning, namely the construction of repetition. The chapter provides a capsule history of how a very few templates of position and juxtaposition have become powered up into a capacious and effective background,[21] and an argument that in recent years the practice of these templates has been changing as a full-blown standardization of space has taken hold based on new modes of address. This standardization of space is gradually leading to the crystallization of a different kind of technological unconscious based on track and trace models which allow much greater 'planful opportunism' – and generate new kinds of spatial and temporal incongruity.

So, my agenda in this book is simple. I want to understand capitalism as a vital intensity, continually harvesting ideas, renewing people, reworking commodities and recasting surfaces – for the sake of profit, of course, but also because capitalism is now in the business of harnessing unruly creative energies for its own sake. Long ago now, Marx depicted capitalism as dead labour haunting the living, but I am not sure that this is an adequate description, for it gives credence to the notion of capitalism as a deadening force when, increasingly, capitalism has a kind of unholy vitality, a kind of double duty, to possess but also to create, to accumulate but also to overflow, to organize but also to improvise.[22] Such a process requires a long tether and, as new adaptive forms of possession have been invented, so that tether has had to become longer still. Thus, we are left with a force exerting something closer to modulation rather than outright control, something which concentrates on the process of process, on the construction of what Knorr-Cetina (2003) calls 'flow architectures'. This is not to argue that the company is being deconstructed, that most labour is no longer slaving away for little reward, that the market doesn't matter or that the laws of supply and demand have been put on hold. It is to argue that by concentrating on just some specific events in the recent history of capitalism which may be counted as, in certain ways at least, novel, it is possible to begin to disclose some institutions and mechanisms which we might well want to think twice about.

Notes

1   Recently Stengers, a writer with whose work I have considerable sympathy, has written in a somewhat similar vein that 'capitalism works like this – grabbing an opportunity and reacting as soon as possible to it. It is completely abstract thought and fits very nicely for young people, for whom it is fun' (2002, p. 252). But though this book documents all the ways in which capitalism has tried to promote new forms of fast thought, as will also become clear, it is also concerned to show that, through the addition of the institutions of the cultural circuit of capitalism, capitalism has added a formal cognitive capacity to its repertoire.

2   Very often, these means of producing stable repetition are based around things – from screwdrivers to paper (Sellen and Harper, 2002) to barcodes – that are coded as insignificant because they are physically small and/or so commonly used that they have sunk below the threshold of visibility. But these things are, in many ways, what lies at the centre of contemporary economies (cf. Finn, 2001). They are the everyday life of globalization.

3   It is quite remarkable how little attention has been paid to these activities, perhaps because they signal how often things go wrong. Yet a good part of the smoothness there is in the world is the result of all those things going on in Yellow Pages and similar directories of the mundane which are hardly ever studied. As interestingly, in this apparatus we find that the mimesis of learning on the job figures as one of the chief means of disseminating knowledge: again mimesis of this kind is still remarkably little studied, given its importance. For a particularly good discussion of the systematic tendency for things to break down, see Urry (2003).

4   Thus, I am much more interested in the formation of stuttering, chattering autopoietic circuits than in the kind of classificatory fields found in, for example, convention theory.

5   Though, as is pointed out in, for example, DiMaggio (2001), the network can take on many forms when it is operationalized.

6   The 'method' that I have used in this book consists of three elements: reading across a wide range of sources (from formal academic accounts through the press (broadly defined) to all manner of informal documents), observant participation (for example, talking on a fairly continuous basis to business people), and, in particular, looking for what I call chains of clues, where one piece of information seems to lead inexorably on to the next in a way which suggests that a trail is being followed but which is really an artefact of looking in the right place at the right time.

7   This bureaucratization drew on, for example, models of small-firm camaraderie in order to stimulate motivation and innovation and can be seen, at least in part, as an attempt by large organizations to mimic small firms (through teams and projects, open office space, high-touch environments, etc.). In one way the new economy can be seen as about the reassertion of bureaucracy, although the rhetoric suggested the opposite. Whatever the case, a whole rhetoric and practice of knowledge creation and integration has now become routine in large firms (cf. Pettigrew and Fenton, 2000).

8   As Gray puts it: 'In evolutionary prehistory, consciousness emerged as a side effect of language. Today it is a by-product of the media' (2002, p. 171).

9   In particular, these new forms no longer rely on the idea of interpretive frames that uncover hidden interior states. Rather they perform directly into the encounter.

10   So, I am not interested in scale, scale switching, etc. which simply resurrect old ways of thinking space. I take it that networks operate at all kinds of 'scales', no one of which is pre-eminent, since all depend on each other (Thrift, 1995; Latour, 2002; Latham, 2002). Little and large? I don't think so. Indeed, I would argue that such a depiction is actively disabling since it fosters lazy views of causality and, indeed, misunderstands how the world is put together. As Latour puts it, following Tarde, 'The macro is nothing but a slight extension of the micro' (2002, p. 122). Or as Tarde himself put it: '[My conception] in brief, is almost the reverse of that of Mr Durkheim. Instead of explaining everything by the so-called imposition of a law of evolution which would constrain larger phenomena to reproduce, to repeat themselves in some certain identical order, instead of explaining the small by the large, the detail by the big, I explain the overall similarities by the accumulation of elementary actions, the large by the small, the big by the detail' (cited in Latour, 2002, p. 125).

11   And, not least, the publishing lags and word limits of so many journals. Ironically, the chapters in this book originally appeared with rafts of footnotes (to which I own up to being addicted) which have had to be excised in order to fit the publisher's word length.

12   But, significantly, Dilbert's brand of cynicism continued to do well. 'This is when I shine,' said Scott Adams (*The Economist*, 14 November 2002).

13   In fact, because of severe measurement problems, no one can really be sure. For an extensive review, see Temple (2002).

14   Though the phrase points to the extreme difficulty commentators have in associating affect with the economy, even though it is clear that affect plays a crucial role in many economic situations and, indeed, that the history of a suspicion of the passions has been the key to a good part of the history of economic thought (see Amin and Thrift, 2002).

15   One major effect was a greater culturalization of the economy, especially in pursuit of intangibles like 'innovation' and 'creativity' (cf. Holmberg et al., 2002). See Osborne (2003) for a wonderful critique of this tendency.

16   The traffic is not all one-way, of course. Ideas like the tipping point (Gladwell, 2000) have circulated back into academe.

17   On this issue, see the excellent paper by Vann and Bowker (2001) on the dissemination of the idea of communities of practice, originally formulated by Jean Lave for quite different purposes.

18   Porter is unambiguously the world's leading 'business intellectual'. A study carried out in 2002 by Accenture put Porter at number 1, followed by Tom Peters, Robert Reich, Peter Drucker, Peter Senge, Gary Becker, Gary Hamel, Alvin Toffler, Hal Varian, Daniel Goleman, Rosabeth Moss Kanter, Ronald Coase, Lester Thurow, Charles Handy, Henry Mintzberg, Michael Hammer, Stephen Covey, Warren Bennis, Bill Gates, Jeffrey Pfeffer, Phillip Kotler, Robert C. Merton, C.K. Prahalad, Thomas H. Davenport, Don Tapscott, John Seely Brown, George Gilder, Kevin Kelly, Chris Argyris, Robert Kaplan, Esther Dyson, Edward de Bono, Jack Welch, John Kotter, Ken Blanchard, Edward Tufte, Kenichi Ohmae, Alfred Chandler, James MacGregor Burns, Sumantra Ghoshal, Edgar Schein, Myron S. Scholes, James March, Richard Branson, Anthony Robbins, Clayton Christensen, Michael Dell, John Naisbitt, David Teece, and Don Peppers.

19 I am uneasy about describing these communities as simulacra (e.g. Ezzy, 2001) as if they were all somehow inauthentic.

20 Already, the proliferation of code is producing a dynamic new ecology. Perhaps we will end up surrounded by a kind of junkyard of old code: 'Though from a distance [it] resembled vegetation, it was neither alive nor dead. It was just some mad old algorithm which, vented from a passing navigational system, had run wild and then run out of raw materials. The effect was of endless peacock feathers a million different sizes: a clever drawing ramped into three dimensions. Mathematics trying to save itself from death. Plush and velvety, surrounded by a vanishingly thin mist of itself, this structure defeated the eye at all scales. It did something strange and absorbent to the light. It lay brittle and exfoliated, fragmenting into a viral dust of itself, a useless old calculation which had accidentally become an environment' (Harrison, 2002, pp. 226–7).

21 I have found it useful to think of these frames as paratexts (Genette, 1999; Jackson, 1999), the frames which order texts. I am quite sure that these frames constitute a potent source of power, since they exist before the event, so to speak. Their *a priori* intervention is a large part of what Bauman (1998) calls the non-terrestriality of power that certain classes seem to experience. However, not all goes smoothly, of course. For example, RFIDs are currently the object of a sustained campaign of resistance from CASPIAN (Consumers Against Supermarket Privacy Invasion and Numbering). The motives of the leader of CASPIAN, Katherine Albrecht, illustrate that we still live very far from a modernist world: 'When I was eight years old, my grandmother sat me down after a visit to a grocery store and told me that there will be a time when people will not be able to sell food without a number, referring to the Mark of the Beast, Revelations 13. I made a promise to myself at eight years old that if there was ever a number to buy and sell food, I would stop what I was doing and fight it' (Rowan, 2003, p. 5).

22 Thus, I share the scepticism of Knorr-Cetina (2003) concerning the apparent predominance of network forms of organization based upon the needs of co-ordination.

2

The Rise of Soft Capitalism

Preamble

This first chapter is concerned with how we might understand 'capitalism' after the cultural turn which has swept across the social sciences and humanities. That task seems pressing. After all, all around us the adverse effects of what we call 'capitalism' seem to be pressing in, in ways which presage more uncertainty and insecurity for everyone.

It is not as if the proponents of the cultural turn do not acknowledge the importance of something called capitalism. They do, in one of three ways. First, capitalism can be generalized out to an all-pervasive cultural formation, usually through its migration into the symbolic realm. Second, capitalism can be elevated into something so self-evident that it can be trundled on whenever a connective explanation is called for. Third, capitalism becomes a reading. It can then be made into a transcendental haunting, both everywhere and nowhere.

In other words, the force of capitalism is acknowledged but it is turned into a necessary but empty foil for the cultural turn, included certainly, but allowed no life of its own, because it is always already accounted for (Morris, 1988).

The cultural turn involves, then, acts of homage to the importance of capitalism, which, at the same time, serve as a means of forgetting all about it and getting on to more interesting things. The results, at least, are clear. 'Cultural' analysis has become more and more sophisticated but it is mixed in with a level of 'economic' analysis which rarely rises above that of anyone who can read a newspaper (Eagleton, 1995).

Why has this situation arisen, and what can be done about it? I want to suggest that this act of amnesia is the result of three shocks which, together, have made it more difficult to 'see' capitalism, in part because these shocks are, ironically perhaps, counterpointed in capitalism itself. But in turn these shocks also provide us with some clues to how we might think about capitalism anew.

The three shocks which have produced the current situation are, in turn, political, technological, and theoretical. The political shock is the increasing stress on subjectivity and self, and the politics of recognition that accompanies it. We live in a world in which reflexivity is a part of the cultural background (Giddens, 1991; Beck, 1992). The technological shock is the rise of so-called information technologies based on telecommunications and the new possibilities of learning and knowledge they offer. The third shock is the rise of new forms of theory, based in part in the first two shocks, which stress decentredness, multiple times and spaces, and the discursive realm. Together, these shocks have obscured the importance of capitalism, by switching attention to other modes of domination, by obscuring or even rendering invisible the critical importance of human skills in what we call technology (Collins, 1990; Schaffer, 1996), and by throwing doubt on the certainty of representation.

Yet, in turn, these shocks have also provided us with new ways with which to approach capitalism, and what I hope to do in this chapter is to point to some of these new ways in an attempt to harness the cultural turn to new understandings of capitalism. Central to the discussion will be the idea that capitalism has become *knowledgeable*. Of course, information and its conversion into knowledge have always been a central concern of capitalism, but the cultural turn allows us to see this more clearly. This is not, however, an innocent activity in which the disinterested academic can simply look down from an Olympian height on what is arising, and for two reasons. First, academics are deeply implicated in the genesis of this more knowledgeable capitalism. Second, this more knowledgeable capitalism is increasingly impinging on what were once regarded as traditional academic preserves.

Therefore, this chapter is in four sections. In the first section, I outline the changing division of labour associated with the production and distribution of knowledge, which makes the relationship between academia and capitalism more complex and more interconnected than previously, and which makes the relationship between the self of the academic and the other of business a more tense and difficult one. In the second section, I accentuate this point by considering the ways in which the dominant discourse of what and how knowledge is has changed in both academia and business from what I call the Joshua discourse to what I call the Genesis discourse. In other words, academia and business have come to think more alike about thinking. Then, in the third section, I want to look at the process by which the international business community has come to adopt this new kind of discourse about what the world economy is like and how it has come to be an instrument of 'regulation'. I argue that this process of institutional and subject formation is giving rise to what I call soft or knowledgeable capitalism. Then, in the final section, I want to point out that soft capitalism, for all the caring and sharing rhetoric, still has hard edges which cannot be wished away but which can be fought in new ways – ways which, to an unknown extent, can turn the major tenets of soft capitalism back on themselves.

The groves of business? The business of academe?

The academic study of business increasingly emphasizes the importance of information and knowledge. There are numerous examples of this statement, but four will do to make the case. First, there is the growth of an information economics based on notions of transaction costs, information asymmetries, spillover effects, intangible and non-homogeneous commodities, and the like (see, for example, Stiglitz, 1994). Second, there is the growth of interest in learning by doing, that is in harnessing the full potential of the knowledge that is incorporated into the bodies of workers, including the potential to innovate (Nonaka and Takeuchi, 1995). Third, there is the growth of interest in a business history which considers the information infrastructures that typify business organizations (Bud-Frierman, 1994). Then, fourth, there is the growth of work that is based on investigating and elaborating the conventions that underlie the success or future of particular urban and regional economies. These conventions are, in effect, particular, culturally specific, information infrastructures, which are seen as the keys to economic success.

Why this interest in information and knowledge? Five reasons seem particularly germane. The first is the massive *increase in information*, consisting of an expansion in the volume of data that can be processed and transmitted per unit of time (Perez, 1985). The second is the increasing emphasis on *innovation*. Innovation necessarily involves the generation and deployment of information and knowledge, but the production of this knowledge is highly problematic since it involves 'non-convexities' (fixed, sunk costs, increasing returns to scale), the inevitable absence of a complete set of markets (since there cannot exist competitive markets for commodities that have yet to be conceived of, let alone invented), lack of homogeneity (since every piece of information produced must be different from any other piece of information produced, or it is not new knowledge), strong asymmetry (since the buyer cannot know all the information until the information is bought), and the degree to which knowledge resembles a public good (since it is difficult to appropriate all the benefits of a particular piece of information, and therefore difficult to exclude others from enjoying the benefits – indeed, it may be undesirable to do so) (Stiglitz, 1994). The third reason is the renewed emphasis on *fallibility*. The transmission of information and knowledge is usually noisy and incomplete, and decision-making can be organized in different ways which can amplify or diminish effects of this noise and incompleteness. Thus, one of the reasons why non-hierarchical organizations have become more popular in business is because they are more likely to give bad decisions a second chance to be rectified. The fourth reason is the increasing emphasis on *learning* in businesses, and most especially on learning by doing, as a means of maximizing an organization's potential. Then there is one final reason, the reason I want to concentrate on in the rest of this section of the chapter: the increasing *interaction between business and academe* (Strathern, 1995a; 1995b; Hill and Turpin, 1995; Readings, 1996). In a sense business has become more academic as academe has become more business oriented. It is no longer possible, if it ever was, to think of academia as an epistemologically privileged sphere. Similarly, it is no longer possible to write off business as though it was the haunt of the epistemologically challenged; business has become more 'intelligent' in a number of ways. To begin with, much of the workforce in many countries, and especially management, has become steadily more qualified. Then, it is possible to see the evolution of an independent intelligence community, produced by the business media (including providers of business information like market researchers), by research analysts and press commentators, and by the continually expanding framework of various forms of business education, all the way from Harvard Business School to Covey 'University'. Again, business has become more responsive to ideas from outside business, partly as a result of this new educational infrastructure.

There are, then, an increasing number of symmetries between academia and business, of which four are particularly striking. First, academia and business share many of the same concerns; for example, they share the need to transform information, of which there is a surfeit, into new knowledge. Similarly, they share the need to construct supple institutional structures which can react swiftly to change. Second, in both academia and business the increasing commodification of knowledge has only pointed to the value of knowledge which cannot be commodified, and especially to the value of practical knowledge – knowledge that cannot be written down and packaged (Thrift, 1985). Thus words like 'practice' and 'skill' have become an important part of the vocabulary of both communities. Third, both academia and business increasingly share many of the same vocabularies, of which the most prevalent is the notion of 'culture'. Fourth, the spaces of knowledge have become as critical to business as to academia. In a world in which more and more information is increasingly able to circulate and circulate rapidly, information *skills* are still highly concentrated in particular locations, in particular offices, in intra-organizational links and in firm networks.

Of course, these symmetries have disturbed the values and procedures of academia. For example, academics from both the right (Hague, 1994) and the left (Plant, 1996) have argued that, increasingly, the kind of static hierarchy of knowledge that was (apparently) typical of the period up to the 1960s – with academics in universities located at the top of the hierarchy as able to offer the best validated knowledge – is being replaced by a flatter, more diverse and more interconnected set of knowledge communities, which mount a real challenge to the pre-eminence of academia by concentrating on learning by doing, often at a distance. Plant puts it in this way:

> As Foucault writes, the 'University stands for the institutional apparatus through which society ensures its uneventful reproduction, at the least cost to itself'. Today's academy still has its sources in Platonic conceptions of knowledge, teaching and the teacher–student relationship, all of which are based on a model in which learning barely figures at all ...
>
> The academy loses its control over intelligence once it is even possible to imagine a situation in which information can be accessed from nets which

UWE LIBRARY SERVICES

care for neither old boy status nor exam results ... Released from its relation to teaching, learning is no longer coded as study and confined to some particular zone, specialised behaviour or compartmentalised period of time. A lecturer no longer controls the process, ensuring the development of well-rounded individuals one step at a time, serial fashion: those once defined as students learn to learn for themselves. (1996, pp. 207–8)

This situation is uncomfortable. There are four possible responses. One is to flee from it. Some of the cultural turn might be interpreted in this way, as a retreat into the attics as the rest of the house is flooded out (although, ironically, it is increasingly a retreat to the examination of consumer products which are produced by capitalism). Another response is to simply condemn it. This is easy enough but gets us nowhere. The third is to embrace it. Plant's ideas, thoughtful though they undoubtedly are, are closer to the designs of modern business than she might think. The fourth response, the one I want to make in this chapter, is to try to face the dilemmas produced by such thinking by realizing that theoretical developments now routinely leak across the old boundaries between academia and business and, in turn, these developments are helping to produce a new form of capitalism, what I call 'soft capitalism'.

The Joshua and Genesis discourses

Discourses are metalanguages that instruct people how to live as people. They are best represented as great rivers of communication, performances propelled into movement by talk and text, enflamed by technologies like books, visual images, and other 'media', guided by procedures like rules and styles, and crowned by significant effects like particular subject positions or emotional states which establish the cultural importance of a discourse at gut level, and allow it to kick in (Gumbrecht and Pfeiffer, 1994; Thrift, 1996b).

One of the prevalent discourses in western intellectual cultures of the last two thousand years, a discourse which has waxed and waned and which has adjusted to historical custom but which still holds to a series of central tenets, has been what Jowitt (1992) calls the 'Joshua discourse'. This is a discourse that is founded on the idea of transcendental rationality, on the notion of a single, correct, God's-eye view of reason which transcends (goes beyond) the way human beings (or indeed any other kinds of things) think, and which imparts the idea of a world that is 'centrally organized, rigidly bounded, and hysterically concerned with impenetrable boundaries' (1992, p. 306). This discourse usually involves a series of linked and self-supporting tenets (Lakoff, 1987), such as that:

• The mind is independent of the body; reason is a disembodied phenomenon.

• Emotion has no conceptual content but is a pure force.

• Meaning is based on truth and reference; it concerns the
  relationship between symbols which represent things in the real world.
  Symbols are meaningless in themselves and only get their meaning
  by virtue of their correspondence to things in the world.

• The categories we use are independent of the world, defined only
  by the internal characteristics of their members and not by the
  nature of the people doing the categorizing.

But, beginning in the 1940s and 1950s with the work of philosophers like
Austin, Merleau-Ponty and Wittgenstein, the Joshua discourse began to
retreat. Further, more recent batterings by other intellectual-practical
communities like cognitive scientists, feminists and social theorists have
produced something close to a rout. So a new discourse has begun to take
hold, a discourse which challenges the idea that a God's-eye view of reason is possible. There are, instead, many rationalities, and these rationalities
are all:

• embodied, relying on our bodily natures

• going to engage the emotions, since feeling is conceptualized and
  conceptualization always involves feeling

• based on a notion of meaning as concerning symbols which are
  constitutive of the world and not just mirrors of it – which are, in
  fact, imaginative processes that rely on our capacity to produce
  images, to store knowledge of particular levels of complexity,
  and to communicate (Putnam, 1981)

• reliant on categories that are not independent of the world but
  are defined by upgraded processes (like metaphor, metonymy and
  mental imaging) which mean that there can be no objectively
  correct description of reality (this does not, of course, mean that
  there is no objective world, only that we have no privileged access
  to it from some external viewpoint).

These tenets (Lakoff, 1987) lead to a view of the world that is very different
from the purified and purifying Joshua discourse, which we might call, after
Jowitt (1992) and Serres (1995a), the 'Genesis discourse'. It is a view of the
world in which 'borders are no longer of fundamental importance; territorial,
ideological and issue boundaries are attenuated, unclear, and confusing'
(Jowitt, 1992, p. 307). It is a view of the world in which knowledge has
become an archipelago of islands of epistemic stability in a sea of disorder,

fluctuations, noise, randomness and chaos. Whereas in the Joshua discourse order is the rule and disorder is the exception, in the Genesis discourse disorder is the rule and order the exception and, as a result, 'what becomes more interesting are the transitions and bifurcations, the long fringes, edges, verges, rims, brims, auras, crenellates, confines ... all the shores that lead from one to another, from the sea of disorder to the coral reefs of order' (Latour, 1987a, pp. 94–5).

Obviously, such a view has a number of consequences, of which two are particularly significant. First, the favoured epistemological stance is, to use Wittgenstein's (1978) feline phrase, 'not empiricism yet realism'. That may sound like a contradiction in terms but it is, in fact, an argument for a limited but not total form of relativism which holds that individuals understand the same domain of experience in different and inconsistent ways and that this is a necessary condition of knowledge (Diamond, 1991). Since even the most disinterested of analysts is engaged in social projects, any *a priori* claim to epistemological privilege is impossible. Second, knowledge is no longer seen as a form of empire-building in which 'a powerful critique is one that ties, like a bicycle wheel, every point of a periphery to one of the centre through the intermediary of a proxy. At the end holding the centre is tantamount to holding the world' (Latour, 1987a, p. 90). At best, knowledge is, in Lakoff's (1987) phrase, 'radial'. That is,

> central truths are true by virtue of the directness of fit between the preconceptual structure of experience and the conceptual structure in terms of which the sentence is understood. But most of the sentences we speak and hear and read and write are not capable of expressing central truths; they are sentences that contain concepts that are very general or very specific or abstract or metaphorical or metonymic or display other kinds of 'indirectness' relative to the direct structuring of experience. Not that they need to be any less true, but they aren't central examples. (1987, p. 297)

Discourses produce power relations. Within them, stories are spun which legitimate certain kinds of constructs, subject positions, and affective states over others. The myths and fables of the Joshua discourse were particularly powerful. Specifically, four of these myths and fables did serious work in producing a particular kind of world which is now so often called 'modern' that we no longer realize the cultural specificity of the description or the strength of the investments we have placed in it. The first of these myths was an old Enlightenment 'chestnut' – the myth of total knowledge. Somehow – though we don't have this facility yet – we could get to know everything that is going on. Every movement of an ant and every rustling of a leaf could be tracked and explained. Every human culture could be laid open to inspection and documentation. Every practical skill could be analysed down to its last detail and then transcended. This myth was supported by a second, that the world was set up in such a way as to allow this: the world was an ordered, homogeneous, quantitatively different multiplicity. The world was defined by oneness, consistency and integrity which, in turn, acted as an ideal terrain on which purified theoretical orders could operate and permeate. The third myth was of a material world which could be separated out from the world of the imagination, from the world of symbols and semiotics. There was no sense, therefore, of a world in which materials are interactively constituted, in which 'objects, entities, actors, processes – all are semiotic effects' (Law and Mol, 1995, p. 277). The fourth myth was one of individuality. This was the idea that knowledge comes from the operation of a god-like gaze which emanates from an individual focal point. Human capacities, therefore, could be framed as being the result of an innate endowment that every individual received at the point of conception. There was, in other words, no grasp of the individual as being a modulated effect (Thrift, 1991), of human capacities as arising out of:

> emergent properties of the total developmental system constituted by virtue of an individual's situation, from the start, within a wider field of relations – including most importantly, relations with other persons. In short, social relations, far from being the mere resultant of the association of discrete individuals, each independently 'wired up' for co-operative or enthusiastic behaviour, constitute the very ground from which human existence unfolds. (Ingold, 1995b, p. 17)

All these myths were often put together in one final myth of how we are now: the myth of the 'modern'. Somehow, human life (in the West at least) had transited into a distinctive historical space where everything was different and, well, modern. Most of all, 'modernity' was characterized by a condition of speed-up and transience which, in its main characteristics, happened to coincide with the four myths outlined above. First, supralunar organizations were involved in a whirl of constant information-gathering which fed into systems of control which produced an 'iron cage' of surveillance and discipline. Second, these organizations were supported by myths of instrumental rationality which allowed the world to be trussed up like a Christmas turkey, with nothing out of place. Third, and here was the lament, these organizations were able to drain sociality out of the world, leaving behind nothing but a systematized shell. Then, fourth, this world was therefore populated by anomic and hard-bitten individuals who had to develop all kinds of asocial survival skills. And there was, of course, a price to pay for this hubris. Not so slowly, but certainly surely, modernity builds towards a climax, usually involving a runaway apocalypse based upon either technology, or the arms race, or mass communications (Norris, 1995) in which, in one way or another, human subjectivity is annihilated.

Now these myths and fables arising out of the Joshua discourse are being recast. Thus, the myth of total knowledge is being replaced by a new one, in which knowledge is both partial and differentiated. The myth of homogeneity is being replaced by a myth of qualitative commotion: 'the best synthesis only takes place on a field of maximal differences' (Serres, 1995a, p. 91). The third myth is being replaced by one in which learning by doing binds the metal and material together. And the myth of the given individual is replaced by the notion of the socially constructed 'dividual', constantly telling stories of their self. The result is a view of the world as a constantly spooling production taking place on many different time scales and over many different spatial scales (Latour, 1993). In other words, the world has to be constantly brought into being through the hard and sustained work of constructing networks of translation and affinity.

Currently, these different myths and fables coexist. For example, contemporary accounts of the world economy after the demise of the Bretton Woods system of international economic management have broken to a greater or lesser degree from the Joshua discourse.

Thus, the first account of the world economy that is on offer is an apocalyptic one. A common reaction to change through history (Bull, 1995), this account reads events like the demise of Bretton Woods and the fall of the Berlin Wall as evidence of a millenarian condition. Laced with phrases like the 'end of history' (Fukuyama, 1992), and *fin de siècle*, such an account provides a cosy rest home for old intellectual habits like teleology and eschatology, as well as satisfying an alluring sense of the dramatic.

A second account of the world economy interprets events like the demise of Bretton Woods and the fall of the Berlin Wall as symbols of a new kind of modernity. Whether posing as 'hypermodernity', 'late modernity', 'postmodernity', 'supermodernity' or what have you, such an account usually retains some of the old features of modernity, most notably a sense of transience, fragmentation and anomie, but then either exaggerates these elements still further (as in Harvey, 1989) or adds in new defining elements (Beck, 1992; Giddens, 1991). This kind of work provides a resting place for social theorists who want to retain grand accounts of the world, but is also home to many social theorists who want to provide more accounts of the contemporary world (Alexander, 1995). However, even the most nuanced of these accounts rarely provide much of an anthropological sense, any sense of the world as a continually practised place in which the human is constantly redefined, and they thereby run the very real risk of exaggerating the differences between this era and previous ones.

That leaves a third, Genesis account of the world economy, one which acknowledges the importance of events like the demise of Bretton Woods and the fall of the Berlin Wall but sees them as both the distillation and the illustration of three of its crucial tenets. First, there is the difficulty of achieving sustained control of human systems, which bubble with a stubborn and constant creativity, and which therefore have a tendency to side-step established orders like the nation state. Second, there is the complexity of what we name in order to escape complexity. Thus systems like 'capitalism' and 'the market' which have apparently triumphed after the two Bs are now revealed, in the apparent absence of opposition, as made up of institutions which are manifold, multiform and multiple. There is no one capitalism or market but only a series of different capitalisms and markets which do not converge on a mean: thus capitalism and the market are seen as powerful – but not all-powerful. Third, there is the need to understand history as an undetermined unfolding, a fullness of events, a 'maximum of matter in a minimum of space' (Perniola, 1995, p. 8). We cannot know history as a clash of giant and opposing, almost natural, forces – tidal waves of economic and social change which sweep across the human shore. We can only know history as a more modest and complexly determined set of 'actor networks' (Latour, 1993; Callon, 1987) – practical orders which allow people and things to be translated into more or less durable entities which can exert force – or alternatively, using another language, as a set of complex systems:

> The development of the complex systems model that seems so salient to us in so many contexts, the model that seems to underlie the organization of our bodies, our groups, our work settings, our world – this model itself repudiates any notion of a structure built on one foundation, an explanation that rests on one principle. In turn the complexly interconnected world in which we now live seems to say that both the model and its implications fit the current nature of reality. All is in flux, order is transient, nothing is independent, everything relates to everything else, and no one system is ever necessarily continuously in charge. (Martin, 1994, p. 250)

Although this latter constructivist account may seem to be the most credible, in part because of the looseness of its storytelling structure which gives more points of entry to those who lack communicative resources, it is not without its own ability to generate relationships of power, and it is important to realize this. Nowhere is this point made clearer than in the intensely practical realm of international business where physical and nervous energies have to be constantly expended on the concerns of the moment. In this realm, just as in the intellectual realm, the Genesis discourse has gradually displaced the Joshua discourse; and, just as in that realm, in doing so it has empowered some groups (such as managers with higher educational qualifications, which increasingly include middle class women) at the expense of others (Van der Pijl, 1994). There is, in other words, as Foucault pointed out so often, no knowledge that is neutral, that is not a part of the power–knowledge couplet. A *cui bono?* question always lies waiting to be answered.

Coping with complexity: the rise of soft capitalism

In this section, I want to show that the kinds of cogitations which have been the subject of the previous sections have gained a purchase outside academic communities, especially in communities concerned with the management of increasingly global business organizations. I want to show that much of the managerial literature since the demise of Bretton Woods and the fall of the Berlin Wall is influenced by the principles of the Genesis discourse, and especially that the world economy is a messy place which we can never know entirely and that business organizations need to both acknowledge this fact and to gear themselves up to take what advantage from it they can. In other words, understanding of the world economy has shifted profoundly, and in a way which is increasingly constitutive. That is, this new managerial discourse is changing the shape of the world economy as much as the changing shape of the world economy is changing it (Daly, 1993).

In presenting this new managerialist discourse, it is important to be clear about its status. First, the discourse is not just an ideology. Thus:

> While it is undoubtedly true that these discourses and practices of work reform have played, and continue to play, an active part in reproducing hierarchies of power and reward at work, or that they have been consciously deployed at various times to attenuate the power of trade unions and their prerogatives for the reproduction of collective interests and the defence of collective rights, it is especially important to note that they are not simply 'ideological' distortions; in other words, that their claims to 'knowledge' are not 'false', nor do they serve a specific social function and answer to pre-formed economic needs. Certainly these discourses of work reform arise in specific political contexts, and have potential consequences, but they are not merely functional responses to, or legitimations of, already existing economic interests or needs. Rather than simply reflecting a pre-given social world, they themselves actively 'make up' a social reality and create new ways for people to be at work. (du Gay, 1996, p. 53)

In other words, the new managerialist discourse must be 'understood primarily as a form of rhetoric ... spoken by managerial professionals not to mention professors of management – in ways that are not necessarily coterminous with organizational practice itself' (Nohria and Berkley, 1994, pp. 125–6). It describes:

> a world that, literally, does 'not exist'. According to those who have developed the term there is no organisation that displays all the characteristics of a 'full' transplantation. The concept of a 'learning organisation' is extremely complex; few would be confident in knowing when they have seen one. 'Network' structures dissolve the boundaries between one organisation and another; with the virtual corporation the disappearing act is complete. (Goffee and Hunt, 1996, p. 3)

It is no surprise, then, that managers and workers presented with these new discourses show some considerable ambiguity (Martin, 1994).

Second, the discourse is not a hermetically sealed, unitary, and static order. It is made up of multiple strands of practice, it is contested, and it constantly changes as its proponents foster new conventions. But, for all that, increasingly it forms a background to how business is practised. Third, the discourse's reach is necessarily partial, geographically and organizationally. It started out within US firms and still retains its strongest hold there. It therefore bears the stamp of a US-style competitive individualism (Martin, 1994). And it is chiefly preponderant in the larger multinational business organizations which have the resources to institute it. 'Most of the world's working population continue to be employed in small or medium-sized (rather than "global") businesses; they earn their living in an identifiable "place"; they have familiar work routines; someone they identify as a "boss"; and so on' (Goffee and Hunt, 1996, p. 3). Even then, not all parts of the discourse are adopted equally: all kinds of combinations are possible. But the point is that it has become a part of the *background* hum of business around the world, soaking further and further into the practical order and used more and more often both to account for decisions and to bring decisions into being (Thrift, 1996a). It is the goal that becomes the means that becomes the reality.

For the new managerialist discourse, the period after the Second World War and before the demise of the Bretton Woods system and the fall of the Berlin Wall was a period in which striated spaces abounded: for one, the buttoned-down personality of the company man (Whyte, 1957; Sampson, 1995); for another, the enclosed, hierarchical world of the multidivisional corporation (Chandler, 1962; 1977), with its monolithic goals of achieving ever-greater size and scale by means of a single corporate strategy realized through a relatively static and formal bureaucratic inner core, which passed information upwards from an 'external' environment and exerted control slowly downwards from a closed-off headquarters. Then there were the rigidities that resulted from rules of nation states, like fixed exchange rates, high tariff barriers, and so on. And, finally, orchestrating the whole, was the idea of a management 'science' which would be able to produce the cognitive wherewithal to predict and thereby control the world. *At least in the rhetoric of the time*, then, the world was an organized place, made up of carefully closed-off spaces which could be rationally appropriated and controlled. (We might, of course, argue about the accuracy of that rhetoric, since any glance at the history of the time hardly suggests the stable, golden age of capitalism that is so often written about. Indeed, as early as 1965 management theorists like Emery and Trist were already writing about organizations that could deal with permanently turbulent environments.)

But from the 1960s on, as the Bretton Woods system declined and then later as the Soviet Union and Eastern Europe split asunder, so the state of permanent turbulence that Emery and Trist wrote about began to look more like a successful prophecy and less like a struggling prescription, and for a series of reasons, including the following. First, there was the floating of exchange rates, the growth of various offshore capital markets, and finally the growth of markets in financial derivatives, which has produced the merry-go-round of monetary transmission, offshore borrowing and lending, and various hedging strategies, flavoured with a dollop of pure speculation, that we take for granted today. Second, there has been the exponential growth of information generated by the intersection of the financial media, information technologies and economic research, which, in turn, have produced both more complex representations of, and more ambiguity in, the business organization's environment: the expansion of information has produced new solutions *and* new problems. Third, there has been the growth of numerous new players in the international business world, which have upset the old competitive equilibrium: the Japanese and Koreans certainly, but also now overseas Chinese firms, third world multinationals, firms from Eastern Europe, and so on. Fourth, there has been the growth of a more differentiated production–consumption nexus in which a more differentiated set of demands on mass producers produces more differentiated consumers, and so on, increasing both the range and the fickleness of many markets. Fifth, there has been a general speed-up in transportation and communications. This speed-up has had numerous differentiated, multiple, and sometimes contradictory effects which mean that it cannot be bracketed within a general description like 'time–space compression' (Thrift, 1995); but that there have been effects which have been sufficiently extensive to allow commentators to write of a world of flows (e.g. Lash and Urry, 1994) seems less open to debate. Sixth, as a result of these and other reasons, national economies have generally performed in a less coherent way which has made it even more difficult to predict economic outcomes.

For the managers of business organizations, the consequences are clear. First, almost any business organization is vulnerable. 'AEG, Boeing, Degussa, Gulf Oil, Sears Roebuck and many other famous enterprises have seen their market shares seriously eroded. Pan Am and other erstwhile leaders have crashed like giant trees in the forest. Other former leaders have, like the Cheshire cat, disappeared leaving only their names behind. Dunlop is now a Japanese brand and RCA a French one' (Stopford, 1996, p. 5). Second, managers are expected to react much more swiftly: 'whereas once we might have expected a new CEO to turn round a struggling business in five years we are now expecting that manager to do so in 12 months' (Goffee and Hunt, 1996, p. 4). Third, large business organizations are, on average, becoming smaller employers and their attraction is perhaps less than it was in the days of the 'company man'. Managers are now more likely both to switch from organization to organization and to find managing or even starting up a smaller firm an appropriate challenge.

Given the scale of these kinds of change, it is perhaps not a surprise that a new discourse (or set of conventions) has been produced which both frames them and forces them. This discourse depends, first of all, on new metaphors which attempt to capture a more turbulent, uncertain and insecure world. At first, the metaphors tended to be ones of excess, overload and saturation. But many of these early metaphors can now be seen as:

> the product of the first hysterical reactions to information technologies. 'Overload' in reference to what? 'Saturated' in reference to whom? The relative, historically contingent nature of these terms is seldom if ever entertained within the discourse, which prefers to present them as timeless. (Collins, 1995, p. 12)

So, very gradually, new visual and linguistic metaphors started to emerge which began to refigure (or, in the jargon, reframe) the business organization's relationship with the world, and the role of the manager within that organization (Buck-Morss, 1995; Crainer, 1995; Morgan, 1986; 1993; Martin, 1994; Collins, 1995). These metaphors were based on the notion of constant adaptive movement – 'dancing', 'surfing', and the like – and of organizational structures that could facilitate this constant adaptation, both by becoming more open to the changing world and by engaging the hearts and minds of the workforce in such a way that the organizations could exist as more open entities:

> We talked of structures and their systems, of inputs and outputs, of control devices and of managing them, as if the whole was one huge factory. Today the language is not that of engineering but of politics, with talk of cultures and networks of teams and coalitions, of influences and power rather than of control, of leadership not management. It is as if we had suddenly woken up to the fact that organisations were made up of people after all, not just 'heads' or 'role occupations'. (Handy, 1989, p. 71)

What each of these new metaphors has in common, then, is a concern with looser organizational forms which are more able to 'go with the flow', which are more open to a world which is now figured as complex and ambiguous, and with the production of subjects who can fit these forms (du Gay, 1996).

In particular, these new metaphors have become embedded through a new managerialism which is becoming hegemonic. The managerial form of the Genesis discourse does not have exactly the same origins as some academic versions, but I would argue that increasingly it amounts to much the same thing, especially because the degree of interchange between the academic and business communities has so greatly expanded: as we shall see, social theory now has a direct line to capitalism.

Amongst the sources of the new international discourse of managerialism can be counted the following. First, the business organization's 'environment' is figured as multiple, complex and fast-moving, and therefore as 'ambiguous', 'fuzzy' or 'plastic'. Of late, most of the inspiration for such a description has come from non-linear systems theory, and especially from the work of authors like Casti and Prigogine (see *Journal of Management Inquiry*, 1994). Second, the business organization is seen as attempting to form an island of superior adaptability in this fast-moving environment. This it achieves in a number of ways, which, taken together, constitute the international business community's 'linguistic turn'. Most particularly, it attempts to generate suitable *metaphors* which allow it to see itself and others in a distinctive (but always partial) fashion (Morgan, 1986; 1993). It tries, as well, to *embody* these metaphors in its workforce, a goal which it achieves via a number of means, including experiential learning – learning which involves placing the workforce in situations which demand co-operative responses to the uncertain and unknown (Martin, 1994). The organization also pays close attention to the resources of *tacit knowledge* (familiar but unarticulated knowledge) embodied in its workforce and to the generation of trust, both within its workforce and with other organizations. Work on tacit knowledge has been almost entirely generated from the writings of Michael Polanyi (Botwinick, 1996) (rather than, for example, Heidegger, Merleau-Ponty or Bourdieu) who, in turn, drew on the ideas of Gestalt psychology. Polanyi's most famous saying, 'we can know more than we can tell' (1967, p. 20), has become a vital part of business discourse, as a way into the problem of mobilizing the full resources of a workforce. In turn, Polanyi's work has underlined the need to generate *trust* or (as Polanyi often called it) confidence, since 'the overwhelming proportion of our factual beliefs continue … to be held at second hand through trusting others' (1958, p. 208). Third, the business organization must therefore be framed as a flexible entity, always *in action*, 'on the move, if only stumbling or blundering along' (Boden, 1994, p. 192), but stumbling or blundering along in ways which will allow it to survive and prosper, most particularly through mobilizing a culture which will produce traditions of learning (collective memories which will act both to keep the organization constantly alert and as a reservoir of innovation: Lundvall, 1992) and extensive intrafirm and interfirm social networks (which will act both as conduits of knowledge and as a means of generating trust). Fourth, the business organization is seen, as has already been made clear, as a cultural entity, which is attempting to generate new traditions, new representations of itself and the world, and increasingly an ethical stance towards the world, because the link between knowledge (as a political economy of information refigured as a culture) and power has been made crystal clear (Pfeffer and Salancik, 1978; Pfeffer, 1992). In other words, the business organization is increasingly built on 'a refusal to accept established knowledge' (Kestelhohn, 1996, p. 7).

Fifth, the business organization must be made up of willing and willed subjects. Thus Foucault's pastoral mode of discipline makes its way into the business organization as a set of new definitions of what it is to be a person:

> Breathing strange new life into the old artistic ideal of the 'organic' – of 'the cultivated moral personality' and 'life as a work of art' … characterizes work not as a painful obligation impressed upon individuals, nor as an activity only undertaken by people for instrumental purposes, but as a vital means to self-fulfilment and self-realization. As Kanter [1992] comments, life in the entrepreneurial corporation has 'a romantic quality'.
>
> By reorganizing work as simply part of that continuum along which 'we' all seek to realize ourselves as particular sets of person-outcomes, self-regulatory, self-fulfilling individual actors – 'enterprise' seeks to 're-enchant' organized work by restoring to it that which bureaucracy is held to have crassly repressed: emotion, personal responsibility, the possibility of pleasure, etc. (du Gay, 1996, p. 25)

As important, in some ways, as the new managerialist discourse itself has been the growth of the agents responsible for its spread across the globe. Together, they form an emergent and increasingly powerful *cultural circuit of capital* which has only existed since the 1960s. This circuit, which is now self-organizing, is responsible for the production and distribution of managerial knowledge to managers. As it has grown, so have its appetites. It now has a constant and voracious need for new knowledge. Chief amongst the producers of the managerial discourse are three institutions: business schools, management consultants and management gurus.

Through the 1960s, 1970s and 1980s formal business education, and especially the master of business administration (MBA) course, has produced a large number of academics and students who act both to generate and to transmit the new knowledge (Alvarez, 1996). In the United States, admittedly the most extreme example, almost one in four students in colleges and universities now majors in business, while the number of business schools has grown fivefold since 1957 (Kogut and Bowman, 1996, p. 14). In the top business schools academics compete with one another to teach students *and* to produce new ideas. Some of these leading schools are now run as *de facto* companies. For example, at Wharton one Dean, Thomas Gerrity, tried to put business process re-engineering into operation:

> In companies re-engineering makes a big fuss of tearing down what it calls functional chimneys and reallocating staff to teams. Mr Gerrity has divided both his students and his professors into teams of six: each student team includes at least two non-Americans; each faculty team includes professors from different academic disciplines. Both are evaluated in teams. Mr Gerrity has also torn down the barriers that divide the school from the University and from the business world. Students now offer consultancy to other parts of the University (on how to bring medical technology to market, for example) and to local businesses. They also study fluffy things like leadership, to the chagrin of many academics but the delight of businesses.
>
> As with other re-engineering exercises, a number of things introduced in its name look like common sense dressed up in fancy language (students are now sent abroad for 'global immersion'). Mr Gerrity has changed the system for granting tenure and awarding annual pay rises in order to shift the emphasis from publishing academic articles (once the only road to success) to teaching and 'leadership'. He has hired a policy firm, Opinion Research, to survey opinion among his constituencies. He has introduced a system of mentoring, so that senior professors can show their juniors how to teach, and quality circles, so that students can tell their teachers what they think of them. (*The Economist*, 13 April 1996, p. 83)

Another generator and distributor of new knowledge has been management consultancy (Clark, 1995). Management consultancy is, without doubt, a growth industry:

> Between 1970 and 1980, the revenue of management consultants registered with the Management Consultants Association doubled; from 1980 to 1987 it increased fivefold. In the UK, over the eleven years 1980–1991 the number of consultants registered with the MCA more than quadrupled to 6963 and their fees increased almost seventeenfold. By the early 1990s there were reported to be 100,000 consultants world-wide. Growth figures in recent years for major players in the global consultancy game confirm the continuing acceleration in business from the late 1980s. Thus the largest company, Andersen Consulting, has been posting 9 per cent growth regularly (and as high as 19 per cent in the recession year of 1992). The second largest player doubled revenue to $1.2 billion between 1987 and 1993. Coopers and Lybrand, third largest (but second in Europe), saw revenue grow 107 per cent over the five years to 1993, and by then had 66,000 staff in 125 countries. (Ramsay, 1996, p. 166)

Using VAT data Keeble et al. (1994) estimated that in 1990 the UK management consultancy industry comprised 11,777 firms with a combined turnover of a little over £2.5 billion. Management consultancies act as a vital part of the cultural circuit of capital. To begin with they provide ideas. For example, Arthur Andersen

> has three research centres and a massive international database, to which all 40,000 consultants are supposed to contribute. The company spent nearly 7% of its budget, or $290 million, on training in 1995, more than any rival. To have a chance of becoming a partner, an Andersenite needs to have put in over 1000 hours of training – some of it at the company's 150-acre campus outside Chicago. (*The Economist*, 4 May 1996, p. 90)

Then, they are responsible for much of the packaging of management knowledge, usually producing formulas which can be applied over and over again in different situations. Using Latour's by now familiar vocabulary,

> each assignment provides consultants with an opportunity to project their special and distinctive competences to clients by 'bringing home' distant events, places and people. This is achieved by (a) rendering them *mobile* so that they can be brought back; (b) keeping them *stable* so that they can be moved back and forth without additional distortion; and (c) making them *combinable* so that they can be circulated, amalgamated and manipulated (Latour [1987a] p. 223). Legge (1994, p. 3) writes that this is precisely what management consultants do when they make the experience of (distant) firms accessible and combinable through the development of (in Latour's terms) equations or packages – such as McKinsey's decentralisation package, Hay MSL's job evaluation package or even Peters' eight rules of excellence. (Clark, 1995, p. 56)

In turn, to make these packages credible to existing and potential clients requires considerable international work, involving a diverse range of social skills (Clark, 1995). And this work is clearly successful. For example, Ramsay (1996) cites reports that, in an 18 month period stretching over 1994 and 1995, 94 of the top 100 British companies had used management consultants.

Then there is one other major generator and distributor of new knowledge: the management guru (Huczynski, 1993; Micklethwait and Wooldridge, 1996). Gurus come in many shapes and sizes. Huczynski (1993) distinguishes between academic gurus like Michael Porter, Rosabeth Moss Kanter, Theodore Levitt, John Kay, Gareth Morgan and Peter Senge; consultant gurus like James Champy, Peter Drucker, Tom Peters, John Naisbitt and Kenichi Ohmae; and hero-managers like Mark McCormack, Akio Morita, John Harvey-Jones, Donald Trump and Lee Iacocca. Then there are other gurus who are less easy to classify, for example Benjamin Zander, conductor of the Boston Philharmonic, who provides inspirational lectures on music as a metaphor for management (Griffith, 1996).

These gurus often only run small operations. But, equally, their operations may be substantial. Most impressive of all is the leadership centre run by Stephen Covey in Provo, Utah.

Having started ten years ago with a staff of two, the Covey leadership centre now employs 700 people and has annual revenues of over $70 million. Mr Covey is building a large campus to house it on the edge of Provo, his home town. But even in its current state, scattered about the town, the centre is a sleek business machine. Its staff are surrounded by enough technology to make a journalist salivate. They have an army of unpaid helpers, thanks to Mr Covey's insistence that the best way to learn his ideas is to teach them. The centre is divided into three core businesses. The first is management training. Throughout the year high-fliers flock to Provo to spend a week reading 'wisdom literature', climbing mountains, discussing personal and business problems and forming into teams. The second is producing personal organisers. These are meant to help people set priorities – so much time for jogging, so much time for your mother-in-law – as well as organise appointments. The third is spinning out new ideas. The centre has a second best seller, 'Principle Centred Leadership'; and a third in preparation, the 'Seven Habits of Highly Effective Families'. (*The Economist*, 24 February 1996, p. 106)

There is no strong dividing line between business schools, management consultancies and management gurus. For example, Thomas Gerrity, the Dean of Wharton, was formerly a member of CSC Index, the consultancy which produced the idea of 'business process re-engineering' and which is now retailing notions of 'organizational agility'. Whatever is the case, it is clear that these three forms of institution are responsible for producing the bulk of management knowledge. That knowledge chiefly comes in the form of a succession of 'business fads' (Lorenz, 1989), of which there have now been a remarkable number. Between 1950 and 1988, for example, Pascale (1991) noted 26 major fads. Certainly the roll call includes quality circles, the paperless office, the factory of the future, intrapreneurship, brands, strategic alliances, globalization, business process re-engineering (including 'core competences') and employability; and more recently, nascent fads and fashions like organizational agility, the accelerating organization (Maira and Scott-Morgan, 1996), complexity theory, and even actor-network theory (Latour, 1995).

In turn, these ideas have to be distributed. The channels and means of distribution are multiple. First of all, of course, there are the business schools, which teach students the new ideas; the management consultants, constantly presenting clients with new ideas and ways of doing things; and the management gurus, taking fees and retainers to distribute their insights. Then, second, there is a rapidly growing business media industry which packages and distributes this knowledge. Management knowledge sells, most particularly since the establishment of the non-academic management book in the early 1980s. For example, Stephen Covey's *Seven Habits of Highly Effective People* has sold more than 5 million copies worldwide since its publication in 1989 (*The Economist*, 24 February 1996, p. 106) and is currently available in 28 languages in 35 countries (it is doing particularly well in China and South Korea). Hammer and Champy's *Re-engineering the Corporation*, published in 1993, had sold 2 million copies worldwide by September 1996, and had been translated into 17 languages. Of course, management knowledge is not just diffused via books (and increasingly tapes and videos). Journals like *Fortune*, *Business Week*, the *Harvard Business Review* and others also dispense such knowledge, as do myriad trade journals. Most broadsheet newspapers also have management knowledge pages: for example, the *Financial Times*, which can claim to be a global business newspaper, started a 'Management Brief' page in 1994 and also produced a major 26-part series on the current state of management knowledge in 1996 (see Crainer, 1995). There are also now a number of specific television programmes which communicate management knowledge.

Finally, there is one more means of dissemination which is particularly important in the case of management knowledge. This is the management seminar, which is a mixture of drill and, increasingly, religious revivalism. Such seminars are big business across the world. There are many kinds of seminar, of course. There are, to begin with, the modest seminars which import skills, usually offered by training companies or management consultants:

> Their advertising literature about short seminars and courses emphasises personal and interpersonal techniques. Such offerings include seminars such as 'Time Management International', 'Liberating Leadership Team', 'Leadership Development', 'Close that Sale!', Karass's 'Effective Negotiating' [named after the management guru Dr Chester Karass] and the one day seminars from Career Track with talks such as 'Management Skills for Technical Professionals' and 'How to Set and Achieve Your Goals'. Attendance at these seminars is substantial if the firm's publicity literature is to be believed. The 'Close that Sale!' seminar claims 59,000 participants from 70 companies. Time Management International claims that 28,000 people participated in its world-wide series of seminars during 1986. Finally, Effective Negotiating claims a world-wide participation rate of 150,000. Such courses are usually of one day's duration. They are offered at a low fee and attract a high attendance, often over one hundred people. They feature a 'high energy' presenter and offer their audiences 'tested techniques' and 'proven skills'. (Huczynski, 1993, p. 186)

But there are also high-profile series of seminars featuring management gurus, often stretching over two or three days, which communicate knowledge which is not easily standardized. Thus:

> Byrne ... reported on a type of executive seminar called a 'skunk camp'. The similarity between his description of it and a religious retreat is instructive. The 'holy man' leading this event was Tom Peters, the co-author of one of the world's bestselling business books. The cost to each participant's company was $4000 and at this particular event the day began with a group jogging session. Following a communal breakfast, the members gathered in the conference room 'waiting for enlightenment'. Byrne reported:

> In walks our rumpled leader. Head down, hands in the pockets of his brown shapeless cords, he paces relentlessly. His voice climbs to the treble clef as he runs through the litany. 'Dehumiliate ... Get rid of your executive parking

spots ... Get everybody on the same team ... There are two ways to get rich: superior customer satisfaction and constant innovation.

Byrne's description has similarities with one reported by Oliver ... of a just-in-time seminar run by Eli Goldratt (co-author of the book *The Goal*):

> Goldratt appeared practically at 9.15 a.m., and in contrast to all the delegates who were wearing suits, he wore neither a jacket nor a tie and was wearing a skull-cap and open-toed sandals. He began by saying he had no prepared slides or any notes. The expression 'the cost world' was used to denote the old order and the 'throughput world' to denote the new one. Towards the end of the session, Goldratt threw out the question, 'Where shall we begin the improvement?' The audience responded with a chorus of cries of 'Us', 'Ourselves' and other similar expressions. (1993, pp. 44–5)

Often, seminars will include books or videos in the price, so that a seamless web of production and reinforcement of ideas is produced.

Increasingly, seminars are being produced on an extraordinary scale. For example, in September 1996 Stephen Covey, Tom Peters and Peter Senge combined forces in an interactive 'supergroup' presentation on 'How To Make Your Team Unstoppable', broadcast by satellite to 30,000 people in 250 cities in 40 countries around the world (in Britain the venue was Birmingham at a cost of £199 per person).

Then, finally, there are management 'audiences'. How many seminars, and of what type, do they attend? What do they get out of them? What do they read and what sense do they make of their readings? How is the knowledge they gain from seminars and readings inscribed in management practices? It is fair to say that we know remarkably little about this aspect of the capitalist circuit of cultural capital: there are only very small amounts of audience research (but see Engwall, 1992). Instead, we have to infer the character and motivations of audiences from general trends, and the few studies there are. Thus, first, we know that managers are becoming better educated almost everywhere. For example, 'as more managers complete MBA-type programmes, they become more sophisticated, and are able to understand and apply more complicated management ideas' (Huczynski, 1993, p. 48). Second, it is clear that managers do read more books (and listen to tapes and watch videos) than previously. Third, at the same time, through the increased 'packaging' of ideas in seminars and books, management ideas have become more accessible. Fourth, managers clearly want and need new ideas. They need them to make their way in organizations, to solve a particular company's problems, to act as an internal motivational device, to guard against their competitors' adoption of new ideas, and simply to provide a career enhancer. In the last case, the new idea demonstrates to others that the manager is creative, up-to-the-minute and actively seeking improvements, thereby increasing that individual's visibility in the organization. Equally, the new idea can act as a defence, can provide a quick-fix solution in a difficult period, or can even simply reduce boredom (Huczynski, 1993). Fourth, the management book or seminar can act to raise or boost levels of belief. Thus, attendees at seminars by management gurus may have already read all the ideas in books, but this is not the point:

> Managers may attend Tom Peters' seminars to become immersed to his personality. In fact, if he was not to say what they have already read, they would come away disappointed. Lorenz ... wrote that 'managers may still pay repeated visits in their thousand to sit at [the guru's] feet, or buy his latest book. One executive at a leading multinational talks of needing his "Drucker fix" every two years.' (1993, p. 201)

Again, seminars may retail experiences of such intensity that they change the terms of what it means to be a person, as can happen in experiential seminars. For example, Martin (1994) documents how the initial cynicism of some participants in these kinds of seminar is gradually overtaken by the experience of the seminar. Sixth, and finally, more managers are now women. Some commentators have argued that much of the change in the metaphorical framing of modern capitalism is a result of the feminization of management knowledge which, at least in part, results from the greater presence of women in management and the workforce (Clegg and Palmer, 1996).

To summarize, what seems clear is that managers themselves search for four main qualities from management knowledge (Huczynski, 1993). The first of these is *predictability*:

> managers want to find ideas that make a constantly changing environment less confusing and threatening; for however brief a period. In order that they do not appear as part of the problem of constant change, management ideas are packaged so that they can be perceived as something already known but able to be reprioritised. The most popular management ideas seem to be those which successfully integrate a number of ideas into a single bite-size whole. The second quality is *empowerment*. Managers want to be told which ideas will achieve what results and which techniques are to be associated with the actions; managers want 'permission' from accredited sources to act. Third, managers want *esteem*. One way of achieving this is to be seen as the champion of a management idea or ideas.
>
> In a number of companies, the promotion of the latest management fad by managers has been used to help them gain company-wide visibility in the promotion stakes. Management idea championing can represent a low-risk way of signalling to those with the power to promote that managers are not averse to change, do not mind challenging established views, but that while they are prepared to look critically at the system in which they work, they will not unduly 'rock the organisational boat'.
>
> Further esteem can be gained if the idea is not of the black-box variety, that is it offers (and is seen to offer) the championing managers the scope to make their own contribution to it. Thus it then gives them greater ownership of the idea in the perception of others. It might be thought that this is a high-risk strategy, since the idea may fail to yield the expected benefits ... [But] assessments of success and failure tend to be very vague in this area, and all parties concerned have a vested interest in not admitting to failure. (1993, pp. 212–13)

Then, finally, managers want *self-belief*. Thinking about the self has a long history in management. For example, Kurt Lewin (1951) invented the so-called 'T-group', an early form of the encounter group which encouraged colleagues to expose their true feelings about each other, while Maslow's (1954) 'enpsychian' management, McGregor's (1960) 'Theory Y' and Herzberg (1965) all emphasized 'the need as a human to grow spiritually' (Huczynski, 1993, p. 71). In other words, managers, like many other contemporary individuals, have, for some time, been enjoined

> to live as if running a *project* of themselves: they are to *work* on their emotional world, their domestic and conjugal arrangements, their relations of employment and the techniques of sexual pleasure, to develop a style of being that will maximize the worth of their existence to themselves. Evidence from the United States, Europe and the United Kingdom suggests that the implantation of such 'identity projects', characteristic of advanced democracies, is constitutively linked to the rise of a breed of new spiritual directors, 'engineers of the human soul'. Although our subjectivity might appear our most intimate sphere of experience, its contemporary intensification as a political and ethical value is intrinsically correlated with the growth of expert languages, which enable us to render our relations with our selves and others into words and into thought, and with expert techniques, which promise to allow us to transform ourselves in the direction of happiness and fulfilment. (Rose, 1996, p. 157)

This emphasis on self-belief as a function of personal growth is perhaps best exemplified by the growth of New Age training which attempts to import New Age ideas via techniques like dancing, medicine wheels, and the use of the I Ching (Heelas, 1991a; 1991b; 1992; 1996; Huczynski, 1993; Roberts, 1994; Rifkin, 1996; Rupert, 1992). New Age thinking has become popular in management for a number of reasons. To begin with its world view, which draws on not only eastern and western spiritual traditions but also quantum physics, cybernetics, cognitive science and chaos theory, chimes with the Genesis discourse. Then, its emphasis on personal development fits with the rise of 'soft skills' like leadership, intuition, vision and the like. In turn, New Age's stress on changing people works in with attempts to change the management (and workforce) subject, particularly because changing oneself or others seems a feasible and certain task compared with many others that management faces.

> Most generally, the idea is to transform the values, experiences and to some extent the practices of what it is to *be* at work. The New Age Manager is imbued with new qualities and virtues, new in the sense that they differ from those found in the unenlightened workplace. These have to do with intrinsic wisdom, authentic creativity, self-responsibility, genuine energy, love and so on. Trainings are held to effect this shift. Furthermore, work itself is typically seen to serve as a 'growth environment'. The significance of work is transformed in that it is conceived as providing the opportunity to work on 'oneself'. It becomes a spiritual discipline. (Heelas, 1996, p. 90)

Whatever the case, New Age training is big business. In the United States $4 billion per year is being spent by corporations on New Age consultants, according to Naisbitt and Aburdene (1990). For example, the New Age think tank Global Business Network is underwritten by major companies like AT and T, Volvo, Nissan, and Inland Steel. Some companies like Pacific Bell, Procter and Gamble, Du Pont and IBM offer, or have offered, their employees 'personal growth experiences' in-house. Thus, IBM provides 'Fit for the Future' seminars which introduce employees to the I Ching. It is claimed that this links internal intuitions with external events. IBM's manager of employee development is quoted as saying that 'it helps employees understand themselves better' (Huczynski, 1993, p. 57). The list goes on:

> Other organisations include those run by Tishi (follower of one of Muktunanda's successors, who has recently, and somewhat controversially, brought the 'Values and Vision' training to Harper Collins in Britain), Branton Kenton's Human Technology Consultants, Emerge (which has worked with Virgin Retail), I and O, Transform Ltd (partly inspired by Rudolf Steiner), the Creative Learning Consultants, Potentials Unlimited, The Results Partnership Ltd, Keith Silvester's Dialogue management training services (influenced by Psychosynthesis), Impact Factory (running the 'Money Factor'), Dave Baun's 'Charisma Training', and Anthony Robbins' 'Unleash the Power Within' weekends. The recently opened London Personal Development Centre alone claims to provide '300 courses, workshops, seminars, and lectures', 'designed to bring new creativity and vision to business'. (Heelas, 1996, p. 64)

In Britain, New Age training therefore also crops up, often in unlikely places. For example, the Bank of England, British Gas, Ernst and Whinney, Mars, and Legal and General have all sent executives to be taught how to do the Whirling Dervish dance, so as to allow their top managers to find inner peace and increase the business potential. Then again, 'the Scottish Office sent thousands of its employees on "New Age Thinking" courses run by Louis Tice of the Pacific Institute which aimed to train the minds of workers to make them "high performance people" in their work and private lives' (Huczynski, 1993, p. 56). Meanwhile Decision Development, a British New Age training company, was offering to boost the spiritual, emotional and creative powers of clients. The company uses the American Indian Medicine Wheel 'to take managers on a journey to discover their spiritual, emotional and creative self. The wheel allegedly enables trainees to access their inner selves by examining their dreams and fantasies' (1993, p. 56). Another company uses 'an inward-focused version of outdoor activities which involves mythical aspects of the "Dungeon and Dragons" variety where managers dress as druids and witches to find a magic elixir to revive a dying child' (1993, pp. 56–7). Some companies are currently using *The Celestine Prophecy* as a focus for training (Redfield, 1994), and this is to ignore the use of 'Star Trek' or Shakespeare as managerial primers (Roberts and Ross, 1995).

What, then, is the task of the reinvented manager in this newly figured world? The new managerialism depends on the notion that the world is uncertain, complex, paradoxical, even chaotic (*Journal of Management Inquiry*, 1994). The manager must somehow find the means to steer a course in this fundamentally uncertain world, which she or he does by six main means (for a comprehensive review, see Ghoschal and Bartlett, 1995). First of all, there is an emphasis on the competitive advantage, in a business world that is increasingly constituted by information that is incurred by knowledge. Whereas managers

> used to think that the most precious resource was capital, and that the prime task of management was to allocate it in the most productive way, now they have become convinced that their most precious resource is knowledge and that the prime task of management is to ensure that their knowledge is generated as widely and used as efficiently as possible. (Wooldridge, 1995, p. 4)

In Drucker's famous words, 'Knowledge has become the key economic resource and the dominant, if not the only, source of comparative advantage' (1988, p. 16). Second, the task of the manager is increasingly seen as the harnessing of extant organizational knowledge and the generation of new organizational knowledge, most especially by tapping the existing tacit skills and talents of the workforce, and then enhancing these competencies by stimulating critical thinking skills which can overcome established prejudices – informally by providing greater communication between workers within the organization so that beneficial practices spread, and formally by instituting means of gaining further qualifications and opportunities for strategic conversation (Badaracco, 1991; Leonard-Barton, 1995; Roos and von Krogh, 1996). Third, the manager no longer aims to produce an overall corporate strategy which is then mechanistically instituted in and through a corporate bureaucracy. Rather, the aim is to produce an emergent 'evolutionary' or 'learning' strategy that is 'necessarily incremental and adaptive, but that does not in any way imply that its evolution cannot be or should not be analysed, managed, and controlled' (Kay, 1993, p. 359). Such a strategy will be based on what are seen as the particular capabilities of a business organization, which are then amplified via informal methods of control which rely on a much greater grasp of the issues involved, and which also mean that whole strata of bureaucracy, most of whose time was taken up with oversight, can be shrunk or, in the jargon, 'delayered' (Clarke and Newman, 1993). Fourth, in order to achieve evolutionary strategies and informal control, the manager has to become a kind of charismatic itinerant, a 'cultural diplomat' (Hofstede, 1991), constantly imbuing the business organization's values and goals, constantly on a mission to explain and motivate an increasingly multinational and multicultural workforce in an increasingly global firm..Not surprisingly, such a task of producing affective effects is not easy. In earlier studies, Mintzberg (1973), Stewart (1976) and Davis and Luthans (1980) all found that managers spent between a half and three-quarters of their time simply talking to people. Stewart, for example, found that 'Management is a verbal world whose people are usually instructed by personal contact rather than on paper' (1976, p. 92).

More recently, Bruns (1997) found that top managers in multinational corporations spent most of their time talking to people, either via electronic means or via direct face-to-face communication. And much of the rest of the time they spent travelling, spending as much as three out of every four weeks on business trips as they personally try to weave the culture of their organization together. In other words, the example of these studies shows that the chief business of business organizations is talk, talk and then more talk in order to achieve some measure of agreement (Boden, 1994); 'conversations are the backbone of business' (Roos and von Krogh, 1995, p. 3). Or to put it another way,

> most of what managers do is discourse: it consists of discussion, ordering, synthesizing, presenting, reporting – all activities that take place through the media of various texts and representations of immediate co-presence. Management mostly concerns words that do things, presented in many various arenas, sometimes personally, sometimes impersonally, sometimes in role, sometimes unscripted and unwarranted by the roles that exist already, the narratives already written. Management, above all, is a performative activity: it does what it says and it says what it does: its utterances and its actions are so frequently fused, so politically meshed. (Clegg and Palmer, 1996, p. 2)

Fifth, the manager must not only weave the organization together but also ensure that, through dedicated networking, she or he can produce and sustain external relationships of trust with other firms, which become vital conduits of information and future business. Through her or his interpersonal skills and cultural sensitivity, the manager builds not only an internal but also an external relational 'architecture' (Kay, 1993). Thus, and sixth, management is no longer seen as a science. Rather, it becomes an art form dedicated to 'the proposition that a political economy of information is in fact coextensive with a theory of culture' (Boisot, 1995, p. 7). In other words, the manager sets out to re-enchant the world (du Gay, 1996).

Thus, as writers as different as Sampson (1995) and Buck-Morss (1995) have noted, the rational company man of the 1950s and 1960s, skilled in the highways and byways of bureaucracy, becomes the corporate social persona of the 1990s, skilled in the arts of social presentation and 'change management'. And the giant multidivisional corporation of the 1950s and 1960s now becomes a 'leaner', 'networked', 'postbureaucratic', 'virtual' or even 'poststructuralist' organization, a looser form of business which can act like a net floating on an ocean, able to ride the swell and still go forward (Drucker, 1988; Heckscher and Donnellon, 1994; Eccles and Nohria, 1990).

The managerial discourse is undoubtedly an exaggeration that, in turn, exaggerates its own importance (Chanlat, 1996; Knights and Murray, 1994). For a start, it reflects 'cultural variations' which are not just variations but root and branch differences. The Japanese firm, with its cultural emphasis on informal reciprocity, is quite clearly a different animal from the US firm, with its emphasis on formal contract (Kay, 1995). And both types of firm are different from overseas Chinese or European firms (Thrift and Olds, 1996). Then again, it overstates the degree to which it has been adopted: many business organizations remain bureaucratic, monolithic and decidedly non-consensual.

But, what seems clear is that this 'new managerialism' is becoming the hegemonic account, both of what the post-Bretton-Woods business world is like, and of how best to exercise corporate power within it, across the world:

> It has contributed to some changes in management practice (however unevenly) and forms of organisational transformation. It has also provided a new and distinctive language of management which has played a significant role in legitimating claims to both organisational and social leadership. (Clarke and Newman, 1993, p. 438)

Most importantly of all, perhaps, the new managerialist discourse has empowered its managerial subjects by presenting them with an expanded opportunity to dream 'global dreams' (Barnet and Cavanagh, 1995). New forms of managerial subject are being produced through the application of an odd mixture of the 'psy disciplines' (Rose, 1996), New Age, and the like. Most particularly, these subjects are being taught to internalize the world as theirs in which to operate with self-esteem and self-confidence (French and Grey, 1996). As Strathern puts it, appropriating actor-network theory:

> How large, Latour asks, is IBM? An actor of great size, mobilising hundreds of thousands of people, it is always encountered via a small handful ... We never in this sense leave the local. The local is not just the people you talk to at IBM or BP but the desks, the paperwork, the connections distributed through the system, that is, the instruments that create a global field. From this point of view it makes no sense to go along with the literalism, that 'global' is bigger than 'local'. It is simply where one is at. But if one never leaves the local, where is the global? It has to be the infinitely recurring *possibility* of measurement – not the scales but *the capacity to imagine them*.
>
> As part of their ability to act, pressed into operation as design or intention, people's sense of scale produces a reflexive sense of context or locale. That is, it is a capacity which prompts comparisons, whether of commensurate things (along one scale) or of things not reducible to a common scale at all. Either way, we can imagine that it enlarges the world ('deepens it': Geertz, 1993, p. 233). If so, we may take such scaling as a technique for knowing oneself to be effective (have relational effects: Law, 1994, pp. 102–3) regardless of agency ... Anthropologists will never understand the power of those who think the world is their market ... unless they appreciate *the energising effect of such expanded horizons*. The expanded horizon, like the world view, is *how things are made effective locally*. (1995b, pp. 179–80, my emphases)

It follows that, as the practical background assumptions with which managers operate have changed, so have the spatial assumptions they make. But these are only just being worked out in practice.

Thus, to the question 'What will the geographies of soft capitalism look like?' there is no easy answer. We can, of course, suggest that these geographies will operate at a range of scales in line with the increased 'granularity' of soft capitalism (Bowker and Star, 1994). At the micro scale, the impact of soft capitalism will be felt in the explicit social engineering of office buildings in order to maximize opportunities for social interaction and thereby learning and innovation. The BMW research and development headquarters is often regarded as the paradigm for this kind of design, with no room being more than 50 metres from any other. At the meso scale, soft capitalism is clearly present in the attempts to set up intrafirm networks and alliances and thereby foster 'learning regions' (Morgan, 1993). These networks provide means of stimulating learning and innovation on a broader spatial scale. Finally, at the macro scale, soft capitalism is present in the burgeoning global information networks of the cultural circuit of capital which 'manage the production and exchange of intangible objects like knowledge' (Boisot, 1995, p. 5) through the production of theories, texts, and practical protocols like seminars which stabilize them, embody them in subjects. In practice, this means a double movement. At one level, it means the frenzy of personal contact reflected in the rise of international business travel. At another level, more and more of the organization's 'values, opinions and rhetoric are frozen into codes, electronic thresholds and computer applications. Extending Marx, then, we can say that, in many ways, software is frozen organizational discourse' (Bowker and Star, 1994, p. 187).

But the example of global information networks shows the rub. Too much of the information circulating in these networks is of an abstract and diffused kind which in fact is predicated upon both information loss and a corresponding increase in ambiguity. What seems certain, then, is that soft capitalism, though global in character, will still be strongly oriented to the local as organizations attempt to replace this information loss and diminish ambiguity. Most particularly, successful organizations will be those that are able to diffuse essentially local tacit knowledge over space through limited amounts of codification and interaction which function as the equivalent of the collective memories of the organization. Thus the main battleground of soft capitalism may turn out to be what Boisot calls the semi-tacit domain:

> Here, people are willing to invest in the acquisition and mastery of codes and categories in so far as they offer participation in the activities of a wider community. Effective communication here depends upon a mix of words and gestures, text and example. Any loss of data entailed by complex coding of messages into words, or by abstracting from a concrete situation, is now compensated by gains in communicative potential offered by an increase in structure. Transacting parties may still need to be co-present, but now no longer necessarily so. The people and things addressed might be elsewhere. Codes and concepts of the semi-tacit domain open large tracts of experience to comparatively effortless shared understanding. (1995, p. 62)

Conclusions: the hard edge of soft capitalism

The hegemony of this new managerialist discourse has four main consequences, each of them uncomfortable. The first is that it has what used to be called 'material consequences' – effects that can be measured out in terms of pain, heartbreak, and shattered lives. Business organizations that take the managerialist discourse on board usually become involved in programmes of direct 'downsizing', cutting back on the workforce with all the human misery this brings – made more of a shock, perhaps, because so many 'redundant' middle management 'layers' have been stripped out, as well as the jobs at the bottom of the occupational hierarchy which are always targeted and forfeited. Business organizations have also been involved in considerable indirect 'downsizing': for example, through programmes that lay off significant numbers of subcontractors so as to produce a core network of closely allied firms. Then, not to be taken lightly, organizational change has brought with it other forms of stress and strain, from the 50-year-old executive who is being shunted into a part-time consultancy to the new graduate who must downsize their expectations of a corporate career. In other words, this new form of the exercise of corporate power is not necessarily any 'nicer' than what has gone before; for all the caring rhetoric, lean can just as easily be mean and learning can mean stomach churning. The sword of management is, as always, two-edged: economic success is, now as then, brought at the cost of the workforce, as much as to its benefit. Most of the angst in the new managerialist discourse is produced by and for the middle class, not the working class.

Then there is a second consequence of this discourse. This is that, for all the commitment to an open-ended view of subjecthood, *in practice* the conception of the person (and the model of action) that is presumed is, more often than not, a narrow one which involves super-exploitation of both managers (who are expected to commit their whole being to the organization) and workers (who are now expected to commit their embodied knowledge to the organization's epistemological resources as well). In other words, the net effect may well be to reduce the different conceptions and comportments of the person which are to hand and, worse, to transfer these reduced conceptions and comportments to other spheres of life (du Gay, 1996).

There is a further consequence of this new managerialist discourse. It makes it even clearer (if this ever needed saying) that there is no intellectual community which can be separated off from other communities, in which the intellectual community has the power to decode the world, whilst all the other communities just slope ignorantly about. As Bauman (1987) has pointed out, the intellectual community has moved from a position as legislator of the world to simply one of a number of interpretive communities. In the case of the relationship between the international intellectual and international business community this tendency has been strengthened by increased traffic between the two communities (for example, as a result of the growth of management education, and the increasing use of intellectual ideas in management), by the growth of an independent intelligence and analytical capacity within international business, and by the growth of the media as powerful disseminators of and traders in ideas between the two communities.

There is one more consequence of the new managerialist discourse. It exposes the problem that there is no theory that is not, or cannot be made, complicit. Just as Marx's and Heiddegger's theories could become some of the ingredients of a totalitarian discourse, so notions of radical indeterminacy can be turned to all manner of ends, not all of which are pure or pleasant. But this is the chief point about discourses: they may contain elements of theory but they are not theoretical. They are practically oriented orders bent to the task of constructing more or less durable social networks and they are constantly redefined in order to cope with the vagaries of that task.

What is certain, what is indeed the only certainty, is that the new view of what we know, whether it is found in the intellectual or business communities, demands a change of style which is also – inevitably – a change of content. We need to move away from the comforting nostrum that we can contain the world in theories, and realize that these theories are not just about seeking out new knowledge but also about telling stories about an uncertain world which can, however briefly, stabilize that uncertainty, and make it appear certain and centred. How else, for example, can we explain the currency of stories like 'postmodernism' which often seem to be simply a means of rolling over old antinomies, thereby providing an unfamiliar landscape with some familiar landmarks. Old habits die hard, and the habit of searching for centred stories that tell all (like the story in this chapter) dies hardest of all – living proof, if proof were needed, of the human need to fend off uncertainty:

> The anxiety would be lessened, tensions allayed, the total situation made more comfortable were the stunning profusion of possibilities somewhat reduced, were the world a bit more singular, its occurrences more repetitive, its parts better marked and separated: in other words – were the events of the world more predictable, and the utility or uselessness of things more immediately evident. One may say that because of their 'fundamental constitution' human beings have inborn (hereditary) vested interests in an orderly structured world free of mysteries and surprises. They also have similar vested interests in being more clearly defined themselves, and having their inner possibilities preselected for them, turned into the source of orientation rather than being a cause of confusion and distress. (Bauman, 1995, p. 141)

Now both the international intellectual and intentional business communities understand the ramifications of this insight. We must learn to live with some of the consequences while striving to prevent them from being turned into a new capitalist orthodoxy.

In this, we may be helped by soft capitalism itself. Soft capitalism, like other forms of capitalism, is shot full with tensions and contradictions. There are three of these that strike me immediately. First, the rise of soft capitalism brings with it the opportunity for new kinds of resistance and subversion in workforces, associated particularly with the rise of electronic telecommunications technologies and with the development of the *appearance* of consensus (see Zuboff, 1988; Jernier et al., 1994; Heckscher and

Donnellon, 1994). Second, a number of the actual tenets of soft capitalism are undermined by their own consequences. For example, it is very difficult to build trust in organizations which are, at the same time, being 'delayered', 'downsized' and 're-engineered':

> Corporate America eliminated 516,000 jobs in 1994, a year in which profits rose by 11%. The most dramatic slimmers included some of the biggest money machines such as Mobil, Procter and Gamble, American Home Products and Sara Lee. Such pruning is hardly conducive to 'trust'. Bosses at AT and T admit that re-engineering has generally undermined employees' trust. An internal survey in British Telecom this year discovered that only a fifth of employees thought that managers could be relied upon to do what they said. (*The Economist*, 16 December 1995, p. 83)

And, third, there is the problem of the motivation of managers. Managers who are taught to be reflexive about themselves, who are increasingly schooled in the ethics of corporate responsibility, and who are expected to work extraordinarily long hours in order to maintain an organization's culture (Massey, 1995), can and do become reluctant, sceptical and even disillusioned (Pahl, 1995; Jacques, 1994; Scase and Goffee, 1989). Thus, amongst such managers, there is an increasing move to values 'involving empathy, connectedness, emotion, ease and green concerns' (Pahl, 1995, p. 180) which, in turn, are helping to provide new models of economic practice.

Unlike previous models of alternative economic practice which were often born out of immanent critiques of capitalism, most of these models tend to be practical critiques, born out of actual attempts to produce new forms of economic institutions which are both immediately feasible and radically democratic, in that they both broaden democracy by bringing in new actors and deepen it by producing new means of giving voice (Amin and Thrift, 1995). Significantly, these institutions have often included quite substantial inputs from business managers looking for new values, and they also often utilize the vocabulary of the new managerial discourses.

There is a diverse range of these new models. Here I will note just three. First, there have been moves towards dispersed corporate ownership which has sparked ideas like 'superstock' and social dividends more generally (Gamble and Kelly, 1996). Second, there is the social investment movement. Beginning in the 1960s, social or ethical investment has now come of age. Even in Britain, which is hardly the most active country in this area, over £900 million of personal and institutional savings are now screened against ethical and environmental criteria. Then, third, there is the social banking initiative, which is made up of a series of different kinds of financial initiatives, including community development banks, community development loan funds, credit unions, community exchange systems (or LETS) and micro-loan funds (Mayo, 1995). Of course, these alternative models may not always set the heart racing, yet they are in the spirit of the times in that they involve an increasingly concerted attempt to set up a counter-discourse, one which is particularist but which is also increasingly able to 'go global'. In a sense, at least, they are about turning soft capitalism back on itself by using its procedures and vocabulary, but to different ends. That, surely, is a worthwhile project.

3

The Place of Complexity

Introduction: thoughts in space

Geographers have always had a problem in coping with complexity; space complicates to the point where it can easily obscure. Thus, the early regional historians of the sixteenth and seventeenth centuries often found themselves exhausted by the sheer magnitude of the task of attempting to record every aspect of a place. Some were discouraged, others never completed their task, one or two were even driven out of their wits (Parry, 1995). Nowadays, with the advent of computing, this same documentary impulse persists, but translated, in the work of 'geocomputationalists', into a manic inductionism. Rather like the top-hatted neo-Victorian engineers from a steampunk science fiction novel, they want to set up an informational dominance over the world.

What we can say is that space complicates because it immediately injects a notion of *distribution*; for all the Derridean notion that we live in an infinite web of meaning, the fact is that this web is differentially distributed. Its elements do not crop up everywhere equally, however often deferred. Spatial distribution, by itself, can therefore begin to account for much of what happens in the world: from the start, the geographical world is a messy one, it does not cohere. On the whole geographers therefore tend to be wary of theories that ride roughshod over ambiguity and polarize complexities. Yet they find it difficult to convey this sense of distribution: too often it ends up sounding like a simple-minded empiricism.

You might have thought, then, that geographers would take to complexity theory like a duck to water. Here, after all, is a body of theory that sees that

> logic and philosophy are messy, that language is messy, that chemical kinetics is messy, that physics is messy and finally that the economy is naturally messy. And it's not that this is a mess created by the dirt that's on the microscope glass. It's that this mess is inherent in the systems themselves. You can't capture any of them and confine them to a neat box of logic. (Arthur, cited in Waldrop, 1993, p. 329)

Here, furthermore, is a body of theory that is preternaturally spatial: it is possible to argue that complexity theory is about, precisely, the spatial ordering that arises from injections of energy. Whereas previous bodies of scientific theory were chiefly concerned with temporal progression, complexity theory is equally concerned with space. Its whole structure depends upon emergent properties arising out of excitable spatial orders over time. And here, most of all, is a body of theory which asks questions about 'instability, crisis, differentiation, catastrophes and impasses' (Stengers, 1997, p. 4) in ways which suggest that there is an obvious affinity between the 'natural' and 'human' sciences, a constant dream of geography.

Yet geographers have stayed on the land, for reasons which are chiefly conjunctural. The links between complexity theory and geography *were* made in the 1970s, but by a group of quantitative geographers, led by major figures in the discipline like Alan Wilson (originally a nuclear physicist), as well as workers from cognate disciplines like Peter Allen (who was, for a time, a part of the Prigogine group in Brussels). These geographers and near-geographers used the forerunners of complexity theory for often technical reasons, for example to add non-linearities to the parameters of location–allocation models, to apply simple catastrophe theory techniques to urban models, or to summarize the form of cities using fractal-based methods (see Wilson, 1994; Batty and Longley, 1995). In turn, given the sceptical reaction to quantitative geography at this time – the subject was going through a series of rapid changes which emphasized Marxian and other mainstream sociological approaches – complexity theory was subsumed as simply a part of the old ways, to be taken with a pinch of salt. Then, adding to this reaction, quantitative geographers interested in complexity theory took most of their energy from what was happening in mathematics, physics and chemistry, rather than from the developments in biology with which the subject has had a long history of intimate relations and from which dissemination might have proved easier (Livingstone, 1992).

In this chapter, I want to produce an account of the dissemination of complexity theory which reinstates the links between geography and complexity theory in three ways. First, I want to take the body of work known as complexity theory seriously. It *does* have interesting and even important things to say. But, second, and at the same time, I want to recognize that, in an increasingly mediatized world, complexity theory is, to an extent, just another business opportunity. It is up for sale and it is being sold. So, third, my account of the long march of complexity theory is tinged with irony and is more than a little ambivalent. In other words, I want to capture a sense of theoretical commitment which is balanced by a sense of the way of the world.

Let me, start, then, by setting out some of the main ideas of complexity theory before moving on to an outline of the chapter. Complexity theory is, it must be stated from the outset, a scientific amalgam. It is an accretion of ideas, a rhetorical hybrid. In this chapter, I assume that the chief impulse behind complexity theory is an anti-reductionist one, representing a shift towards understanding the properties of interaction of systems as more than the sum of their parts. This is, then, the idea of a science of holistic *emergent* order; a science of qualities as much as of quantities; a science of 'the potential for emergent order in complex and unpredictable phenomena' (Goodwin, 1997, p. 112); a more open science which asserts 'the primacy of processes over events, of relationships over entities and of development over structure' (Ingold, 1990, p. 209). Put another way, complexity theory concerns the study of the behaviour of macroscopic collections of [interacting] units that are endowed with the potential to evolve in time. Their interactions lead to coherent collective phenomena, so-called emergent properties that can be classified only at higher levels than those of individual units. (Coveney and Highfield, 1995, p. 7)

Or as one of the key proponents of complexity theory, Chris Langton, puts it:

From the interaction of the individual components [of a system] … emerges some kind of property … something you couldn't have predicted from what you know of the component parts … And the global property, this emergent behaviour, feeds back to influence the behaviour … of the individuals that produced it. (quoted in Lewin, 1993, pp. 12–13)

Complexity theory is an economy of concepts based around this emergent or self-organizing impulse, usually involving a series of what might be thought of as 'question marks' (Stengers, 1997) like non-linearity, self-organization, emergent order, and complex adaptive systems (Jencks, 1996). Most of the many writers on complexity theory will then usually lay claim to a whole series of fields of study which they assert are a part of this impulse, including chaos theory, fractal modelling, artificial life, cellular automata, neural nets, and the like, and to a companion vocabulary which has become both technical and metaphorical: chaos, attractors, fractals, emergent orders, self-organization, implicate order, autopoiesis, life at the edge of chaos, and so on .

In this chapter, I want to look at the recent history of complexity theory as an account of how it has travelled and what that travel might mean. The first section therefore offers an account of the geography of complexity theory, looking at how the metaphors of complexity theory have circulated around the world through the three different but related networks of science, business and New Age. This geography has not, as I will show, been a simple diffusion outward from a point. Rather, the propagators of complexity theory have been present in more than one of these networks, and these networks have therefore imported these concepts, processed them, and re-exported them – sometimes even back from whence they came – showing, once again, the difficulty of controlling interpretation since the act of communication is always at one and the same time an act of dissemination. Then, in the second section, I will consider how complexity theory might be seen as one of the harbingers of something more, the emergence of a structure of feeling in Euro-American societies which frames the world as complex, irreducible, anti-closural and, in doing so, is producing a much greater sense of openness and possibility about the future. The conclusion to the chapter then provides a cautionary gloss on this interpretation.

The spaces of complexity: some metaphorical geographies of complexity theory

My rap on this is that we are moving from a point where a lot of talk about molecular biology and genetics is ideology or culture … So we are moving out of that to what I am calling biosociality where a whole form of identity, both individual and group identity, and a vast army of cultural, political, social, theoretical institutions, practices of all sorts, are emerging very rapidly around truths. So I am interested in that Foucauldian sense of seeing truths have emerged, been produced, and then circulated. (Rabinow, 1995, p. 449)

Complexity is a multi-headed monster that can wreak havoc on investors who have assets to protect, preserve and enhance. Our International Fund Services people know how to handle complexity – no matter how great it is. (CITCO Group Advertisement, *The Economist*, 26 July 1997)

This section of the chapter tells us a story of three networks, singing a song to themselves and to each other. The networks I want to tell of are global science, global business and global New Age. And the song I want to follow is called 'complexity'.

Why have I chosen these particular three networks? First, because they are important determinants of our everyday lives. Science, business and New Age all matter to people: their discourses are touchstones of many practices. Second, because one of the processes that allows them to sing is a common one – mediatization. These are networks which are increasingly playing to publics created and driven by the media. Third, because these networks trade with each other. And why have I chosen this song? First, because it is current. The chief ideas of complexity are presently active across a vast terrain of practice – from the photographs of Eliot Porter (Gleick and Porter, 1991) to the thoughts of archbishops (Richardson and Wildman, 1997), from redefining business strategy (Beinhocker, 1997) to redefining Marxism (Owen, 1996). Second, because at the moment there are concentrated attempts to trade complexity theory into other networks. This is a process which it is possible to follow, if not in real time, then at least not so far behind.

Let me begin, though, with some reflections on how we might construct a geography of complexity theory. Though I am well aware that theory consists of more than metaphor, I will treat complexity theory as a set of metaphors concerning holistic emergent order, since this reduction at least has the merit of making it possible to produce a manageable account. And what I am primarily interested in, as a result of this discussion, is the means by which metaphors of complexity theory are able to travel and gradually become a *commonplace* structure of intelligibility. I will prime my account by undertaking some definitional work.

First of all, I assume that scientific metaphors, like other metaphors, are generally indefinite. This is not a disadvantage. To the contrary, it is why they are so powerful, because they can be *performed* in and to many different situations. As Game and Metcalfe put it:

Whereas literal knowledge aspires to the inert status of information, metaphor works with indeterminacy to keep meaning safe from the final clarification that is its obituary. Meaning's play is not a game watched from the outside but one in which we live and throughout which we understand. We may fantasize about mastering literal knowledge, fixing it in our memories or reference books or filing cabinets, but metaphors in knowledges cannot be processed, always maintaining reserves of wisdom beyond our present understanding. When someone criticized the lack of likeness in Picasso's portrait of Gertrude Stein, Picasso advised the person to wait. In the same way, the meaning of rich metaphors keeps blooming; people think further by growing into them, awakening to their implications. Traditions of thought grow stale with the declining productivity of their key metaphors …

Metaphoric activity is not the same as the culture's reality, but we are sceptical of the literal claim to re-present reality. Reality cannot really be seen, because we cannot see the world from the outside. Our knowledges are ours, mediated through us and projecting us into the world. We cannot fix or imitate the world as it really is. As Benjamin noted, 'Perhaps there is none of [man's] higher functions in which his mimetic faculty does not play a decisive role' … By letting us live (in) the world, metaphors enliven our understandings. Weber was too modest when claiming that the faculty for compassion or empathy lets us understand other people: it underlies all metaphoric truth.

We do not come empty-handed to our performances and metaphors. When metaphor engages us, we respond through the emotions and memories that reverberate with the role. (1996, pp. 50–1)

In particular, I would argue that metaphors are often at their most powerful when they are at their most diffuse: then their very breadth of meaning allows many meanings to be enlivened by them.

Second, I assume that complexity theory is deeply metaphorical. Certainly, some of its more subtle proponents see it precisely as an attempt to replace one set of metaphors with another:

the point of this exercise is not to conclude that there is something wrong with Darwin's theory because it is already linked to some very powerful cultural myths and metaphors. All theories have metaphorical dimensions which I regard as not only inevitable but also extremely important. For it is these dimensions that give depth and meaning to scientific ideas, that add to their persuasiveness and colour the way we see reality. The point of recovering this and the influences that act within current Darwinian theory is simply to help us to stand back, to take stock, to contemplate alternative ways of describing biological reality. (Goodwin, 1994, p. 32)

To connect with the previous point, I do not therefore assume that because metaphors of complexity theory come from science they are necessarily 'clearer'. This is to ignore one of the main functions of scientific metaphors in their early stages, which is to act to clear a semantic space within what may well be an obdurate scientific tradition. The case of Darwin's development of the metaphors of evolution is instructive. Campbell argues that Darwin was not able to 'explain the precise mechanism by which the earth and organism interact. However as a "place-holding illusion" – a means to identify and reserve a place within convention where a scientifically detailed explanation could be developed – it is a significant advance' (1990, p. 66). Gross glosses this statement thus: 'This seems exactly right. Darwin's form of argument is by nature not well-specified and it's just this lack of precision that accounts for its usefulness at this point in the process of discovery' (1996, p. xxiii).

Third, I would want to point to the importance of considering scientific metaphors as functioning in a number of registers, as ably demonstrated in the work of Barbara Maria Stafford (1992; 1994; 1996). In this chapter, I will chiefly consider the metaphors of complexity theory as verbal constructs, but what is equally important to remember is that science nearly always works with 'visual intuitions' as well (Lyne, 1996). This is a particularly germane observation in the case of complexity theory whose metaphors nearly all strongly depend upon the visual register (Hayles, 1991; 1996). It is difficult to think of complexity theory without its accompanying visual rhetoric: the obligatory fractal images of the Mandelbrot set, the spirals in the Beloussov–Zhabotisky reaction, the life cycle of the cellular slime mould, and the like. The 'new scientific perception is exercised metaphorically and literally through visualisation' (Wright, 1996, p. 234), the result of the interaction of advances in computing power with traditions of mathematical and biological representation that hark back to the invention of topology.

I want to relate how the new(ish) metaphors of complexity have been able to travel. To do this, I will take certain themes from actor-network theory as important. In particular, I will implicitly appeal to notions like translation (with its four stages of problematization, *intéressement*, enrolment and mobilization), to the role of intermediaries and to the agency of inscription devices. It may be thought that actor-network theory is an ideal vehicle for considering travelling metaphors. After all, this is a 'theory' that tells stories of quasi-objects which circulate a 'queer sociology that is emerging from the careful study of instruments, lieutenants, representatives, objects, angels and characters – to name but a few of the delegates with whom we build our daily life' (Latour, 1988a, p. 34). Again, actor-network theory tells stories of continuous attempts to make networks longer, of the constant extension of material-semiotic feelers, so that in a sense, and in line with actor-network theory's 'ethnographic' principle of following the actors, the networks end where the actors say they end. Actor-network theory also points to the fact that metaphors do not come empty-handed to a situation. They are always part and parcel of wider networks of practice, involving all manner of intermediaries and inscription devices, which co-produce them as 'objects which are both plastic enough to adapt to local needs and constraints of the several parties employing them, yet robust enough to maintain a common identity across sites' (Star, 1989, p. 46). The semiotic and the material are two sides of the same coin (Shapin, 1998). And consequently actor-network theory argues that metaphors do not lie still. They are always transmuting, pushed this way and that by the work of redefinition of one local knowledge by another that results from a host of different, rhizomatically multiplying agendas. For example, in the case of science,

> theory building is deeply heterogeneous: different viewpoints are constantly being addressed and reconciled ... Each actor, site, or node of a scientific community has a viewpoint, a potential truth consisting of local beliefs, local practices, local constraints, and resources, none of which are fully verifiable

across all sites. The aggregation of all viewpoints is the source of the robustness of science. (Star, 1989, p. 46)

In other words, semiosis is constant, unremitting and always entangled, and the story is in what is linked, not what something is.

But the case of complexity theory also points to some of the weaknesses of actor-network theory as practised, if not in theory (see Grint and Woolgar, 1997). In particular, many applications of actor-network theory in effect frame actor networks as discrete entities, pulling various bits of the world into them as and when it suits their purposes. The result is that a crucial dimension of actor-network theory – crossings, movement, travel – is under-emphasized; many of the wranglings and tanglings of re-presentational practices are thereby missed. I want to make up some of this weight in two ways. One is to take a leaf out of the growing body of work on cross-cultural consumption and interaction more generally, which stresses how greater interconnectedness can actually produce very diverse 'habitats of meaning' (Hannerz, 1996). Creolization produces all manner of creative responses out of what might appear to be quite similar materials. Another is to take a leaf from literary approaches to science, typified by the work of Gillian Beer and others (Beer, 1996; Gross, 1996; Spufford and Uglow, 1996) which also emphasizes how crossings, traffic, 'lateral encounters' can all produce fresh perceptions.

> Terms move across from one zone to another, for ideas cannot survive long lodged within a single domain. They need the traffic of the apparently *in*appropriate audience, as well as the tight group of co-workers, if they are to thrive and generate further thinking. An engrossing question is what happens when *unforeseen* readers appropriate terms and texts …
>
> Encounter, whether between peoples, between disciplines, or answering a ring at the bell, braces attention. It does not guarantee understanding; it may emphasize first (or only) what's incommensurate. But it brings into active play unexamined assumptions and so may allow interpreters, if not the principals, to tap into unexpressed incentives. Exchange, dialogue, misprecision, fugitive understanding, are all crucial within disciplinary encounters as well as between peoples. Understanding askance, with your attention fixed elsewhere, or your expectations focused on a different outcome, is also a common enough event in such encounters and can produce effects as powerful, if stronger, than fixed attention. (Beer, 1996, pp. 1–2)

In science, the concepts of complexity have a complex genealogy: they did not come naked into the world; they are already tangled and braided. Most proponents of complexity theory claim a set of ancestors in what is, in itself, an interesting rhetorical exercise. In mathematics, there is Henri Poincaré. In computing, there is Alan Turing and John von Neumann. In biology, there is D'Arcy Thompson, Jacob Von Uexkull, J.B.S. Haldane and, latterly, by adoption, Gregory Bateson. And so on. Yet what is clear is that by the late 1970s, as a result of manifold additions to the theory of non-linear dynamical systems and exponential advances in computing power, nearly all of the key components of complexity theory were already in place. For example, the late Conrad Waddington's (1977) *Tools for Thought* already regales the reader with most of the main themes of complexity theory, save for 'artificial life', a creation of the late 1980s, and 'life at the edge of chaos', a term first used in print by Langton in 1990 (Lewin, 1993). In the 20 years since Waddington's book, many of the elements of complexity theory have, in their various guises, become an important part of scientific discourse. But equally, it is crucially important to note that the success of complexity theory has only been partial and its future as a new scientific paradigm – as opposed to the success of some of its individual elements – is by no means assured. For example, in biology a reductionist molecular approach (typified by the human genome project) still holds sway.

Yet ironically, perhaps, the key moments of complexity theory – chaos, attractors, non-linearity, emergent orders, self-organization, implicate order, autopoiesis, life at the edge of chaos – have moved very rapidly into other parts of western society than science, and they seem to be producing a refiguring of the world far more rapidly than Darwin's plots ever did. Indeed, it might be possible to argue that it is outside science that complexity theory is being most successfully propagated.

Thus, complexity theory has reached into academic subjects like economics (Arthur, 1994; Barnett et al., 1996; Mirowski, 1994), regional science (Isard, 1996), architecture (Benjamin, 1995; Jencks, 1996), literary theory (Owen, 1996; Argyros, 1991; Hayles, 1990; 1991; Livingston, 1997), history (DeLanda, 1997; Ferguson, 1997), sociology (Byrne, 1996; Eve et al., 1997; Elliott and Keil, 1996; Khalil and Boulding, 1996) and anthropology (Benitez-Rojo, 1992; Martin, 1994). It has become the stuff of art, film, drama, and imaginative fiction (de Lillo, 1990; Waterson, 1996a; Egan, 1996; Jones, 1994). It has become inscribed in consumer objects (such as Donna Karan's new scent 'Chaos'). It has become a New Age selling feature (as in Chaos Magic in Neal's Yard in London). It has even become a focus of garden design (as in Charles Jencks's garden in Dumfries).

But, why is it that these metaphors have been able to travel so fast? A cynic might argue that it is because as these metaphors have travelled, so they have become almost completely meaningless. Flexibility produces lack of friction which produces fatuousness. But I think there are three more deep-rooted reasons.

One is that science has become common cultural currency in a way that it never was in Darwin's time (see Beck, 1992; Thrift, 1996a):

> the general culture incorporates scientific and quasi-scientific language, authority and modes of explanation into its talk about matters of common interest, including human behaviour, psychology, gender relations, the environment, and the nature of the cosmos, to name but a few. Thus science is a resource for the invention and performance of rhetoric in a variety of social contexts. (Lyne, 1996, p. 128)

Another reason is that, since the 1960s, what Gibbons et al. (1994) call a 'Mode 2' knowledge regime has grown up based on a much greater diversity of knowledge producers, distributors and audiences. The Mode 2 knowledge regime produces knowledge which is closer to applications, which is transdisciplinary, heterogeneous, heterarchical, organizationally diverse and reflexive.

At the core of this new Mode 2 knowledge regime is an expansion in the number of knowledge producers, coupled with a corresponding expansion in the number of specialist knowledges that are able to be produced. Or, put another way, a number of new, and in time autopoietic, knowledge-producing actor networks have come into existence, with consequences for both the conditions of knowledge production and what is thought of as knowledge. These actor networks, whose purpose is to generate and transmit knowledge, have translated the metaphors of complexity to their purposes and then circulated them in these mutated forms.

Then, last, these metaphors can travel faster because they circulate in heavily mediatized networks. In part, these networks exist to circulate information, often in heavily processed forms, which can attract audiences, and so profit.

I want to concentrate on the actions and interactions of three of these networks, one of which is a relatively old global actor but has taken on a new mediatized lease of life, the other two of which are relatively new.

The first of these networks is science. Science has changed over the last 20 years. It was always an international endeavour. But now it has become cosmopolitan on an entirely different scale. Thus, Rabinow writes of modern molecular biology as an entirely different kind of scientific animal from those of the past:

> Molecular biology, for example, has taken up the current conjuncture through an increased use of electronic means of communication, of data storage, of internationally coordinated projects like the human (and other organisms) genome mapping projects. The circulation and coordination of knowledge has never been more rapid or more international. Articulating and sustaining these goals is extremely expensive. Heads of major laboratories may well spend the majority of their time raising money, making contacts and forging alliances. The appearance in the last two decades of 'start up' biotechnology companies funded by venture capital and stock offerings, first in the United States and increasingly in Asia, India and Europe, has reshaped both the financing of research and (probably) its directions. Capital is international. While the principle of the international status of science has been in place for a long time, the form that it is taking in the biomedical sciences today is quite distinct. What kind of scientific life is it that is constantly travelling, constantly negotiating over resources, constantly engaged in competitive claims of priority, expanding in multiple arenas? (1996, p. 24)

A vital part of this new, even more cosmopolitan science (see also Shapin, 1998) is clearly mediatization. Books, television programmes, and the like sell science. And in turn, science sells books, television, and the like. Indeed, to a greater and greater degree, science is dependent upon media exposure, so that science and the media have become more and more closely intertwined.

Complexity theory is now one of the major scientific media exports. Numerous books have appeared over the last five years extolling its virtues, some by journalists but many by some of the founders of complexity theory (e.g. Gell-Mann, 1994; Goodwin, 1994; Kauffmann, 1995). Indeed, especially through the auspices of the Santa Fe Institute (SFI), set up in 1984, these founders, and other scientists, have clearly attempted to produce a site which would not only do research on complexity theory but also act as a centre for its dissemination. Thus, the Institute has acted to circulate complexity theory workers through its doors so as to produce a global 'family':

> The word family is appropriate because SFI is a rather loose organization. The president, Edward Knapp, is assisted by two vice presidents and an office staff of about a dozen remarkably dedicated workers. There are only three professors, of whom I am one, all with five year opportunities. Everyone else is a visitor, staying for periods ranging from a day to a year. The visitors come from all over the world, and a number of them pay frequent visits. The Institute holds numerous workshops, lasting a few days or sometimes a week or two. In addition, several research networks have been organized on a variety of interdisciplinary topics. The far-flung members of each network communicate with one another by telephone, electronic mail, fax, and the occasional letter, and they meet from time to time in Santa Fe or sometimes elsewhere. They are experts in dozens of specialties, and they are all interested in collaborating across disciplinary boundaries. Each one has a home institution … but each one also prizes the Santa Fe affiliation, which permits making connections that are somehow not so easy to make at home. These home institutions may be great industrial research laboratories, universities, or national laboratories (especially the nearby one at Los Alamos …). (Gell-Mann, 1994, p. xiii)

The Institute, as part of its 'family' strategy, has moved into numerous fields outside the natural sciences, including archaeology, linguistics, political science, economics, history and now management. Thus, the family strategy is a means of disseminating complexity theory both within and without science. Indeed, in certain senses, it might be seen as a strategy to make complexity theory so well known outside the networks of science that it will become better respected in science.

But it is not a strategy without its critics in the networks of science. The Santa Fe Institute is often seen as publicity-seeking to a fault:

> I … came across some downright negative assessments of the Santa Fe Institute's venture. For instance, Oxford University ecologist Robert May told me that what the Institute does is 'interesting but biologically trivial'. The computer models are too far from real biology for his taste and are irretrievably simplistic. 'Well Bob *would* say that, wouldn't he' was one rebuttal I heard in Santa Fe. Bob has a reputation for arrogance as well as brilliance. 'I don't think Bob really knows what's going on here,' Stu [Kauffman] told me. 'If he did, I think he'd see things differently.'
> Bob did concede that the Institute is crammed with talent, and then said that one of the things it seems most talented at was generating hyperbole. Jack Cowan, the University of Chicago mathematician who gave Stu Kauffman his first faculty position back in 1969, agreed. 'Don't get me wrong,' he said, 'there's a lot of good work at the Institute, but I often come away wondering where some of it is leading.' Jack, a member of the

Institute's science board, has long experience in research on complex dynamical systems. 'There have been examples of tremendous progress in understanding complex systems, but there have also been episodes of unbounded hype,' he told me. 'Remember catastrophe theory?' (Lewin, 1993, pp. 184–5)

The second of these networks has come into existence since the 1960s. The cultural circuit of capital, which I have already outlined in Chapter 1, is now self-organizing and is responsible for the production and distribution of managerial knowledge to managers. As it has grown, so have its appetites. It now has a constant and voracious need for new knowledges - including complexity theory.

Why have metaphors of complexity circulated in this burgeoning network of business practices? There are at least five reasons. The first of these is receptivity. From very early days, management thinking expounded systems theory approaches which directly link to complexity theory (see, for example, Emery, 1969). The intellectual ground was therefore, so to speak, prepared. The second reason is technological. As business has turned to information technology, so it has come into contact with an environment which is common between it and much of the science of complexity theory, allowing for much easier transfer of ideas. So the technological ground was also prepared. Third, the cultural circuit of capital needs a constant flow of ideas/metaphors: indeed this flow is a condition of its existence. These ideas, often called 'business fads' (Lorenz, 1989), roll by year after year. For example, between 1950 and 1988 Pascale (1991) noted 26 major fads and they have continued apace ever since. In this milieu, ideas of complexity theory are likely to receive a warm welcome. Fourth, a part of the work of the cultural circuit of capitalism is to inscribe metaphors in the conduct of business organizations and business bodies. In particular, the management seminar has proved a fertile means of introducing ideas of complexity into embodied corporate practices. At their most effective, they can produce strong shifts in what it means to be a person (Martin, 1994). Here, then, the circuit of cultural capitalism interacts with the new 'psy disciplines' (Rose, 1996) and a part of that interaction is metaphors like complexity. Then, fifth, the production of complexity theory is bound up with business, in the way that so much modern science is. For example, the Santa Fe Institute, perhaps the chief 'propagandist' for complexity theory, has had a long connection with Citicorp, is interested in the application of certain ideas in complexity theory to financial markets, and has spawned companies such as Prediction (again, chiefly involved in predicting the movement of financial markets) (Waldrop, 1993; Lewin, 1993). Now it is making a determined push into management by retailing ideas of complexity and life at the edge of chaos (Beinhocker, 1997). In 1997, for example, the Santa Fe Group and Knowledge-Based Development ran a series of seminars for business people in Phoenix and London on 'Complexity and Technology: Organizing for Innovation', featuring the founders of complexity theory like Brian Arthur, Murray Gell-Mann, John Holland and Stuart Kauffman, and also management gurus like John Seely Brown from Xerox PARC (see Seely Brown,

1997) and David Whyte (a poet and corporate consultant). Later in 1997, seminars were organized in Dallas, Sante Fe and Chicago by the Santa Fe Center for Emergent Strategies on 'Complexity in Business: Organizing for Emergent Strategies'. The blurb for this latter series of seminars argued that:

> It is increasingly recognized that the rapidly changing business environment makes extended strategic planning less and less useful. Strategy is becoming more an ongoing process and less a set of annually produced distant targets. Instead of fighting volatility, some companies are starting to respond with greater agility and with less bias towards new ideas. These new ideas, which form the basis for new company models and behaviors, can rarely be antic-ipated far in advance or in useful detail. Rather, they will emerge from the interactions between the company and all the environments in which it operates.
>   Strategy should be emergent and subject to continuing reassessments and alterations. In this way a company can keep pace with its marketplace, its competition and the new technologies that will change it. (Santa Fe Center for Emergent Strategies, 1997)

Goodwin summarizes the particular economy of concepts that are on offer to businesses (which have the advantage that they already fit well into many current ideas of management thinking):

> Business corporations have been among the first to see the potential rele-vance of these ideas to management structure and creative organisational change. Since their everyday experience is 'living on the edge', any insights into dynamic structures that facilitate adaptive response are welcomed. The suggestions of complexity theory for business practice are a flattening of the management hierarchy, distribution of control through the system with fluid networks of interaction between the parts, and the necessity of periods of chaos for the emergence of appropriate new order. The move towards a more anarchic, spontaneous dynamic is clearly threatening to the controlling man-agers, but it appears to be the path to creativity and diversification. This in no way guarantees survival, just as there is no long term survival guaranteed to adopted, adapting spaces in evolution. What it allows for is innovative expression, which has intrinsic value for the members of the enterprise, as well as providing the best chance of the organisation's persisting in a con-stantly changing corporate world. All the participants in this sector of social organisation can then experience a higher quality of life, since they have greater freedom, more opportunities for creative play, and richer interactions – good for them and good for the organisation. The primary goal would not then be to survive through maximisation of profits, but to make possible a fuller and more creative life for all members of the company and thus to maximise the chances of appropriate collective responses to perpetually changing circumstances. (1997, p. 117)

In turn, this economy of concepts can become a new management 'para-digm' of emergence and self-organization, which can be marketed as a set of simple principles that change 'how we design, lead, manage and view organizations' (Wheatley, 1994, publisher's blurb) (see Table 3.1). In other words:

Like Newtonian science before it, twentieth century science has grown out of a deep shift in general culture, a move away from absolute truth and absolute perspective toward contextualism; a move away from certainty, toward an appreciation for pluralism and diversity, toward an acceptance of ambiguity and paradox, of complexity rather than simplicity. Also like Newtonian science, this new science focuses the associated cultural shift and helps us to articulate the new paradigm. It provides us with the new concepts, new language, and new images that new paradigm thinking requires. Quantum thinking is new paradigm thinking. Both can help us rethink the structure and leadership of organizations, and initiate change processes that will allow business to thrive in the new paradigm. (Zohar, 1997, p. 9)

Table 3.1 Change in management paradigm

Old paradigm	New paradigm
Reductive	Emergent
Insulated and controlled	Contextual and self-organizing
Parts completely define the whole	Whole is greater than the sum of its parts
Top-down management	Bottom-up leadership
Reactive	Imaginative and experimental

Source: Zohar, 1997, p. 53

The third network that I want to describe consists of New Age practices. New Age consists of a set of organizations which are much less coherent than the cultural circuit of capitalism but which, since the 1960s, have also become a functioning international circuit. Like the capitalist circuit of cultural capital, the New Age circuit depends upon a constant throughflow of new ideas, even though these are often painted as rediscoveries of older knowledge; 'New Agers are averse to traditions ... yet New Agers continually draw on traditions' (Heelas, 1996, p. 27). The producers of these ideas are diverse. There are, first of all, various new religious movements and communities such as Erhard Seminars Training (est) and Findhorn. Then there are networks such as the Wrekin Trust. Then there are centres of spirituality and healing, camps and gatherings, and businesses. The ideas are distributed through a whole series of means. The chief of these is almost certainly the seminar or workshop. Introduced in the early 1970s, the seminar or workshop has become a pivot of New Age practices. Other forms of distribution like books, tapes, videos, managers and journalists are also becoming more important, as any glance at the New Age section of bookshops will show: 'in the space of half a decade, Americans have doubled their consumption of New Age books to 10 million a year' (*The Economist*, 5 April 1997, p. 58). Not to be forgotten, either, are other more informal means of interaction: e-mail discussion groups, small publishers and informal publications, and the general interaction in camps, gatherings and cafés. What is distinctive about the New Age circuit, compared with the cultural circuit of capitalism, is the much greater active participation by audiences; in other words audiences are, to a much greater extent, a part of the process of idea formation. Given the emphasis on self-spirituality and on syncretism in New Age this is, perhaps, to be expected.

Complexity theory seems to provide a ready-made vocabulary with which to talk self-spirituality and to battle against certain self-limiting images and beliefs, and it is no surprise that metaphors of complexity have become steadily more popular in New Age since the 1980s. There are four main reasons for their popularity. First, they can very easily be interpreted as a language of the self and self-making: there are emergent properties, there is self-organization, and so on (Capra, 1996). Second, they have provided a new vehicle for dissemination of older and more general New Age and New Agey ideas, such as Lovelock's Gaia (Capra, 1996; see also Lewin, 1993, and Goodwin, 1994, for the way in which these ideas have made their way into complexity theory). Third, they have provided symbolic authority for a relatively small and insecure network; the use of 'scientific' metaphors adds a touch of legitimacy, and it is not far from here to *Blackfoot Physics* (Peat, 1994) and *The Quantum Self* (Zohar, 1990). Fourth, some scientists themselves seem to lean, in their more popular writings, towards connecting complexity theory with elements of New Age thinking. Most of these popular writings at some point wax a little mystical, for example by making some reference to eastern religions. According to Waldrop, complexity theory makes it 'entirely too easy to come off sounding New Age and flaky' (1993, p. 23), but Stuart Kauffman (1995), one of the doyens of the Santa Fe Institute, seems less than concerned. Here is how he finishes his popular book:

> We have only just begun to invent the science that will account for the evolving emergent order I see out of my window, from a spider weaving her web, to coyote crafty on the ridge top, and we at the Santa Fe Institute and elsewhere proudly hope that we are unlocking some kinds of secrets, to all of you making your ways by your own best efforts and best lights.
>
> We are all part of this process, created by it, creating it. In the beginning was the Word – the Law. The rest follows, and we participate. Some months ago, I climbed to the first mountain top I have been able to reach since my wife and I were badly injured in a car accident. I climbed to Lake Peck with Phil Anderson, Nobel Laureate in physics and good friend at the Institute. Phil is a dowser. I once was astonished to see him pull a forked twig off a tree and march across a hilltop holding it. I pulled off a forked twig and followed him. Sure enough, whenever his twig dropped toward the ground, so too did mine. But then I could see him ahead of me. 'Does it work?,' I asked him. 'Oh, sure. Half of all people can dowse.' 'Ever dig where your stick pointed?' 'Oh no. Well, once.' We reached the peak. The Rio Grande Valley spread below us to the west; the Pecos wilderness stretched out to the east; the Truchas Peaks erupted to the north.
>
> 'Phil,' I said, 'if one cannot find spirituality, awe, and reverence in the unfolding, one is nuts.' 'I don't think so,' responded my dowsing, but now sceptical friend. He glanced at the sky, and offered a prayer: 'To the great nonlinear map in the sky.' (1995, p. 307)

To summarize, what I have tried to show, so far, is how the practices of three diverse actor networks, whose main purpose is the production of new knowledges, have produced a rapid diffusion of metaphors of complexity which, in turn, have been changed by the new networks in which they can circulate. But the trade in metaphors of complexity is not just between the network of science (which itself is now a more heterogeneous set of networks than in the past, which includes significant commercial interests) and the other two networks; it is also between the two newer networks as well. Thus, both business and New Age are united in their commitment to technologies of the self, from the cultural circuit's vision of an entrepreneurial self who makes the corporation healthy, wealthy and wise to the New Age network's cultivation of self-spirituality. It is no surprise then, given these imperatives, that New Age technologies have migrated into business, or that business has migrated into New Age. In both cases, metaphors of complexity have travelled with them, from different directions from the networks of science, often in mutated forms. And there is one more twist. It can, I think, be agreed that the increasing visibility of complexity theory outside science promoted by institutions like the Santa Fe Institute is part of a strategy to disseminate ideas of complexity *back into a science* which has sometimes been resistant to them. If complexity theory becomes a part of the general culture atmosphere then it must be breathed in by science as much as by other cultural producers.

There are certainly interesting examples of linkage, of which I will mention just three. First, there is the travelling from science into New Age. For example the biologist Brian Goodwin is now Director of Studies at the Schumacher Centre at Dartington, near Totnes, a generator of alternative concepts with a heavy emphasis on environmentalist values. In 1997 he toured Britain in dialogue with a number of artists concerning 'the creative "edge" between order, chaos and complexity in the natural world' (Arnolfini, 1997).

Second, there is the travelling from New Age into business. For example, a number of New Age training consultants (not that they would call themselves that) now retail complexity ideas as part of wider set of New Age and New Agey ideas that can be injected into businesses (Brown, 1997; Heelas, 1996):

> As freelance technicians of the sacred, working channels face the challenges of a volatile market that offers clients a constantly expanding array of therapeutic and spiritual options. To survive and prosper in such an environment, professional channels must learn to broaden their practice, to deal successfully with fickle clients, and to protect their intellectual property within the constraints of New Age values that are hostile to modernity. (Brown, 1997, p. 144)

Complexity theory offers 'channels' a means of presenting New Age assertions as neutral laws of the universe, legitimated by science. After all, 'even in the 1990s, insurance companies and HMOs are not ready to endorse the use of energy from the Pleiades, for healing or anything else. They are even less inclined to pay for it' (1997, p. 170). But science is a different matter.

Third, there is the travelling from science into business. We have seen the example of Goodwin's writings, but there are others. For example, Darah Zohar, a consultant who also teaches at Templeton College, Oxford University, has published books replete with complexity ideas (e.g. Zohar, 1997) as a means of broadening out the business of business so that it 'no longer restricts itself to manipulating things and nature and people for profit. Rather business becomes a spiritual vocation in the largest sense of that word' (1997, p. 154). In turn, these ideas can be inscribed by consultants at management seminars. For example, Peter Isaacs, Director of Training at Peter Chadwick Ltd, a fast-growing UK-based consultancy company, describes an approach based on the 'New Science':

> the challenge laid before us during those days we worked with Darah and her colleague led us to undertake a journey to 'rewire our corporate brain'.
>   Adopting some of the leading-edge thinking, we restructured ourselves into a collection of self-organizing networks. Each network in turn focused on key issues, whether these were market, sector, or lateral learning opportunities, that could benefit both ourselves and our clients. At the same time, we repositioned ourselves in the marketplace. It became our trademark to promote what at first seemed a very anti-consultant message: 'For change to be sustainable, it must ultimately come from within.' The new science was a crucial element in changing our company thinking. (1997, p. 155)

Mapping all of these metaphorical travellings and encounters would require a research project I cannot undertake here. But one thing is clear: the importance of space. Actor networks construct spaces and times and they do this work of construction in many registers at once (Latour, 1997). There are four main ways in which the space–time geographies of these networks have helped to shape their function as shifters of metaphors.

First, they provide a map of *where counts*. In the case of science, there are the main sites where complexity theory is produced which are, in turn, part of a quite specific international geography of where science as a whole is produced which is, perhaps, best summarized by studies of citation counts. In the case of the cultural circuit of capitalism, the map is of the main poles of managerial innovation like Boston, and the sites of managerial seminars. In the case of the New Age network, the map is (or has been) chiefly one of margins (Hetherington, 1996). In Britain, for example:

> Travelling [outside the north-west] one often encounters more on offer. Activities are most numerous in the capital city, Islington, London and – more specifically – Neal's Yard ... Then there are the more rural heartlands of the movement: Glastonbury, the Totnes region, the Welsh borders, Central Wales, and places along the 'Celtic' littoral including the Isle of Arran. East Grinstead is also worthy of note, being home, for instance, to the British headquarters of the National Pagan Association, the Rosicrucians and Scientology. (Heelas, 1996, p. 108)

In North America a similar kind of map could no doubt be drawn, taking in especially California, Arizona and New Mexico.

Second, the cultural valuation of the landscapes inscribed on these maps provides a *force of identity*. Thus science gains extra validation from certain stock landscapes such as the two Cambridges. Business also has its stock of familar landscapes on both sides of the Atlantic. New Age sites in Britain are often woven together into a mystical geography centred on, for example, notions like Avalon. In North America, more attention is usually given to Native American cultural sites, closeness to nature, and wilderness with, for example, desert and canyon landscapes providing a particular resonance. Third, these are geographies of *interaction*. In the networks of science and business, conferences, symposia, seminars, workshops and other forms of face-to-face interaction are supplemented by mediated communications. These are both worlds of 'frequent fliers and frequent faxers' (Hannerz, 1996, p. 29). In the New Age networks, face-to-face interaction, in seminars and workshops, at festivals and gatherings, and in cafés tends to be more important. And, fourth, space provides a *vocabulary* of journeys, travels, maps, shifts, and transformations which give the metaphors of complexity a semiotic force which is, at the same time, intended to imply transformation and diffusion.

At certain sites, networks can physically coincide, and these sites can provide particularly important points for the transmission of metaphors since they allow direct interaction and negotiation to (quite literally) take place. For example, as I have pointed out above, one of the major scientific centres of complexity theory has been the Santa Fe Institute. The Institute, has, from the start, attempted to reach across disciplines – into economics, for example (Arthur, 1994). But what is also interesting is just how much, in work emanating from the Institute, the surrounding landscape is regarded as an illustration of the importance of complexity metaphors: the New Mexico desert landscape provides a kind of ground. Then, even more interesting, Santa Fe is one of the key centres of New Age in the United States. We can see, here, how networks both interweave in spaces, and interweave spaces. Thus in Lewin's book *Complexity*, Chaco Canyon in New Mexico is figured as a landscape of complexity, as a site of a sophisti-cated Native American society which seems to have suffered a catastrophic collapse (and thus provides a conundrum for complexity theory to solve), and as a place which 'is also important to today's New Agers, who flock to the canyon for their own ceremonies, complete with borrowed Buddhist chants, meditation techniques, and crystals' (1993, p. 5).

The times of complexity: complexity theory as an aspect of seeing complexity

That life is complicated may seem a banal expression of the obvious, but it is nonetheless a profound theoretical statement – perhaps the most important theoretical statement of our time. (Gordon, 1997, p. 3)

I hope to have shown that metaphors of complexity have been able to travel rapidly through the burgeoning 'Mode 2' knowledge actor networks, constituting their own object as they go. So far, the tone of the chapter has been, if not sceptical, then certainly uncommitted. This is not, after all, a realist tract. But now I want to suggest that metaphors of complexity may be a sign of something of wider cultural interest and most especially a greater sense of openness and possibility concerning the future, based upon new cultural senses of time that acknowledge that things are complex and cannot be easily apprehended, upon models of time that are not foundational but still allow grip. In other words, I want to suggest that a new structure of feeling is emerging, a new 'cultural hypothesis' (Williams, 1978) concerning how we anticipate and frame the future which operates at 'the edge of semantic availability' (1978, p. 23) to which the metaphors of complexity theory are both a call and a response.

By way of preamble, I need to make it clear that I am not against the use of scientific metaphors outside science. On the one hand, there is certainly room to exaggerate their powers. For example, in many of the books on complexity written by practising scientists there seems to be an obligatory final chapter which suggests the ways in which the metaphors of complexity will refigure science and will then go on to provide an explanation of the whole world by providing a new world view. Then, it's off into every domain of current intellectual effort imaginable with every kind of false or tawdry analogy possible, as if to prove that these inheritors of systems theory can forget all about equifinality.

On the other hand, however, metaphors of complexity can focus cultural debate. For example, French social theory has undoubtedly been informed in productive ways by ideas drawn from science. Ideas from systems theory, topology and the like have been used in French social theory since their invention. Again, there is a long tradition of what might be called 'philosophical biology', 'an area of enquiry which although neglected in the English-speaking reception of continental philosophy, was of decisive importance for modern thinkers such as Kant, Hegel and Nietzsche and which has enjoyed a high profile in twentieth century France thought (Bergson, de Chardin, etc.)' (Ansell-Pearson, 1997, p. 17). More recently, the use of scientific metaphor has been extensive in French social theory as a means of getting at what Guattari once called 'a processual calling, a processual passion' (1996, p. 260). Thus, Jacques Derrida is often noted as a writer who has drawn on precursors of complexity theory like systems theory, the writings of Gregory Bateson, and the work of Jacques Monod and François Jacob, in interesting ways. In particular, his insistence on the primacy of the *écart* within the 'trace' (of survival over life, of translation over text) bears a strong resemblance to some current biological thinking: 'whereas biologists have traditionally taken reproduction to be the defining feature of living systems, the category of fluctuation is now considered to be logically prior to that of reproduction' (Johnson, 1993, p. 196). In other words,

> the continuous chain that extends from writing (technology) to the biological to evolution is a subset of the more general category of the trace. The enveloping context or condition of possibility is therefore something much wider than

the bio-social or the bio-anthropological, the essentializing alliance of 'life' and (at the apex of evolutionary ascent) 'man' being a central tenet of logocentric thinking. Similarly, systems theory, though indebted to modern neo-Darwinian biology, with its use of concepts such as teleonomy and equifinality, goes on to formulate a theory of self-organizing and self-regulating systems of which 'life' is but a special case, a regional instance. One arrives therefore at a non-biological theory of evolution in which the testamentary structure of survival (in the delegation and translation of the trace), the supplementary *überleben* over and above (before and after) the economy of life, is the organizing principle. It is striking to record Bateson practising what is basically the same metaphorical inversion as Derrida ... the terminology differs, but the basic idea, that symbolic systems, or more precisely the translations between symbolic systems, are the considerations of the possibility of life, rather than the reverse, remains the same. (1993, pp. 193–4)

Similarly, Michel Serres draws on notions from biology, systems theory and thermodynamics to fashion an early statement which echoes down through his later work (e.g. Serres, 1995a; 1995b) and which refers to biology, information theory, and the work of Jacques Monod (whom he knew as a friend):

It is no longer necessary to maintain the distinction between interpretative knowledge, or 'deep' knowledge, and objective knowledge. There is only one type of knowledge and it is always linked to an observer, an observer submerged in a system or in its proximity. And this observer is structured exactly like what he observes. His position changes only the relationship between noise and information, but he himself never effaces these two stable presences. There is no more separation between the subject, on the one hand, and the object, on the other (an instance of clarity and an instance of shadow). Thus separation makes everything inexplicable and unreal. Instead, each term of the traditional subject–object dichotomy is itself split by something like a geographical divide (in the same way as am I, who speak and write today): noise, disorder, and chaos on one side; complexity, arrangement and distribution on the other. Nothing distinguishes me ontologically from a crystal, a plant, an animal, or the order of the world; we are drifting together toward the noise and the black depths of the universe, and our diverse systemic complexions are flowing up the eutopic stream, toward the solar origin, itself adrift. Knowledge is at most the reversal of drifting, that strange conversion of times, always paid for by additional drift, but this is complexity itself, which was once called being. Virtually stable turbulence within the flow. To be or to know from now on will be translated by: see the islands, rare or fortunate, the work of chance or of necessity. (1982, p. 83)

I could go on to, for example, the work of Deleuze and Guattari, and especially to Deleuze's middle period 'biophilosophy' (see Ansell-Pearson, 1997) and Guattari's (1996) later work which, with its emphasis on 'chaosmosis', owes a clear debt of honour to the work of writers like Prigogine and Stengers.

But hopefully the point is made. In this more positive spirit, I want to suggest some of the ways in which the metaphors of complexity theory are being used in cultural debate as a means of clearing old ground and creating new. Four of these ways strike me as particularly important. First, the example of complexity theory shows how quickly scientific metaphors can now be co-opted by society as a whole, especially when forced by some of the networks I have identified. In the case of metaphors of complexity, I think it would be possible to argue that these metaphors have found and will find particularly fertile ground in contemporary western society because they can be bent to the *reflexive* turn, which, for all the undoubted exaggerations of Beck and Giddens (Alexander, 1995), still seems to be important. Certainly, writers as different as Capra (1996) and Maturana and Varela (1992) make these kinds of links to the self, and often make them quite explicitly.

Second, and at the same time, the metaphors of complexity theory tell us something about how the *rhetoric* of contemporary science is being mediatized. The persuasive metaphors of complexity are bolstered by the persuasive techniques of a media industry which is hungry for material. The rise of popular scientific publishing is little remarked upon, yet it is clearly important, especially now it has been linked to other networks like the capitalist cultural circuit and New Age. Complexity theory, in other words, becomes another means of systematizing and then commodifying ideas.

Third, the metaphors of complexity theory are also useful as a means of clearing a semantic space which might allow us to think again about the world in more explicitly *spatial* terms. There is the refiguring of 'internal' and 'external' processes which the metaphors of complexity theory lend themselves to, in the same manner as Deleuze's notion of the fold. Or, there is the way in which the metaphors of complexity theory seem to link to notions of spaces of flows, as in the work of Lash and Urry, or Serres's emphasis on message-bearing systems.

But I want to turn to, and end with, one more clearing, upon which I will concentrate most of my remaining attention. I want to argue that the metaphors of complexity theory make it easier to think about *time* in new ways (Turner, 1997), and especially the structure of the future as open, as full of possibility and potentiality, even as pliant. They allow this sense of time to be constructed in a number of registers, of which I will point to just three.

The first of these is a shift in western notions of *personhood* (see Strathern, 1999). As the number of possibilities of personhood has multiplied – through the division of labour, the sexual revolution, postcolonial imaginings, and so on – so the notions of persons as consisting of a set of complex, multivalent and more open subject positions has taken hold. These 'fractal' persons are irreducible to a single dynamic (Strathern, 1996):

> Complex personhood means that all people (albeit in specific forms whose specificity is sometimes everything) remember and forget, are beset by contradiction, and recognize and misrecognize themselves and others. Complex personhood means that people suffer graciously and selfishly too, get stuck in the symptoms of their troubles, and also transform themselves. Complex personhood means even that those called 'other' are never ever that. Complex personhood means that the stories people tell about themselves, about their troubles, about their social worlds, and about their society's problems are entangled and weave between what is immediately available as a story and

what their imaginations are weaving towards. Complex personhood means that people get tired and some people are just plain lazy. Complex person-hood means that groups of people will act together, that they will vehemently disagree with and sometimes harm each other, and that they will do both at the same time and expect the rest of us to figure it out for ourselves, intervening and withdrawing as the situation requires. Complex personhood means that even those who haunt our dominant institutions and their systems of value are haunted too by things they sometimes have names for and sometimes not. At the very least, complex personhood is about conferring the respect on others that comes from perceiving that life and people's lives are simultaneously straightforward and full of enormously subtle meaning. (Gordon, 1997, p. 405)

The second register is how those in the West regard *things*. It is possible to argue that our attitude to things has become more open and that things have become more open to us. To begin with, because we are surrounded by a more and more complex ecology of things (Williams, 1991; Thrift, 1996a). Then, because these things increasingly have the capacity to interact with us; indeed they have increasingly become designed to do so (Latour, 1991). Again, because we are increasingly configured to interact with things; we have become more 'charitable' to them (Collins, 1990). And, finally, because many more things have become multifunctional and therefore able to be fitted to many situations (Knorr-Cetina, 1997). The way in which this openness is most often captured is through the notions of actor-network theory, an anti-essentialist attempt to weave the social and the technical together by stressing the construction of more or less durable actant networks:

Actor-network theory stresses the contingent nature of networks and network theory. There is a constant need to establish and reproduce the network. In part, this can be achieved through material embodiment. Indeed, networks based solely on human relations tend to be very weak. Hence, an important question is not whether constituent members of a network are human or non-human but: 'which associations are stronger and which weaker?' (Latour [1987b] p. 40). (Grint and Woolgar, 1997, p. 24)

While actor-network theory is about reducing contingency, its purpose is also therefore about emphasizing the contingency of the world and the many possibilities that are open at any point. Indeed in some of its more extreme manifestations (e.g. Law, 1997; Law and Mol, 1996), actor-network theory has become contingency incarnate, the gaps and uncertainties having become almost as important as the networks:

Similarities and differences. And here is a further difference. Perhaps there is no pattern, no overall pattern. Perhaps, then, it is not simply that we can't describe a single and coherent pattern … Perhaps there is no single and coherent pattern. Perhaps there is nothing except practices. Perhaps there is nothing other than stories performing themselves and seeking to make connections, practical and local connections, specific links.

In which case? In which case we are no longer in the business of epistemology. Of trying to find ways of telling about the links that exist between bits and pieces of complex objects. Instead … we are in the business of creating links, of making them, of bringing them more or less successfully into being. Which means in turn that we are no longer trying to find good ways of narrating and describing something that was already there. Instead, or in addition, we are in the business of ontology. We are in the business of making our objects of study. Of making realities, and the connections between these realities, of making the realities we describe. Of trying to find good ways of interacting with our objects, ways that are sustainable, ways that are making it possible to link with them. (Law, 1997, pp. 8–9)

The third register, and the one which, given the geographic theme of this chapter, I want to end by considering, is a reframing of *space–time* as a series of possible worlds, what Lewis (1973) calls 'unactualized possibilities', what Casti (1991; 1996) calls 'would-be worlds'. It is remarkable how little attention has been given to these kinds of cultural imaginings by social scientists, the multiplicity of sequences that lurk at every fork of the present. These are shadow worlds about which we can never be certain. But, they can still promise a kind of understanding 'which comes from locating an actual in a space of possibilities' (Hawthorn, 1991, p. 28). In other words, 'they raise the ghost of another possibility in order to investigate the groundwork of the real; they raise it in order to lay it again' (Spufford, 1996, p. 274) by attending to

the complexities that start to emerge if we abandon distinctions between possibility and impossibility. And in particular, a sharp distinction between possibility and impossibility. Between, for instance, objects out there (permissible) and object-and-subject couplets (impossible). Between object-singularity (permissible) and object-multiplicity, the decentred object (impermissible). Or between that which is real (permissible) and that which is fantastic (impermissible). (Law and Mol, 1996, p. 12)

Consideration of this kind of openness has perhaps been most developed in the investigations by Morson (1994) and Bernstein (1994) of the power of closed narrative models of time, in which events are 'foreshadowed', becoming posthumously 'historical' by virtue of a belief that, 'in one way or another, the future must already be there, must already exist substantially enough to send signs backward' (Morson, 1994, p. 7). By way of contrast, Morson and Bernstein advocate more open narrative models of time which 'recognise a middle realm of possibilities that could have happened even if they did not' (Morson, 1994, p. 6), a 'sideshadowed' realm of unactualized possibilities which can both restore the presentness of the past and simultaneously open up the present by demonstrating how

each counterlife is compressed of limitless countermoments, and how each thought takes shape as only one realization amid the counterthoughts that hover as its side shadows, multiple alternatives existing in a potential space and ready to be brought, by the quickening of imagination or desire, out of the shadows and into the light of formal expression. (Bernstein, 1994, p. 7)

Taking their cue from novels of the nineteenth and early twentieth centuries, these authors also point to the current interest in postmodern narrative forms of the kind outlined by Gibson (1996), Brandt (1997) and Livingston (1997). Such narrative forms attempt to produce new narrative topologies, geopoetics, constellations and 'chaologies' in which space and time are figured as the result of 'the connection among entities' (Latour, 1993), and so can slide in many directions. Thus we arrive at a polymorphic aesthetics of the 'multiple proliferations of spaces' (Gibson, 1996, p. 13), an aesthetics which

> must turn away from laws and regulations to exchanges and interferences, connections and disconnections between spaces. It must choose against Kant, in opting for what Kant saw as 'denaturation', a confounding of different knowledges ... It must concentrate on perturbations and turbulences, multiple forms, uneven structures and fluctuating organisations. (1996, p. 13)

To summarize. It seems to me that complexity theory must be seen, then, as in a direct line of scientific thinking from topology through Einsteinian relativity theory, quantum theory and the like which has now become part of a progressive recasting of popular Euro-American beliefs about time and space as dimensions *open to possibility*. Thus, the buttoned-down Newtonian/Darwinian 'time of the victors' gives way to a new disclosive sense of time and space in which 'order is not the law of things but their exception' (Serres, 1982, p. xxvii), but which also allows certain kinds of emergent order to become possible and to be more easily acknowledged (Massey, 1997). Or, to quote Serres again: 'we have not, nor shall we ever again, fail in dealing with spaces' (1982, p. 53).

Conclusions

This chapter is clearly only a starting point for what should be a much larger project. In it, I have tried to use complexity theory both as an object of study and as a means of making some observations about the changing sense of what is possible in Euro-American cultures. In particular, I have suggested that the metaphors of complexity theory are important signs of new senses of time which are more open to possibility. However, I want to end the chapter with an important injunction. One interpretation of the latter part of the chapter might be that older senses of time based on linear notions of progress and discrete, synchronized spaces are being knocked on the head by newer 'postmodern' senses of time founded on cultural diversity and desynchronized spaces of flows (see, for example, Adam, 1990; 1995; Nowotny, 1994; Urry, 1994). This may be. But another interpretation is that this more open time is actually simply a continuation of the older time senses by other means. What we are tracking is an expansion of the older Euro-American mindset, not its extinction, as the future becomes a space of possibility for subjects who believe that anything is possible, given the means, the result of

> the cultural place that is given to enablement itself. Euro-Americans imagine that they can do 'more' things than they once could, crystallised in the hypostatisation of technology as 'enabling' ... I suspect that above all they

take for granted, quite simply, that *given the technology* they can do anything. If technology is society made durable, it is at the same time ability made effective. (Strathern, 1996, pp. 46, 49)

Seen in this way, the changing sense of temporalization I have hinted at might be simply a continuation of imperialism by other channels, but now in time rather than space (Osborne, 1995; Frow, 1997). In which case, what we may be seeing in the guise of expanded possibility is simply business as usual.

4

Virtual Capitalism: The Globalization of Reflexive Business Knowledge

Introduction

The analysis of capitalism is beset by scripts which prevent us from seeing many of the new things that are going on. These scripts are typified by a paper by Altvater and Mahnkopf (1997). For these two authors, the triumph of the world market comes on apace, forced by various mechanisms which have intensified a tendency to 'global disembedding' in which the market has increasingly become separated from its social bonds. These mechanisms are of four types. First, the money form takes on a new, more aggressive stance: 'there emerges a global financial system as a monetary sphere decoupled from the real economy' (1997, p. 451). Second, the economy becomes globalized as 'commodification envelops the global system' (1997, p. 451). Third, temporal and spatial co-ordinates are compressed by the expansion and acceleration of money and other forms of commodification. We live, therefore, in a world time of 'all-encompassing contemporaneity' (1997, p. 456) produced by new means of transportation and communication. Then, fourth, these developments produce new environmental stresses and strains, as natural resources are used up and not replaced.

Elsewhere, I have taken strong exception to these kinds of scripts (see Thrift, 1995; 1996c). Their tone is that of the seer, able to navigate the currents of history with aplomb. Their assumptions are often mistaken, based on bad or outmoded historical research, and on long-standing intellectual habits like technological determinism whose pervasiveness has only recently been acknowledged. These scripts, in other words, tell their stories with a kind of supernatural confidence which is more appropriate to the old Norse sagas than to the soap operas of everyday economic life.

In this chapter, I therefore want to take issue with scripts like those of Altvater and Mahnkopf, by starting to write another tale. I will begin in the same place as Altvater and Mahnkopf – with the triumph of the global market – but then draw rather different lessons. Instead of seeing this triumph as the apogee of capitalism, I will suggest that what it points to is just how tentative, tendentious and uncertain the global capitalist 'order' really is. The world that capitalism has wrought is a world, exactly as Marx pointed out, of chronic uncertainty and instability. Capitalism is, in other words, hoist by its own success.

So how can capitalist firms establish some control of their circumstances, in a world which they increasingly regard (and increasingly frame as such, so to a certain extent producing a self-fulfilling prophecy) as inherently uncontrollable (Thrift, 1995)? I will argue that this vision of uncertainty has pushed those who run capitalist firms into taking a virtual turn (Carrier, 1996; Miller, 1996), a turn towards 'theory' – but, as I shall make clear, towards *a quite particular form of theory*.

The chapter is therefore in two main sections. In the first section I will consider the *practical* forms of theory, based upon the dictates of the moment, that are crucial to the running of capitalist organizations. The second section then builds on this base by considering the rise of reflexive management theory over the course of the twentieth century. This theory is a form of virtualism which, as I point out, has its own self-reproducing institutional set-up – a set-up which is currently undergoing its own form of globalization, as I will underline by using the example of Asia. However, as I note in the conclusions to the chapter, the term 'virtual' needs some qualification in the case of capitalism.

In both sections, my chief source of inspiration will be work on concrete material practices such as are currently found under investigation in research on material culture, the sociology of science, and actor-network theory. This body of work grounds theory in specific arenas of practice, and by situating knowledge in context, questions what might be meant by terms like 'concept' and 'idea' which, though often enough bandied about as the very stuff of theory, are always engrained in practices (Thrift, 1996a).

Practical capitalism

I need to start by briefly describing my sense of how the global capitalist economy is, for this is a very different sense from those of writers like Altvater and Mahnkopf who constantly confuse the logic of theory with the logic of practice. First, I do not believe that the capitalist economy has become progressively more disembedded, in the sense of more abstract and more abstracted. The capitalist economy has become more distanciated (Giddens, 1991), certainly, structured through time and over space by all manner of machines and other devices, but this has produced a multitude of time and spaces which interact in complex ways with each other. Again, this distanciation has produced a thickening of communication; in many senses, capitalist firms live in a more intimate and connective world than ever before. Second, I do not believe that money functions as something apart from a 'real' economy which, by implication, acts as a social corrosive. Money acts in complex ways, depending upon the networks in which it is deployed. Money, in other words, is not one thing; it consists of many different instruments working to many different purposes (Leyshon and Thrift, 1997). Third, I do not believe that we live in a time of all-pervasive contemporaneity. To return to the first point, all manner of times are constantly being constructed by particular networks which tread their way differently around the world. Some of these times are fast, and some of them are slow; there is no mean (Thrift, 1997a). Fourth, I do not believe that the capitalist economy has become globalized in any strong sense. The world 'capitalist' economy is 'profoundly mixed' (Mann, 1997, p. 480). It is a raucous conglomeration of competing priorities, some transnational, some not. In other words, my world capitalist economy is a tentative creation, constantly generating new networks which sometimes prove durable and sometimes not. Just because it is full of tools of ordering does not mean that it is ordered. Just because it uses fast technologies does not mean that it is fast. Just because it has its ideologies, does not mean it is ideological. Rather, its existence demonstrates the multiple, multiplex ways in which profit can be searched out and realized (Latham, 1996).

How, then, might we think about theory *in* capitalism, rather than of the theories *about* capitalism that abound? Let us start with a picture: Hans Holbein's famous painting of *The Ambassadors* (1533). In this painting is a sign of the new confidence in business and trade which is, at the same time, one of the reasons for this confidence. The sign is one of the first books for business people, placed significantly under the globe, a German book called *A New and Well Grounded Instruction in All Merchant's Arithmetic in Three Books Compiled by Peter Apian, Astronomer in Ordinary at Ingolstadt* (Latour, 1988a; Conley, 1996; Foister et al., 1997).

But academics have, I think, manipulated this and other such signs as the first stirrings of political economy. And, being academics, they have tended to see the birth of political economy as a pivotal event: here is the beginning of a discourse, a textual outfitting of the world which constitutes notions of economy (Foucault, 1970).

Similarly, academics have tended to assume that one of the descendants of political economy – economics – is the theoretical language of business. Over the years, economics, or so it is thought, has provided the theoretical backbone of business. Thus, the world is made into a reflection of theory.

But I have become less and less convinced by this kind of story. No one can deny that political economy, and then economics, have been important through recent history, but I am not at all sure how important they were or are in business. Where they *are* important is as discursive elements of state governmentalities, justifying state action in producing arenas which the state enacts as 'economic'. But, on the whole, I believe that capitalist firms play to different drums. I make this judgement for four reasons.

First, it is possible to simply argue that much economics has never been quite as important in business as is often made out. It is true that economics is taught to MBA students, sometimes in profusion, as at the hardline economics business schools like Stanford (and many German business schools). It is also true that many business people will have been taught some formal economic theory. But what strikes me is how little economics is actually ever *used* in business. The one exception to this rule is financial economics, which is used in the financial markets and is one of the backbones of corporate finance. More generally this strain of economics manifests itself in audit operations and in standard measures like return on capital employed (ROCE). But such economics seems to me to function

UWE LIBRARY SERVICES

as legitimation, as a kind of discursive principle which can be referred to but which often bears about as much relation to the conduct of business as the high court judge does to the shoplifter.

Second, capitalist business is performative (Thrift, 1997a). By this I mean that it is a practical order that is constantly in action, based in the irreversible time of strategy (Bourdieu, 1977). Whilst it has its contemplative aspects, based in the time of learned knowledge, it is chiefly an order of the moment, and a means of crafting the moment. Tasks have to be carried out. Reports have to be made. Plans for the next two years cannot be made in two years' time. There is no 'if only ...' (Boden, 1994).

Third, capitalist business is based in a material culture. Its devices – from the vast number of intermediaries required to produce trade, through the wide range of means of recording and summarizing business, to the different layouts of buildings that discipline workers' bodies – are not an aid to capitalism; they are a fundamental part of what capitalism is. This depiction is hardly unusual. For example, there are elements of it in the work of Braudel. More recently it has been taken up by actor-network theorists (Latour, 1986; 1993). But its consequences are only just being thought through.

Fourth and finally, capitalist business is based in a notion of 'theory' which is of a different order from more formal theory; it is based on problematization and problem spaces rather than a succession of scholarly theories which roll by and are judged according to particular criteria of correctness. The problem is that academics tend to marginalize and (implicitly at least) demean such theory through a number of associations: its lack of formality; its source in social groups which are regarded as 'practical' rather than theoretical; its closeness to technological devices; its allegiance to the empirical; its fixation on the moment. But, in turn, the denigration of such 'theory' can be constructed as a problem for more formal notions of theory, since

> these problematising voices tend not to be much concerned with 'epochal' theories or systems, or with abstract conceptions of society, and yet, some suggest, it is these voices that have often proved decisive, setting the terms under which sociological theories can place themselves 'in the time' or, alternatively, shaping the criteria which strip their truthfulness away. (Osborne and Rose, 1997, p. 80)

So, I want to interpret the sign of Peter Apian's book in a different way, as one of the first sightings of new forms of practical business 'theory', based on what I will call the promotion of intelligence about competence within specific problem spaces. Such thinking on 'how to solve', usually by modest example, specific problems has a long and still only partially told history in business, and more generally (Osborne and Rose, 1997).

I want to argue that, in the sphere of business, three different but related variants of this theory exist, each of them with their own specialist communities which produce and disperse these intelligences and competences. Such communities include not only specific kinds of people but also specific kinds of device which are a vital part of the means of producing and distributing intelligence. Elsewhere, these spheres have been called by terms like 'regimes of calculation' (e.g. Porter, 1995) but for my purposes, as will become clear, this depiction conjures up too great a sense of a pursuit of objectivity through numerical means. I prefer, then, to call them 'theoretical networks'.

The first such theoretical network I have called book-keeping. Until recently the history of accounting was something of a backwater, but in the last 10 years it has become a major centre of intellectual endeavour, thus making it easier to frame a brief history of the network. The early growth of the network was clearly based around three practices. The first of these was the abacus or counting board:

> By the late eleventh and twentieth centuries, treatises on elementary calculations were, by and large, treatises on the use of the counting board, and there was a new word, *abacus*, meaning to compute. In the sixteenth century counting boards were so common that Martin Luther could off-handedly refer to them to illustrate the compatibility of spiritual egalitarianism and obedience to one's betters. (Crosby, 1996, p. 44)

But the counting board was a device for computing, not recording:

> Its users of necessity erased their steps as they calculated, making it impossible to locate mistakes in the process except by going back to the beginning and repeating the whole sequence. As for permanently writing down the answers, that was done in Roman numerals. (1996, p. 111)

Thus another important practice, one which allowed not only better calculation but also better recording, was imported from Arabic Spain. This was calculation using Arabic numerals. Even given the usefulness of these numerals it took some 300 years from their introduction in the twelfth century for the process of 'pen reckoning', as Arabic numerals were called, to become current throughout Western Europe, even though such numerals did not erase themselves as calculation occurred – and so could be checked – and allowed calculating and recording to be done with the same symbols.

Finally, there is the invention of double-entry book-keeping. Living in a blizzard of transactions, as they did, merchants and other business people had to have some sense of how to track each transaction, and this problem was solved by the evolution of a two-column system of debits and credits, probably originating in Venice at the end of the thirteenth century. This system was then supplemented by the practice of entering each entry twice, keeping what was, in effect, a double account. In turn, the procedure spread across Europe, chiefly through manuals on book-keeping.

Nowadays, the book-keeping network is most often associated with the computer, but it is important to understand the extent to which automated practices of book-keeping have been evolutionary. Thus tabulating and calculating machines were introduced in the 1880s into accounting departments. Later punch-card systems and various electromechanical devices for sorting and analysis were also used (Yates, 1994). Thus by the time the computer appeared the protocols of automated book-keeping had already been established.

A second theoretical network consists of the crystallization of organizational practice in written procedures: codes and algorithms, organizational values, opinions and rhetorics, as well as skills, are frozen into devices like operating manuals, company rules and procedures, company handbooks, posters, and the like. The network has its origin in two devices. The first is instruction manuals. These are the first attempts to objectify practical knowledge (Thrift, 1985). Such manuals date from the sixteenth century. Then, second, there is the recording and compiling of lists and subsequently reports, which collect and draw up information which could not have been written down hitherto:

> List-making has frequently been seen as one of the fundamental activities of advanced human society. Thus Jack Goody (1971; 1987) has argued that the first written records are lists (of things, of equipment). Michel Foucault (1970) and Patrick Tort (1989) have, in their different ways, claimed that the production of lists (of languages, races, minerals, animals) revolutionised science in the nineteenth century and led directly to modern science. Latour [1987b] has proclaimed that the prime job of the bureaucrat is to compile lists which can be shuffled and compared. These diverse authors have all turned their attention away from dazzling end-products in the various forms of Hammurabi's code, mythologies, the theory of evolution, the welfare state, and so on. They have instead looked at the work involved in making these productions possible. They have dusted off the archives and discovered piles and piles of lowly, dull, mechanical lists …
>
> List-making is fundamental for co-ordinating activity distributed in time and space … when lists are used to co-ordinate important work that is distributed widely over time and space, a corresponding complex organisational structure and infrastructure must evolve (Yates and Orlikowski, 1992). Negotiations over the content of the list became reified – frozen – and often take quantitative form, especially if the items are numerous, costly, or critical for other operations. The judgement calls are still there, but now involve multiple actors including individuals, organisations and technologies. The decisions about division of labour remain, but now entail bureaucracies as well as spot judgements. As all the authors cited above have concluded, large-scale co-ordinated work is impossible without lists. As well, those lists entrain whole series of substantive political and cognitive changes in the classes they inventory. (Bowker and Star, 1994, pp. 188–9)

Both these activities were measurably boosted by the new office technologies which were produced from the mid nineteenth century onwards – technologies which not only recorded, copied, duplicated and stored information, but, in effect, through these different activities, created it. In particular:

> The first mass-produced typewriters appeared in 1874, aimed at a large market of court reporters, authors and other specialised users. Typewriters operated by experienced typists could produce documents at three times the rate of pen and paper, thus increasing the speed and lowering the cost of producing them. Beginning in the 1880s and 1890s, firms adopted the typewriter

just in time to show the already rising costs of their increased internal and external written communication. (Yates, 1994, p. 32)

At the same time, prepared forms became common in businesses. These forms not only reduced the time spent recording information but also encouraged consistency and made it easier to extract information as necessary. (Around the turn of the century, the tab function was added to typewriters precisely in order to aid the typist in typing tables and filling out forms.) Duplicating activity was also becoming easier. Carbon paper, hectographs, and stencils were used to produce large numbers of copies, culminating in the invention of the mimeograph in the late 1890s. Filing systems also became more common, with the introduction of vertical filing to the business world at the 1893 Chicago World's Fair. In turn such systems were used to produce systems of indexing and organizing which were much proclaimed in management periodicals and textbooks. The card file also became more common and had many of the same effects. Thus, by the time of the computer, many business procedures, codes and algorithms had already settled out and had only to be adapted to the new medium (Pellegram, 1997).

In some cases values, opinions, rhetorics and skills are frozen in the written word or number. But just as likely they are encapsulated in visual representations: graphs, maps, charts, diagrams, which envision the organization and give it its position in the 'economy' (Buck-Morss, 1995). For example,

> graphs were widely adopted in the early twentieth century to make information more accessible and compelling to those using it. While graphic representations of data had existed for at least a century, they had been used primarily for government statistics and later for experimental data in science and engineering. Advocated by systematisers and engineers-turned-managers, graphs gained considerable popularity as a way to make the information gathered and analysed available to decision-makers in an efficient and compelling form. (Yates, 1994, p. 36)

Often these visual representations sink into the background, serving no other purpose than to provide a stance from which to act into the world. For example:

> After a 90-minute session at Andersen [Consulting], which involved a particularly complicated diagram, the question was asked: 'Why do you draw so many charts?' After a moment of thought, the reply came 'I don't know. Everyone here does.' (O'Shea and Madigan, 1997, p. 85)

Visual representation keeps evolving. Much has been made of the impact of the computer, but perhaps the most potent managerial tools of the last few decades have been the humble flipchart, the overhead projector, and the slide projector, all used in a vast number of different situations to produce, organize and represent the thinking of groups.

That said, in the last 20 years, a new crystallization of organizational practice has become possible through the development of computer software of a bewildering range and variety which imposes standards but also offers choices. In turn, software has become intelligent in its own right, and capable of producing complex representations.

The third network is the most recent. Though its history can clearly be traced back in time – for example, to Robert Owen or to Quakers like the Cadburys and Rowntrees – its origin is usually identified with managerial experiments in the 1940s and 1950s in Britain and the United States arising out of psychology. In Britain, the work of psychologists like C.S. Myers and Elliott Jacques at the Tavistock Institute, as well as the work of Eric Trist on coalmines in Haighmoor, were seminal. In the United States the invention of training groups and the founding of the National Training Laboratories (NTL) by psychologists like Lewin, Lippitt, MacGregor and Argyris, in Bethel and then nationwide, are regarded as founding moments. From these beginnings there has developed an alternative tradition of management, one which stresses human interaction and self-fulfilment as general elements of organizational successes. Indeed, one might argue that this network has, to a considerable degree, developed in direct opposition to the other two networks, as a conscious effort to supplement, extend, or even undermine them. Kleiner (1996) shows how this network was built up in piecemeal fashion from all manner of sources until the 1970s, dependent upon the enthusiasms of particular managers and corporate whim. But in the period since the 1970s, it has become highly successful as the inculcation of 'soft' management skills like team leadership, creativity, emotional thinking, and the like. This success has been for four reasons. First, the network was able to find a home in extant institutional bases like business schools and, increasingly, management consultants. Second, it was able to promote itself through the power of the media. Indeed, this network is strongly coupled with the media, as instanced by its reliance on inspirational books for managers, business growth, and the like (Thrift, 1997a; Micklethwait and Wooldridge, 1996; Crainer, 1997a; Carrier, 1996). Third, it has been able to produce believers who have considerable investments in the network, especially in the human resources sector which it has largely driven. Fourth, and finally, it has been able to produce and make general its own (interactional) devices. These include all manner of transactional trainings and therapies (Heelas, 1996; Brown, 1997). But they also include far more mundane but equally effective means of interaction. Thus, business lunches and seminars and conferences are now regarded as a background hum in business. But they all had to be invented. For example, social events/seminars as means of selling business were probably invented by Marvin Bower of McKinsey as a way of selling services to target companies. The first such event was held in 1940 and was called a 'clinic dinner'. Conferences about business strategy (which are also marketing tools) probably originated with Bruce Henderson of Boston Consulting in the 1960s. They were used as a means of starting or keeping up relations with top corporate management (O'Shea and Madigan, 1997).

These three networks are not necessarily opposed to each other. They interact in most business organizations, sometimes in opposition, sometimes in uneasy coexistence, sometimes in concord. And, out of this interaction new practices are produced. As an example, one of the most significant of these practices in recent times has been the rise of new forms of business indicator. These indicators can be interpreted in a number of ways. They can be seen as the movement of book-keeping culture into the humanist network, as an example of the rise of 'audit culture' (Power, 1997; Strathern, 1997). Equally, however, they might be seen as the spread of humanist forms into book-keeping networks. But, more likely, they are a new hybrid form. Thus, the so-called balanced scorecard approach (Kaplan and Norton, 1996) aims to complement standard financial indicators with a whole range of other indicators of business success stressing 'softer' attributes like leadership, human resource management, business process management, customer and market focus, and information utilization and quality, which are, in turn, broken down into further items. For example, in one British financial services firm,

> scorecards are displayed on desktop machines in each branch. Each branch manager can only see information for his or her branch, each area or regional manager can only see information for the relevant area or region, and so forth. The headline screen displays a distillation of statistics for each area – for example, the customer services survey uses 50 items, but these are compressed into just five components. A further 70 screens can, however, be accessed for further levels of data. (van de Vliet, 1997, p. 80)

Each of the items has to be effective if the whole is to work, and each item is meant to correspond with 'a "defined desired state", "written in an active, almost emotional way", to create a positive mental image' (1997, p. 80). Another example is the rise of 'relational software' – systems which instantly call up a client's personal details, thereby allowing high levels of personal interaction. Again this example can be interpreted in two ways: as the movement of the book-keeping culture into the humanist network, or vice versa. More likely, again, this is a hybrid.

'These days it seems like any idiot with a laptop computer can churn out a business book and make a few bucks. That's certainly what I'm hoping': reflexive capitalism

The key point of this chapter is that capitalist 'theory' is of a practical bent. But what is interesting is that increasingly, over the last 30 years or so, capitalist business *has* taken a more reflexive, virtual turn. This turn is not a total one. It is concentrated in larger firms and the more dynamic small and medium enterprises. But that it exists can no longer be doubted.

Some words of caution are necessary, however. First, much of what I will describe has had direct antecedents in practical theory. Thus the seminar, which is now so essential to the practices of reflexive capitalism, is an outgrowth of previous practices. Similarly, many of the packaged books and 'how to' guides that circulate in such profusion in business are really only developments of company procedures and guides. Second, reflexive theory and practical theory remain tightly locked together. Whilst the language of the reflexive turn is often stratospheric, the fact is that it has to reconnect to practical theory if it is to be sold on in quantity. In other words, reflexive theory is likely to be commodified at an early stage and must stand up to the rigours of the market.

The reflexive turn is based on a body of management theory which has arisen from a large number of sources. To begin with, management theory has clearly had a long history of its own. For example, even at the turn of the century there was the systematic management movement in the United States and, a little later, the scientific management of F.W. Taylor. The *Management Review* was founded in 1918, the *Harvard Business Review* in 1922, the American Management Association in 1925. By the end of the First World War, Arthur D. Little (originally an engineering firm) included management advice amongst its services, and James McKinsey set up his consulting firm in 1925.

But, arguably, management theory came into its own after the Second World War through the incorporation of a large and eclectic body of knowledge including organization theory, economics, and actual business practice (including, most especially, the use of case studies as exemplars of success) and, increasingly, other 'softer' sources of inspiration, including sociology and psychology. Currently, its most visible manifestation is the 'business fad' (Huczynski, 1993; Shapiro, 1995; Thrift, 1997a). In the past, such fads have included management by objective, quality circles, just-in-time manufacturing and, most famously of late, business process re-engineering (Hammer and Champy, 1993; Coulson-Thomas, 1997) and core competences (Hamel and Prahalad, 1994). More recent fads have included ideas such as the balanced scorecard (Kaplan and Norton, 1996), the living company (de Geuss, 1997), and, most particularly, knowledge as capital (Nonaka and Takeuchi, 1995). For example, 1997 saw at least two books published with exactly the same title, *Intellectual Capital* (Stewart, 1997; Edvinsson and Malone, 1997). These marketable 'philosophies' are the basic quanta of business knowledge. They are the means of tapping the moment by creating the spirit of the moment. They are

> part of a tried and tested formula that evolved after Tom Peters, a McKinsey co-consultant, gathered wealth and fame in the wake of *In Search of Excellence*, published some 15 years ago and the most successful business book of modern times. The response: get an article in the *Harvard Business Review*, pump it up into a book, pray for a best-seller, then market the idea for all it is worth through a consultancy company. (O'Shea and Madigan, 1997, p. 189)

Whilst fads come round like the seasons, they are only the most visible part of the system of reflexive business knowledge. Many other knowledges circulate as well, chiefly through the constant, unremitting hum of courses and seminars.

How has this autopoietic system been able to come about? There are four different reasons. The first of these is an interlocking institutional set-up. Elsewhere (Thrift, 1997a) I have described this set-up in some detail. It consists, to begin with, of the business school. Business schools have, of course, been extant for some time. For example, the first business school (Wharton) was set up at the University of Pennsylvania in 1881. The University of Chicago and the University of California both established undergraduate schools of commerce in 1899. Stern (New York), Amos Tuck (Dartmouth) and Harvard followed in the next decade (Mark, 1987; Micklethwait and Wooldridge, 1996). But their heyday has been since the 1960s. Currently, more than 75,000 students are awarded MBAs every year in America, 15 times the number in 1960. Every year, around the world, 250,000 people sit the GMAT entrance examination for MBA courses (Micklethwait and Wooldridge, 1996). The business school has produced new, more reflexive knowledge in three ways. First, it has systematized and then reproduced existing business knowledge. For example, the case study method, at one time so beloved of Harvard Business School, is able to be used as a means of reflecting back on business. Second, it has synthesized existing academic knowledge and ingested it into businesses. For example, the primary route for much organization theory into business has been from journals like the *Administrative Science Quarterly* into the business school and so into business. Then, third, it has produced new knowledge by producing modes of interchange and knowledge creations hitherto unknown. For example, the close interaction with more mature MBA students who may well already have business experience means that academic knowledge is put to the test.

Another element of the institutional set-up is the management consultant. Since the 1960s, like the business schools, management consultancy has grown massively. Such consultants actively trade in reflexive knowledge and they do so more and more conspicuously. For example, Arthur Andersen, with revenues of $5300 million in 1996 and an international staff of about 38,000 consultants, has its own 'university' at which it trains consultants by the thousands and, increasingly, promotes conferences and video conferences. This is the former girls' school at St Charles, Illinois, which is now known as Andersen Consulting College. And, since Andersen believes in the growth of an 'infocosm', consultants communicate through a computer communications system called Knowledge X-Change aimed at integrating the organization's business knowledge. Most recently, it has established a 'thought leadership' centre near its technology centre in Palo Alto. But there is a rub:

> Whatever the product – downsizing, growth, or something else – consultants need to sell ideas. The problem is that what consulting has to sell isn't always new, and certainly isn't always fresh. It is an unusual industry because it builds its knowledge base at the expense of its clients. From a more critical perspective, it is not much of a stretch to say that consulting companies make a lot of money collecting experience from their clients, which they turn around and sell in other forms, sometimes not very well disguised, to other clients. (O'Shea and Madigan, 1997, p. 13)

A final element of the institutional set-up is the management guru. Though they had existed before – Peter Drucker is a case in point – management gurus came into their own in the early 1980s on the back of a new brand of high-energy management theorists led by Tom Peters (Micklethwait and Wooldridge, 1996). Many of these consultants now have their own very successful consulting companies (as in the case of Michael Porter's company, Monitor). Management gurus are high-profile embodiments of management fads, whose business is to produce and, more importantly, to *communicate* these fads by performatively energizing their audiences.

A second reason has been the growth of the media. The growth of reflexive business theory is intimately associated with the media: management has become a cultural industry. In particular, business fads depend upon media firepower: fads can only fly if they can find an audience (Jackson, 1997). This has, of course, been recognized for a long time. But the significant association with the media dates from the success of Peters and Waterman's *In Search of Excellence*, published in 1982, which demonstrated the potential size of the market. Since then, each year has seen a flood of management books, tapes and videos.

> In 1991 McGraw Hill published 25 (business) titles; in 1996 it published 110. Marketing budgets at the esteemed ... Harvard Business School Press are estimated to have almost doubled in the last four years. In the UK alone 2931 business titles were published in 1996, compared with a paltry 771 in 1975. (Crainer, 1997b, p. 38)

Sometimes ghostwritten, the books can relate management to almost any aspect of human life, from jazz (Kao, 1997) to computer hacking (Phillips, 1997).

The business media have their own institutional structure. This consists of a number of institutions. To begin with, there are the various institutions of the press, including business pages and business journals. Then there is book publishing. And, increasingly there are radio and television programmes and video. For management theory to take off, it must become interwoven with the media. For example, books that reach the top bestseller lists take on their own momentum, becoming the subject of presentations by business gurus and being actively marketed by management consultants that have often produced them, or had a hand in producing them. Similarly, increasing numbers of journals are being published by management consultants in order to push ideas. Another set of institutions consists of media consultants and press officers who interact with the media, attempting to sell ideas to it. A symbolic date for this set of institutions was the appointment in 1980 of a press officer by Bain and Company, which had been the last bastion of consultant standoffishness towards the press. Even Bain and Company were forced to recognize the necessity of media coverage in their business, a necessity which has been underlined by the recent widespread case of advertising by some management consultants: 'Robert Duboff of Mercer Management says that "ten years ago, if I'd suggested we advertise,

I'd have been shot; five years ago I'd have been whipped"' (Wooldridge, 1997, p. 16). Then, finally, there is the audience for business ideas. About this audience we know very little (see Thrift, 1997a). But that it is extensive and rapidly growing in size there can be no doubt.

A third reason has been the growth of new business practices, as well as the transformation of some older ones. Three such practices stand out. One is the whole area of human resources. Human resources managers have become a staple of most firms since the 1970s. Another is the growth of marketing, spurred on by the simultaneous growth of computers and psychology. In particular, since the beginnings of consumer psychology in the 1940s and 1950s, marketing has taken on a markedly more psychological tinge (see Miller and Rose, 1997). The final practice is the growth of interest in leadership, communication, and other 'soft skills': recently, for example, there has been much interest in emotions and emotional leadership (e.g. Cooper and Sawaf, 1997).

A fourth reason is simply momentum. Once a system becomes autopoietic it has its own push. For example, more and more business people have been educated in institutions like business schools which teach reflexive management theory and they provide a ready audience for management ideas subsequently. Again, such people are likely to demand these skills when they attain positions of responsibility, thus pulling candidates skilled in reflexive theory into the system. Similarly, a growing number of managers have themselves worked in management consultancies and, in any case, 'bosses who have had a taste of management theory, either at business schools or working for consultancies, may be more inclined to listen to consultants than those who have not' (Wooldridge, 1997, p. 4).

'Good ideas have flight': the globalization of reflexive capitalism

What is clear is that this institutional set-up – and with it the management ideas which mobilize it – is rapidly globalizing. It is worth considering in some detail how reflexive capitalism is journeying and, in order to achieve this, I want to concentrate on the example of Asia.

Asia, of course, has some quite different business traditions which need to be acknowledged. To begin with, its trade networks have been spatially extensive for many thousands of years. Its theoretical networks have been extant for many hundreds of years, based on the use of the abacus and on indigenous forms of book-keeping, which are only now being fully researched (Goody, 1996). Its economic ethics (such as 'rationality') have been varied and, though they may have been based to a greater extent on the family than in the Occident, equally, as Carrier (1995), Goody (1996) and others have pointed out, this depiction has often suited both East and West as signals of their difference (as for example in notions of collectivist and individualist spirits of capitalism).

But if Asia's business history has been a different one, it is worth remembering that this is a relative judgement. Asia has still shared much of its economic history with the rest of the world: it has never been a hermetically sealed economic zone. Thus, it is no surprise that Asia has been drawn into the practices of reflexive capitalism. Bolstered by a massive increase in physical and electronic communication and therefore in general interconnection, and forced by the problems of economic success, such as the increasing scale of business organizations, the need to ensure management succession in what have been family-run firms (Dumaine, 1997; Hiscock, 1997a; 1997b) and a general shortage of managers, the paths of entry have chiefly been through the reproduction of the institutional set-up of reflexive capitalism in Asia.

The business school is a fairly recent invention in Asia, with most dating from the late 1960s or 1970s. Many Asians still attend business schools outside Asia; indeed, until recently the spiralling demand for MBAs could not have been satisfied from within Asia. But Asia now has many business schools, with the number expanding all the time, and more and more Asians are attending them. Many of the schools are wildly oversubscribed, even given fees which are often well above average national incomes. For example, in India in 1996, 40,000 students took the entrance examinations for the six Indian Institutes of Management (at Ahmedabad, Calcutta, Lucknow, Bangalore, Calicut and Indore) but only 1000 were accepted. In China in the same year, there were 4000 applicants for a 20 month MBA course at the China Europe International Business School in Shanghai, but only 65 were accepted (Micklethwait and Wooldridge, 1996).

The management consultant is another important part of the institutional set-up in Asia. Until recently, expansion into Asia has been rather haphazard. For example, McKinsey is only now opening an office in Bangkok, while

> BCG's Tokyo office opened before its London one because one of the partners, James Abbeglen, had a passion for Japan. Booz-Allen arrived in Indonesia in the early 1980s because the head of one of the country's biggest banks, BNI, had walked into the firm's New York office and asked them to work for him. (Wooldridge, 1997, p. 6)

However, most management consultants have Asian expansion plans which are more advanced in some countries than others (for example, market penetration is still low in Japan). But these expansion plans are dogged by a number of problems. First, establishing an intangible product in a market dominated by family firms who have often been suspicious of playing outside is difficult. It can take a decade or more for 'pioneers from head office to establish a viable outpost, staffed by locals and earning its keep' (1997, p. 6). Second, recruitment and retention of staff are difficult when well-qualified people are at a premium, equally because when consultancy hires and trains local recruits, this inevitably boosts their market value, making them difficult to keep. Third, the balance of western and local employees needs to be kept. But the emphasis on multiculturalism in management consultancies is not always easy: many clients from emerging markets would rather take advice from foreigners. In particular, 'Chinese family companies tend to put more faith in grey-haired westerners than in Chinese MBAs just out of business school' (1997, p. 6). Fourth, it is difficult for consultants to publicize their activities: many Asian clients do not like their name used in firm publicity.

Yet, against these problems, management consultancies are still expanding rapidly in Asia. For example, Andersen Consulting now has 4000 people in Asia while McKinsey's Indian office is the company's fastest-growing (Micklethwait and Wooldridge, 1996).

Management gurus are also becoming influential in Asia. Indeed, for many, it is one of their most important stamping grounds, as typified by books like Naisbitt's *Megatrends Asia* which are tailored to the market. A number of superstar gurus regularly tour the region. For example, Tom Peters currently charges $95,000 per one day (usually seven hour) seminar (including in India!) (Crainer, 1997a):

> For many western gurus, Asian speaking tours offer much the same enticements that the musical variety do for elderly rock stars. The money is good ($25,000 a seminar), the audience large and relatively uncritical, and there is also a chance that you can find an Asian anecdote or two to spice up your performances back home. (Micklethwait and Wooldridge, 1996, p. 57)

Then there is the extensive Asian business media. Apart from business-oriented newspapers, the region contains a large and lively battery of magazine titles such as *Asia Inc.*, as well as a large market for western business titles.

It follows that business ideas have circulated in Asia. Three kinds of idea have been prominent. One is the standard self-improvement literature which emphasizes leadership, self-discipline, and other skills. These kinds of books clearly sell well. For example, Zhang Ruimin is the President and Chair of the Chinese Haier Group which employs 13,000 people in plants in China, Malaysia, Indonesia and the Philippines, chiefly in the manufacture of home appliances. The Haier Group is known for its aggressive management style which has made Zhang Ruimin into one of the few famous managers in China (*The Economist*, 20 December 1997, p. 119). He told the *Financial Times* (3 November 1997, p. 16) that

> he has a profound interest in US business thinking – an avid reader of western business books, Mr Zhang has just finished Peter Senge's *The Fifth Discipline* [1990], which he appreciated for its emphasis on what he describes as the idea of 'a people-nurturing business'.

Another set of ideas has been thoroughgoing business fads and fashions. For example, the bible of business process re-engineering, *Re-engineering the Corporation* (Hammer and Champy, 1993), has sold 17 million copies worldwide, including 5 million copies in Asia. Whilst few companies have taken up the approach lock, stock and barrel, there have been Asian examples.

The third set of ideas has been home-grown, based around the Asian and especially Japanese experience (see, just most recently, Hampden-Turner and Trompenaars, 1997; Chin-Ning, 1996). And, in turn, these ideas have spawned home-grown management gurus, most notably Japanese gurus like Kenichi Ohmae (a former McKinseyite) and, more recently, Ikujiro Nonaka, whose book with Hirotaka Takeuchi, *The Knowledge-Creating Company*(1995), has become a business bestseller, as well as Korean gurus like Chan Kim (now at INSEAD).

We can argue about the influence of these three kinds of idea on Asian managers, but that they are beginning to have an effect seems undeniable. For example,

> in a massive pan-Asian survey of business people in 1995 roughly half of the respondents had bought a book by a western management writer in the previous two years (although it was noticeable that roughly the same proportion admitted that they had not finished reading it). (Micklethwait and Wooldridge, 1996, p. 57)

In turn, increasingly these ideas can no longer be seen as a purely western cultural form. They are being simultaneously co-produced in many parts of the world as the institutional set-up of reflexive capitalism expands into many areas of economic growth, and most especially, Asia.

Conclusions

In conclusion, reflexive theory is moving into the business world, producing a virtual sphere of operation that did not exist before, a sphere which complements practical business theory but still differs from it. However, in contrast to the spread of virtualism in other spheres of human life, there are two crucial differences in the virtual sphere of capitalism. First, as already pointed out, it will always be close to practical theory. There are structural reasons why reflexive management theory must stay down-to-earth, even though it now forms its own institutional set-up. Second, and related, reflexive business knowledge is *performative*. All knowledge involves embodied performance, usually in defined contexts which are a part of that knowledge and the trust in which it is held: thus the scientist in her or his laboratory, the academic in her or his lecture theatre, and so on. But reflexive business knowledge is of a particularly performative character. It is based, to begin with, on specific training in the skills of interaction and presentation. This training is extensive in nearly all walks of business life (see du Gay, 1996; Kerfoot and Knights, 1996). Then, and following on from this point, embodied performance is increasingly central to the communication of business knowledge. The management seminar, whether led by a management guru or someone much less visible, is a fundamental part of business life. At any one time at numerous sites around the world these studied interactions are taking place (Thrift, 1997a). Management theory relies, more than other forms of virtual knowledge, on a conglomeration of performed and book knowledge, and the two are not exclusive but form part of a chain of production and communication. Then, finally, management theory itself stresses embodied performance as an important aspect of the 'human capital' which businesses increasingly attempt to foster: the expressive potential of the body must be harnessed. Thus, the process of social relationship must be managed as a commercial resource in its own right. In turn, this means more attention must be paid to the self and its ability to relate, through the body, to others.

In other words, it cannot be doubted that something akin to a virtual capitalism now exists which is beginning to produce, perhaps for the first time, an 'international language' of capitalism. But this virtualism is, for all that, still resolutely based in the practical order of business.

5

Cultures on the Brink: Re-engineering the Soul of Capitalism on a Global Scale

*Co-author **Kris Olds***

> Where do you produce your entrepreneurs from? Out of a top hat? ... There is a dearth of entrepreneurial talent ... We have to start experimenting. The easy things – just getting a blank mind to take in knowledge and become trainable – we have done. Now comes the difficult part. To get literate and numerate minds to be more innovative, to be more productive, that's not easy. It requires a mindset change, a different set of values. (Senior Minister Lee Kuan Yew, quoted in Hamlin, 2002)

Introduction

It is a near constant in the history of capitalism that what there is to know about the conduct of business is surrounded by a garland of institutions which not only impart that knowledge but attempt to codify and improve upon it, so producing new forms of conduct. But since the 1960s this roundelay has accelerated as the institutions of business knowledge have joined up to form a fully functioning 'cultural circuit of capital' (Thrift, 1997a; 1997b; 1999b; 2002). This cultural circuit of capital is able to produce constant discursive-cum-practical change with considerable power to mould the content of people's work lives and, it might be added, to produce more general cultural models that affect the rest of people's lives as well. Indeed, it would not be too much of an exaggeration to say that the omniscience once claimed by Marxism-Leninism in large parts of the world as a means of rehabilitating the economic, social and cultural spheres has now passed to the fleeting ideological products of the cultural circuit. These are the equivalent of capitalism's commissars.

But we cannot stop there. For the discursive and practical tenets of this world have increasingly become entangled with state action, producing new practices of government that are also redefining who counts as a worthy citizen. In other words, the kind of subject positions that are deemed worthy of managers and workers are increasingly similar to the kinds of subject positions that define the worth of the citizenry (and, it might be added, other actors like migrant workers). This is particularly true of that network of global cities where these tenets are most likely to be put into action (Olds, 2001).

In turn, we can also begin to see how global corporate power is deployed nowadays. More often than not translated by the cultural circuit of capital, the discursive style of state policy has become ever more closely aligned with the discursive style of corporations. They both share a common background of expectations of how, and on (and in) what terms, the world will disclose itself. But we should be careful here. The products of the cultural circuit of capital tend to see the world as fast-moving, ambivalent, difficult to predict, and on the brink, and this frame of mind (which can equally be found now in much state policy) does not make for an easy imperium.

The different centres of 'calculation' (if calculation is quite the right word) that make up the cultural circuit of capitalism can perhaps best be thought of as shifting assemblages of governmental power, made more powerful by their strictly temporary descriptions and attributions. It is a set of assemblages which – fuelled by the raw material of events as sieved through the discursive-cum-practical sequences of the cultural circuit – are in constant motion, constantly inventing new moves.

We want to use the world 'assemblage' here in a Deleuzean way to signal that we want to think of these centres of calculation not as homogeneous and tightly knit structures, or even as loosely linked constitutions, but rather as 'functions' that bring into play particular populations, territories, affects, events – 'withs'. They are therefore to be thought of not as subjects but as 'something which happens' (Deleuze and Parnet, 1987, pp. 51–2). Assemblages differ from structures in that they consist of co-functioning 'symbiotic elements', which may be quite unalike (but have 'agreements of convenience') and coevolve with other assemblages, mutating into something else, which both parties have built. They do not, therefore, function according to a strict cause and effect model.

In turn, the denatured notion of assemblage makes much more room for *space*. Assemblages will function quite differently, according to local circumstance, not because they are an overarching structure adapting its rules to the particular situation but because these manifestations are what the assemblage consists of. Indeed, the cultural circuit of capital allows the knowledges of very different situations to circulate much more freely (and rapidly) and to have a much greater say than previously within a space which is precisely tailored to that circulation, consisting of numerous sites and specialized route ways.

In this chapter, we want to look at one of these spaces, a space which is attempting to recast itself as a 'global schoolhouse' for business knowledge. Singapore, a Pacific Asian city-state with a population of 3.9 million (of whom about 600,000 are foreigners), is a rapidly evolving laboratory for the corporate interests of both the cultural circuit of capital and the state. But while Singapore is a very intense example, we would argue that the trajectory it has set out to follow – towards a kind of *kinetic utopia* – is one which many western and some Asian states (e.g. India or Malaysia) would like to emulate to a significant degree. This is a space where accumulation becomes the very stuff of life, through persuading the population to become its own prime asset – a kind of people mine (in a mineral sense) of reflexive knowledgeability.

This chapter therefore consists of five sections, including these introductory comments. In the second section, we go on to consider the cultural circuit of capital, concentrating especially on the role of business schools as the key nodes in this circuit. In the third section, we will consider the Singaporean state as both testbed for, and to some extent progenitor of, a number of the ideas that have been circulating in the cultural circuit. The fourth section is then concerned with a study of the actual process of negotiation between state and the cultural circuit of capital in which a number of elite 'world-class' business schools established formal presences in Singapore between 1998 and 2000. Finally we offer a few speculative comments about the future direction of the Singaporean management experiment, for the phase that we focus on in this chapter was designed to lay the groundwork for a much more ambitious goal of transforming Singapore into an 'enterprise ecosystem', not just for Singaporeans but for the entire Pacific Asian region (ERC, 2002b).

1. The cultural circuit of capital

The world may consist of a constantly moving horizon of situated actions, learning experiments and makeshift institutional responses, but that does not mean that it cannot be held together. Since the 1960s, one of the more impressive of these holdings together has been the link-up of a series of institutions to produce and disseminate business knowledge. In particular, this circuit arises from the concentration of three different institutions – management consultants, management gurus and especially business schools – all surrounded by the constant swash of the media, which in itself constitutes a purposeful part of the circuit.

Management consultancies date from the late nineteenth and early twentieth centuries. But their heyday has been since the 1960s, when companies like Bain and Company and McKinsey began to gel into vast consulting combines. Consultancies subsequently became the important producers and disseminators of business knowledge through their ability to take up ideas and translate them into practice – and to feed practice back into ideas.

Management consultancies were helped in these ambitions by the oracles of business knowledge, *management gurus*, nearly all of whom were (or are) consultants. Gurus packaged business ideas as aspects of themselves (Micklethwait and Wooldridge, 1996). Though they existed before the 1980s, gurus have become particularly prevalent since the phenomenal success of Peters and Waterman's *In Search of Excellence*(1982), 'a Zen gun that was fired 20 years ago' (Peters, 2001). Gurus tend to embody particular approaches to business knowledge through performances that are meant to both impart new knowledge while also confirming what their audiences may already know (but need bringing out or confirming). Increasingly, gurus come replete with moral codings: 'they do not only tell managers how to manage their organisations, they also tell them what kind of people they should become in order to be happy and morally conscious citizens with fulfilling lives' (ten Bos, 2000, p. 22).

But the primer for the system of producing and disseminating management knowledge is now the *business school*. Though a small elite of business schools was formed in the late nineteenth and early twentieth century in the United States, the main phase of expansion took place much later – from the late 1940s on – on the back of the master of business administration (MBA) degree. In the rest of the world, business schools only slowly came into existence until, in the 1950s and 1960s, they began to open and expand in Europe and then in Asia. They now form the most visible tips of a vast global business education iceberg, one that turns over billions of dollars per year.

Producers of business knowledge necessarily have to have a voracious appetite for new knowledge since it is the continuous conveyor of new knowledge that keeps the system going. In particular, this means a central bank of knowledge that can be stripped of many of its local contingencies and can therefore be made mobile across the globe. So for example ideas like 'complexity theory' (Thrift, 1999b) or 'community of practice' (Vann and Bowker, 2001) can be made into ready-made resources that give up a hold on certain aspects of the world for the sake of portability. But while the universalizing nature of much business knowledge is evident, business schools also produce rich case studies of actual corporate strategy that more often than not recognize the socio-spatial embeddedness of firms and market processes. The case study method is a prominent one in many business schools, with upper-tier schools such as Harvard Business School, the Richard Ivey School, Darden, and INSEAD producing the bulk of the 15,000 plus cases that now circulate through business school classrooms and corporate education centres. Given the interdependencies between business schools and corporations, business school academics have relatively deeper access to the primary 'movers and shapers' (Dicken, 1998) of the global economy than the vast majority of social scientists.

The kinds of knowledge that are pursued in business schools necessarily range widely, of course. So there is functional knowledge of all kinds – from principles of accounting and finance to logistics. Then, there is knowledge that is organizational and strategic. And, finally, there is knowledge that is especially concerned with subjectification – how to be a 'global leader', for example (Roberts, 2002). But, whatever the case, what is effectively being pursued is a constant process of adaptation through continuous critique of the status quo (Boltanski and Chiapello, 1999). The critical feedback loop produced by the cultural circuit of capital is meant to produce a kind of dynamic equilibrium in which the brink (the 'edge of chaos') is the place to be.

Weaving in and out of this set of actions and ideas are the *media* – key means of transport, amplifiers, and generators of business knowledge in their own right. Through the vast range of different general and special media outlets which now exist, and through the vast range of general and special media intermediaries which vie to get their ideas circulated in these outlets, the media act to force the production of ideas. Newspapers such as the

Financial Times also shape institutional conduct at a wide variety of levels via their regular surveys and ranking exercises. In addition, business knowledge is also circulated via the continual production of conferences, seminars, workshops, and the like as the meeting has increasingly been turned into a means of dissemination, which is itself sold as a product.

Through these different sets of institutions which make up the cultural circuit of capital, dispersed knowledges can be gathered up and centred, practical knowledges and skills (including soft skills like leadership) can be codified, the miasma of too much information can be cut down and simplified, and large numbers can be made into small and handleable numbers. But three points need to be made here. First, we are *not* claiming that the knowledge being produced is somehow false, for example because it is caught up in 'fashion'. The hard and fast lines between the kind of studied objectivity which, in its various forms, academic knowledge still strives for and the mutable contingencies of management knowledge were long ago broken down by surficial models of relativist or quasi-relativist approaches to knowledge, and the continuous process of osmosis between academic and management knowledge. But, second, that does not mean that we consider management knowledge to be neutral. The process of instrumentalized commodification which calls it into being brings with it a set of highly politicized values which cannot be denied (Vann and Bowker, 2001; Dezalay and Garth, 2002a) – values that underlie the influential spread of neoliberal policies through much of the world. Still, and third, both academic and management knowledges increasingly share certain values: a commitment to conceiving the world as continuously rolling over, continually on the brink; a commitment to fantasy as a vital element of how knowledge is constructed; and a commitment to tapping the fruitfulness of the contingency of the event.

One element of management knowledge which we want to foreground here is the constant attempt to produce new, more appropriate kinds of *subjects*, what we might call 'souls' that fit contemporary and especially future systems of accumulation. In pursuit of high performance, both workers and managers must be refigured. Of course, this kind of explicit engineering is hardly new. F.W. Taylor and others plotted bodily configurations which they believed would produce better workers at the end of the nineteenth century. Similarly, by the middle of the twentieth century, managers were beginning to be expected to embody themselves in ways that would make them better leaders. But the emergence of the subject as a quite explicit focus of management knowledge has taken on a new urgency of late, boosted by the growing power of human resources departments and the growing body of knowledge and practice devoted to such practices. In particular, we can see much greater attention being paid to attempts to produce 'knowledgeable' subjects – by harnessing tacit knowledge, by producing communities of practice within which learning is a continuous activity, by working with and making more of affect, by understanding the minutiae of embodied time and space, and so on. In other words, a partially coherent set of practices of 'government of the soul' (Rose, 1999) is starting to be produced by the cultural circuit of capital, a kind of instrumental phenomenology which can produce subjects that disclose the world as uncertain and risky but also able to be stabilized (in profitable ways) by the application of particular kinds of intense agency that are creative, entrepreneurial and businesslike.

2. The state and the global schoolhouse

Of course, other organizations have interests in producing pliant but enterprising subjects, not least the state. And, as has been shown many times now, a considerable part of this interest has come about as states have become more and more aligned with global corporate interests, redescribing themselves as guarantors of economic growth through their ability to produce subjects attuned to this objective. *Enterprise* becomes both a characteristic and a goal of the new supply-side state. Nearly all western states nowadays subscribe to a rhetoric and metric of modernization based upon fashioning a citizen who can become an actively seeking factor of production, rather like a mineral resource with attitude. And that rhetoric, in turn, has been based upon a few key management tropes – globalization, knowledge, learning, network, flexibility, information technology, urgency – which are meant to come together in a new kind of self-willed subject whose industry will boost the powers of the state to compete economically, and will also produce a more dynamic citizenry.

Many of the states of Asia have bought into this rhetoric of a knowledge economy, often with good reason. Thus, beyond the purely economic advantage that is seen to arise from it, there is also its ability to both respect and minimize ethnic difference and to provide an unthreatening (or difficult to critique) national narrative (cf. Bunnell, 2002). Of these states, perhaps the most enthusiastic participant has been the paternalist but ultimately pragmatic state of Singapore (Low, 1999), an independent city-state since 1965. Indeed, it would not be entirely unfair to say that Singapore has become a kind of management primer come true, with the fantasies of the serried rows of management texts in its main bookshops embodied in the person of its citizens and its 'professional' migrant workers. In Singapore accumulation often seems to have become the work of life, a passion of production (and consumption – Singaporeans are expected to be 'prosumers') in its own right.

Periodically, prompted by circumstance, Singapore refocuses its economy. In the process this 'modern day garrison state' reworks a post-independence discourse of *survivalism*. Frequent tropes include both real and manufactured concerns about the country's small size and its resultant openness to competition from Malaysia, Hong Kong and most recently China; the gradual rundown of its traditional long-term geographic advantages (such as the port); and its lack of natural resources and consequent dependence upon its people. This concern seemed to be confirmed by the

Asian economic crisis of 1997–8 which meant that Singapore, though on the edge of events, saw its growth rate fall from 8 per cent in 1997 to 1.5 per cent in 1998. Singapore reacted predictably, with a 15 per cent wage cut, a 30 per cent reduction in rentals on industrial properties, and the liberalization of its financial sector (allowing for more foreign bank presence in the domestic banking sector). But the crisis also hastened a longer-term strategic shift fuelled especially by the later downturn in information technology industries, as well as more general concerns about a sluggish world economy.

The government of Singapore, a technocratic 'soft-authoritarian' government that has been controlled by the People's Action Party (PAP) since 1959, is responsible for reshaping the economy. The Ministry of Trade and Industry (MTI) is the most important formal institutional mechanism for economic governance. While the MTI has only one functional department – the Singapore Department of Statistics – nine statutory boards (semi-independent and well-resourced agencies) under the MTI jurisdiction carry out policy and programme work. The most significant MTI statutory boards are:

- the Singapore Economic Development Board (EDB)
- the Singapore Productivity and Standards Board (PSB)
- the Singapore Trade Development Board (TDB).

The Singapore EDB (http://www.sedb.com) was founded in 1961 to formulate and implement economic development strategy for Singapore (Schein, 1996; Low, 1999; Chan, 2002). While relatively well resourced and staffed by Singaporeans, the EDB is open to the cultural circuit of capital through regular visits by management gurus and consultants – figures like Tom Peters, Gary Hamel and Michael Porter (the latter having worked with the EDB since 1986, anointed as a 'Business Friend of Singapore' in 2001).

While the EDB is the shaper and mediator of most economic change within Singaporean territory, a powerful guidance role is played by select committees that report on a one-off or *ad hoc* basis. An example of the former is the Committee on Singapore's Economic Competitiveness that reported on Asian crisis related matters in 1998. An example of the latter is the Economic Review Committee (ERC) (http://www.erc.gov.sg), a Singapore-based network of state and private sector representatives responsible for making recommendations to generate structural shifts in economy and society. The most recent ERC was set up by Prime Minister Goh Chok Tong in October 2001 with a mandate 'to fundamentally review our development strategy and formulate a blueprint to restructure the economy, even as we work to ride out the current recession'. The Committee's composition is revealing: nine members of the government or government functionaries (including the President of the National University of Singapore), two union representatives, and nine private sector representatives (including Arnoud De Meyer, the Dean of INSEAD's Singapore campus). Arnoud De Meyer also serves on the Sub-Committee on Service Industries in the ERC.

While the current ERC was given a relatively new mandate in 2001, it is building upon initiatives first established in the mid 1980s to promote the *services* sector as actively as manufacturing, thereby firing up 'twin engines' in a city-state drive for more diversified economic growth (ERC, 2002a). This service-oriented agenda subsequently merged with the trope of the 'knowledge-based economy' (KBE) that began circulating at a global scale in the 1990s. As Coe and Kelly (2000) demonstrate in the Singaporean case, this phrase first surfaced in a speech by the Prime Minister in 1994. By 1998 the phrase was gaining some currency. By 1999 it was in wholesale circulation, having 'seemingly entered the common vocabulary of all Ministers, bureaucrats and media commentators in Singapore' (Coe and Kelly, 2000, p. 418; also see Coe and Kelly, 2002).

In line with the goal of transforming Singapore into 'a vibrant and robust global hub for knowledge-driven industries', the EDB accordingly announced its detailed *Industry 21* strategy, a strategy whose product would be a Singapore capable of developing:

> manufacturing and service industries with a strong emphasis on technology, innovation and capabilities. We also want to leverage on other hubs for ideas, talents, resources, capital and markets. To be a global hub and to compete globally, we require world-class capabilities and global reach. The goal is for Singapore to be a leading centre of competence in knowledge-driven activities and a choice location for company headquarters, with responsibilities for product and capability charters.
>
> The knowledge-based economy will rely more on technology, innovation and capabilities to create wealth and raise the standard of living. For our knowledge-based economy to flourish, we will need a culture which encourages creativity and entrepreneurship, as well as an appetite for change and risk-taking. (http://www.sedb.com, accessed 20 May 2001)

As this quote and Lee Kuan Yew's statement at the start of this chapter make clear, this strategy involves constructing an assemblage made up of a different set of 'withs', and not least a major cultural change which consists of an upgrading of Singapore's labour force so as to make it more knowledgeable and entrepreneurial through a continuous process of learning.

An important part of the *Industry 21* strategy is the creation of a 'world-class' education sector which would import 'foreign talent', both to expose Singaporean educational institutions to competition (thereby forcing them to upgrade), and to produce a diverse global education hub attractive to students from around the Asia–Pacific region. In theory this cluster of educational institutions would produce and disseminate knowledge at a range of scales, supporting local and foreign firms in Singapore, state institutions in Singapore, and firms and states in the South East, East and South Asian regions.

Significantly, much of this educational strategy was concerned with those key institutions of the cultural circuit of capital, business schools. In turn, this hub would hypothetically act as the core of a series of industrial clusters, through spinoffs and the like in industries like medicine, engineering and applied sciences.

This education upgrade strategy hinged on attracting 10 world-class educational institutions to set up independently or in collaboration with Singaporean partners by the year 2008, plus a series of large corporate training concerns. In fact, by mid 2002 that target had been nearly been reached with eight major educational institutions having signed agreements (see Table 5.1), three of them elite western business schools.

Table 5.1 Substantial foreign university initiatives in Singapore by date of establishment (as at August 2003)

Johns Hopkins University (JHU)   Three medical divisions of JHU were established in January 1998: Johns Hopkins Singapore Biomedical Center, Johns Hopkins Singapore Affiliated Programs, and Johns Hopkins-National University Hospital International Medical Centre. These institutions facilitate collaborative research and education with Singapore's academic and medical communities. Web link: http://www.jhs.com.sg
JHU's Peabody Institute is also collaborating with the National University of Singapore (NUS) to create the Singapore Conservatory of Music (now known as the Yong Siew Toh Conservatory of Music). An agreement was established in November 2001. Web link: http://music.nus.edu.sg/index.htm

Massachusetts Institute of Technology (MIT)   The Singapore-MIT Alliance (SMA) was established in November 1998. Local alliance partners include the National University of Singapore (NUS) and Nanyang Technological University (NTU). The focus is on advanced engineering and applied computing. SMA-1 runs until 2005, and involves approximately 100 professors and 250 graduate students (who receive MIT certificates). A new phase (known as SMA-2) will run from July 2005 to 2010, with deeper MIT degree granting capacity. Web link: http://web.mit.edu/sma

Georgia Institute of Technology (GIT)   The Logistics Institute-Asia Pacific (TLI-AP) was established in February 1999. TLI-AP is a collaboration between NUS and the Georgia Institute of Technology. TLI-AP trains engineers in specialized areas of global logistics, with emphasis on information and decision technologies. TLI-AP facilitates research and the acquisition of dual degrees and professional education. Web link: http://www.tliap.nus.edu.sg

University of Pennsylvania (Penn)   Singapore Management University (SMU) was officially incorporated in January 2000. Wharton School faculty from the University of Pennsylvania provided intellectual leadership in the formation of SMU's organizational structure and curriculum. The Wharton-SMU Research Center was also established at SMU. 306 students were enrolled at SMU in 2000, 800 in 2001, 1600 in 2003, with eventual enrolment levels expected to top out at 9000 (6000 undergraduates and 3000 graduate students). A US$650 million campus is currently being built in Singapore's downtown. Web link: http://www.smu.edu.sg

INSEAD   INSEAD, the prominent French business school, established its second campus in Singapore in January 2000. A US$40 million building was built to enable Singapore-based faculty, and European campus visiting faculty, to offer full- and part-time courses as well as executive seminars. As of February 2003 there were 255 MBA students in Singapore. In February 2003 INSEAD formally decided to launch phase two which will involve doubling the size of the Singapore campus. Web link: http://www.insead.edu/campuses/asia_campus/index.htm

cont.

University of Chicago   The University of Chicago Graduate School of Business (GSB) established a dedicated Singapore campus in July 2000 to offer the Executive MBA Program Asia to a maximum of 84 students per programme. The curriculum is identical to the Executive MBA Programs in Chicago and Barcelona, and faculty are flown in from Chicago to teach on it. Web link: http://gsb.uchicago.edu

Technische Universiteit Eindhoven (TU/e)   The Design Technology Institute (DTI), jointly administered by National University of Singapore (NUS) and Technische Universiteit Eindhoven, was established in May 2001. The courses and projects offered by DTI aim to provide a balance between basic engineering concepts, and product design and development. TU/e has strong links to Philips, both in the Netherlands and in Singapore. Web link: http://www.dti.nus.edu.sg

Technische Universität München (TUM)   The National University of Singapore (NUS) and the Technische Universität München established a Joint Masters degree in Industrial Chemistry in January 2002, and a Joint Master of Science in Industrial and Financial Mathematics in late 2003. The German Institute of Science and Technology (GIST) in Singapore co-ordinates these education programmes, as well as executive training and contract research. A significant proportion of specialists from industry are involved. Web link: http://www.gist-singapore.com

Carnegie Mellon University (CMU)   Carnegie Mellon University signed a Memorandum of Understanding with Singapore Management University in January 2003 to collaborate on the development of a School of Information Systems (SIS). The MOU runs from 2003 to 2007. The School will be SMU's fourth since it was established in 2000. Web link: http://www.smu.edu.sg/sections/schools/information.asp

Stanford University   Stanford University and Nanyang Technological University (NTU) signed an official Memorandum of Understanding in February 2003 to offer joint graduate programmes in environmental engineering. The Stanford Singapore Partnership education programme began in June 2003. The programmes will be a mix of distance education with student and faculty exchanges. Web link: http://www.ntu.edu.sg/CEE/ssp/Index.htm

Cornell University   A Memorandum of Understanding was signed in February 2003 between Nanyang Business School (NBS), Cornell University's School of Hotel Administration, and the International Hotel Management School (a Singaporean entity), to set up a joint Cornell-Nanyang Business School of Hospitality Management. The School will be established by 2004 and offer joint graduate degrees while facilitating research on the Asian hospitality industry. Web link: http://www.hotelschool.cornell.edu

Duke University   A Memorandum of Understanding was signed in June 2003 between Duke University Medical Center and the National University of Singapore, to establish a graduate medical school in Singapore by 2006. Web link: http://medschool.duke.edu

Karolinska Institutet (KI)   A Memorandum of Understanding was signed in July 2003 between the Stockholm-based Karolinska Institutet and the National University of Singapore to operate joint postgraduate programmes in the areas of stem-cell research, tissue engineering and bio-engineering. Web link: http://info.ki.se/index_en.html

Indian Institute of Technology (IIT)   The multisited Indian Institute of Technology gave in-principle approval, in May 2003, to the idea of establishing a Singapore campus in 2004. The IIT campuses involved include Bombay, Chennai, New Delhi, Kharagpur, Kanpur, and Roorkie. The exact modality of presence is currently being worked out in conjunction with the Singapore Economic Development Board

This striking development trend is likely to continue: in August 2003 Singapore's Trade and Industry Minister (George Yeo) stated that a foreign university is likely to be permitted (within the next year) to establish a large university campus in Singapore to offer a comprehensive curriculum from liberal arts to engineering. This is without taking note of the numerous corporate organizations which have set up training facilities in Singapore, including the New York Institute of Finance (set up in 1997) which trains senior financial executives and professionals, Motorola University South East Asia, Cable and Wireless, Citibank, ABN Amro, St Microelectronics, Lucent Technologies, and so on.

In summary, elite institutions of higher education are recognized by the Singaporean state as playing a fundamental role in restructuring the economy via the refashioning of the local citizenry, while simultaneously providing retooling opportunities for the 75,000–100,000 professional migrants who use Singapore as a temporary base. The key idea is the creation of a virtuous circle: draw in the 'best universities' with global talent; this talent then creates knowledge and knowledgeable subjects; these knowledgeable subjects, through their actions and networks, then create the professional jobs that drive a vibrant KBE. As Tharman Shanmugaratnam (Senior Minister of State for Trade and Industry) puts it, the government seeks to create 'a new breed of Singaporean':

> We have strong institutions and a highly credible government. We start from a position of strength, both financially and socially. All we want to have now is a stronger individual, more adaptable to the business world with a global mindset and concrete experience. (*Straits Times*, 17 March 2002, p. 18)

And, again, elite business schools are perceived by the state to support (and attract to Singapore) the highly prized 'global talent' associated with transnational corporations.

3. Negotiating the global schoolhouse

But these bare facts hide much of the process by which international educational interests were initially brought into alignment with the Singaporean state. Therefore in this section we look at the way in which that alignment took place by concentrating on the counterposed strategies of the Chicago GSB, INSEAD, and Wharton with the Singaporean state. Much of this section is based upon dialogue with people associated with new business schools in Singapore and with the National University of Singapore (NUS), as well as life experience and fieldwork in Singapore between 1997 and 2003.

The Singaporean state had to make some significant changes of emphasis in order to accommodate these educational institutions with the aim of fashioning new subjects, while simultaneously branding Singapore as a global business education site.

The first change of emphasis relates to enhancing the *depth of linkages* between foreign universities and Singapore. Given that education can be viewed as a 'service', it is helpful to delineate four modes or channels for the provision of educational services to 'foreign' consumers (Kemp, 2000): (1) cross-border supply (e.g. distance education); (2) consumption abroad (e.g. foreign students studying in the United States); (3) commercial presence (e.g. supplier of education on an established campus, or via the formation of a joint venture); and (4) presence of natural persons (e.g. academics travelling to a foreign country to run courses). Until the mid 1990s, Singapore was strongly incorporated into the first two modes of educational service provision. But a shift began occurring in the mid to late 1990s when Singapore formally permitted and indeed encouraged foreign universities to establish relatively *deeper* commercial presences in the city-state. However, this change of emphasis was selectively applied to western universities deemed to be of 'world-class' stature.

The second change of emphasis related to the *educational model* that Singapore followed at the tertiary level. A geo-institutional realignment took place that demoted the long-hegemonic British-based educational model, replacing it with the American model:

Kris Olds: I'm not assuming here, but is there a preference for universities from a particular geographic region?

Lily Kong: I think again this is interesting, because when we were talking about benchmarking issues, up to about three or four years ago, we were still talking about looking towards Britain and an RAE [research assessment exercise] kind of model of evaluation and benchmarking. And it was quite clearly and quite starkly [altered] with this particular DPM's [Deputy Prime Minister's] entry into the educational arena. I think it was around 1997, 1998 maybe. And there was a very clear, I think, and marked shift towards a North American, and in particular, a United States kind of a model, and at that point in time there also was this talk about being the Harvard of the East. It wasn't just North America, or just USA, but Harvard specifically. The institutions that we now look towards are of course more varied, more realistic perhaps, but certainly it is very much a United States sort of thing.

The reframing of the geo-institutional reference point for Singapore's higher education system took place quickly, and was driven by the Deputy Prime Minister and Minister of Defense (Tony Tan):

LK: The common belief is that DPM Tony Tan came to know the North American system quite well, in part through his son who studied there [in Boston]. That may have influenced the way he thought about the higher education system.

Janice Bellace of Wharton echoed Lily Kong's comments. Tony Tan, though, was in no way the only Singaporean politician to look favourably upon the American system. Senior Minister Lee Kuan Yew (2002) has also pushed the American model *vis-à-vis* the development of more 'entrepreneurial culture':

Lee Kuan Yew :   The difference between British and American values cannot be more profound. The US is a frontier society. By and large there were and are no class barriers. Everybody celebrated getting rich. Everybody wanted to be rich and tried to be. There is a great urge to start new enterprises and create wealth. The US has been the most dynamic society in innovating, in starting-up companies to commercialize new discoveries or inventions, thus creating new wealth. American society is always on the move and changing. They have led the world in patents, striving to produce something new or do something better, faster and cheaper, increasing productivity. Having created a product that sold well in America, they would then market it worldwide.

When I saw America's amazing recovery in the last 10 years after it had lost so much ground to industries in Japan and Germany in the 1980s, I appreciated in full the meaning of Americans being 'entrepreneurial'. But for every successful entrepreneur in America, many have tried and failed. Quite a few tried repeatedly until they succeeded. Quite a few who succeeded continued to create and start up new companies as serial entrepreneurs. This was the way America's great companies were built. This is the spirit that generates a dynamic economy.

This said, it is important to place our comments about these two admittedly powerful individuals (Lee and Tan) in context: the late twentieth and early twenty-first centuries are an era in which American universities have generated increasingly positive (of the most part) attention in many parts of the world.

In turn, it is also clear that this move towards the United States was in part an attempt to increase Singapore's economic visibility across the Pacific, with select Americans being associated with producing this prized 'entrepreneurial culture'. For many Americans, especially elite business school faculty, Singapore did not exist in their geographical imagination, or else it was viewed casually as an authoritarian hothouse, Asian style.

Janice Bellace/SMU & Wharton: I want to stress that few people have visited Singapore. A significant number of Wharton faculty have been to Hong Kong, and some have been to China. And since the 1980s, everybody has managed to get to Japan. But Singapore is a place that people just have never visited. So for most of the Wharton faculty, it was unknown. The question I heard repeatedly was, 'What's Singapore like?' In the first two years here, the big challenge has been to get Wharton people out here, just to come out to visit. As you would expect, nearly everyone who has come out has been pleasantly surprised. The first surprise is that it is not like Hong Kong. Many people didn't realize that everything is in English here, and how modern and prosperous it is. The second surprise, and you can quote me on this, is that Singapore is not some sort of a police state. For many Wharton faculty, their vague impressions of Singapore are based on articles like those in *The Economist*. I tell my colleagues that they don't understand what *The Economist* means when they call Singapore 'the nanny state', and that some mistakenly assume it is like former communist Eastern European states. I tell them to think about how a British nanny interacts with the children. She exhorts them to behave themselves and to improve themselves. It might seem strange in the US if the head of the government in a major speech were to tell the people to speak better English, but to Singaporeans it seems natural for the Prime

Minister to say that, and they simply view it as something the government should say if it is important for the economic vitality of Singapore. Once Wharton faculty visit and experience how Singaporeans act in everyday life, they better understand exactly what is meant by 'the nanny state'.

The third change of emphasis was concerned with *freedom of speech for foreign academics*. Some of the principles that the Singaporean government held dear had to be shifted a little – but only a little – in order to accommodate academic concerns:

> *Arnoud De Meyer:*   I don't want to put words in their mouths but they really don't care about publishing research results in journals that nobody reads. What they are concerned about is publishing in non-academic journals with wide circulations in Singapore. More specifically, there are three specific areas that we have to be careful about. First, we cannot get involved in any activity that stimulates racial or religious tensions. If we do so, we are going to get immediately cracked up. Second, and they didn't phrase it this way but this is my reading of it: Singapore has two big Muslim countries as neighbours and we have to be careful, we cannot start insulting Muslims, etc. And third, they basically said that if we get ourselves involved in local politics, we better get our bags packed ... We as faculty said that we have no problems with the first two areas because we are not in the business of creating racial or religious tensions, and we are not in the business of insulting countries. Local politics, we are not interested in it, because Singapore is far too small for our interests. So it was like yes, we can live with it.

> *KO:* Was this a written agreement or was it just a verbal understanding?

> *ADM/INSEAD:* This was a verbal understanding; we don't have that on paper, but it was very consistent throughout our conversations.

The comments of Arnoud De Meyer were matched in tone by Janice Bellace and by Gary Hamada, Dean of the University of Chicago GSB (as cited in Boruk, 1999). In other words, the Singaporean state made it relatively clear (in comparison with its policies towards indigenous universities and academics) that greater academic freedom was being permitted. The schools were aware, however, that certain subjects were highly sensitive due to local and regional concerns. The government's stance did cause the three western business schools to consider whether they could engage in teaching and research consonant with their own policies on academic freedom. They concluded that they could conduct their type of work in what is a relatively more authoritarian political context.

These three changes of emphasis – deeper foreign university presence within Singaporean space, a different kind of educational model, and relatively more academic freedom – laid the foundations for the stretching of the institutional architecture of elite western universities across global space. The realignment of Singaporean priorities was clearly not enough, however, to draw in elite universities that had already embarked upon globalization drives. What also mattered was government support via the powers and capacities of the developmental state (e.g. targeted financial subsidies), along with doses of bureaucratic persistence and persuasion. For example, the EDB played an important role in courting select universities in R&D-rich contexts (e.g. Boston). However, universities are less hierarchical than the transnational corporations Singapore is used to dealing with. As Tan Chek Ming, Director of EDB Services Development, put it, 'Every faculty member has to agree. All you need is one person to disagree and the whole deal will be thrown out of alignment.' In this context:

> [EDB] team members act as tour guides, flying in faculty staff for a look-see trip to Singapore. The usual highlight is a meeting between the dons and senior Cabinet Ministers, namely Deputy Prime Minister Tony Tan, who oversees university education, Education Minister Teo Chee Hean, and Trade and Industry Minister George Yeo.
>
> These meetings are important, stresses Mr Tan, as they send a strong signal to the visitors of the political will and commitment in drawing reputable universities to Singapore. Team members also double up as property agents, scouting around for suitable premises in Singapore to locate the foreign university. They also help look into the legal and financial aspects of setting up shop in Singapore. (*Straits Times*, 24 June 2001, p. R1)

In order to tempt business schools, the EDB played up Singapore's cosmopolitan nature, and then used tangible material resources in the form of financial and other incentives. For example, INSEAD received $10 million in research funding over four years, plus soft loans, reduced land values (about one-third of the commercial price), easier-to-get work permits, housing access, and so on. The University of Chicago GSB received several million dollars' worth of subsidy via the renovation of the historic House of Tan Yeok Nee building they now use as their 'campus'. Finally, the government of Singapore effectively funds the Wharton–SMU Research Center (http://www.smu.edu.sg/research) at SMU, providing monetary and in-kind support for research projects, seminars, scholarships and the like.

These forms of material support are clearly important, and short- and long-term financial opportunities needed to be viewed favourably by the three business schools before they would commit the necessary intellectual and material resources required to stretch complicated institutional fabric across space. But there were some additional factors that led the cultural circuit of capital into Singapore space: the city-state's strategic geographical position within Asia (boosted by Changi Airport, an efficient award winning airport 20–30 minutes taxi ride from all three campuses), 'quality of life' for expatriates, the fact that many alumni were Singaporean, and the large number of transnational corporations with presences in Singapore. All of these factors were often put together as 'international feel' or a genuinely 'cosmopolitan nature' – characteristics associated with global cities (Olds, 2001; Sassen, 2001). As Arnoud De Meyer of INSEAD put it:

> ADM/INSEAD: We developed a business plan and finally chose Singapore because it stood out in terms of government support for business, and for us the 'international feel'. I often say, and you would be able to relate to this, that Singapore is more international than Hong Kong. Hong Kong is a

Chinese city. I remember when I took two groups of faculty and major administrators for a tour of Hong Kong, Kuala Lumpur and Singapore. When visiting each city I brought them outside the central business district. I brought them to Woodlands, in the case of Singapore, to show them an HDB [public housing] environment. Some of our faculty and administrators might live in such areas, or else in expatriate enclaves yet often be forced to interact with such areas. I still remember when one of my colleagues made an interesting remark: she said that when she went to Hong Kong and she got out of the city, she really felt that she was in a 'Chinese' city. When she went to KL [Kuala Lumpur] she saw Indians, Malays, Chinese and Caucasians on the streets but she never saw them together. But when she went to Woodlands [in Singapore] she saw these people together. Or the fact that all taxi drivers understand English. That was part of why we felt comfortable here. It's little things like that.

The selection process in all cases was relatively systematic:

ADM/INSEAD: I initiated INSEAD's Asia campus feasibility study in June 1995. In 1996, I visited 11 cities in Asia amidst my other work. At this time there was a lot of pressure from the [INSEAD] Board to move fast. We had six criteria to judge the potential of each of the locations. We wanted, from the very beginning, to have faculty stationed in Asia because the Euro-Asia Centre was already flying faculty in and out. The additional objective of establishing an Asia campus for INSEAD was to develop our faculty. This idea of linking the establishment of an Asia campus to the development of our faculty makes us very different from Chicago or Wharton.
The first criterion we considered was quality of life for professionals.
The second criterion related to good communications infrastructure. There also had to be a bit of time-zone overlap between our French campus and the prospective Asian campus. The time-zone differential effectively excluded Japan because of the eight-hour time difference during part of the year. In other words, time-zone overlap with respect to telephone usage becomes much more complicated in Japan.
Third, we wanted to have a place that had 'international' appeal.
Fourth, we wanted a place that had other good universities. We were aware that even with 50 faculty in Singapore, we would be a very small group and we wanted interaction with other scholars, a place with a lot of flow of people so that we would have visitors.
The fifth point is that we looked for a place where there was government and business support for the concept.
There was probably a sixth element, that of the perceived 'neutrality' of the place, although it was really an afterthought. For example, KL [Kuala Lumpur] is less neutral than Singapore. Similarly, Shanghai is less neutral than Singapore.
Cost was actually not part of our decision criteria. It would be foolish to say that it was irrelevant but it was not a major issue. When we developed that grid of five to six criteria and related it to the 11 cities that I looked at, about eight disappeared very quickly. Shanghai was impossible in terms of its politics. Perth was too far away in terms of communications. Tokyo and Osaka fell through very quickly as well. In short, applying this grid to the potential cities led to a number of them falling out very quickly. We were left with KL, Hong Kong and Singapore. But in each place we were considering three different development models. Here, in Singapore, we have a free-standing campus. In KL we were looking at a joint venture with a number of large companies. In

Hong Kong, we were looking at either a free-standing campus, a small subsidiary, or a takeover/joint venture with an existing business school.

As Arnoud De Meyer's last comment points out, there are a variety of modes of entry to Singapore space, and the government of Singapore allowed the business schools to identify their own mode of entry (versus forcing them to engage in joint ventures, as is required in Malaysia). Though each of the three schools (Wharton, INSEAD and Chicago) were simultaneously globalizing their business education and research programmes, INSEAD chose a relatively high-risk new product strategy, building a completely new offshoot of INSEAD, with some of its own priorities and research agendas (in comparison with the larger Fontainebleau campus). At the other end of the spectrum of risk was the Wharton approach via intellectual influence on a local provider. Through collaboration with the Singapore government in the establishment of Singapore Management University, most risk for Wharton was dispersed to the state. Finally, the Chicago GSB was somewhere in between, seeking to export its fixed products more efficiently. It had already established a new subsidiary campus in Europe (Barcelona) in 1994, and it wanted to reproduce a similar model in Pacific Asia.

These three divergent models were, in part, prompted by willingness to take financial risk but also by the forms of business knowledge that were being developed and diffused. INSEAD has a more heterogeneous and institutionalist view of business knowledge. This form of knowledge requires the formation of relatively deep regional (i.e. Asian) knowledge and networks. In contrast Chicago has a very explicit, fixed and universal model, based on economics, statistics and the behavioural sciences.

Beth Bader/Chicago: When we planned to establish our two international campuses in Barcelona and Singapore, we wanted to offer an educational product identical to what we offer in Chicago. Since the quality of our faculty members is so integral to the quality of our MBA programmes, we felt that the only way to assure that the programmes offered in Barcelona, Singapore and Chicago were identical was for the same faculty to teach in all three programmes. So our regular Chicago-based faculty members 'commute' to Barcelona and Singapore for one week at a time to teach in these programmes. Each faculty member makes two trips to deliver his or her course in two one-week modules, rather than two 90-minute sessions per week over 10 weeks, for example, as in our full-time programme in Chicago. NPNow clearly, the limitation of this model is that we cannot expand very much. We admit 84 students per year to each of the three branches of the Executive MBA programme. Because of the limitation on faculty resources, we do not have any plans to add to the size of our existing programmes or to establish additional campuses.

As Beth Bader's comments imply, the Chicago School trains up students via a universal programme that need not account for significant difference across space. Gary Eppen, the GSB's Associate Dean, put it even more bluntly: 'Demand curves don't slope up in Taiwan. Demand curves slope down everywhere in the world.' The GSB teaches 'fundamental concepts that you should be able to apply wherever you are' (Dolven, 2000, p. 49).

Conclusions

This chapter has sought to describe the way in which the cultural circuit of capital has become aligned with the state and has thereby increasingly become involved in global geopolitical interventions. These interventions are producing new forms of governmentality that privilege the mass production of knowledgeable and enterprising subjects, subjects who can simultaneously optimize their relationship to themselves and to work. We paid particular attention to the case of Singapore as a story of how what are still relatively loose functions that bring into play populations, territories, affects and events can find *common cause* in particular places, at particular times, and can coevolve new strategies of government which are intended to recode Singapore's citizens. The injection of new knowledges into Singapore space is designed to create 'a new breed of Singaporean', one that will be more entrepreneurial, connected to the world, yet (so the state hopes) still committed to 'our best home'. Moreover, these new strategies of government are designed to enable the local and regionally based professional migrants (expatriates) to discipline themselves through a continual 'upgrading' process, spur on restructuring in indigenous universities, and simultaneously 'brand' Singapore as a suitable hub for 'global talent'.

So far as Singapore is concerned, the strategy of bringing the cultural circuit of capital and the state together as a relatively loose and opportunistic assemblage is clearly intended to be a critical element of 'remaking Singapore', one which if successful may lift Singapore further out of the South East Asian region, flinging it into an orbit where its region can be the globe itself.

> ADM/INSEAD: The locational advantages of Singapore and the nearby region (including Johor Bahru in Malaysia and Batam in Indonesia) are eroding. Singapore is being challenged by China, Vietnam and some parts of India. In other words geographical proximity is not as valuable as it once was. How do you replace that? At the level of the Singapore government, an idea is developing that Singapore should 'move out of the neighbourhood'. So I see the development model being focused on remaking Singapore into a centre of excellence that is linked to Tokyo and San Francisco and Munich, rather than being a service centre for the region. Is this a good idea? I'm not sure. That's very difficult for me to judge, but I do see a policy that is moving in this direction. It is clearly a big bet; one that is being pursued at the top level of government.

Of course, as Arnoud De Meyer implies, no strategy is without risk. One risk is that the strategy of attracting the cultural circuit of capital will be too successful and that the pile-up of new educational institutions of one sort or another will grow beyond what Singapore can deliver. Indeed in September

2002 the ERC recommended that Singapore become a 'global schoolhouse' for an 'additional 100,000 international fee-paying students and 100,000 international corporate executives for training' (ERC, 2002b) – a challenging policy goal for both the state and the cultural circuit of capital, to put it but mildly. Another risk is that the informal agreement on academic freedom for these foreign universities will be tested, just as foreign media freedoms in Singapore are tested from time to time. One more risk is that contradictions may emerge between economic sectors in this small island nation: a services sector, and services employees, that demand high quality of life, versus a fast-growing chemicals sector, one that is injecting increasing volumes of noxious emissions into the atmosphere of the coastal zones. In any of these cases, the elite brand name business schools may move on to pastures new, in which case an Asian tiger may find itself having caught a rather larger tiger by the tail – a tiger which can consign it to the place where all the old management ideas go. What is clear, then, is that the future shape and effectiveness of the set of assemblages that are associated with making 'literate and numerate minds to be more innovative, to be more productive' has yet to be fully worked through.

6

It's the Romance, Not the Finance, that Makes the Business Worth Pursuing: Disclosing a New Market Culture

Introduction

In this chapter, I want to consider the invention of a new economic form, the so-called 'new economy'. This form was invented by a series of stakeholders as a means of providing new behaviours which confirmed its existence. It was a canonical case of trying to forge facts to which everyone would agree to submit (Callon, 1998). Forging this new economic form was a Herculean task, involving vast expenditures without any necessary return. And it worked – partly because of the power the various stakeholders had to *define what the facts consisted of*, partly because of the ability a number of stakeholders had to *train up bodies* whose stance assumed this world, and partly because of the provision of *measures of behaviour* that offered confirmation. Act as if it's the case and new regularities are produced which 'have the obduracy of the real' (Callon, 1998, p. 47).

Yet, what is also remarkable is how open-ended this process of achieving mass was. For a long time the new economy was little more than a signature which gathered associations – information technology, novelty, business revolution, youth. But this spectral gathering was able to gather flesh and form a kind of frame.

To summarize my argument, rhetorics and frames produced practices and knowledges which have consequences. But this was not a mechanical causality. Rather, the new economy was a performative legitimation, a realignment of knowledge and power which could take in and work with middle class management bodies and desires by shifting 'between different evaluation grids, switching back and forth between divergent challenges to perform – or else' (McKenzie, 2001, p. 19). This new kind of free-associating management narrativity clearly could not last since, as we shall see, it depended for its existence on extraordinary levels of financial subsidy, but it has laid down a new style of doing business which cannot just be reduced to its time. Elements of this style will continue on, as new forms of property, as new kinds of 'expressive organization' (Schulz et al., 2000) and as a legacy of new technologies, some of whose most important impacts have yet to be felt.

These thoughts provide an agenda for this chapter, one of five sections. In the first section, I will outline how the concept (or better, perhaps, brand) of 'the new economy' was constructed by stakeholders like the cultural circuit of capital, as a new institutional-cum-ideological calculus. The second section then considers the means by which the new economy was incarnated into business. I will suggest that, above all, this involved the romantic notion of a kind of passion for business: thus Komisar's bestselling injunction that 'it's the romance, not the finance, that makes the business worth pursuing' (2000, p. 93). In other words, the new economy was an attempt at mass motivation which, if successful, could result in a new kind of *market culture* – or a spiritual renewal of an old one. Then in the third section, I will argue that we should be careful about this attempt to build a conviction capitalism. In very specific ways, the new economy *was* framed by finance – in terms of venture capital, the prevalence of shareholders, and the distribution of wealth. I will argue that, as a first cut at least, the new market culture was better interpreted as a material-rhetorical flourish intended to produce continuous asset price inflation. In other words, the passion play of the new market culture was framed by another calculative agency with its associated metrics, which acted to both produce and discipline it. Then, I will come to what is often considered to be the core of the new economy, namely information and communications technology (ICT). My aim is to show that many of the new developments in ICT are the results of a technological forced march induced by the rhetorical push of the cultural circuit of capital and the resultant sheer weight of investments from finance. In large part, ICT was created anew by the new market culture. Finally, I will conclude by considering what the legacy of the new economy may prove to be. I will argue that this will prove to be rather longer lasting than commentators like Frank (2000) have been willing to countenance.

2. The new economy

Nowadays the idea of the new economy has been stabilized; it consists of strong non-inflationary growth arising out of the rising influence of information and communications technology and the associated restructuring of economic activity. All kinds of other features can be – and usually are – associated with this core definition: for example, the growth of small high-tech firms, the increasing importance of mobile and highly skilled talent, the rise of entrepreneurship, and the centrality of venture capital. And it is almost second nature for commentators to produce grand rhetorical flourishes such as the death of the business cycle or virtually unlimited growth. What seems certain is that the new economy is both a description and, at the same time, an assumption of what constitutes a normal future. For example, all kinds of counties, cities and regions now want to be a part of a new economy.

But where did this idea arrive from, and who were its chief progenitors? The 'new economy' as a description was first used in the 1980s. At the time there was no clear economic model. Rather this has had to be developed, and that work was mainly done in the 1990s (although a new economy genealogy can certainly be traced back to the 1960s). It was made durable in the media, in academia, and, most importantly of all, in people's own houses through the advent of the personal computer and subsequently the Internet and the World Wide Web. Thus, the World Wide Web first appeared in November 1993 and the Mosaic web browser became publicly available in February 1994. But large numbers of people did not discover the web until 1997 – not entirely coincidentally the time of the concerted acceleration of the NASDAQ stock index and the movement of price–earnings ratios into hitherto uncharted territory.

What seems certain is that by the mid 1990s the new economy had already become a stable rhetorical form, in common usage in business and government, and seeping into popular culture. In effect the new economy had become a kind of *brand*, compounding in one phrase the attractions and rewards of a new version of capitalism.

So, how had an innocuous phrase become the chief watchword of capitalism, to the extent that by the late 1990s even the *Financial Times* had declared itself the 'newspaper of the new economy'? I want to argue that its strength and speed of diffusion was the result of the existence of five stakeholders willing to give it push. Of them, undoubtedly the most important was an institution I have elsewhere called the 'cultural circuit of capital'. This circuit, which has chiefly come into existence since the 1960s, is a machine for producing and disseminating knowledge to business elites (Thrift, 1997a; 1997b; 1999a; 1999b).

The three chief producers of this knowledge are business schools, management consultants and management gurus. Business schools were first founded in the late nineteenth and early twentieth centuries in the United States. However, save for a small elite, the main phase of expansion in the United States took place much later, from the 1940s on, on the back of the MBA. In the rest of the world, business schools were slow to be founded, but in the 1950s and 1960s they began to open and expand in Europe and subsequently in Asia. Nowadays business schools are the jewels in the crown of a vast global executive education market, calculated to be worth in excess of \$12 billion per annum, of which they generate about one-quarter of the value (Crainer and Dearlove, 1998).

Management consultants also date from the late nineteenth and early twentieth centuries. Often described as unacknowledged legislators, management consultants offer advice to business on such a large scale that a case could be made that they have simply become an extension of firms. Whatever the case, it is clear that they are important producers and disseminators of business knowledge, able to take up ideas and translate them into practice and to feed practice back into ideas (Micklethwait and Wooldridge, 1996; Clark, 2001). As we saw in Chapter 4:

Whatever the product … consultants need to sell ideas. The problem is that what consulting has to sell isn't always new, and certainly isn't always fresh. It is an unusual industry because it builds its knowledge base at the expense of its clients. From a more critical perspective, it is not much of a stretch to say that consulting companies make a lot of money collecting experience from their clients, which they turn around and sell in other forms, sometimes not very well disguised, to other clients. (O'Shea and Madigan, 1997, p. 13)

Finally, management gurus are chiefly a phenomenon of the later twentieth century, consisting of various well-known academics, consultants and business managers who have been able to package their ideas as aspects of themselves. Though there is a clear genealogy, modern management gurus date from Peters and Waterman's *In Search of Excellence*, published in 1982. Gurus tend to develop formulaic approaches to management, which play down context for the sake of rhetorical force.

Producers of business knowledge necessarily have a voracious appetite for new knowledge which can continue to feed the machine of which they are a part. So they do not just produce knowledge from within. They are also constantly on the hunt for knowledge from without which can be adapted and brought within. Thus almost every aspect of human knowledge is available for incorporating – and huge amounts of it have been (Thrift, 1999a)!

These producers generate a range of different kinds of business knowledge. Put schematically, it is possible to say that this knowledge has three main functions. The first is the provision of general principles of business life – 'do this, don't do that' – a kind of grammar of business imperatives. The second is as a primer which tells managers how to attain particular goals. The third is an intelligence-gathering function – concerned with how business practices are working out. In other words, what is being produced is a process of endless, relentless, and continuous critique of the status quo (Boltanski and Chiapello, 1999).

These three producers could not exist in their modern form without a symbiotic relationship with the media which both publicize and distribute their wares. In particular, we can consider three main ways in which the media intervene. The first is through the production of standard media like books, magazines, newspapers, Internet sites, and television. The importance of journalists as translators of business ideas, coupled with the way in which the media provide outlets for the knowledge producers to display their wares, are underlined by these media (Furusten, 1999). A second element is the increasing scale of specialized business media. These range all the way from industry-specific magazines to the new breed of consultancy-sponsored magazines (such as *Strategy and Business*) which emulate the *Harvard Business Review*. Since the mid 1990s a whole set of new economy magazines has come into existence, either in print or on the web (e.g. *The Standard*). The model provided by *Fast Company*, first published in 1995, has proved particularly influential, leading to a large number of copycat magazines (e.g. just in the United Kingdom, *Business 2.0, Red Herring, e-Business, Revolution, The International Standard*). In turn *Fast Company's* format has been copied back into the mainstream business journals like *Fortune*. A third element is the growth of media intermediaries – press officers, publicity consultants, design consultants, advertising agencies, and so on – which have become more important as business ideas have increasingly come to resemble brands. Then, a fourth element has been the re-engineering of the face-to-face meeting through the continual production of conferences, seminars, workshops, and the like. These events serve both as disseminators of new business knowledge and as motivational fuel.

The new economy could not have taken off without this cultural circuit. But it was not the only stakeholder. There were others. To begin with, there was government. By the mid 1990s governments around the world were latching onto the idea of a new economy and were attempting to make it their own through a series of reports. Particularly active in all of this were intergovernmental bodies like the OECD and the EU for whom the new economy provided both a means of justifying their existence and a new means of authentication (e.g. European Union, 1997; Anderson, 2000). Governments launched initiatives aimed at preparing for and instituting a new economy – which already existed – some way into the future. The reasons for the attractiveness of the 'weightless' new economy for governments were many: increasing closeness to business, the use of many new economy ideas in government, a sense of imminent threat, new justification for government intervention, a search for a kind of youthfulness, and so on. They were typified by the annual Davos meeting of the World Economic Forum, often described as the Parliament of Managers (Lapham, 1999; Thrift, 1997a). Here, the hope was that through information technology the leviathan of capitalism could be invested with a human face.

Another set of stakeholders were non-business-school academics, and especially economists. Initially economists were slow to take up the new economy, although their ideas (e.g. on endogenous growth) were sometimes drawn upon by new economy gurus (e.g. Romer, 1990). But in the late 1990s many economists began to take serious note, and acted as key legitimators by providing validation through empirical studies as well as elaboration (e.g. Quah's 1997 weightless economy). Economists, in other words, began to produce a formal body of knowledge which could act as serious confirmation of more general (and rather flighty) business knowledge. In their hands the new economy took on weight.

Then there was another group of stakeholders: the managers themselves. Managers provided a growing audience for the new economy for a series of different reasons. For older managers the new economy was something to keep in touch with. For younger managers it was something to be part of. It was talking the talk and walking the walk. It was both a rhetorical frame for producing business effects and a source of ideas about how business (and the management self) should be conducted.

There was one final stakeholder, and that was information and communication technology itself. ICT has now reached the point where it can be counted as having its own agency, of a sort. That agency comes from four separate directions. First, there is the simple matter of sunk costs. Massive amounts of expenditure have been laid down on ICT which means that it has to be used, even if at first its use is highly inefficient. Many of the results of ICT come from massive, even excessive, expenditures which force the world in a particular direction. Second, it produces an expectation of usage, complete with its own morality: 'good' companies have and use ICT. Third, it provides new means of apprehending the world, although often not in the ways originally expected (see Brown et al., 2001, on groupware). Fourth, through software, rules of conduct are laid down which are the informational equivalent of walls and barriers, roads and tolls, junctions and crossroads, and which have similar effectivity.

The push provided by these five stakeholders set up a frame of action and expectation, a new set of market rules and commensurabilities. Just as importantly, the institution of the frame also depended upon a vision of what was outside it. In this case, it was the 'old economy' of heavy industry, bureaucratic ways, deficit of entrepreneurial spirit, and general lack of economic sparkle. This othering was crucial since it provided an economic negative, a mirror world of all the things that cannot and must not be.

Management body: it's the romance

This is all very well, but it suggests a level of engagement with the new economy which is merely (or perhaps not sufficiently) gestural. But effective social movements need to create background, a taken-for-granted world which, if you like, assumes the new economy's assumptions. In this section, I will argue that this necessarily meant providing a *performative* politics of incarnation. Management had to become convincingly embodied in new ways.

So what kind of management body was required by the new economy? On this the cultural circuit of capital was clear and its ideas are still being played out in businesses around the world. There were four ways in which the management body was to be shaped.

To begin with, at a number of levels the management body had to *do more*: 'All of us can do more, and be more, and contribute more, and help each other more' (Lewin and Regine, 1999, p. 268). The management body had to make more of itself. That meant working harder but it also meant spreading the body around more.

So, second, the major body had to be *passionate*. Managers had to be continuously active in pursuit of visions and goals, continuously wary of 'spinning the wheels'. But that required being able to engage the emotions, not just cognitive skills, in order to design the moment so that it would engage others.

Third, the management body had to become more *adaptable*. Bodies had to be involved in continuous learning so that these firms could learn faster, on the ground that learning faster than their competitors was now the main competitive advantage that firms had (de Geuss, 1997; Senge et al., 1999). But this was a particular kind of learning based on the production of emergence rather than the reproduction of routines. Therefore it was necessarily open-ended: 'if we believe that people in organizations contribute to organizational goals by participating inventively in practices that can never be fully captured by institutionalized processes then we will minimize prescription, suggesting that too much of it discourages the very inventiveness that makes practices effective' (Wenger, 1999, p. 10). The learning had to be carried out in a new way which would maximize invention, sort for creativity. Such chronically inventive learning has a number of characteristics. To begin with, it is generally the work not of individual genius but of shared community. Then, it is learning that takes place in the doing; it is worked out in the working out. And, last, it is 'playful'. That is it involves constant cultural prototyping which, because it is prepared for surprise, is more likely to happen across viable solutions (Schrage, 2000).Finally, the management body had to be *participative*. Management bodies had to work through persuasion as well as command. They had to engage the 'soul' (Lewin and Regine, 1999). This means investing the community with a sense of purpose and common ownership through deliberate working on relationships. The idea was that the management body would be sensitized to the social dynamics of the organization and could achieve continuous modulation rather than bureaucratic control (Deleuze, 1990a). The management body could go with the flow, providing smaller but more effective interventions as and when necessary. The heavy bureaucratic hand was replaced by the light touch of the 'change agent'.

Producing management bodies that can conform to these strictures involved a whole series of technologies of government of the self which could achieve these goals. But this did not prove as problematic as might be thought, for three reasons. First, it was, at least in certain senses, simply another stage in the trek of a romantic US-style individualism and was therefore already culturally attuned to its heartland. Here yet again was the open frontier consisting of limitless possibilities, the self-made person, the elemental force of entrepreneurialism, and all the other tropes that populate so many of the writings on the new economy, all celebrations of a particular way of life which was now, so the story went, being reasserted. Whether this was the case, or the new economy was in fact the platform for a sub-Nietzschean individualism, I will leave to another day. Second, this was also the time of the therapeutic model of the self and its associated tropes: the stress on emotions, on good communication, on psychological knowledge, and so on (Rose, 1999). Therapeutic models had become so prevalent that they operated as a part of the general cultural background:

> Social institutions no longer bind and determine the self as they once did. More and more areas of life (vocation, beliefs, sexual identity, etc.) are now areas of choice, determined by the individual self. The therapeutic ethos is thus characterized by a conspicuous self-referencing. (Nolan, 1998, p. 9)

Third, over a considerable period of time, a management ethos had existed which was based on producing more open bodies which could develop a series of soft skills like intuition, leadership and other conducts of conduct. In part, this movement started as a reaction to the workplace authoritarianism of Taylorism but it gradually began to take on its own dynamic, ably documented by Kleiner (1996), which began to get into its stride with the work of Emery and Trist in the UK in the 1940s, and with the work of the National Training Laboratories in the US in the 1950s. For Kurt Lewin and Ron Lippitt, the answer to the problem of good organizational development was to make managers more authentic by changing their internal competences and ultimately their behaviour so that they could enact different, more democratic and less top-down organizations. By the 1960s such thinking had become standardized, even stylized, by other currents like countercultures (as in est) and a nascent New Age tradition, so producing a range of technologies which were intended to change styles of embodiment in order to produce better managers.

Thus, by the 1990s a rich archive of continually validated work on the management body already existed, ready and able to be applied to the new economy. This work spawned three technologies in particular. The first of these was *organizational*, and consisted of technologies that brought bodies into alignment. In particular, optimal alignment was considered to occur through the use of teams and projects. Indeed, so widespread had the use of teams and projects become that, by one estimate, in 2000, 80 per cent of all *Fortune 2000* companies had over half their employees working in teams:

> In response to this trend, the US Department of Labor has suggested that schools begin training students in such competencies as team work and project management. Scientists, engineers, technicians and so forth increasingly see themselves as engaged in the project, not the company. With this kind of organisation, today's companies have learned to sustain even the 20 per cent annual average employee turnover experienced in their IT departments. (Flores and Gray, 2000, pp. 24–5)

However efficacious they may or may not be, the fact is that teams and projects are now regarded as the main way in which bodies can be aligned to produce creativity. The intention is to produce concerted periods of time in which people can come together productively to push through a particular creative project. This will involve designing rapid team start-ups (through the use of facilitators, 'check-ins', and other means of producing intense dialogic conversation) which will build both trust and new ideas, and careful time management. In turn, all over the world, offices are being redesigned to cope with this way of working. 'Hives' and 'cells' are being replaced by 'club' and 'den' environments (Duffy, 1997).

The second technology was *inspirational* and consisted of the careful design of events which would enable organizations to interact on a larger scale. A whole series of these technologies now exist, from conferences and seminars through to courses and workshops. Their purpose is in part to dis-seminate information but it is also in part to keep the current of inspiration going. Many of these events are minutely plotted and the smaller of them use a number of summative body techniques, from performance (e.g. the-atre, dance, opera), through body control techniques like Aikido or the Alexander Technique, to various forms of ritual (especially of the New Age variety).

The final technology to emerge was *ideological*. Each organization had to have narratives which would sustain it, especially in circumstances in which there might be constant jumping between projects, in which the organiza-tion was likely to be dispersed over many locations, and in which there might be high personnel turnover. Thus the vogue for corporate storytelling, corporate websites, and the like. Thus also, on a different level, the iconog-raphy of the new economy – the dressed-down fashion styles, the there but not there spaces like Silicon Valley, the technological rhetoric (from the webpage layouts to their print equivalents) – all wrapped together by a vast outpouring of business books, magazines and television series, each of them telling exemplary stories of what it is like to be in and a part of the new economy.

In each of these cases what we see are formats intended to change the body by changing space and time. From the vagaries of the modern office, through the controlled otherness of the event, through to the iconological formats, what we see are attempts to change the background of space and time by changing the way the body lives (Thrift, 2000b):

> By changing space, by leaving the space of one's usual sensibilities, one enters into a communication with a space that is psychically innovating. For we do not change place, we change our nature. (Bachelard, 1966, p. 15)

Change the rate of embodied interaction, and change space and time; change space and time, and change the nature of embodied interaction. Make room, in the process, for possibility. This is also the virtuality of Deleuze applied, the constitution of a landscape of assemblages, circulations and multiplicities, a new conjunctive synthesis. For what is being built is a new machine which comprises not individuals in interaction but rather interrelationships of *assemblages*:

> An assemblage can be made up of elements which are generative, neuro-physiological, linked to infancy, to the family, to mass media, and so forth. The concept of assemblage draws on the assemblages created by certain sur-realist painters and sculptors. The simplest example is the famous *Bull's Head* created by Picasso in 1942: in this assemblage, a bicycle handlebar placed on a saddle invokes a bull's head. On the basis of separate elements – heteroge-neous elements placed in relationship to one another – an assemblage breathes life into the elements that compose it and induces a novel percep-tion of reality. (Elkaim, 1997, p. xvi)

But, of course, such a process of manager-making had a notable downside. For the romance of the new economy also produced exclusivity. In a world where the passion and romance of work had to be displayed on a 24/7 basis, where 'work today has to be half work, half play' in part because 'we spend our whole lives at the workplace' (Bronson, 1999, p. xxxiv), those with other responsibilities found it hard to play. In particular, for all the talk of female values, women were actually a declining element of the new economy. Thus, in 1986 women represented 40 per cent of the US technology sector workforce; in 1999 they represented only 29 per cent. Again, women represented only 3 per cent of the board members of new economy companies compared with 11 per cent of *Fortune 2000* companies. One of the reasons was that women were not well represented in relevant educational sectors: only 28 per cent of US computer science graduates are women. Another reason is the general increase in managerial work hours which in the United States, Britain and some other countries (Massey, 1995; Schor, 1993) is now striking. Indeed, one study of dot.com companies found that 'the hours worked are longer, the travel is more onerous and time at home is limited. The new economy company increasingly mirrors the old, but without a supportive infrastructure' (Skapinker, 2000, p. 23). In other sectors of the economy, flexible work arrangements are much more common. And then one other reason is that the ultracapitalist romance of the new economy played to a certain kind of male role model. The artist obsessed with their work becomes the entrepreneur seeking the concepts which make up the soul of the new economy:

> The media has mythologised stories of entrepreneurs sleeping in dingy motel rooms, or on the office floor, slaving away at the computer until the early hours, sometimes forgetting to eat or to take a shower. They wear rumpled clothes, drink beer and play in their few free hours. Eventually they become billionaires. Just how much of this is reality and how much is myth is irrelevant. The point is that it has become the industry's image, and it is not a role many women see themselves playing. As they cannot place themselves in such a culture, many may choose to shun the industry. (Griffith, 2000, p. 12)

It's the finance

Many of those working in the new economy wanted to believe in more-than-business. For them, the new economy 'isn't primarily a financial institution. It's a creative institution. Like painting and sculpting, business can be a venue for personal expression and artistry. At its heart more like a canvas than a spreadsheet' (Komisar, 2000, p. 55). But there is another way of understanding the new economy and its rhetorical claims, one that reintroduces finance not as inimical to passion but as the central passion of the new economy. Business missionary becomes financial mercenary. For another way of understanding the new economy is as a ramp for the financial markets, providing the narrative raw material to fuel a speculative asset price bubble which was also founded on an extension of the financial audience.

On this interpretation, the real genesis of the new economy was probably the initial public offering made on 9 August 1995 by Netscape, the Internet browser company which is now part of AOL. Initially set at $28 a share, the price of its stake doubled during the day and then kept on going up, so setting off the Internet feeding frenzy which was to last five years. And this interpretation of finance as the ruling passion of the new economy has much to commend it. After all, many of the key innovations of the new economy were clearly financial. Most particularly, there was the growth of venture capital companies, able to specialize in funding the technological innovation; the growth of the initial public offering (which provided powerful necessities for managers and members who generally held stock options, produced funds for expansion, and allowed investors to cash out without waiting 10 or 20 years); the increased use of stock options as compensation; and the creation of a labour market of entrepreneurial workers willing and able to take the risks, which formed a 'mobile attack force', constantly on the move to the projects most likely to be successful (Mandel, 2000).

This financial interpretation therefore produced a frame around the frame of the new economy; the new economy became a command performance whose script (aided by extravagant props and acting) played so well to financial audiences that they were willing to pay the ever-increasing costs of admission. In other words, the new economy became a theatre which could be used to both push share prices up and extend share ownership.

Of course, the demand for shares of economic assets has always been strong in the financial sphere, but the demand has chiefly circulated within a relatively small circle, made up of institutional investors and a comparatively small number of individual investors. However, in the last two decades of the twentieth century, this demand began to become more general, the result of the increase in the number of those who have investments, either directly or indirectly. This growth resulted from four sources. First, and most importantly, there was the growth of pension funds and other institutional investors (Clark, 2000). Pension funds now own many of the key sectors of the US economy, and nearly half of the British and Dutch economies. In effect pension funds (which themselves account for more than 40 per cent of investments in venture capital funds) dramatically multiplied those who had indirect investments in the shareholder economy. Then, second, there was the growth of new aggregate investment vehicles. Of these, the most important must be the mutual funds (unit trusts in the UK), which grew strongly in the United States from the early 1980s to the point where by 1998 there were nearly two shareholder accounts per family (Shiller, 2000). In part, the reason for the proliferation of these funds can be linked to a third source, the growth of individual shareholder choice (Martin and Turner, 2000). In the United States this was given an enormous boost by the growth of defined contribution (401(k)) pension plans which allowed employees the opportunity to have their pension contributions paid into a tax-deferred retirement account. They then control the investments in these accounts and must allocate them among stocks, bonds, and money market accounts. Elsewhere, individual shareholders were growing in number even without this boost. Finally, there was the growth of employee stock options, shares issued through privatizations, and other means of boosting share ownership. Through the 1980s and 1990s these became more general.

This growth in the number of shareholders (both directly and indirectly) and in shareholder choice was buttressed by the increasing mediation of finance which meant that narratives like the new economy could travel further and more forcefully than before. This mediation came about through four processes of authority. The first was the constitutive role of the media which now acted as the main conduit of market information for most shareholders. The scope of business reporting expanded massively and much of this played to shareholders, as typified by the success in the US of channels like CNBC, CNNFn and Bloomberg which produced an uninterrupted stream of business news, much of it aimed at investors. So pervasive has their occurrence become in the United States that

> traditional brokerage firms found it necessary to keep CNBC running in the lower corners of their brokers' computer screens. So many clients would call to ask about something they had just heard on the networks that brokers (who were supposed to be too busy working to watch television!) began to seem behind the chase. (Shiller, 2000, p. 29)

A particularly important subsidiary element of this newly mediated sphere of the economy was advertising: the sheer scale of current financial advertising needs to be acknowledged, not so much for its impacts (which are debatable) as for its ability to set up a new background in which investing is a normal practice.

The second, related process of authority was the growth of financial literacy. This has been remarkable. Shiller (2000, p. 33) notes a 1954 New York Stock Exchange survey which showed that only 20 per cent of the US public even knew enough to describe what a share was. Now this is basic knowledge for many. Yet the consequences of this growth in financial literacy have yet to be explored. 'It occurred to no one that the public might one day be as sophisticated in [financial] matters as the professional' (Lewis, 2001, p. 33), but this has increasingly proved to be the case.

> The Bloomsberg News Service commissioned a study to explore the phenomenon of what were now being called 'whisper numbers'. The study showed that whisper numbers, the numbers put out by the amateur Web Sites, were mistaken, on average, by 21 per cent. The professional Wall Street forecasters were mistaken, on average, by 44 per cent. The reason the amateurs now held the balance of power in the market was that they were, on average, more than twice as accurate as the pros – this in spite of the fact that the entire financial system was rigged in favour of the pros. The big companies spoon-fed their scoops directly to the pros; the amateurs were flying by radar. (2001, p. 33)

Then a third process of authority was the general growth of financial advice, ranging from the kind of advice that was being doled out by the star media analysts like Mary Meeker through brokerage services to personal financial advisers. Such advice produced a kind of proxy financial literacy which is heavily oriented to the promotion of share ownership. And, finally, there was the fact that business interest increasingly ran to the dictates of shareholder sentiment (Williams, 2000). Through the advent of measures of performance like shareholder value, the share price of a company has become a crucial determinant of what is regarded as business success. In turn, these new processes of authority led to a continuation of stories like the new economy day by day, to the point where public relations became a crucial element of many aspects of economic life – from the IPO to managing shareholder sentiment – and increasingly therefore economic life came to resemble the media industry with fashions, stars and favourite stocks.

The importance of this change should not be underestimated. As Kurtz puts it:

> a decade ago, those chronicling the ups and downs of Wall Street spoke to a narrow audience comprising mainly well-heeled investors and hyperactive traders. But a communications revolution soon transformed the landscape, giving real time television coverage and up to the second reports immense power to move jittery markets. This mighty media apparatus had the ability to confer instant stardom on the correspondents, the once obscure market gurus, and the new breed of telegenic chief executives. CNBC was now as important to the financial world as CNN was to politicians and diplomats and, like Ted Turner's network, it had the power to change events even while reporting them. This was America's new national pastime, pursued by high powered players and coaches whose pronouncements offered the tantalizing possibility that the average fan could share in the wealth. (2000, p. xxvii)

So, for example, financial journalists no longer just reported. They were players (but with no real penalty for being wrong):

> Financial professionals entered some weird new head space. They simply took it for granted that a 'financial market' was a collection of people doing their best to get onto CNBC and CNNfn and into the Heard on the Street column of the *Wall Street Journal* and the Lex column of the *Financial Times*, where they could advance their narrow self-interests. (Lewis, 2001, p. 33)

Running the new economy story through this financial machine had enormous benefits for a number of actors: it added value to particular shares (so, for example, benefiting managers whose salaries are attached to share value), it proved analysts' worth and made media stars of some of them, it demonstrated the worth of the system as a whole, and so on. In particular, a new story will have grip on this machine if it can change the investment categories through which the economy is thought. And in the 1990s the new economy became an investment category of its own, as an obsession with high-technology shares, with markets like NASDAQ and so on. In other words, telling the new economy story worked, and worked to the extent that it began to redescribe market fundamentals.

So great was the demand for shares in this category that, for a time, the new economy became an irresistible force. For example, in the UK fund management firms like Foreign and Colonial and Philips and Drew which tried not to get sucked into the technology bubble fared poorly. Pension funds gave them the cold shoulder. And the growth of indexing added to the whole effect, making it well-nigh impossible to ignore technology stocks (*The Economist/*, 21 October 2000, p. 145). Indeed, as Mandel (2000) has argued, one way of interpreting the new economy story was as a means of persuading investors of all kinds to take on riskier investments. In this sense, it might be seen as a means of fostering innovations that could otherwise not have taken place. Or it could be seen quite differently – as a means of drawing investors into taking on debt. It is worth remembering that in the five years to 2000 business and consumers took on $4 trillion in debt (Mandel, 2000) and the US savings rate in 2000 was only 0.8 per cent, a 67 year low. Seen in this way, the new economy comes to resemble a financial instrument like junk bonds.

The strength of the story was only added to by the growth of the technology which most symbolized the new economy, the Internet. The Internet is an active technology which can give people a sense of mastery in their everyday life (not least through share investing):

> Because of the vivid and immediate personal impression the Internet makes, people find it plausible to assume that it also has great economic importance. It is much easier to imagine the consequences of advances in this technology than the consequences of, say, improved shipbuilding technology or new developments in materials science. Most of us simply do not hear much about research in these areas.
>
> Spectacular US corporate earnings growth in 1994, up 36% in real terms as measured by the S&P composite real earnings, followed by real earnings growth of 8% in 1995 and 10% in 1996, coincided roughly with the Internet's birth but in fact had little to do with the Internet. Instead the earnings growth was attributed by analysts to a continuation of slow recovery from the 1990–91 recession, coupled with a weak dollar and strong foreign demand for US capital and technology exports, as well as cost-cutting initiatives by US companies. It could not have been the Internet that caused the growth in profits: the fledgling Internet companies were not making much of a profit yet, and indeed they still are not. But the occurrence of profit growth coinciding with the appearance of a new technology as dramatic as the Internet can easily create an impression among the general public that these two events were somehow linked ...
>
> What matters for a stock market broker is not, however, the reality of the Internet revolution, which is hard to discern, but rather the public impressions that the revolution creates. Public reaction is influenced by the intuitive plausibility of Internet lore, and this plausibility is ultimately influenced by the ease with which examples or arguments come to mind. If we are regularly spending time on the Internet, then these examples will come to mind easily. (Shiller, 2000, pp. 20–1)

In turn, such impressions had knock-ons. For example, managers started to consider how they could insert their companies into the high-valuation categories, often with little concern for longer-term consequences.

The consequences were clear. By one estimate about $150 billion was raised for venture capital and public stock offerings in the five years from 1995 to 2000 to finance the new economy story. In turn, this led to major income and profit for certain sectors, precisely those addressed in this chapter (Tomkins, 2000). In particular, very large amounts of money went into the cultural circuit in the form of consultancy fees (especially to specialist consultancy firms like the Gartner Group, Forrester Research and Jupiter Communications), public relations company fees and the like. Most spectacular of all were the benefits that accrued to the media from publicity: advertising agencies, television, network, radio stations, billboards, newspapers and magazines. Others who benefited included the financial sector, investment banks, venture capitalists, and their investors (especially institutional investors like pension funds). Those who lost were the investors who acquired shares and failed to sell them in time: mutual funds, pension funds, some corporate investors, and, inevitably, large numbers of ordinary investors (especially young first-time investors).

So by disclosing a new world, 'the new economy', money was made and spent – and it was made, and invested to be made and spent again, in large quantities. Little wonder that Lewis has argued that for a time Silicon Valley was a 'little experiment of capitalism with too much capital' (1999, p. 254). But what was being described was not so much new knowledge as new business impressions and sensitivities, a new *mood* of engaging activity (Spinosa et al., 1997; Flores, 2000; Flores and Gray, 2000), a new style of doing capitalism.

In turn, the new economy share boom had enormous effects on wealth distribution, and these should not be gainsaid. It is worth remarking that in the United States, for example, since the beginning of the 1980s, Americans' financial wealth has grown from $7 trillion to $32 trillion, but this growth has been unevenly spread. In 2000, for example, the richest 2.7 million Americans, comprising the top 1 per cent of the population, had as many after-tax dollars to spend as the bottom 100 million put together. (Meanwhile, the poorest one-fifth of households had an average income of $8800, a decline from the 1970s.) More to the point, since the beginning of the Clinton administration (roughly paralleling the growth of the new economy) the incomes of the richest one-fifth rose twice as fast as those of the middle fifth (Reich, 2000).

But there is more. These figures do not include deferred income, stock options and the like, which have mainly gone to the top fifth. And most notably of all, they do not include increases in the values of stock portfolios. On one estimate, 85 per cent of the increases in share values went to the top 10 per cent of earners, and over 40 per cent to just the top 1 per cent (Reich, 2000).

Thus, the new economy story has had great purchase on the world. But, to slightly rephrase Komisar, it's the romance that produces the finance that makes the business worth pursuing. The romantic journey ends here. For stories of economies have usually proved to be about ownership, and this story was no exception. As the figures above show, the youthful countenance of the new economy masked social relationships which were still regressive. The new economy built new connections but at the same old cost. To this extent, it was simply a new received economic doctrine of the elite masquerading as a democratic or even aesthetic impulse (Gregory, 1997).

Creating a new market culture

We come then to information and communications technology (ICT). What can we say about what was often regarded as a central preserve of the new economy, given the previous discussion? The first point to make is that the new economy depended upon the sheer amount of expenditure on ICT able to be unlocked by the cultural circuit and finance working in lockstep. The scale of this investment cannot be gainsaid and it resulted in what might best be described as a kind of forced technological march. The second point to make is that the cultural circuit also produced a process of constant technological critique (Boltanski and Chiapello, 1999). Thus, rather more rapidly than in the past, innovations were communicated and their opportunities and problems were fed back. In particular, the cultural circuit was able to produce two important forms of technological feedback very rapidly which jointly equated to a much greater diffusion of technological expertise – and what counted as technological expertise. One was the ability to track and comment upon how new technologies fitted into organizations. The other was the ability to track and comment upon consumer response (in part because of the existence of a set of consumers who were themselves to a degree producers). In turn, this process of constant technological critique meant that ICT technological changes could become akin to those of the cultural industries, involving rapid changes in function and style which were constitutive and not just a by-product, and competences which were much more evenly distributed between producers and consumers. A third point to make is that this meant that what counted as technology was redefined. Technology was increasingly counted as a subset of knowledge more generally, in part because of trends in management thinking which equated technology with knowledge or informational capital (e.g. Burton-Jones, 2000). More generally, what counted as information and communication technology could increasingly be framed as cultural, as software and software engineering became more dominant. Thus, the kind of easy technological determinism that had been a part of the mindset of the ICT industry became something more subtle and more likely to be culturally inflected by content. A fourth point follows on. New privileged groups were created by ICT who took ownership of a cultural style being retailed by the cultural circuit and more widely. These 'bourgeois bohemians' (Brooks, 2000; see also A.W. Frank, 1997; T. Frank, 2000) regarded 'hip as the official capitalist style' (Frank, 1997, p. 224) and a part of this style was advertising the presence, actual or implied, of ICT. The actual manifestation could be of several kinds, of course, from the ethereal concept artist to the hard-living entrepreneur. But they could all fit into a bobo style which was simultaneously calculatedly irreverent and profoundly complacent about the world.

To summarize the argument so far: the success of the new economy arose from its ability to disclose, to bring out, a new kind of market culture as a frame in which technology could be constantly modulated and so constantly redefined – to the advantage of many stakeholders. In other words, the triumph of this new culture resulted from an act of redescription which provided a peculiarly open means of framing the world, as a set of becomings which kept the possible possible and thereby initiated a new style of doing business. In a certain sense this was simply a successful commercial restatement of Euro-American culture's fundamental tenet that everything is possible given the technology (Strathern, 1999), but if that was so then it was also about producing more effective means of making this restatement effective, new holdings that could create a new viewpoint.

Screaming 'uncle'

So now it's all over. The new economy has been scorched, scotched, even scuttled. Both the rhetorical and the financial push are gone. The gilded age is tarnished (Remnick, 2000):

> Only yesterday, so it seems, Wall Street equity analysts almost unanimously proclaimed a new economic paradigm. Out with these old equity valuation models, out with fusty concerns about earnings (actual or predicted), out with the business cycle, in with network effects, burn rates, and global scale. Forget, ugh, prudence: caution is the new recklessness. Nowadays, as one reputable member of the breed then put it, the only danger is to be out of the market.
> Well, for the shrewd advice (as NASDAQ tottered at around 5,000) many thanks. For all those 'busy', 'hold' and 'accumulate' recommendations on stocks that cost $100 last year, and now cost $1.50, thanks a lot. (*The Economist*, 6 January 2001)

So, everywhere, there were signs of a new economy in a serious downturn. In February 2001, for example, Cisco Systems, one of the new economy bellwethers, missed its earnings expectations for the first time in six years. Inventories were building. Firms had started to cut back on ICT spending. And Morgan Stanley Dean Witter's Mary Meeker, who made $15 million in 1999 telling people to buy Priceline when it was at $165 a share and Healtheon/WebMD when it reached $105 a share, went silent as their values collapsed.

Not surprisingly, those who have promulgated the new economy worry what will come next – and how they can survive it. One of the key rhetorical sites of the new economy, the business magazine *Fast Company*, shows all these concerns (Thrift, 2000b). Bylines like 'Weathering the Internet Storm', 'It's Crunch Time for the Net', 'Act II for the New Economy' and 'How To Win in the Next Economy' document an increasingly fraught state of mind (while the halving of the size of the magazine as advertising revenues have plummeted, and its takeover by a part of Berkelsmann AG, an old economy company if ever there was one, show a business model forced to conform). Meanwhile websites like fuckedcompany.com, with their counts of jobs scuppered daily, show what the decline of the new economy means: lost jobs, lost hopes, lost passions. Now all the writing is about business basics: sustainable business, good management, grassroots adoption of products, and so on (e.g. Anders, 2001).

It is easy to be cynical about the new economy. As I read the nth management book or article on the inevitability of change, the desirability of constant experimentation, and the necessity of creative dissent, it was difficult not to gag. This seemed all too like Frank's (2000) 'age of incantation'. But I think it is important not to be quite so dismissive. Frank's wonderful polemic on 'the long summer of corporate love' (2000, p. 356) is so concerned to root out all believers that it cannot see that new practices might have arisen from this frenzy of capitalist experiment (Thrift, 2001b). But elements of the new economy will live on. To write it off as simply a discourse is to misunderstand discourse's materiality. To begin with, it is by no means certain that the widespread adoption of technologies and new modes of industrial organization over the last five years has not generated growth in the output produced from a given amount of labour and capital. Then, a global software industry has been produced in a quite remarkably short space of time. And, as Chandler and Cortado (2000) point out, software is profoundly discontinuous with the past, not only in how it has appeared in the economy, but in how it is sold and what it is. There has been nothing quite like it before. Most importantly of all, though many of the investments in the new economy will be written off, many of the practices and products of the new economy will carry over into what follows, from new forms of property (Rifkin, 2000) to new kinds of 'expressive' corporate organization (Schulz et al., 2000). Most particularly, the extraordinary wave of investment that splashed over North America and parts of Europe has produced a flood of innovations whose effects will be with us for a long time to come. Innovations like wireless communication, pervasive computing and certain new kinds of software program (such as peer-to-peer systems like Groove) will produce an intensification of everyday life that will finally, I suspect, produce some of the enormous changes in the social and cultural structures of the Euro-American world that new economy enthusiasts constantly (and tiresomely) predicted (French and Thrift, 2001; Thrift, 2001b). The new economy may have screamed 'uncle' but it has left a legacy, not all of which is bitter.

7

Performing Cultures in the New Economy

Introduction

This chapter is intended to provide a symptomatic reading of some of the practices of modern western business (see also Thrift, 1996a; 1997a; 1999a; 1999b). I want to argue that something new is happening to western capitalism – not as new as some of its more evangelical proponents would argue, no doubt, but not just business as usual either. That something new is preparation for a time that Walter Benjamin once forecast, the time when the emergency becomes the rule.

For, so the stories go, firms now live in a permanent stage of emergency, always bordering on the edge of chaos. So firms must no longer be so concerned to exercise bureaucratic control. Indeed, through a variety of devices – cultivating knowledge workers, valuing teams, organization through projects, better use of information technology, flattened hierarchies – they will generate just enough organizational stability to change in an orderly fashion and sufficient hair-trigger responsiveness to adapt to the expectedly unexpected. Firms will therefore become faster, more agile (e.g. Illinitch et al., 1998). They will be able to live life in a blur of change.

Such a turn towards the rule of emergency demands new disciplines and skills of managers. 'Organization man' is gone. In his stead, new subject positions must be invented. Managers must become 'change agents' – able, through the cultivation of new disciplines and skills, to become the fastest and best.

Obviously we need to be careful. For a start, the vast bulk of business consists of the reiterative rollover of practices laid down many centuries ago, practices like double-entry book-keeping, invoicing and filing and the like, which have changed much less than those who want to believe that we live in the new would be willing or would want to concede. Then, much of what I have written so far draws on analyses which are, by their nature, rhetorical. 'For all we read about bold companies managing in new ways, most enterprises continue to noodle with functionally organised many-tiered hierarchies, the mechanistic model of a century ago' (Colvin, 2000, p. F5).

So how has the new discourse of permanent emergency obtained so much grip? I want to argue that the best description of its effectivity is provided by the word 'style', a word which gives the right sense of an intention or a modulation rather than a wholesale changeover of practice but which, nonetheless, does not suggest something trivial. Of course, style is one of the key words in the social sciences and humanities at present, suggesting the need to understand a change in the style of engagement governing a repertoire of practices. Generally speaking, style is a means of making different things significant and worthy of notice: 'a style governs how anything can show up as anything' (Spinosa et al., 1997, p. 20). Style will therefore include the creation of new metaphors, stories, concepts, percepts and affects but will, at the same time, contain considerable ambiguity; indeed this ambiguity is a crucial part of the power of style.

What I want to argue in this chapter is that the new style hails managers in new ways. What we are seeing, in particular, is the gradual unfolding of an attempt to engineer new kinds of 'fast' subject positions which can cope with the disciplines of permanent emergency. This is a project which involves much more direct engineering of the management subject than has heretofore been attempted. Further, and crucially, it involves the production of new spaces of intensity in which the new kind of managerial subject can be both created and affirmed. This is a project, in other words, which relies on the construction of an explicitly geographical machine.

The chapter is therefore in three sections. In the first section, I will outline some of the pressures that face contemporary managers, pressures which I argue are leading to attempts to institute a new regime of managerial governmentality centred on the creation of a maximally creative 'fast' subject position. In the second section, I then move to an examination of some of the spaces of intensity through which the new subject position is being engineered, spaces of visualization, spaces of embodiment and spaces of circulation. The chapter then concludes with a number of speculations about the viability and potential bent of the nascent form of governmentality. Fast subjects, I will argue, may well turn out to be fragile subjects able to be held together only with certain costs.

Before I follow this agenda, however, I want to make a number of methodological points. First, as already stated, this is a synoptic reading. It is not, therefore, intended to be a buttoned-down piece of research. Second, that said, it is not any old story. It is based on a series of different research strategies: reading what managers themselves read, visiting all kinds of business websites, sustained conversations with numerous managers and management consultants over the last five years or so, presentations to audiences which have included managers and management consultants, and so on. Third, the shape and style of the chapter is intended to simulate the fast-moving nature of the new discourse which aims to produce effects through action, not simply reflect on already made possibilities (Bourdieu, 2000). In a sense, I want to push a little way into the future.

1. Practising manager

What is the forcing ground of new ways of doing 'manager'? I think it can be said to be time. Of course, since the industrial revolution, time has been a watchword of capitalism. But modern economies are based upon a particular fine-grained approximation of time, arising out of two linked developments.

The first of these developments is the increasing attention given to the measurement of *short-term financial performance*. For example, the rise of a metric like 'shareholder value', a term introduced in the 1980s by US management consultants, is both indicative of the construction of a broader field of financial visibility and, by increasing still further the pressure to increase returns, a spur to new means of corporate governance (Froud et al., 2000; Lazonick and O'Sullivan, 2000; Williams, 2000). In turn, such measures have bred other measures which make more and more parts of the business organization visible to the financial gaze and so become a means to check that all parts of the business are doing equally well – at least by financial yardsticks. In turn, other measures have come into existence (often, ironically, as attempts to critique and fend off simple financial metrics like shareholder value) which attempt to summarize and often quantify all kinds of non-financial indicators like market share and quality, such as the so-called 'balanced scorecard' approach (Kaplan and Norton, 1996). The net result of the spread of these measures is that not only workers but also managers now find themselves part of a panoptic (or at least oligoptic) world based on shorter and shorter time horizons. In other words, managers too have become a part of Power's (1997) 'audit explosion', the rise of an orientation to constant checking of performance.

The second development is a general speed-up in the conduct of business, chiefly although not only because of the increasing use of information technology. In particular, the increasing speed of production and consumption (which itself seems to problematize these two terms) means that firms are forced to launch new products more frequently. It means that firms are forced to compress product development cycles, especially through so-called 'concurrent engineering' – performing historically sequential activities in parallel (see Fine, 1998). And it also means that firms are driven closer to the chief actors in their world – competitors, suppliers and customers – and must react to them more quickly.

The emphasis on constant measurement of all aspects of business performance and the increasing speed of business practice put the business organization – and the manager – under growing pressure to constantly perform as the whole process of reproduction of products and services becomes subject to more and more demanding disciplines in ways which are inevitably self-reinforcing, since successful competition between firms seems to increasingly depend upon success in adopting them.

So managers must learn to manage in what is framed as a faster and more uncertain world, one in which all advantage is temporary. In such circumstances, hierarchical organizations based upon long-term strategic planning clearly will not suffice. To use the words of a well-known management guru (Kanter, 1992), giants must learn to dance. And nowhere is this terpsichorean imperative more apparent than in the need to produce rapid and continuous innovation. Under such circumstances, it is therefore no coincidence that *knowledge* has come to be seen as a resource in its own right. Knowledge becomes an asset class that a business must foster, warehouse, manage, constantly work upon, in order to produce a constant stream of innovation (Thrift, 1997a; 1997b; 1999b). New positions in the managerial division of labour – like the knowledge officer – have even been produced which are symptomatic of this recognition.

In turn, this increasing pressure to innovate has led to a much greater emphasis on *creativity*. In the rhetoric of the times:

> There is more room for creativity than ever. Smaller and smaller groups of smart people can do bigger and bigger things … Now there's sobering news: you're only as good as your last great idea. The half-life of any innovation is shorter than ever. People, teams and companies are feeling the heat to turn up new products, services and business models. What's the reward for one round of successful innovation? Even greater pressure to revisit your success, and to unleash yet another round of innovation. (Muoio, 2000, p. 152)

Of course, innovation has always been an important part of a business organization's practice and self-image, but what we now see is a much greater attention being paid to fostering the powers of creativity that will lead to innovation, most particularly through models which eschew the black-boxed model of information processing in favour of an emphasis on what von Krogh and Roos (1995; von Krogh et al., 1998) call 'creative' knowledge. Thus, creativity becomes a value *in itself*.

On the one hand, then, remorseless pressure towards the short term. On the other hand, remorseless pressure to be creative. Managers must somehow learn to manage in this more uncertain world in which all advantage is strictly temporary, whilst also conforming to the rigours of audit.

Against this background what is striking are the efforts to produce new kinds of 'fast' management subject able to swim in this world. They must be calculating subjects able to withstand the exigencies of faster and faster return. Yet, at precisely the same time, they must be subjects who can be creative. It is this project of new managerial subject formation that I want to address in this chapter.

Such a project requires finding a whole variety of different methods of acting upon others in order to produce subject effects. Still the best means of understanding this process are Foucault's brief writings on 'governmentality' (Foucault, 1991; Dean, 1999). In these pieces, Foucault concentrates on the *practices* of power – famously 'the conduct of conduct' – all those endeavours to shape, guide and divert the conduct of others, including the ways in which one might be urged to control one's own passions, to govern oneself. In other words, what Foucault wanted to consider was the formation of theories, programmes, strategies and technologies for the 'conduct of conduct':

> To govern is to act upon action. This entails trying to understand what mobilizes the domains or entities to be governed: to govern one must act upon these forces, instrumentalize them in order to shape actions, processes and outcomes in desired directions. Hence when it comes to governing human

beings, to govern is to presuppose the freedom of the governed. To govern human beings is not to crush their capacity to act, but to acknowledge it and to utilize it for one's own objectives. (Rose, 1999, p. 4)

If 'governmentality' is taken to be the modern version of rule, then what is being suggested is that increasingly to rule properly means ruling in the light of particular and specific characteristics that are taken to be immanent to that over which rule is exercised. In other words:

The activity of government is inextricably bound up with the activity of thought. It is thus both made possible by and constrained by what can be thought and what cannot be thought at any particular moment in our history. To analyse the history of government, then, requires attention to the conditions under which it becomes possible to consider certain things to be true – and hence to say and do certain things. (1999, p. 8)

An important element of governmentality is space. Why? Because to govern it is necessary to render visible the space over which government is to be exercised. And this is not a simple matter of looking; space has to be re-presented, marked out. And these governable spaces

are not fabricated counter to experience; they make new kinds of experience possible, produce new modes of perception, invest percepts with affects, with dangers and opportunities, with saliences and attractions. Through certain technical means, a new way of seeing is constructed which will 'raise lived perceptions to the percept and lived affectations to the affect'. (1999, p. 32)

This stance means that I am interested not in management identity as such (cf. Knights and Willmott, 1999), but rather in the means by which spaces can produce identity effects, the ways in which spaces figure as, to use that well-worn Foucauldian phrase, 'technologies of the self'. I am interested, in other words, in how spaces can be used to produce collective bodies and identifications 'through the inscription of particular ethical formations, vocabularies of self-description and self-mastery, forms of conduct and body techniques' (Rose, 1999, p. 47). This means that I think not that managers are unrelenting drones but rather that, like all of us, they are the products of (increasingly engineered) circumstance. Nowadays, this kind of view is often gathered under the sign of 'performativity' understood as the temporalized regulation and constant recitation of norms (Butler, 1990; 1993). What I want to suggest is that practices have citational force because of the spaces in which they are embedded and through which they do work. As I have argued elsewhere (e.g. Thrift, 2000a; 2000c), this kind of view runs counter to the predominant model of performativity which is based on socio-symbolic signification (and on a corresponding politics of recognition) in that it makes more room for non-representational qualities which are a crucial part of spaces of subjectification and which allow some of the more active and positive aspects of citational force to become known and worked upon (e.g. McNay, 1999). Such a move also tracks the move to pastoral models of discipline which are so characteristic of modern societies – models which allow more space for a self-regulating subject. This move can be seen in the world of managers who are being locked down by regimes of perpetual training which also, at the same time, demand an opening up of their imaginative powers. The gendered dimension of this move is, I hope, obvious (cf. Wajcman, 1998).

This brief excursion allows us to sort out the agenda for the rest of the chapter. For what I now want to consider is a series of procedures which both show up and value the new things which are necessary to create 'fast' subjects, the subjects of the new managerial governmentality. I have called these procedures, rather glibly, *sight*, *cite* and *site*. But what I am trying to suggest by deploying these words is precisely how bound up these new procedures are with the productions of *new spaces* – spaces which by being more active, more performative than those of old, can help to foster creativity (Thrift, 2000a; 2000c). Thus sight (new spaces of visualization), cite (new spaces of embodiment), and site (new spaces of circulation).

I want to conclude this section by making four extra points. The first of these is that most of these spaces have only become possible because of the advent of information technology. Information technology is pivotal in numerous ways. To begin with, it is one of the main products of the new economy. Then, it is one of the main signifiers of the new economy. Information technology signifies youth, speed, excitement, buzz, and being appropriately tooled up is therefore essential for a modern manager – Palm Pilot, portable, mobile, favourite software and websites, etc. But there is more to it than this. The very ubiquity of information technology – the burgeoning ecology of everyday computing devices – means that information technology increasingly becomes background as a means of storing and working with knowledge, as a new expressive medium, as an image of bodily change, and as a means of producing new geographies. For example, in the case of new spaces of visualization, we will see it used – more often than not – through a crude technological determinism which maps the characteristics of technologies on to subjects – as a means of hailing the new management self ('web-ify yourself', 'becoming fast', 'becoming digital', etc.). But we will also see it used as a stylistic glue, holding new kinds of text together. In the case of new spaces of performative embodiment, we will see that computer software is part of the model of embodiment. And in the case of new spaces of business circulation, information technology is a key moment of agency. It has its own voice.

The second point is that it would clearly be ludicrous to suggest that the project of governmentality I describe in more detail below has a total grip. It is quite clearly confined to certain parts of certain western national economies. It is most prevalent in the United States (and especially states like California, with a long history of constructing of the managerial self: see Kleiner, 1996), but it is spreading rapidly through all western economies, usually as a key element of the 'new economy' or 'knowledge economy' package (see, for example, *Business Week*, 31 January 2000). Similarly, this project is more likely to be found in certain industries, especially those that characterize themselves as 'fast'. For example, for manufacturing industry Fine (1998) has produced a classification of industries based on their 'clock-speeds', which seems a very appropriate indicator. No doubt a similar classification could be produced for service industries with advertising or management consultancy in the van. Then there is firm type. The project is more likely to be found in large firms than small, but with significant exceptions, for example, high-technology small firms, and small services firms dependent upon project work (cf. Grabher, 2000). And, there is also management type. The project of governmentality is most likely to be found where highly educated managers exist, especially those in lines of work (like human resource management) which are intimately connected to fashioning the self (Thrift, 1997a; 1997b; 1999b). But it cannot be easily tied down to any managerial specialization. Indeed this would be to miss the point: that this project is concerned with a style of being that many managers often *want/* to attain. For example, working as a manager in a top-heavy bureaucracy can be frustrating and the new project gives resources for both critique and action.

Then there is a third point. Managers *are* often cynical and sceptical about the practices I describe below, aided by professional debunkers like Lucy Kellaway (2000) and 'Dilbert' (Adams, 1996). There is a saying which managers constantly use to describe their reaction to training – '10 per cent is worth doing but you don't know which 10 per cent' – which summarizes the reaction of all but the most evangelical. However, this does not mean that these practices have no grip. Some of them, indeed, are powerful in their own right (cf. Martin, 1994). But even when their touch is light, they can still be brought to bear. They can be used by frustrated managers to produce change in stodgy organizations. They can be used by ambitious managers as a career platform. They can be used by fractious managers to justify a change of job or setting up a small firm. They can be used by managers going through personal crises to work those crises out. Managers, in other words, can be hailed in many ways.

I end this section with one more point. The project of governmentality I outline here is still nascent, still hesitant. It has not yet precipitated out into general understanding, and it may fail. 'Fast' subjects, as I will argue in the concluding section of this chapter, may well turn out to be fragile subjects only able to be held together with certain costs which ultimately may turn out to be too great to bear.

2. Performing manager

Sight (seeing truth)

To refigure the subject of business, so that it sees new things from new perspectives, requires considerable resources: what is being produced are new means of picturing business power and identity which frame the world in a different way. Business magazines have often been used as a means of undertaking this reframing. When *Fortune* was launched in the United States in 1930, it was as a bullet aimed at the heart of American business's self-image. 'Where,' asked Henry R. Luce in the prospectus, 'is the publication that even attempts to portray business in all its heroic present-day proportions, or that succeeds in conveying a sustained sense of the challenging personalities, significant trends, and high excitements of this vastly stirring civilization of business?' (cited in Hugh, 2000, p. 8). So Luce's *Fortune* was high price, and included high-quality journalism and photography; the writers and editors even invented new journalistic forms like the 'corporate story' and the history of top companies. *Fortune* set the tone for how business would see itself. This was a world which was serious, masculine, 'business-like'. Pictured in suits, against the background of compact offices and boardrooms, business managers were *in control*. And the control of business was a sober and serious affair. Smartly dressed, arms crossed, photographed face-on or from below.

But since the 1980s, this way of framing business has been coming under siege. Beginning, I suspect, with the financial markets of the 1980s in which were to be found younger business people who wanted to be recognized as cultural and not just business figures, and continuing with the publication of a series of glossy business journals (for example, in the UK, the now defunct journal *Business*), a new means of framing business has gradually come about. A new style of business magazine has come into existence, of which the most visible (in a number of ways) is *Fast Company*. Founded in 1995 in the United States, published out of Boston but with a number of regional offices, the magazine is currently issued 10 times a year. *Fast Company* is 'the handbook of the business revolution': 'More than a magazine; it's a movement ...'. In effect, *Fast Company* is a cultural weapon aimed at changing business's self-image, by focusing the insights of the 'new economy', an economy based on constant and unremitting change, high technology and adaptation as a way of life. It is both a material and a semiotic manifesto.

A symptomatic reading of *Fast Company* suggests that it achieves five things. First, it is an attempt to produce a new 'virtual' rhetoric, aimed at visualizing the values of the new economy. To this end, much of its format is based on visual devices which simulate speed and change, for example picture layouts, which mimic high technology (through devices like pixelized pages that look like computer screens) and which involve constant adaptation – by, for example, scanning, embedding and mixing images together. Much of the phatic imagery – the name given to signals which maintain discourse or dialogue but have little or no ultimate meaning, such as panels, framing devices, rules and motifs – is clearly intended to simulate computer screens. Thus, one cover designer argues that 'even when I'm not working on a computer, people think that I am because my art is very hard-edged and because I use a lot of bright, simple colours' (*Fast Company*, December 1998, p. 18). Second, and following on, the magazine is highly pictorial. It is a magazine for browsing, with many articles broken down into segments – which also demand a considerable degree of visual literacy, of the kind associated with computer-intermediated layouts (Stafford, 1994; 1996; Cubitt, 1998; Wood, 1998). Third, the magazine is based upon a semi-naturalistic depiction of business people. They are often photographed in casual preppy clothes, in action (although there are also power shoots of people in suits). This democratic depiction of business is enhanced by numerous characteristic biographies which are meant to act as role models for those working in the new economy. Fourth, the emphasis is on youth. Even when subjects are over 50, they are often dressed and depicted in youthful ways: running, jumping, rarely standing still. Fifth, the magazine assumes an active audience 'like us' which will respond to its articles. It has a large website, which allows participation in online polls. And there is a readers' network, called 'Company of Friends', which has more than 18,000 members. Communication is all.

How might we see *Fast Company* as a cultural project? It is clearly an attempt to produce a new community based around the idea of a new economy, which will embody particular values and produce new foundational stories: 'You are already like me' or 'You can become like me'. But it is, I think, more than this simple appeal to simulate. Most of all, I think that it can be seen as an attempt to boost the cultural capital of business. Business becomes funky, youthful, sexy, caring, fun. Business becomes where it's at, not just work but popular culture. Why might this be? I think it must be seen, above all, as an attempt to boost the cultural capital of business. In most studies of the distribution of economic, social and cultural capital in developed countries (e.g. Bourdieu, 1984; Lamont, 1992) managers are seen as occupying a high position in terms of economic capital but a much lower position in terms of cultural capital. But now, this positioning is changing. In part, it is changing because new generations of better educated managers brought up with the cultural preoccupations of their class and time – and keen to gain the respect of these cultural preoccupations – have come into existence. In part, it is changing because business is being seen and is seeing itself differently. As a knowledge business, it becomes a major site of cultural intensity with faster turnover times nearer to those of 'creative' industries like, say, popular music or film, which have become some of its chief exemplars. And in part it is changing through the offices of projects like *Fast Company* which provide both rallying points and means of diffusion.

Cite (embodying truth)

It is February 2000. In a marquee in the grounds of Ribby Hall holiday village near Blackpool, 40 managers from Asda, Britain's third largest supermarket chain, are being inducted into the spirit of the squirrel (making work worthwhile), the way of the beaver (control of achieving the goal) and the gift of the goose (cheering others on). It is all part of a proprietary American management training system called Gung Ho! (Blanchard and Bowles,

1998) apparently based on Native American customs and designed to motivate managers:

> Sue Newton of Asda said: 'we have devised a three-day event for managers
> to put it into practice among all their colleagues. Our aim is to make the
> event a memorable experience – there are valuable lessons to be learnt about
> motivation, team work and leadership. (Steiner and White, 2000, p. 1)

A little bit unusual perhaps, but no longer remarkable. For in the last 10
years, management training – now estimated to be a $250 million business
worldwide – has taken a markedly performative turn, one that is based on
the much more explicit design of the business of trainings. Take the case of
Asda's events:

> The events, involving 40 managers, run twice a week in a marquee made up
> to look like a woodland scene. Coir matting covers the floor, which is crossed
> by a stream running to a model of a lake complete with model beavers
> building dams.
>   Plastic geese hang from the ceiling in a V-formation, while models of squir-
> rels are dotted among painted trees. Group discussions are held in mock log
> cabins to create what Asda calls 'a rough and ready feel'. Staff have to pre-
> pare their own evening meals to encourage team working.
>   As they sit round a mock fire, managers are told stories showing them ways
> in which Gung Ho! can be implemented when they return to civilisation (fire
> regulations ban the real thing). (2000, p. 1)

Why such a performance? I think such events have to be seen as another of
the means of making the invisible visible now being used by business, in this
case the citational force of the body. Where has such a motivation come
from? There are two main strands of practice that inform this move (Thrift,
1997b; 1999a).

First, there is that whole stream of work concerned with management
trainings, stemming from experiments at the Tavistock Institute in London
in the 1940s and 1950s, the National Training League experiments in the
United States in the 1950s, various counter-cultural experiments in the
1960s, and so on (cf. Kleiner, 1996), which are now exemplified by a whole
series of practices which work on the management body, from encounter
groups, through various forms of programming, to outward bound courses.
Then, there is a diverse stream of work produced by those in management
studies (and especially human relations) on subjects as diverse as the minutiae of management talk, ambiguity, cultural difference, emotional investments, even humour (Hatch and Ehrlich, 1993), which has made its way
into actual management practice in all sorts of ways, but especially through
a raft of popularizing books and trainings, as in, for example, the current
vogue for *emotional thinking* (cf. Marcus, 1998).

Arising out of these practices of inscription onto the management body,
therefore, have been a whole series of practices which stress citational force
and especially the use of the body as a central element of organizational
processes of *learning* which can produce 'better' (i.e. more productive, more

valuable) business through active participation in heightened practices of *interaction*. Such work on experiential learning dates from the 1970s (e.g. Argyris and Schon, 1974; 1978) and became very powerful in the 1990s (Argyris, 1991; Senge, 1990; Senge et al., 1999). In other words, what is at stake is unlocking the potential of the management body, and most particularly the potential to innovate.

But to enable this process to happen the body must be made visible so that it can be worked upon. The key difference with many previous ways of making the body visible is that this cannot happen in an unduly prescriptive way, as in, for example, the various forms of drill often applied to workers, but must be of a participative nature using interaction of a relatively open-ended kind:

> If we believe that people in organizations contribute to organizational goals by participating inventively in practices that can never be fully captured by institutionalized processes, then we will minimize prescription, suspecting that too much of it discourages the very inventiveness that makes practices effective. We will have to make sure that our organizations are contexts within which the communities that develop these practices may prosper. We will have to value the work of community-building and make sure that participants have access to the resources necessary to learn what they need to learn in order to take actions and make decisions that fully engage their own knowledge ability. (Wenger, 1999, p. 10)

If this process of community-building is successful, then what will be produced will be an organization which will be committed to innovation. Most particularly, it will be able to unlock its managers' imagination and *creativity*.

Many solutions to the engineering of the managerial imagination (Clegg and Birch, 1999) are on offer. However, nearly all of them involve the production of spaces of 'serious play' (Schrage, 2000) which, through partially engineered processes of inspiration, can produce innovation. The idea is that managers will be 'prepared for surprise', both in their openness and adaptability to unexpected events and in their ability to see productive anomalies:

> Innovation requires improvisation. It … isn't about rigorously following 'the rules of the game' but about rigorously challenging and revising them … innovation is less the production of how innovators think than a by-product of how they behave …
> The essence of serious play is the challenge and thrill of confronting uncertainties. Serious play is about improvising with the unanticipated in ways that create new value. Any tools, technologies, techniques or toys that let people improve how they play seriously with uncertainty is guaranteed to improve the quality of innovation. (2000, pp. 1–2)

But being prepared for surprise is not easy. Roughly speaking, we can say that it consists of activating three qualities. The first of these is cultural (Arbile, 1998). All successful learning and creativity needs to engage the passions and senses of the 'whole brain' of the company through what Hamel and Prahalad (1994, p. 134) call the fostering of strategic intent, a sense of mission which is 'as much about the creation of meaning for employees as it is about the establishment of direction'. The second is the establishment of innovative groups which are more than the sum of their parts because they are able to deploy group-generated transactional knowledge through techniques as different as brainstorming a problem, role play, purposeful shifts in metaphors, shock experiences, visits to new environments, developing empathy through detailed observation, benchmarking, and so on (Leonard and Rayport, 1997; Leonard and Strauss, 1997; Leonard and Swap, 1999; Lester et al., 1998). The third is the design of thinking spaces which allow groups to create. This can simply mean highly malleable and adaptive spaces which allow a multitude of options and sensory registers or it can mean spaces which are highly specific means of producing innovation (see Leonard and Swap, 1999, Chapter 5).

Each of these three qualities requires, in effect, the ability *to 'stage' learning through the explicit design of memorable events* (Pine and Gilmore, 1999) – events which, above all, generate passion. Given these requirements, it is no surprise that so many business organizations have tended to draw inspiration from the performing arts, as a means of giving life to community, creativity, and space. The performing arts are a rich archive of knowledge and techniques for making community, tuning creativity and enlivening space (Thrift, 2000a; 2000c). Four examples of this tendency will suffice.

The first arises out of the increasing desire to generate commitment through 'strategic stories'. The organization is constructed as a community with its own narratives. For example, Nike has a corporate storytelling programme, first launched in the 1970s, and a number of senior executives spend much of their time acting as corporate storytellers. When the programme started it was an hour-long lesson given to all new employees. Now orientation lasts two days and the company envisages the process lasting a week and taking place at 'Nike University'. The storytellers concentrate on innovation and on heritage:

> When Nike's leaders tell the story of how Coach Bowerman, after deciding that his team needed better running shoes, went out to his workshop and poured rubber into the family waffle iron, they're not just talking about how Nike's famous 'waffle sole' was born. They're talking about the spirit of innovation … 'Every company has a history,' says Dave Pearson, 43, a training manager and storyteller. 'But we have a little bit more than a history. We have a heritage, something that's still relevant today. If we convert people to that, chances are that they won't view Nike as just another place to work.' (Ransdell, 2000, pp. 45–6)

Much of this modern corporate storytelling has been inspired by the 'computers as theatre' movement (Laurel, 1993) and this is emphasized by the vogue for 'digital storytelling':

> Dana Winslow Atchley III, 57 … uses modern tools – computers, scanners, video – to update the ancient craft of telling tales. He helps companies to harvest their artefacts, to surface compelling stories – and to render these stories in ways that are engaging and exciting …

Digital storytelling is more than just a technique. In fact, it's become something of a movement among both artists and business people. One convert is
Bill Dauphinois, 53, of Price Waterhouse Coopers (PWC). He's been using it
to teach members of the accounting and consultants group about the PWC
brand. Dauphinois has collected stories about PWC's founders, patrons, and
clients, and he's captured these stories on digital video and housed them on
a PC. Now he travels regaling employees with video tales of the firm's core
values.

'Brands are built around stories,' says Dauphinois, 'And stories of identity
– who we are, where we've come from – are the most effective stories of all.
This is a powerful way to bring them to life.' (Pink, 1999, p. 32)

The second example is the use of artistic genres which both communicate
and create corporate values and strategy by amplifying new thinking. For
example, there is currently much interest in applying different modes of
theatre – platform theatre, matching theatre, improvisational theatre and
street theatre – to actual business situations (Pine and Gilmore, 1999).
Take the case of Barbara Waugh, Hewlett Packard Laboratories
Worldwide Personnel Manager. She has used 'readers' theatres' both in
the labs and in the company as a whole to present options and explain
strategies. For example, in one play put on by employees for an audience
of colleagues, the issue was whether to extend benefits to long-term partners of gay and lesbian employees. 'Combined with dramatized evidence
of discrimination and hardship, senior management reversed its original
(negative) decision. The drama placed managers in the uncomfortable
position of experiencing firsthand what colleagues had told them about in
general terms before' (Leonard and Swap, 1999, p. 70). In another play,
her interest was to produce a new corporate research style:

The last thing she wanted was to preach through PowerPoint. So instead of
creating bullet point slides, she drew on her experience with street theatre
and created a 'play' about HP Labs. She worked passages from the surveys
into dialogue and then recruited executives to act as staff members, and jun-
ior people to act as executives. The troupe performed for 30 senior managers.
'At the end of the play the managers were very quiet,' Waugh remembers.
'Then they started clapping. It was exciting. They really got it. They finally
understood.' (Mieszkowski, 1998, p. 152)

The third example is the tendency to use actual artistic groups to enliven
trainings and to help the process of thinking creatively about situations. For
example, in the UK, there are currently about 80 groups of actors, dancers,
artists, musicians, and so on working in this area, either acting out situations
and halting the action at key points to solicit feedback or producing means
of thinking more creatively in teams.

Companies are beginning to wake up to the advantages of a more creative
approach to team-building – one that is altogether less threatening and more
enjoyable. No more ropes, no more freezing mud. All hail, then, to the arts
which is producing the new source of inspiration when it comes to bringing
out the best in your employees.

Marks and Spencer, Sainsbury's and Allied Domecq are using the UK companies to embrace this new approach to management training. Oxford Stage Company, based in Warwick, ran a workshop for Sainsbury's showing how much can be communicated through body language alone. Trade Secrets, another touring company, ran a series of communication workshops in Sainsbury's stores to accompany a national tour of *Twelfth Night*. The staff's thrill at undertaking Shakespeare for the first time (no mean feat in itself) was matched by their enthusiasm for the games and exercises.

Body and Soul, based in Gloucestershire, has workers dancing along in harmony – by teaching them Rio Carnival-style salsa percussion. Employees without a musical bone in their body are eventually transformed into rhythmic pulsating beasts. It helps to increase their self-confidence and teaches them to work together …

Clients include City merchant banks, along with companies such as Pfizer and Virgin, Our Price. Mr Brotherton says 'It's very good for self-confidence and teamwork. The barriers come down, people take their shoes and socks off and start dancing. They find out an awful lot about each other …

But it is with the arts that management theory is really coming into its own … Living Arts, based in London, gets participants to stage their own performances with the help of performers and technical staff drawn from opera, theatre, circus and film.

One group of UK business consultants on a 'bonding' trip to Lisbon were given a week in which to create an entire opera – a refreshing variation on the usual team-building games. The effect was exhilarating. One participant said 'You forget most conferences within two days. We will remember this retreat in detail until we are 85.'

Tim Stocki, ABSA's (Association for Business Sponsorship of the Arts) director of programmes, reports steadily rising demand for this approach to training. 'This is a growth area,' he says, 'After years being taught to think logically and focus on the bottom line, employees are now being encouraged to think laterally and creatively. This is where artists are ideal.' (McKee, 1999, pp. 26–7)

The fourth example, upon which I want to concentrate most of my attention, is the use of dramatic techniques to challenge entrenched ways of proceeding, thereby producing more creative outcomes. Many of these techniques for creating drama, and thereby creativity, are now used in business trainings. Just a few instances will suffice. There is, to begin with, the chief exemplar of the creative company, the London-based advertising agency St Luke's (Law, 1999; Lewin and Regine, 1999). St Luke's set out to break the mould by operating as a co-operative, locating outside the main London advertising cluster, and organizing itself in order to promote maximum creativity. For example, there is a carefully designed calendar of events (Monday Meetings, Flag Meetings, Shareholders' Day, St Luke's Day) intended to provide a structure of motivation and celebration. St Luke's has become so successful that special business tours now take place around the office space (Grabher, personal communication). Or take the Richmond, Virginia-based marketing agency, Play, a small firm which delivers 'creative concepts'. In turn, about 30 per cent of the agency's revenue comes from teaching other companies to be more creative:

The 20 or so staff members in the room are instructed to invent their own superheroes, create circumstances for them, figure out their superpowers, and invent Clark Kent-like alter egos ... These folks aren't goofing off. They aren't fooling around. They're not even acting strangely. They're actively engaged in real work for an important client with a tight deadline. But they are trying to be creative – which means, they insist, that they can't sit in boring meetings, in boring conference rooms, and expect to guarantee much beyond boring ideas.

Play's undeniably playful workplace affects the company's overall approach to the hard work of creativity ... When you turn work into a place that encourages people to be themselves, have fun and take risks, you unleash their creativity. (Dahle, 2000, p. 170)

Or take Rob Smith's 'Thinking Expeditions', run from Estes Park, Colorado:

A Thinking Expedition combines creative problem solving with challenging outdoor experimental learning – similar to an Outward Bound Boot Camp for the mind. 'It's an accelerated unlearning process,' Smith explains, 'Their days are intense, full and demanding. There are no scheduled meals, no scheduled breaks. We deliberately design the expedition to put people out of their "stupid zone" – a place of mental and physical normalcy – so that they can start to think independently, explore what they don't know, and discover answers to obtain mission critical problems.' (Muoio, 2000, p. 152)

Or take the Ehama Institute, the province of a Native American tribe which teaches ' creative development' through ritual and ceremony. The Institute mixes the 'earth wisdom' of Native American spiritual traditions and the tenets of the learning organization as a means of producing 'sustainable cultural change'.

But the instance I want to concentrate on is the work of a firm called Business Development Associates, a $30 million consultancy established in 1989 which now has 150 associates, working from offices in Alameda in California, Santiago in Chile, Colonia Polanco in Mexico, and Frankfurt in Germany. It has carried out consultancy in the United States, Canada, Mexico, Chile, Ireland, Italy and Switzerland. The company is, in a certain sense, idiosyncratic but it is also exemplary of a certain performative means of proceeding, and fascinating because of its strong allegiances to transferring certain kinds of academic theory into practice.

The company is based around the charismatic and intensely interesting figure of Fernando Flores. At a very early age, Flores was placed in charge of Chilean state-owned corporations by Salvador Allende. In rapid succession he became Minister of Economics and then Minister of Finance. During this time, he was instrumental in the large-scale project to apply cybernetic theory to practical economic management problems (Beer, 1975).

After the fall of the Allende government, he was imprisoned for a number of years. On release, he moved in 1976 to the United States where he began a PhD programme at the University of California, Berkeley, drawing together several fields – philosophy, computing, operations research and management. In particular, he drew on the work of Heidegger and speech act theorists like Austin and Searle to understand language as a constitutive medium and communication as a structure of commitments to act (Flores,

1998). Instead of 'send message', 'make report' and 'make promise' (Winograd and Flores, 1987, p. 171):

> From Heidegger, Flores learned that language conveys not only information but also *commitment*, and that people act by comparing assessments and promises. Computers, he concluded, would be more effective if they recorded and traded commitments, rather than simply moving information. (Rubin, 1999, p. 199, my emphasis)

Using this kind of insight, Flores finished his dissertation in 1979 and proceeded on a chequered career which has included the setting up of a number of software and consultancy firms. He also completed an important and influential book on software design (Winograd and Flores, 1987) which argued that computers were essentially concerned with communication rather than computation: 'Computers are not only designed in language but are themselves equipment for language. They will not just reflect our understanding of language, but will at the same time create new possibilities for the speaking and listening that we do – for creating ourselves in language' (1987, p. 79). It is clear that Flores already regarded training as a complementary element of this approach to design, since 'it is impossible to completely avoid breakdown by means of design. What can be designed are aids for those who live in a particular domain of breakdowns. These aids include training' (1987, p. 165). The trainings were devoted to teaching the fulfilment of promises and commitments in day-to-day work operation: 'how to train people to improve their effectiveness is working with others. This training in "communication for action" reveals for people how their language acts participate in a network of human commitment' (1987, p. 179).

Flores's ideas are set down most fully in a recent book with Charles Spinosa, a Shakespeare scholar and Vice-President of Business Development Associates, and Hubert Dreyfus, the renowned philosopher (Spinosa et al., 1997). For these authors, innovation cannot be reduced to a series of stable and regular procedures, a systematic means of dealing with the facts of the world. Innovation is, instead, about opening up new spaces for human action by cultivating *sensitivity to anomaly*, that is purposely attempting to change the way we see and understand things so that what counts as a fact is changed. The approach, then, is 'attempting to develop sensitivities, not knowledge' (1997, p. 39).

In turn, the book also provides a 'composite' account of Flores's turn to this approach:

> Our representative ... started out as an executive level director of national economic planning. He thought that the primary concern of a person in his position was to ensure that his office produced the best possible model of the economy, which could then be used as a guide to improve the efficiency and functioning of every economic institution in society. Though he was trained both to develop such models and to evaluate the models others developed, he seldom found time to do this work. Instead he was constantly talking, he explained this and that, to that and this person, put person A in touch with person B, held press conferences, and so forth. It seemed to him that he was

doing nothing substantial. And if we think of work as a matter of performing certain tasks to produce certain products, little, indeed, was being done. This entrepreneur, however, did not simply inure himself to the fact that what he was doing was different from what he thought ought to be done. Rather, he retained the oddity in his life as an anomaly.

Holding on to an anomaly as an anomaly is not an easy matter to describe. It is a matter of constantly being sensitive to the anomaly as happening in one's life. In our case, the entrepreneur remained sensitive to the fact that his work was not producing any concrete or abstract theory but that he was working nonetheless. Because he was sensitive to the anomaly, it eventually led him to take a course on the theory of speech acts and in that course he found a key to the anomaly. He came to realize that this anomalous aspect of his work was actually its central feature. He saw that work no longer made any sense as the craftsmanship of writing this or that sentence or the skilled labor of bringing this or that widget into shape but that currently work was becoming a matter of coordinating human activity – opening up conversations about one thing or another to produce a binding promise to perform an act. (1997, pp. 45–6)

In turn, this notion of conversation and promise as central components of work has led to the practices of Business Development Associates, which are aimed at the redescription of the nature of particular businesses, and then through trainings the implementation of changes of identity that will produce this redescription, a shift in the ingrained domain. They aim, in other words, to increase sensitivity to anomaly, and therefore foster creativity by changing the status of things within the community through the production of speech acts which confer 'new identities, duties, rights, affects and values' (Flores, 1998, p. 21). The practices are intended to produce trust through total commitment to speech as embodied action which can create new values and new worlds:

> Talk all you want to, Flores says, but if you want to act powerfully you need to master 'speech acts': language rituals that build trust between colleagues and customers, word practices that open your eyes to new possibilities. Speech acts are powerful because most of the actions that people engage in – in business, in marriage, in parenting – are carried out through conversation. But most people speak without intention; they simply say whatever comes to mind. Speak with intention and your actions take on new purpose. Speak with power, and you act with power. (Rubin, 1999, p. 144)

To this end, Flores uses scripts which are aimed at conjuring up moments of truth and trust in which transformation can occur. Speech becomes a kind of weapon to batter down prejudices and preconceptions: 'To speak in language that practices action, you must practice *assessments* (to work on truth) and generate *commitment* (to work on trust)' (1999, p. 149). Assessments are often brutal because 'if we are asked to give conditions under which we would give up being who we are, we tend to fight rather than switch' (Flores, 1998, p. 23). They are aimed, in effect, at ridding speech acts of the taint of defeat through scripted call and response. Commitment involves making bold promises which drive action by asking more of managers, and ultimately build trust: 'value is produced by a story. Value lies in creating new possibility' (Flores in Rubin, 1999, p. 151). And these stories require body:

> In a flash, Flores becomes Ryan. He rounds his shoulders into his chest, recedes into himself, and says in a wimpy voice 'I think it will give us advantages.' Then he shouts, 'There is no energy in that story. You need to put your body into it, there is no truth. And without that you can't sell the idea, not even to yourself.' Flores is standing. Spit is flying from his mouth. He conveys the message with his whole body. 'Ryan, you are a Dilbert leader. You never take a stand. And here you are listening to Felix, who is resignation personified. You know what mood you are in? The life-is-tough mood. Don't be too optimistic. Next year, we'll lose a little less than this year. If you live in a mood, you are blind to it. The last time I made that mistake, I was in prison for three years.' (1999, p.151)

What, then, can we say about the new means of embodying fast subjects? That bodies can be trained to *act* their way out of the new management dilemmas through new techniques of the self, based especially in the lore of the humanities. Activity becomes a means of making the fictive fact. It is imagination reincarnated. It is a citational force.

Site (geographies of truth)

Let me now move to the final set of procedures I want to discuss: locational practices. For new means of producing creativity and innovation are bound up with new geographies of circulation which are intended to produce situations in which creativity and innovation can, quite literally, take place. I will mention three of these geographies of circulation as currently being particularly important.

The first of these is the constant quartering of the globe by executive travellers. For some time, it was assumed by many commentators that the volume of business travel would ultimately begin to decline as the effects of information technology bit. Yet, in fact, this does not seem to be happening: business travel volume continues to increase as workforces become more and more mobile.

> Personnel [are spending] less of their time working in offices. It may be necessary for them to attend corporate premises for meetings with colleagues but, increasingly, more time will be spent working on projects at home and spending time away from the office with customers and business partners. In the United States roughly 25 per cent of the labour force is mobile in this sense. In the United Kingdom the figure is 35 per cent and growing. By 2010 this [may] reach over 60 per cent – a staggering change in the patterns and culture of work. (Scase, 1999, p. 7)

In part at least, this increase in the volume of business travel seems to be the result of attempts to engineer knowledge creation. This process of engineering is oriented toward settings which privilege face-to-face interaction on the grounds that:

> All the technology in the world does not – at least yet, and maybe never – replace face-to-face contact when it comes to brainstorming, inspiring passion, or enabling many kinds of serendipitous discovery. A study of geographically dispersed product development has found that team members conducting complex tasks *always* would have preferred to have a 'richer' medium (that is, one supporting more channels and more interaction) than they actually had to use. Fax is fine for one-way communication; e-mail for two-way, asynchronous and relatively emotionless communication; telephone for communications that require no visual aids; and video conferencing if no subtlety in body language is necessary. But face-to-face communication is the richest multi-channel medium because it enables use of all the senses, is interactive and immediate. (Leonard and Swap, 1999, p. 160)

But, increasingly, information technology is a means of allowing these kinds of creative interactions to take place because it provides a means for managers to be in on more face-to-face meetings around the organization whilst still keeping in touch with home base, rather than a means for the home base to control the periphery. The home base comes visiting. Control, or more accurately modulation, is executed through *the circulation itself* (Latour, 1993). For example, take the case of the chief knowledge officer of Price Waterhouse Coopers (PWC), Ellen Knapp:

> Her life requires dedication and organisation. The resolutely cheerful Ms Knapp says that her blessings involve a constitution immune to jet-lag, two children who are grown up, and two extremely efficient assistants, whom she compares to Mission Control at NASA. She grabs exercise whenever she can and sticks to activities and hotels she knows well (London's Ritz wins points for having rewired its rooms). Price Waterhouse Coopers (PWC) tries to make life easier for her, scheduling meetings at hubs (all the West American partners, for example, meet in Los Angeles); it has also started a 'hotelling' policy at its offices, where itinerants like Ms Knapp are given a desk and telephone connection when they arrive. 'My place of work,' she says 'is simply where I am.'
>
> This sounds endearingly modern. All the same, it is hard not to feel tired just listening to Ms Knapp describe her work. With all this endless flitting around, no wonder that executives are increasingly complaining about stress. The overworked American is, in truth, often an overtravelled American.
>
> All of which prompts the question: are these journeys really necessary? Ms Knapp is, after all, a chief information officer. Surely one of the points of all the computer hardware that PWC has bought (not to mention the even bigger pile it has encouraged clients to buy) is to make big companies seem smaller. Company intranets are supposed to be ways to swap knowledge. Cheaper telecoms are meant to be killing distance. Why go to Frankfurt or talk to colleagues who could read an e-mail or join a video conference?
>
> The answer seems to be that technology is more help as a way of keeping the peregrinating Ms Knapp in touch with home than in getting far flung offices to collaborate. As Ms Knapp points out, technology depends on trust. PWC has nearly 150,000 people in 152 countries: a bossy e-mail from somebody you had never met could put you off them ... Ms Knapp thinks that

you have to meet people first: 'it is important to gesticulate'. A bubbly lady, her powers of persuasion would indeed be diminished by e-mail.

Merely knowing other people and persuading them to share knowledge is only half the battle. If juggernauts such as PWC are to be more than the sum of their parts they must get people to spark off ideas from each other – and that seems to depend on direct contact. Anecdotal evidence suggests that for every heralded example of something designed 'virtually' by two people in different locations, a lot of other new products are dreamt up during idle banter by the coffee machines. (*The Economist*, 9 January 1999, p. 76)

And this brings us to the second geography of circulation, the construction of office spaces which can promote creativity through carefully designed patterns of circulation (Duffy, 1997; Worthington, 1996). Office space is organized in such a way that it 'can maximise learning through providing the apparatus for much more face-to-face interaction' (Duffy, 1997, p. 50) and can be saturated with prodigious amounts of information technology, which both enable and expand the opportunities for this interaction: 'the conventions that determine office layout, predating the punch card, have little relevance in a world of work' (1997, p. 51). The design logic of the new office therefore moves from the old 'hive' and 'cell' spaces, based on institutionalized clerical processes and individualized enclaves which demonstrate the incremental rewards of career longevity respectively, towards 'den' spaces and 'club' spaces, bringing integrative spaces generating transactional knowledge via interactive group work and connected team projects on an as-need basis, respectively. Thus the space requirements of offices are increasingly engineered. For example, increasingly explicit information technology strategies are used to break down the barriers between formal and informal working by enforcing mobility. Fixed offices become rarer and instead managers have 'touchdown' areas. At the extreme are offices like those of Andersen Consulting in Paris which have no fixed abode space: consultants book space as and when they need it: their possessions are kept on a trolley. Then, the space requirements of offices increasingly include all manner of meeting spaces: conference rooms, meeting rooms, play spaces, kitchens, and so on. At the extreme, it is possible to build indoor streets with cafés, restaurants, indoor pubs, or, even, in the case of one Canadian company, a Zen garden. And, the engineering of office space can go even further, down to the smallest of spaces. For example, ranges of high-interaction furniture have been designed, from furniture for meeting rooms which can be rapidly moved about, to break-area furniture which, based on careful observation, enables people to interact.

There are many examples of these new office spaces (see Duffy, 1997). Here, I will fix on just one. This is the new British Airways headquarters designed by Neils Torp and opened in 1998:

> When BA decided to abandon the ancient office building beside Heathrow's runways, Bob Ayling, its boss, made up his mind to 'move his office, change the culture'. Mr Ayling ... has long believed that the airline retains a bureaucratic hangover from its days in the public sector. He wants to use the new offices to make a decisive break with the past.

Step inside BA's front door and you soon understand that things have changed. After passing the receptionists, lined up like check-in desks, you walk between two giant wheels from the undercarriage of a jumbo jet. The main corridor, linking six small office blocks within the complex, is a village street, complete with cobbles and wayside trees. The core of the building deliberately tries to ape an English village square. Workers arriving from the basement car park have to walk across the square to get to their office space. The aim is to ensure that people's paths cross, easy informal communications.

John Wood is the airline's director for the Pacific Rim market. Like other BA employees, he does not have his own office. In the two weeks a month that he is not travelling he has a touchdown area next to the team area where his staff work. Previously, BA clung to old bureaucratic norms, with bosses on a floor to themselves far away from their staff.

Mr Ayling says that when he wants to talk to one of his directors, he is forced to walk through the building, meeting people on the way and exchanging a few words. 'I learn more in a couple of days than I used to in month,' he says.

The building is more than a traditional corporate headquarters; it also houses a training department right by the village square, complete with a mock-up of a jumbo jet's first class cabin. On any day, 100 front-line cabin crew or ground staff are there on a course. Mr Ayling hopes this too will break down barriers between head office and staff in the field.

It takes more than a world-class architect … to make such an idea work. BA has invested £10m ($16m) in fancy IT; staff wander round with digital cordless telephones that double as their desk phones. Employees can even order groceries electronically from a local store and have them delivered to their car in the garage before they go home. (*The Economist*, 1 August 1998, p. 88)

Then there is one more geography of circulation, the increasing move towards constructing new institutions which can promote knowledge exchange and sharing by bringing different actors together via information technology. There are now a multitude of these institutions of exchange, both intracompany (such as Arthur Andersen's Knowledge X-Change, intended, via information technology, to promote continuous exchange of knowledge between partners) and intercompany (such as the numerous 'thinking studios' which have been set up on the Internet, some of which feature spectacular attempts to create virtual simulations of landscapes of information exchange as in the Strategic Horizons webpage). An attempt is thereby being made to produce a 'flocking' of business organizations and people around particular creative intensities, on the principle that innovation often comes from taking ideas across boundaries. For example:

To facilitate 'productive flocking' the Marketing Council and London Business School have created an Innovation Exchange, a network of companies keen to foster creativity by swapping ideas and sharing experience. Launched on Tuesday by Stephen Byers, Trade and Industry Secretary, the exchange provides a website for member companies, access to search on innovation and a programme of workshops and seminars. (Willman, 1999)

The construction of these institutions is heavily dependent upon technical issues like speed and interoperability but also demands outline human skills like facilitation (Senge et al., 1999). The goal is to provide virtual clustering, the clusters being intellectual 'stages' through which creativity can be unleashed.

Conclusions

I have tried to outline a new style of doing business, one in which certain things that were previously invisible are now made visible and so available to be operated on. This creation of visibility is, I hope I have shown, intimately bound up with the construction of new spaces of action in which the previously unremarked becomes marked and objectified, and a new fast subject position can be formed.

This, then, is the first conclusion. What we can see is a new set of embodied resources being brought into the world for capitalist firms to operate on and with – resources that might well prove to be on a par with, say, the invention of perspective, double-entry book-keeping, filing, various means of production management, and so on. These resources are both new businesses practices and means of creating new kinds of previously unavailable products. We are, if you like, witness to the birth of a new ecology of business.

And the rhetoric of this new business ecology is all nice. This is a world where business is smart and fast but it also has values and reaches out to the community. This is, if you like, a kind of Land's End capitalism, dressed down and tasteful, participative and community oriented, responsible. Or maybe it is something else, and this is my second conclusion. Maybe what we are seeing is a new phase of imperialism. In the nineteenth century, a great map of mankind was developed by the ideologues of western nations based upon the distinguishing characteristics of race. The peoples of the world were able to be distributed in order of priority according to racial characteristics. Now perhaps a new great map of personkind is coming into existence, a map based upon other attributes of personhood and, most specifically, potential for innovation and creativity. On the border of this map we would see a frieze of particular creative types, no doubt with *Homo siliconvalleycus* in the evolutionary lead. And instead of maps of climate or characteristics like skull type, there would be major airports and educational systems. Yet, the net result might, I suspect, be surprisingly similar to the old map – with a few exceptions made for new entrants like the Japanese, non-residential Indians and overseas Chinese.

And this downside is accompanied by another, which is my third conclusion. This is that for there to be faster subjects, there have to be slower ones. Not just in the sense that the new geographies of circulation depend upon a large, static workforce, from Ellen Knapp's 'mission control' to all the people servicing the information technology and the aeroplanes, but also in the sense of all those workers who, living in this marginal world of perpetual training and forced teamworking, have been shorn of a vocabulary of protest (Crang, 1999; Sennett, 1998). But then – and this is the fourth conclusion – this fast world cannot last. It is critically dependent upon an American business model of short-term returns which has its limits. Maybe the emphasis on a permanent state of emergency is the most successful one at this conjuncture (McKenna, 1997) but it has its problems. For example, by 2000 *Fast Company/* was already expressing concern over the increasing prevalence of 'built to flip' rather than 'built to last' companies, based on the practice of selling up 'quick companies' that realize instant profits:

> The hard truth is that we're dangerously close to killing the soul of the new economy. Even worse, we're in danger of becoming the very thing we defined ourselves in opposition to. Those who kindled the spirit of the new economy rejected the notion of working just for money; today, we seem to think that it's fine to work just for money – as long as it's a lot of money. (Collins, 2000, p. 132)

In other words, managers had come to see themselves as *entitled* to make money; a sure sign of a boom in decay.

But more than this – and this is my final conclusion – there is no guarantee that the process of producing fast subjects, which are capable of functioning in this fast world, can or will succeed. This is subject formation in process, and a legitimate language and body of knowledge is still being created. Indeed, what is interesting about current management literature, from the popular to the academic, is the amount of space given over to the stresses and strains of being a member of the new economy: sometimes it seems as if all that managers have found are ways to oppress themselves as well as workers (Schor, 1993). Is it possible for a manager to achieve 'balance', to 'live lightly', to be a 'sustainable person' – and be a change agent? Or is it the case that 'the more you have the less you feel you have. The faster I go, the faster I need to go' (Barlow, 1999, p. 85)? Which could hardly be a better description of capitalism. And 'How thin can I spread myself before I'm no longer there?' (1999, p. 85). Which could hardly be a better description of the perils of the new subject position and the parallel necessity to act into it.

8

The Automatic Production of Space

Co-author **Shaun French**

Introduction

This chapter is an attempt to document the major change that is taking place in the way that Euro-American societies are run as they increasingly become interwoven with computer 'software'. Though this change has been pointed to in many writings, it has only rarely been systematically worked through. This, then, is the first goal of this chapter – to systematically register this change and its extent. We hope to show how, in only 50 years or so, the technical substrate of Euro-American societies has changed decisively as software has come to intervene in nearly all aspects of everyday life and has begun to sink into its taken-for-granted background. But simply registering this change is not enough. Our second goal is to explain why it has been so effective. And here we point to software's ability to act as a means of providing a new and complex form of automated spatiality, complex ethologies of software and other entities which, too often in the past, have been studied as if human agency is clearly the directive force. In other words, what we believe we are increasingly seeing is the automatic production of space which has important consequences for what we regard as the world's phenomenality – new landscapes of code that are now beginning to make their own emergent ways.

But it has to be said that the description 'software' is not an easy one to work with because, in the literature, all kinds of different meanings of 'software' are routinely conflated, with the result that different kinds of efficacy are muddled up. Thus, at the most general level, software is often considered to be part of a more general structure of writing, a vast Derridean intertext which has gradually become a system without edges and which includes all manner of 'coded' writings rooted in a base cybernetic metaphor (Johnson, 1993; Hayles, 1999; Kay, 2000). In such a conception, software is both a measure of how writing is now done, and a new kind of cultural memory based upon discourses of information as pure digital technique (Hobart and Schiffman, 1998). In a second guise, software can be considered as another step in the history of writing as a supplement to spoken language: here we have Derrida's critique of phonocentrism and logocentrism made flesh (Derrida, 1998; Aarseth, 1998).

> An ever-increasing number of people are spending more hours per day using written – that is, keyboard – language rather than spoken language. Within a few years, computers will be enriching nearly every household of the developed world. Human life in these countries is centering on, and contracting to,

electronic text and international networking, and moving away from speech. Soon written language might be more prominent world-wide than spoken language. A different sort of language is emerging from this artificial interfacing: an 'oral written language' occupying a special position between spoken and written language. Computers now regularly communicate with one another, too, through writing – that is, through written programming languages – without human mediation. Writing has, in this way, transcended humanity itself. We have redefined the very meaning of writing itself. (Fischer, 2001, p. 316)

Within this general shift, software can be thought of as a set of new textualities: programming languages, e-mail and other forms of 'netspeak' (Crystal, 2001), and software packages, each with their own textual protocols and paratexts, which have produced their own linguistic turn. Then, in a third guise software can be thought of as the product of the actual writing of code, as the outcome of the 'practised hands' (McCullough, 1998) of a comparative handful of people who are able to mobilize skills that even now are difficult to describe to produce effective forms of code (Lohr, 2001). Such skilful interaction between humans and machines has been the object of numerous studies in the human–computer interaction (HCI) and computer-supported co-operative work (CSCW) literatures which all show that there is no straightforwardly observable exchange between discrete purified entities called 'human' and 'machine' but rather a series of conversations which demonstrate that software is not a simple intermediary, but rather a Latourian 'mediary' with its own powers (see, for example, Thomas, 1995). Then software has one more guise. It can be couched as the guts of a set of commodities: websites, software packages, games, animated movies, and so on, which are dispensed via the medium of the screen and have become part of a more general cultural ambience. The ubiquity of the screen (see McCarthy, 2001) guarantees software's cultural hold, letting it assume a central economic and cultural place.

Whatever the guise, software clearly stands for a new set of effectivities. But, of course, such a statement begs a whole series of important questions. For example, how does software relate to hardware? Is it, as in Kittler's (1997) extreme reaction, the case that there is no software, only hardware? Or is it that the hardware is now secondary? And, as another example, given that software has a hold on the world, what is the exact unit of efficacy? A line of code? An algorithm or a program? A complete 'informational ecology' (Nardi and O'Day, 1999)? And, as one more example, is software's address now somewhere between the artificial and a new kind of natural, the dead and a new kind of living, or the material and a new kind of material semiotics? These are not questions we can hope to answer fully in such a short chapter but, hopefully, we can start to open them out, for what is certain is that software is displacing some of our fondest conclusions about our contemporary age and cultural idiom as it provides us with 'new and different means of informing' (Hobart and Schiffman, 1998, p. 268). We will attempt this opening out through a chapter which is structured in five sections. In the first section, we will consider the nature of software. Our argument here is that software consists of a series of 'writing acts' which have changed our expectation of what can show up in the everyday world. This definitional section having given software a kind of voice, we can then move on to consider through a simple audit – no more, no less – how that voice is increasingly heard in everyday life as software achieves presence as 'local intelligence'.

Then, third, we will consider the ways in which all this software has been transmuting and, in particular, how it is beginning to recognize and play to apparently human characteristics like emotion and is therefore starting to take on some of the characteristics of corporeal intelligences (just as corporeal intelligences are beginning to take on some of the characteristics of software: Collins and Kusch, 1998). In the penultimate section, we will attempt to touch on the 'absent presence' of software in everyday life, by outlining three different geographies of software: (1) how and where software is produced; (2) the rise of new informational standards of conduct; (3) new forms of creativity and play. In the conclusion, we will try to sum up and extend our narrative by considering software as a new form of gathering, what we might call 'semi-artificial life' (Borgmann, 2000).

The machinations of writing

In this section, we want to begin our account of software by briefly considering its nature. In doing so, we have to face up to the fact that software is often considered to be a 'technology', and is then able to be negatively assimilated into the domain of thought as a figure or metaphor representing some social else, thus allowing it to be captured within a linguistic or semiotically contrived field, rather than disclosed as an agent of *material complexification* (Hansen, 2000). But software cannot be reduced to this kind of textualism, even though it can be regarded as a text. That would be to domesticate its generative alterity, to simplify what can be regarded as intent, and to draw a veil over a politics of the shifting boundaries defining 'objects' which is so crucial to the contemporary 'human' sciences (Oyama, 2001).

For a long time, much of the human world has been on automatic, has expanded beyond the immediate influence of bodies and has made its way into machines. The expansion of humanity beyond bodies has taken place in two ways: as a result of the invention of writing and then print; and as a result of the invention of various machines, with line-by-line instructions and rude mechanicals. This is 'software' and 'hardware'. In the past, these two means of manipulating the world have often been held separate. But now what we are seeing is an age in which writing is able to take on many new mechanical aspects – an age of software, but software becoming so pervasive and complex that it is beginning to take on many of the features of an organism. But this is an organism with a passion for inscription which goes to show that 'the logocentric repression of writing is to an extent only now visible and understandable in the light of recent developments in contemporary science' (Johnson, 1993, p. 191).

We believe that this gradual evolution of software into what Clark (2000) calls 'wideware' is extraordinarily important for understanding the current direction of Euro-American cultures, and especially the nature of western cities. Increasingly, spaces like cities – where most software is gathered and has its effects – are being run by mechanical writing, are being beckoned into existence by code. Yet, remarkably, this development has gone almost unrecorded. Why so? There are four immediate reasons, we think.

First, software takes up little in the way of visible physical space. It generally occupies micro-spaces. Second, software is deferred. It expresses the co-presence of different times, the time of its production and its subsequent dictation of future moments. So the practical politics of the decisions about production are built into the software and rarely recur at a later date. Third, software is therefore a space that is constantly in-between, a mass-produced series of instructions that lie in the interstices of everyday life, pocket dictators that are constantly expressing themselves. Fourth, we are schooled in ignoring software, just as we are schooled in ignoring standards and classifications (Bowker and Star, 1999). Software very rapidly takes on the status of background and therefore is rarely considered anew.

It would be easy at this point to fall back on some familiar notions to describe software's grip on spaces like cities. One would be hegemony. But that notion suggests a purposeful project whilst software consists of numerous projects cycling through and continually being rewritten in code. Another notion would be haunting. But again the notion is not quite the right one. Ghosts are ethereal presences, phantoms that are only half-there and which usually obtain their effects by stirring up emotions – of fear, angst, regret, and the like. Software is more like a kind of traffic between beings, wherein one sees, so to speak, the *effects* of the relationship. What transpires becomes reified in actions, body stances, general anticipations (Strathern, 1999). We would argue, then, that software is best thought of as a kind of absorption, an expectation of what will turn up in the everyday world. Software is a new kind of phenomenality which can 'touch the ontic' (Spivak, 1993, p. 30). Software is, in other words, a part of a 'technological unconscious' (Clough, 2000), a means of sustaining presence which we cannot access but which clearly has effects, a technical substrate of unconscious meaning and activity. 'It is, after all, against the natural unity of self-heard voice that Derrida places technicity, the machine, the text, writing – all as bearers of unconscious thought' (Clough, 2000, p. 17). Increasingly, therefore, as software gains this unconscious presence, spaces like cities will bear its mark, bugged by new kinds of pleasures, obsessions, anxieties and phobias which exist in an insistent elsewhere (Vidler, 2000; Thrift, 2001a). Software quite literally conditions our existence, very often 'outside of the phenomenal field of subjectivity' (Hansen, 2000, p. 17).

Thus we come to a more general reason why software remains so little considered. We still cleave to the idea of spaces like the city as populated by humans and objects which represent each other via words and images, which makes it very difficult to mark this new territory (cf. Downey and

McGuigan, 1999). Software does not fit this representational model, the 'theatre of proof' (Phelan, 1993), for its text is about words doing things, about determinate presentations in particular contexts 'below the "threshold" of representation itself' (Hansen, 2000, p. 4). Because software 'affects our experience first and foremost through its infrastructural role, its import occurs prior to and independently of our production of representations' (2000, p. 4). Seen in this way, software is perhaps better thought of as a series of 'writing acts' (rather than speech acts) of a Bakhtinian or Derridean kind, which have a 'heuretic' rather than an analytical dimension (Ulmer, 1989), based upon the inventive rather than the analytic, in which language is both message and medium. Thus:

> Within the previous instauration, founded on the alphabet, the only way to access theory *per se* was through metaphor, every concrete manifestation of the idea being equivalent to its deformation. Metaphors were necessary because the intellect was otherwise incapable of grasping the idea of true illumination. With the new instauration, the artefacts of theory are no longer metaphors. Instead, the object is no longer the deformation of the idea, but is its real embodiment. Now the idea, or thought, rests within, or out of, the object itself. (Lechte, 1999, p. 141)

It then becomes something of a moot point whether this means that software – as a non-representational form of action – 'does not rely on the activity of thinking for its ontogenesis' (Hansen, 2000, p. 19) or whether it is simply another kind of distributed thinking in which yet more human functions are delegated into 'the automatic, autonomous and auto-mobile processes of the machine' (Johnson, 1999, p. 122), as part of a process of externalization and extension of the vital based, for example, on the apprehension of the human body as simply 'too slow' (Stiegler, 1998). Whichever the case, what we can see is that what counts as 'life' itself comes into question as new material syntheses emerge and embed themselves (Doyle, 1997).

In the rest of this chapter we will therefore chiefly call on two theoretical technologies to understand software. One is a whole series of theoretical elements which are now merging which, when taken together, constitute a 'theatre of promise' in their emphasis on the how of practice, their attention to hybrid human–object networks (cyborgs, actants, ethologies, and the like) and their devotion to the task of repopulating the spaces of modernity with these new inhuman figures. The other is the emphasis on the performativity of writing. Drawing on work as diverse as Derrida and performance studies, this other 'theatre of promise' constitutes a series of plays with scriptural space and time which are intended to extend the nature of writing whilst retaining its 'prophetic touch' (Johnson, 1993; 1999).

Mapping software

To begin our audit of software's locations, let us try to understand just how much things have changed by journeying back to the 1970s. In a remarkable and unjustly neglected paper, Ron Horvath (1974) argued that much of the interior of western cities had become a new kind of machine wilderness, which he called 'machine space'. He saw this new territory, 'devoted primarily ... to the use of machines' (1974, p. 167), as a desolate and threatening one, because it gave priority to machines over people. Horvath was writing chiefly of the automobile and he mapped out in detail the 'expanding realm of machinekind' (1974, p. 187) by paying attention to the increasing amount of space being given over to cars in American cities and the consequent deathly effects. Yet now we see something of the same kind of machinic expansion occurring on as great a scale (Mackenzie, 1996). But even though software has infused into the very fabric of everyday life – just like the automobile – it brings no such level of questioning in its wake.

Indeed the automobile is a good place to start our audit since automobiles are increasingly stuffed full of software. Reporting on the explosion of electronics within motor cars, the Economist Intelligence Unit (EIU) (2000) predicts, for instance, that within a very short space of time electronics will constitute more than 30 per cent of an executive car's total value. Such vehicle electronics are increasingly driven by smart software, developed by individual companies and through partnerships such as the Intelligent Vehicle Initiative (IVI) in the United States. Work within the IVI includes the development of intelligent collision avoidance systems; traffic, location and route guidance; driver condition monitoring systems; and obstacle and pedestrian detection systems. As we write, Ford UK is currently marketing its Mondeo model on the basis of its intelligent protection system (IPS). A neural network of sensors embedded within the Mondeo enables the IPS to assess the severity of any impact, instantaneously adjusting the car's safety systems to maximize their effectiveness. Similarly the new Jaguar X-type, based on the Mondeo platform, not only has a now familiar computerized navigation system, but also has voice activation of some controls and a new feature called Jaguar Net which integrates telephone and satellite location and automatically transmits an emergency call if there is an accident in which an airbag is deployed. The number of car components with these kinds of embedded systems is such that the EIU report predicts that as early as 2001 passenger cars will appear on the market with 'vehicle intranets' connecting all the various onboard computers.

These intelligent vehicle programmes are paralleled by a growing number of intelligent transportation initiatives. For instance, the US IVI is integrated within a wider Intelligent Transportation System (ITS). Drawing on developments in Australia, Japan and Europe, ITS America (www.itsa.org), an amalgam of public and private bodies, seeks to foster the wider development, employment and integration of intelligent transportation systems to create a more efficient, safer, and cost-effective transport network. Areas targeted by the ITS include the collection and transmission of information on traffic conditions; the reduction of accidents and congestion; and the development of sophisticated navigation and route guidance systems for drivers. More specific examples of intelligent traffic systems include the development of intelligent software for traffic lights. Employing fuzzy logic, intelligent traffic lights are, for instance, able to read and react to changing traffic conditions, thus providing enhanced performance *vis-à-vis* conventional fixed-time controlled lights (Khiang et al., 1996).

But it is easy to move beyond automobiles and roads in the search for urban software. Elevators (lifts) are another integral part of the infrastructure of cities which have become increasingly software rich. From being held up as an exemplar of a 'stupid machine' in the early 1980s, elevators, as James Gleick points out, have now surpassed even the motor car in terms of their software richness. According to Gleick, smart elevators now pack 'more computing power than a high-end automobile, which is to say more computing power than the Apollo spacecraft' (1999, p. 24). By adding microprocessors, again programmed with fuzzy logic, smart elevators or 'elevators with algorithms' have

> learned to skip floors when they are already full, to avoid bunching up, and to recognize human behavior patterns. They can anticipate the hordes who will gather on certain floors and start pounding the DOWN button at 4.55 p.m. each Friday. (1999, pp. 24–5)

The infusion of software into the urban infrastructure not only has impacted upon older urban technologies, but is also a vital part of newer technologies. Despite only being a relatively new addition to the fabric of cities, security surveillance or CCTV systems are in the process of being revolutionized (Graham, 1998). In October 1998 the London borough of Newham became the first place in the world to employ smart CCTV to monitor public spaces (*The Guardian*, 10 February, pp. 14–15). Developed by Visionics, the Faceit surveillance system uses cutting edge facial recognition technology to scan for criminals: 'mimicking the brain, the software scans and measures distances between the major landmarks of the face, reducing them to a heap of pixels' (2000, p. 14). Following Newham, a similar anti-crime smart CCTV system, Satnet, has been introduced to the West End, while Cromatica, designed to monitor crowd flows and congestion and to prevent suicides, has been tested on the London Underground (*New Scientist*, 25 September 1999; 11 December 1999; 21 October 2000).

Is there any way of making a more general assessment of software in the city? Conveniently, the millennium bug (Y2K) provided a close approximation to such a general audit. A brief examination of the UK Audit Commission's (1998) report on Y2K immediately brings into sharp relief the degree to which software and related embedded systems have infused everyday urban life. In addition to traffic lights and lifts the Audit Commission lists car park barriers, central heating boilers, building security systems, burglar and fire alarms, accounting software, vehicle fleet maintenance systems, local authority revenue systems, child protection registers, benefit systems, emergency service communication systems and medical equipment as just some of the areas with the potential to seriously disrupt everyday life as a consequence of their reliance on embedded and computerized systems.

Other notable landmarks of 'Bugtown UK' included the banking industry, gas, water and electricity supply, food retailing, the post office, the police force, the fire brigade, hospitals and emergency services. In the case of hospitals the Audit Commission used the following passage to warn of the extent of the potential problem: 'The year 2000 project manager at one NHS trust is quoted as saying: "The [potential] problem extends to all areas of the hospital – lifts, diagnostic equipment, X-ray machines, anaesthetics, breathing equipment and monitors"' (1998, p. 11). The year 2000 problem was a global problem, and similar kinds of audits were carried out all over the world.

In the event, of course, the disruption caused by the 'millennium bug' was negligible and there have since been questions raised as to how much of a true threat Y2K ever posed. Nevertheless, if it achieved nothing else, Y2K served to amply illustrate the extent to which software has seeped into everyday life.

If, until now, much of this infusion of software into everyday life has gone largely unnoticed, newer technological developments will, by virtue of their closeness to bodies, be much more readily apparent (though not necessarily visible). This is the world of *local intelligence* in which everyday spaces become saturated with computational capacities, thereby transforming more and more spaces into computationally active environments able to communicate within and with each other. This change is taking place as a result of two main developments. The first of these is the move to 'ubiquitous', 'everywhere' or 'pervasive' computing – computational systems which are distributed through the environment in a whole range of devices, 'a physical world invisibly interwoven with sensors, actuators, displays and computational elements, embedded seamlessly in the everyday objects of our lives and connected through a continuous network' (Weiser et al., 1999, pp. 2–3).

NPThis is the world of 'information appliances' foreseen by Norman (1998) in which each of us will, in a sense, put our own computing needs together as and when necessary. 'Information appliances should be thought of as systems, not isolated devices' (1998, p. 253) so that 'instead of one massive device that occupies considerable space on our desk top, we will have a wide range of devices that are designed to fit the tasks that we wish to do' (Norman, 2000, p. 12). Today, of course, we only have access to the first generation of appliances meant to inform everyday life, devices which still too often bear the mark of 'computing', chiefly personal digital devices (like the Palm Pilot), mobile phones, recordable CD players, portable MP3 players, personal voice recorders, interactive pagers, Internet radios, and so on, which have some computing capacity and can often communicate with each other. But increasingly, this kind of computing will likely make its way out into many more kinds of devices and become personally tailored (see Bergman, 2000). This is a move away from an Internet-inspired idea of computing as concerned with the provision of specific stand-alone high-technology devices which provide analyses and representations of information, to computing as distributed through a whole series of devices used as and when – and where – appropriate. 'Less fuss and bother. Simpler, more convenient devices. Great flexibility and versatility. New modes of interaction, of learning, of conducting business and recreation' (Norman, 1998, p. 261).

The second development is the move to position the Internet – the obsession of the 1990s – as but one element of a computing revolution: 'the use of the Internet [will be] so pervasive, so natural, and so commonplace that the very notion of calling something an "Internet appliance" will be completely unnecessary' (1998, p. 269). Rather we will exist in a broadband world in which the Internet will be a permanently available 'cloud' of information able to be called up through a number of appliances scattered through the environment. These appliances will be something more than portals for information. Rather, like many other devices which will not have Internet connections, they will be 'practice-aware', responding to and aware of the context in which they are used through an array of wireless and other sensors, continuous locational information read from global positioning system (GPS) references, and the like. In turn, this means we are moving away from machines that simply respond to machines that interact because they are aware enough of the context in which they operate to be able to do so. This means more than simply better human–machine interfaces (though these will be a part of this new interactivity: Johnson, 1997). And it means more than simply the redesign of the overall encounter with a machine, so that it becomes a more satisfying experience (see Dryer et al., 1999). Rather it means that a whole set of appliances (which 'compute') will, through a process of cultural absorption into practices, sink down from the representational into the non-representational world, so becoming a part of a taken-for-granted set of passions and skills (Thrift, 2000a).

At present, this world of local intelligence is still some way off. But not that far off. Two examples will suffice to make the case: mobile phone technology, and so called 'wearables'. With the advent of third-generation (3G) technologies, the software running mobile phones and mobile phone networks is becoming ever more sophisticated such that, just like the car or the elevator, the mobile is set to become 'smarter' (*New Scientist*, 21 October 2000). Mobile phones incorporating speech recognition technology to allow hands-free dialling and access to functions are already in common use. In addition, work is under way on installing Bluetooth and other wireless communication chips, in addition to SIM cards, into 3G phones. Such chips will allow communication with other Bluetooth devices within the immediate vicinity (roughly a house-shaped bubble) of the mobile phone user. This would allow, as one simple instance, the retailers in city centres and shopping malls to send a '"10 per cent off" coupon to your mobile's screen as you approach' (2000, p. 33). Following on from this kind of approach, it is clear that messages soon will be pinned in mid-air using GPS:

Messages [will not] actually be kept in the air; they're stored on a web page. But that page's web address is linked to co-ordinates on the Earth's surface, rather than the organisation. As you move about, a GPS receiver in your mobile phone or PDA will check to see what has been posted on the website for that particular spot. If you're in luck a snippet of info left as a recording by someone who passed there previously will pop up on your screen or be whispered into your earpiece. (*New Scientist*, 1 December 2001, p. 16)

Already, prototype systems like Hewlett Packard's Cooltown (http://cooltown.hp.com) are attempting to produce spaces in which universal open messaging is commonplace.

The way in which mobile telephony has already become a part of everyday life – producing new forms of social action, from the new kinds of 'hyper-coordination' promoted by text messaging (and the new kinds of 'flocking' that is made possible), to the invasion of public space by private and work lives, to new kinds of affective social performance – shows, in turn, the way that even very basic forms of local intelligence can have substantive cultural effects (see Townsend, 2000; Laurier and Philo, 2001; Brown et al., 2002).

A second example of nascent local intelligence is provided by wearable computing which has begun to develop strongly in the last five years as a means of providing computing that is always ready and available by virtue of being present in items of clothing: 'it's always on, it's always accessible and it's always part of you' (Billinghurst, n.d.). 'It therefore exists within the corporeal envelope of the user' (Bass, 1997). Though commercial wearables will at first consist of items like Levis IGD+ (developed in partnership with Phillips and featuring the Xenium speech recognition phone), which are little more than bulky multipocketed jackets able to contain various pieces of electronic kit, the future might be very different. Cyberjackets will probably be the first step. Such cyberjackets will, for example, be able to alert and guide a wearer to interesting shops. 'Shopping jackets' are, however, only one of a whole host of potential wearable applications developed to transcend the conventional user/PC paradigm. For example, the Belgian company Starlab has unveiled layers of i-wear with memory, communication, interface, power, connectivity and computational abilities (www.starlab.org).

More recently, it has become possible to create computationally active textiles which are able to weave circuit substances into cloth, so creating the possibility of ever more corporeally sensitive interfaces (Post et al., 2000). By installing computing systems into jackets, trousers, hats, shoes, glasses, and the like, wearable pioneers like Mann have sought to radically reconfigure the way in which we use computers. Smart clothing transforms computation into 'intelligent assistance', actively rather than passively engaging with the user (MIT website: ww.wearcam.org/computing.html). Thus, wearables can not only assist in locating shops but also act as more general navigation aids and mobile payment systems, provide security access to buildings, assist engineers and mechanics in the field, record conversations, meetings and other events, act as mobile Internet and phone portals, augment vision and memory and a host of other activities. And, as in the case of mobile phones, a key requirement of future wearable systems will be the need to communicate, through the employment of wireless protocols like Bluetooth, with each other and with other systems embedded in the fabric of everyday life.

The trend towards local intelligence will hardly stop at mobile phones and wearables, as a glance at any journal like *Personal Technologies* shows. Computational ability is being embedded in household white goods, in furniture (including beds and couches), even in carpets (Omojola et al., 2000; Paradiso et al., 2000).

However, it is also important to note that some of the most important imprints of local intelligence will come from the increasing ability afforded by Bluetooth and similar wireless protocols to produce a multitude of 'invisible' embedded systems, communicating not with human users but with each other, so producing a genuine 'mechanosphere'. In certain contexts it may even be, as *New Scientist* (21 October 2000, p. 33) predicts, that communication between people will become subservient to machine-to-machine communication. So, for example, 'the number of phone calls between people will be overtaken by machines talking to machines on behalf of people', with results such as:

> As soon as your washing machine is installed, it will be on the air to your Bluetooth controller, asking if it can contact its manufacturer over the Net. A year later you'll trip over a repair engineer who's been e-mailed by the washing machine because it has a worn bearing. (2000, p. 33)

In concluding this section of the chapter, it is important to note that this kind of actual and prospective audit should not give the air of a kind of technological finality for two reasons. First, the new generation of intelligent devices is already being socially and culturally inflected in quite different ways in different cultures. A good current example is the radically different pattern of use of mobile telephony and PDAs and laptops in Europe and North America. Quite unexpectedly different practices have already grown up on both sides of the Atlantic in relation to the take-up and use of these two technologies (see Brown et al., 2002). Then, second, software itself hardly constitutes a smoothly functioning and well-versed set of procedures. This is a point worth expanding. To begin with, software consists of many often incompatible languages which are constantly changing:

> I learned to program a computer in 1971; my first programming job came in 1978. Since then, I have taught myself six higher level programming languages, three assemblers, two data-retrieval languages, eight job-processing languages, seventeen scripting languages, ten types of macros, two object definition languages, sixty-eight programming library interfaces, five varieties of networks and eight operating environments – fifteen, if you cross-multiply the different combinations of operating systems and networks. I don't think this makes me particularly unusual. Given the rate of change in computing, anyone who's been around for a while could probably make a list like this. (Ullman, 1997, p. 101)

Then, software is built up from many different components, many of which are 'legacy systems' which have existed for many years. In effect, many different programmers still live in the code (Downey, 1998):

Software gets to age. Too much time is invested in it, too much time will be needed to replace it. So unlike the tossed-out hardware, software is tinkered with. It is mended and fixed, patched and reused ... I once worked on a main-frame computer system where the fan-folded history of my COBOL pro-gram stood as high as a person. My program was sixteen years old when I inherited it. According to the library logs, ninety-six programmers had worked on it before I had. I spent a year wandering its subroutines and serv-ice modules, but there were still mysterious places I did not touch. There were bugs on this system no one had been able to fix for ten years. There were sections where adding a single line of code created odd and puzzling outcomes programmers called 'side effects': bugs that come not directly from the added code but from some later, unknown perturbation further down in the process. My program was near the end of its 'life cycle'. It was close to death.

Yet this system could not be thrown away. By the time a computer system becomes old, no one completely understands it. A system made out of old junky technology becomes, paradoxically, precious ...

The preciousness of an old system is axiomatic. The longer the system has been running, the greater the number of programmers who have worked on it, the less any one person understands it. As years pass and untold numbers of programmers and analysts come and go, the system takes on a life of its own. It runs. That is its claims to existence: it does useful work. However badly, however buggy, however obsolete – it runs. And no one individual completely understands how. (Ullman, 1997, pp. 116–17)

In other words, programmers function against a background of 'ignorant expertise':

The corollary of constant change is ignorance. This is not often talked about: we computer experts barely know what we are doing. We're good at fussing and figuring out. We function well in a sea of unknowns. Our experience has only prepared us to deal with confusion. A programmer who denies this is probably lying, or else is densely unaware of himself. (1997, p. 110)

No wonder that most software is only properly tested out through a process of trial and error in real applications (Mackenzie, 1996).

Again, as numerous writers have pointed out (e.g. Winograd, 1996; Norman, 1998), software is rarely designed well, so that the capacities of most programs are underused:

One of the main reasons most computer software is so abysmal is that it's not designed at all, but merely engineered. Another reason is that implementers often place more emphasis on a program's internal construction than on its external design, despite the fact that as much as 75 per cent of the code in a modern program deals with the interface to the user. (Winograd, 1996, p. 5)

Then, software does not always do as it is bidden by programmers or is used as it is meant to be by users. It is inescapably a joint production, a feature which is especially noticeable when the program is applied:

Writing a software program ... is a way of addressing a problem in an original manner. Each team of programmers redefines and resolves, although differently, the problem it is faced with. The actualization of the program during use in a work environment, however, ignores certain skills, reveals new kinds of functionality, gives rise to conflicts, resolves problems, and initiates a new dynamic of collaboration. The software carries with it a virtuality of change that the group ... actualizes in a more or less inventive way. (Lévy, 1998, p. 25)

To conclude this section, one last point also needs to be made. The simple fact of the matter is that software, in the shape of embedded systems, is now so widespread that we are no longer able to be sure of its exact extent. As the Audit Commission stressed in relation to the difficulties encountered in identifying Y2K affected equipment, 'the presence of the embedded system may not be obvious *even to a trained observer* ... [and some] systems may also be extremely difficult to locate or test' (1998, p. 11, emphasis added). Yet the Commission estimated that even as far back as 1996 some 7 billion embedded systems were being distributed worldwide.

Breathing new life into software

Any audit of software in cities can therefore by its very nature only ever be partial and incomplete, and ours is no different. Indeed this recognition, more than anything else, illustrates just how extensive the distribution of this form of 'machine space' has become. But this may only be the beginning. Continuing developments within computer science suggest a much greater role for software than has so far been apparent as the machinic writing of software itself changes its form and capabilities.

Such change arises out of a general move away from formal well-specified programs towards programs which stress the situatedness of action, the importance of interaction and adaptation, and emergent properties. Such notions have existed for a long time now, spurred on by the ethnographic study of human–computer interaction and by more general developments in the social sciences and humanities (e.g. Suchman, 1987). But, of late, these kinds of programs, using a diverse range of methodologies – from fuzzy sets to neural networks to generative algorithms to the data mining techniques of bio-informatics and bio-computation – have become much more prevalent (Bentley, 2001). Here we note just one of these developments, the growth of the so-called 'soft computing' movement. Soft computing encompasses a range of methods which stress appropriate rather than precise models.

Fuzzy computation is a set of techniques most often associated with the work of Zadeh at the University of California, Berkeley from the 1960s, on fuzzy sets, fuzzy logic and complex systems theory. In general terms fuzzy computation was born from a recognition that existing programming methodologies which relied upon precise and detailed models were inappropriate for dealing with complex, uncertain and vague systems or problems (Ruspini et al., 1998). Similarly, techniques of *evolutionary computing* grew out of a recognition of the limitations of precise modelling techniques for many empirical problems. Drawing upon natural theories of 'reproduction, mutation and the Darwinian principle of survival of the fittest', evolutionary computing seeks to harness the 'power of natural selection to turn computers into automatic optimization and design tools' (http://evonet.dcs.napier.ac.uk/evoweb: Heitkötter and Beasley, 1999).

The term *soft computing* is closely linked to both fuzzy computation and evolutionary computation. In attempting to define soft computing Zadeh (1994, emphasis added) states that 'the role model for soft computing is the *human mind*'. Soft computing is distinguished by its tolerance of 'imprecision, uncertainty and partial truth' (Zadeh, 1994), in contrast to conventional hard computing with its emphasis upon 'crisp classifications' and perfect information. As Bonissone stresses:

> when we attempt to solve real-world problems, we realise that they are typically ill-defined systems, difficult to model and with large-scale solution spaces ... Therefore, we need hybrid approximate reasoning systems capable of handling this kind of imperfect information. (1998, D1.1:2)

Increasingly, many soft computing approaches have begun to share a general characteristic: a turn to biology and the natural sciences for inspiration. In particular, theories of evolution have inspired a host of alternative programming techniques, of which one of the most influential has been the genetic algorithm (GA). As with many other soft computing methods, GAs have provided the building blocks for some of the most sophisticated software applications, particularly artificial intelligence systems. It is therefore worth very briefly examining the rationale behind the genetic algorithm, both in its own right and as an exemplar of soft computing techniques.

The genetic algorithm was developed in the 1970s by Holland at the University of Michigan as a mechanism for addressing complex problems with very large 'solution spaces' (Sipper, 2000; Holland, 1975). To tackle large solution space problems, Holland developed a 'model of machine learning which derives its behaviour from a metaphor of some of the mechanisms of evolution' (Heitkötter and Beasley, 1999, p. 1). As with other types of evolutionary computing, GAs work by seeking to evolve solutions to a given problem. To achieve this the GA employs a specific mode of *genetic representation* (see Table 8.1). A population of *individuals* or bit *strings* of data, analogous to chromosomes in human DNA, is initially generated, each of which represents a possible solution. This first generation of candidate solutions is then evaluated in the context of its environment, its fitness to the problem in hand. On the basis of this fitness and the *genetic operator* employed, a new generation of individuals is born (Heitkötter and Beasley, 1999; Goldberg, 1989; Sipper, 2000; Belew and Vose, 1997). By employing the principle of 'survival of the fittest' along with that of genetic diversity, each new generation produced should include solutions that are better than those of the previous generation. Of critical importance in understanding the power of the GA is that it removes the necessity of having a predetermined solution to a problem. Programmers simply have to determine an appropriate fitness function and genetic operator (Davis and Steenstrup, 1990).

Table 8.1 Comparison of biological and genetic algorithm terminology

Biological	Genetic algorithm
Chromosome	String
Gene	Feature, character, or detector
Allele	Feature value
Locus	String position
Genotype	Structure
Phenotype	Parameter set, alternative solution, decoded structure
Epistasis	Non-linearity

Source: Goldberg, 1989, p. 22

The genetic algorithm, along with the various other soft computing techniques, has been particularly important in the development of artificial intelligence (AI) systems. AI incorporates a wide variety of specific applications, from artificial life, robotics and recognition technologies through to data mining, expert systems and intelligent agents. One of the distinguishing features of all these various types of AI system is the fact that they operate within the very same large solution spaces in which conventional hard computing approaches have shown themselves to be so ill-equipped. It is no surprise then that soft computational models have been mobilized to address such complex and indeterminate problems. Indeed much of the impetus behind the development of soft computing and the like has come from the desire to develop artificial life systems, biometrics and other smart technologies. This is little surprise since, beginning with the early days of cybernetics, there has been constant interchange between biology and computing as, for example, in the case of neural nets (Hayles, 1999; Helmreich, 1998; Anderson and Rosenfeld, 1999; Oyama, 2001).

Turning back to our audit, soft computation can be found in a great number of the embedded systems that populate cities. Intelligent traffic lights, elevators, automobiles and washing machines are programmed with fuzzy logic, as are many intelligent transportation systems (www.its.org). Genetic algorithms are helping to run medical diagnostic and monitoring equipment, data mining technologies, credit scoring and behavioural modelling systems, traffic management systems and call centre telephone routing technologies. More generally, genetic algorithms are being utilized in artificial life worlds such as Tierra, financial market models, flexible production systems, telecommunication networks and even by the UK's Channel 4 to assist in the scheduling of television advertisements (Helmreich, 1998; Evonet, www.evonet.dcs.napier.ac.uk). Self-learning software is also being mobilized within the field of biometrics and in technologies of recognition (for example, in visual recognition systems).

These techniques have enabled machines and objects to begin to take on some of the characteristics of corporeal intelligence. Smart software has begun to breathe new kinds of life into a multitude of everyday things. This is not to suggest that software or for that matter computer systems have ever been dead (see Downey, 1998; Ullman, 1997, p. 117), but to propose that the 'romantic reaction' (Turkle, 1991, cited in Helmreich, 1998, p. 140) to hard, rationalistic computing has helped software begin to take on many of the characteristics normally associated with biological life.

This new form of machine is no more starkly illustrated than in the case of a range of technologies designed to recognize and act upon the human body: the face, the voice, handwriting and, perhaps most remarkably, mood and emotion. The first and second of these, facial and speech recognition, form part of a wider school of biometrics technologies, designed to recognize individuals from their distinguishing traits. Other biometrics technologies developed for a range of security uses include electronic fingerprinting, iris coding, hand geometry and palm print recognition. As we have shown, facial recognition technologies are already becoming a reality within cities, as are commercial voice recognition packages such as those developed by the Belgian company Lernout & Hauspie (L&H) and those incorporated within the Xenium mobile phone. L&H are developing not only speech recognition applications for use within call centres, consumer and business electronic packages, toys and wearables, but also text recognition products.

Research institutes such as the MIT Media Lab have also conducted considerable work within the area of 'affective computing' – computational systems with the ability to sense, recognize, understand and respond to human moods and emotions. Picard (1997; 2000) argues that to be truly interactive computers must have the power to recognize, feel and express emotion:

> Not all computers need to 'pay attention' to emotions or to have the capability to emulate emotion. Some machines are useful as rigid tools, and it is fine to keep them that way. However, there are situations in which human–computer interaction could be improved by having the computer adapted to the user, and in which communication about when, where, how and how important it is to adapt involves the use of emotional information. (2000, p. 1)

Plutowski (2000) identifies three broad categories of research within the area of affective or emotional computing (www.emotivate.com/Book): emotional expression programs that display and communicate simulated emotional affect; emotional detection programs that recognize and react to emotional expression in humans; and emotional action tendencies, instilling computer programs with emotional processes in order to make them more efficient and effective. Thus, specific projects at MIT (www.media.mit.edu/affect) have included the development of affective wearables such as affective jewellery, expression glasses, and a conductor's jacket designed to extend a conductor's ability to express emotion and intentionality to the audience and to the orchestra. Other projects include affective carpets, affective virtual reality avatars which represent the changing emotional state of their users in the real world, affective toys such as the 'Affective Tigger', and Orpheus, an affective CD player which selects music in alignment with current mood.

Affective computing is already making its way into the commercial world. Basic emotional expression and detection technology is being employed through the use of 'embodied conversational agents' (see Cassell et al., 2000; Pesce, 2000) – icons which are able to mimic conversation not only through better linguistic skills but also through employing a range of the non-verbal behaviours associated with affect like facial expression, gesture and posture. Such agents therefore operate not only in the representational register (as in, for example, representing concepts) but also in the non-representational register (as in spatializing or providing rhythm to a conversation). Such icons now encompass a whole range of agencies, including not only roles in games but also intelligent avatars like virtual pets and virtual friends, and the intent to go one better is also clear:

> Just like real creatures, some agents will act as pets and others will be more like free agents. Some agents will belong to a user, will be maintained by a user, and will live mostly in that user's computer. Others will be free agents that don't really belong to anyone. And just like real creatures, the agents will be born, die and reproduce ... I'm convinced that we need (these agents) because the digital world is too overwhelming for people to deal with, no matter how good the interfaces we design ... Basically, we're trying to change the nature of human–computer interaction ... users will not only be manipulating things personally, but will also manage some agents that work on their behalf. (Maes, cited in Suchman, 2001, p. 9)

So genetic algorithms beget something which is meant to approximate life. Whether, as Suchman (2001) convincingly argues, these icons are often based on faulty attributions of interactive agency to machines, the fact remains that these faulty attributions are now constitutive. By enabling and amplifying non-verbal communication between humans, between humans and machines and ultimately between machines and machines, these icons seek to greatly enhance the usefulness of embedded systems.

Software writing space

Wherever we go, then, in modern urbanized spaces, we are directed by software: driving in the car, stopping at the red light, crossing the road, getting into an elevator, using the washing machine or the dishwasher or the microwave, making a phone call, writing a letter, playing a CD or a computer game: the list goes on and on. Given that we have established the prevalence of mechanical writing in the spaces of everyday life, we now need to begin to establish exactly how that effectivity comes about. In this section we will argue that this effectivity stems from three different but intersecting geographies. The first of these geographies is the most obvious, the large and complex geography of the writing of software, of the production of lines of code – a geography which takes in many different locations and many different languages and which has been built up progressively since the invention of programming in the 1940s. And this geography of writing can only grow, especially given the demands of a modern economy which is built on software (see Chandler and Cortado, 2000) and the consequent need to produce more and more lines of code – whether we are talking of the 3000 or so lines of code that an electric toothbrush may now use, or the millions of lines of code that inhabit a personal computer (Lohr, 2001). 'Business cycles and Wall Street enthusiasms will come and go, but someone will have to build all the needed software. Programmers are the artisans, craftsmen, brick layers, and architects of the Information Age' (2001, p. 7).

Software programming is still itself little understood. As we have seen already, it is a curious blend of science, engineering and artistry. On the whole, studies of the programming labour process (e.g. Orr, 1996; Perlow, 1997; Downey, 1998; O'Riain, 2000) do not capture its exact blend of writing skills and are unable to explain why some people are quite clearly better at programming than others. As Knath (1997) has observed:

> There are a certain percentage of undergraduates – perhaps two per cent or so – who have the mental abilities that make them good at computer programming. They are good at it, and it just flows out of them ... The two per cent are the only ones who are really going to make these machines do amazing things. I wish it weren't so, but that is the way it has always been. (cited in Lohr, 2001, p. 9)

Whether new developments like grid programming can overcome the reliance on those few who can manipulate the few basic higher-level languages (like C and its variants), or whether large amounts of programming will end up being automated – software produced by software – remains to be seen.

Though software programming has a long history spun out of many locations, its geography has now stabilized. To begin with there are, of course, all those institutions that teach programmers to write code: universities, schools and colleges, computer institutes, and so on. But the geography of programming is most often linked to centres of software production. This geography can be apprehended in two ways. One is the large and complicated geography of those humans who *write* software. 'The globalization of the information technology industry is seen to result not in a virtual economy but in a global industry organized around and through certain key plans and regions. Within these global workspaces, relations among workers constantly cycle through phases of cohesion and fragmentation, as worker solidarity is mobilized for principles of innovation but disowned by the structure of careers in the labor market' (O'Riain, 2000, p. 179). The geography of software production is concentrated into a very few key places and regions: Silicon Valley (Kenney, 2000), New York (Pratt, 2000), London, and a number of subsidiary and sometimes mass production software locations (often concentrating on tasks like consulting, testing and support) in countries like Ireland and India (O'Riain, 2000). However, because writing software requires skills which are still in short supply, especially for newer languages, software writers from all over the world often gravitate to the main software-writing centres (Kenney, 2000).

The other is a much wider network of production which takes in many consumers as well. Since the founding of the free software movement in 1983 by Richard Stallman, open-source software has become a massive collective project (McKelvey, 2000). This has been particularly the case since the founding of Internet languages like Linux and Perl, which are essentially software that has been communally enhanced by thousands of software writers worldwide (Moody, 2001). The much trumpeted Linux – with its familiar Penguin logo – was born from three sources: a team of professional corporate developers attempting to solve their organization's needs, commercial software companies, and individual programmers. More interesting in many ways is Perl (Practical Evaluation and Report Language). Created in 1987 in Santa Monica by Larry Wall, Perl is now known as the 'duct tape of the Internet'. Made visible by the familiar logo of the camel, signifying an entity often thought to have been made by a committee – but which still works – Perl is a kind of mechanical writing culture with something like a million users (Moody, 2001). Perl does not operate according to the strict logics necessary to write earlier generation programming languages. Rather, Wall, a linguistics expert, created it to mimic 'expressive' written languages on the principle of 'there's more than one way to do it'. Perl is, in other words, a language which allows a large amount of creative expression, on the principle that 'easy things should be easy and hard things should be possible' (Wall et al., 2000, p. 4). Thus Perl is not a minimalistic computer language but has the capacity to be fuzzy and to migrate. However:

> Wall's achievement goes much further than simply a great language. Perl was one of the key enabling technologies that made possible the last wave of interactive web sites, and hence e-commerce itself. It established yet another field – that of programming languages – where the net-based open-development process had produced better results than those traditionally employed within software companies to create their black box products. (Moody, 2001, p. 134)

And, at least in part, this was because of the openness of the development process: 'if you have a problem that the Perl community can't fix, you have the ultimate backstop: the source code itself. The Perl community is not in the business of renting you their trade secrets in the guise of upgrades' (Wall et al., 2000, p. xvii).

Whatever the language it is clear that open software is being written in many locations at once, but even here there is a very definite hierarchy of places and people.

The second geography is one of power. Power is built into software from its inception. For example binary code is premised on the Leibnizian conception of permitted/not permitted. But, that said, software has no fixed foundations beyond the logical and material technologies of micro-informational processing, so we must find a body of work that can play to this characteristic. This we do through the Foucauldian notion of governmentality.

Foucault's chief concern was with an analysis of government which took as its central concern *how* we govern and are governed within specific regimes, and the conditions under which such regimes are able to emerge, continue to persist, and are transformed. According to Dean, an analytics of government therefore works through four dimensions of problematization:

1   characteristic forms of visibility, ways of seeing and perceiving
2   distinctive ways of thinking and questioning, relying on definite vocabularies and procedures for the production of thoughts (e.g. those derived from the social, human and behavioural sciences)
3   specific ways of acting, intervening and directing, made up of particular types of practical rationality ('expertise' and 'know-how'), and relying upon definite mechanisms, techniques and technologies
4   characteristic ways of forming subjects, selves, persons, actors or agents. (1999, p. 23)

We can see straightaway that software intervenes in each of these dimensions. It has changed characteristic forms of visibility by informationalizing space, so producing new objects of analysis. It has changed ways of thinking and questioning by producing new analytic procedures. It has changed the nature of expertise by producing new templates for decision-making. Finally, it is changing the nature of human subjects by producing enhanced capabilities and by questioning not just what techniques of the self consist of, but whether the self is a meaningful governmental category.

Software is now, therefore, a key technology of government for both the state and commerce. But it is more than just a potent juridical intermediary. Increasingly software is becoming the practice of government. What were corporeal routines that could be questioned have seemingly become incorporeal routines that lie below the level of explicit discourse, that are no longer disclosed.

Seen in this way, what then does software consist of, outside the physical fact of lines of code? In essence, we can say that it consists of rules of conduct able to be applied to determinate situations. But these rules of conduct operate at a distance, so that too often the code seems to have little to do with the situations in which it is applied.

Instead of seeing the program as a real instrument affecting the lives of real people, programmers sometimes see it as a game, a challenge to their ingenuity. The alienating quality of the computer permits us to overlook the human consequences of a programming design or error. An assignment to link scattered databases in different quarters, for example, becomes nothing more than a problem to be solved; the programmer does not notice the resulting diminution of privacy and the increased opportunities for mischief that can result. (Kohanski, 1998, p. 22)

Again, programmers themselves argue about exactly what it is that they are producing and who makes the decisions about the decisions incorporated into the code (Kohanski, 1998; Ullman, 1997). The remarkably few ethnographies of the labour process in the software industry (e.g. Orr, 1996;

Perlow, 1997; Downey, 1998; O'Riain, 2000) hardly mention the issue, even though it is surely crucial.

What we can say is that code is law of a kind. But it is not so much law considered as a set of rules as law considered as a set of possible stories framing encounters (Lessig, 1999), new *adaptive* standards of conduct. Taken together, these stories write out standards of conduct which can work in all kinds of situations at all kinds of scales. These stories can be simple blocks. They can be encryptions. They can be overall architectures. So, code has different effects on conduct, from the given of the green, amber, red of traffic lights, to the fact that only 23 people can be present in an AOL chat-room at once (originally a choice of code engineers), to the amount of information able to be collected on each person and translated to commercial advantage. Within certain highly coded domains, this information can be wielded in almost absolute terms:

> AOL space [is] different from other places in cyberspace – it is easier for AOL to identify who you are, and harder for individuals to find out who you are; easier for AOL to speak to all its 'citizens' as it wishes, and harder for dissidents to organize against AOL's views about how things ought to be; easier for AOL to market, and harder for individuals to hide. AOL is a different narrative world; it can create other different worlds because it is in control of the architecture of that world. Members in that space face, in a sense, different sets of laws of nature; AOL makes those laws. (Lessig, 1999, p. 70)

In a sense, what software is able to achieve is a standardization and classification of urban situations in ways which were formerly impossible. It forms a new chapter in what Bowker and Star call the 'categorical saturation' of the modern world:

> Although it is possible to pull out a single classification scheme or standard for reference purposes, in reality none of them stand alone. So a subproperty of ubiquity is interdependence, and frequently, integration. A systems approach might see the proliferation of both standards and classifications as purely a matter of integration – almost like a giant web of interoperability. Yet the sheer density of these phenomena goes beyond questions of interoperability. They are layered, tangled, textured, they interact to form an ecology as well as a flat set of compatibilities. That is to say, they facilitate the collection of heterogeneous 'dispositif techniques' [Foucault] … They are lodged in different communities of practice such as laboratories, records, offices, insurance companies and so forth. There *are* spaces between (unclassified, non-standard areas), of course, and these are especially important to the analysis. It seems that increasingly these spaces are marked as unclassified and non-standard. (1999, p. 31)

Seen in this way, the governmentality of software is perhaps best approximated by Deleuze's (1990a) notion of 'societies of control' in that it provides a set of modulations which constantly direct how citizens act (and who, therefore, is important). Those modulations are often simply opportune. For example, many of the most malign effects of code have arisen when systems are linked in ways which provide new opportunities for surveillance, for example by providing previously unavailable kinds of information. 'As a product manager once told me, "I've never seen anyone with two systems who didn't want us to hook them together"' (Ullman, 1997, p. 85). But increasingly the modulation will be purposeful. As software becomes increasingly context-aware, so it will be able to adjust rules to circumstances, providing a new kind of mechanical stance to judgement which may well begin to redefine what counts as law.

Numerous examples of new software classification and standardization entities exist. We will fix on one particularly potent one – the humble spreadsheet. Low-cost spreadsheet programs first appeared in 1979 with the introduction of VisiCalc (for Visible Calculator) for the Apple II computer, developed by Daniel Bricklin, Robert Frankston, and Dan Fylstra (see Lohr, 2001). Within five years over one million spreadsheets were being sold annually worldwide. Spreadsheets became ever more ubiquitous as a result of additional design work and the ability to be used on a PC (leading to the successor program Lotus 1-2-3 for the IBM PC, and to Microsoft Excel), as well as more recently to a Linux spreadsheet program. Certainly, within 10 years it could already legitimately be claimed that many businesses had become 'spreadsheet cultures'. Subsequently, spreadsheets have continued to evolve with the addition of a WYSIWYG (what you see is what you get) interface (with many word processing facilities), as well as sophisticated graphical display capabilities.

The spreadsheet was able to be adapted so rapidly for two reasons. First, it functioned as a high-level programming language which could easily be made task-specific through just a few functions. As Nardi (1995) points out, the spreadsheet was accessible (even in its early completely text-based programming formats) because it used very simple control constraints which meant that results could be achieved almost immediately with relatively little effort by the user. The sacrifice of the flexibility and generality characteristic of most programming languages paid dividends in producing much greater expressivity. Second, the spreadsheet format mimicked the structure of the paper ledger sheet, so that it was already familiar and able to be inserted into the everyday life of business. Yet:

> The spreadsheet is fundamentally different from earlier programs for financial calculation, with their unbridgeable separation between programs and data – responding to a nearly unbridgeable separation between program and accountant. The key innovation was not in the interface elements or the software structure but rather in the virtuality provided to the user – the underlying world of objects and their behavior. The spreadsheet virtually combines the regular structure of the familiar ledger sheet with an underlying structure of interlinked formulas. The non-technical user can build a complex financial model incrementally, and can explore the model through successive iterations of inputs. This quantitative change in ease meant a qualitative change in how people worked with data. (Winograd, 1996, p. 230)

Thus managerial behaviour was profoundly changed by the generation of new kinds of information *and* interaction, new 'everyday business lives':

> The artfully crafted spreadsheet – here is how we can cut costs! Here's how we should restructure this deal! – could and did prove as politically explosive a document as the declaration of independence or the communist manifesto. Spreadsheet software breathed new life into the old adage 'figures don't lie, but liars figure'. As budgets and forecasts were used to find previously unimagined opportunities, traditional perceptions of power, politics, productivity, and profit all dramatically shifted. Finance-driven organizations often found themselves reorganizing around their spreadsheets. (Schrage, 2000, p. 39)

The spreadsheet therefore had impacts in a number of ways. To begin with, it provided new opportunity for interaction. Then, it furnished managers with rhetorical energy: there is a rhetoric of spreadsheets that results in more or less persuasive forecasts ('spreadsheet rhetoric is about turning what appears to be a dispassionate logic of numbers into presentations that mute opposition even as they enlist allies': 2000, p. 47). Again, the spreadsheet asked new questions, tested new ideas and provided new business opportunities (such as new financial products). They were 'a medium for serious play as much as for crunching hard numbers' (2000, p. 44). And, best of all, they provided a new language. Thus Schrage exaggerates only slightly when he writes that:

> The multinational, multibillion dollar institutional leader Asea Brown Boveri, nominally headquartered in Europe, insists that English is its primary language, but in practice the dominant language of ABB is spreadsheet. Indeed, several senior managers observe that it is communication, disagreement and negotiation over spreadsheet forecasts and projects that drive business at ABB. 'Yes, I think it is better to be more fluent in your spreadsheet forecasts than in English,' says a senior ABB executive. 'Our numbers are probably more important to us than our words.' (2000, pp. 46–7)

In other words, spreadsheets created new stories of government, not least by producing new intellectual stimulation. The artefact of spreadsheet program created new coalitions, new forces, new realities. In turn, their persuasiveness as a model allowed them to migrate outwards from business and finance into the city as a whole. They had found a 'design foothold'. So, for example, specialist spreadsheet programs are now available for applications as diverse as car purchase, class notes and assignments, diving decompression, seed cultivation and trading, landfill gas production, archaeological digs, laboratory management, chemical properties, music production and real estate management.

> Now that the spreadsheet is widely available, it has come to be used for many tasks that have nothing to do with figures. A spreadsheet can be used for anything that calls for calculating regular arrays of values that are interconnected by regular formulas – especially for those actualities that call for exploring alternatives. Professors use spreadsheets for grading courses, scientists use

spreadsheets for interpreting data from experiments, and builders use spreadsheets for keeping track of materials. New kinds of spreadsheets have been developed that fill the cells with visual images, sounds, and other data representations, interleaved by formulas that perform calculations in the appropriate domain. (Winograd, 1996, p. 231)

But Foucault's notion of governmentality has a negative side. Though it stresses the positive role of power, it overwhelmingly concentrates on the realm of constraint, whether legislated or self-imposed. But there is a third kind of geography of software, what Hobart and Schiffman (1998) call 'the realm of play'. The general profusion of software, its increasing complexity and consequent emergent properties, all count as means of producing playful idioms which have not been captured by dominant orders. Software's very indeterminacy and lack of closure provide a means of creating new kinds of order:

> Play is 'freedom', wrote Huizinga, yet it also 'creates order, *is* order'. In its creative activity, play does not imitate or reflect or correspond or map directly to an outside world, although the resulting order it produces might eventually do so. Play's own order is not derivatively mimetic but *sui generis* methectic, as the Greeks would say in reference to the theatre, a 'helping-out-of-the-action'. By now it should be abundantly clear that information in the contemporary idiom means process, always in motion, always abetting the action of life's drama. Less clear, perhaps, this motion has direction, not towards any telos, purpose, or end, but following with its rules the arrow of time. From the time-bound movement of information play there can emerge novel, unforeseen structures, 'order for free'. (1998, 259)

The creative phrasing of play can be put another way, as a tending of the virtual. Software has creative potential which is more than just possibility. As Lévy puts it:

> The possible is already fully constituted but exists in a state of limbo. It can be realized without any change occurring either in its determination or nature. It is a phantom reality, something latent. The possible is exactly like the real, the only thing missing being existence. The realization of a possible is not an act of creation in the fullest sense of the word, for creation implies the innovative production of an idea or form. The difference between the possible and the real is thus purely logical.
>
> The virtual should, properly speaking, be compared not to the real but the actual. Unlike the possible, which is static and already constituted, the virtual is a kind of problematic complex, the kind of tendencies or forces that accompanies a situation, event, object, or entity, and which involves a process of resolution: actualization. This problematic complex belongs to the entity in question and even constitutes one of its primary dimensions. The seed's problem, for example, is the growth of the tree. The seed *is* this problem, even if it is also something more than that. This does not signify that the seed knows exactly what the shape of the tree will be, which will one day burst into bloom and spread its leaves above it. Based on its internal limitations, the seed will have to invent the tree, co-produce it together with the circumstances it encounters. (1998, p. 24)

Seen in this way, software does not have to be seen as simply a form of constant and unbending recital. It can be redefined as an experimental tool such that

> rather than being defined principally through its actuality (a solution), the entity now finds its essential consistency within a problematic field. The virtualization of a given entity consists in determining the general question to which it responds, in mutating the entity in the direction of this question and redefining the initial actuality as the response to a specific question. (1998, p. 26)

The given solution, then, proceeds to a different problem. So software which may be designed to produce defined and determined responses can in certain circumstances – as the example of spreadsheets shows – act as a spur to forms of creativity which can transgress these standard forms of classificatory arrangement: there are new forms of 'yes' as well as 'no' (Lunenfeld, 1999). Software is, then, being used in remarkably creative and craft-laden ways – from advances in animation which are redefining kinetic events (Wells, 1998), through work on new forms of music using musical instrument digital interfaces (MIDIs), through work on new forms of theatre and dance (Sparacino et al., 2000), through the pairing of artists and technologists (Harris, 1999), through to the work of technologically sophisticated artists like Char Davies who use software to create new virtual art forms which recognize that 'whenever people experience a piece of software – whether it be a spreadsheet or a physics simulation – [they can] experience beauty, satisfaction and fun or the corresponding opposites' (Winograd, 1996, p. xix). Such aesthetic uses all depend on software programs, from the early (mid 1980s) Macintosh programs like MacPaint and MacDraw to complex contemporary multimedia programs like Director. Such software can be said to proceed in a number of different but related ways. To begin with, it can be used to extend the range and meaning of the body, not least by conjuring up various affective states (McCullough, 1998). It is interesting that so many creative software projects have been concerned with the body, both representing it in new ways and questioning its bounds as it is constantly augmented (e.g. Allsopp and de Lahunta, 1999). Indeed new software developments like haptic computing promise to extend the range of informationalized embodiment still further, producing interfaces between software and body which will allow effects of unparalleled subtlety to be created. As Tenhaaf notes: 'the body seems … to know itself in a minutely expressive way that may by definition not be conscious, but that may nevertheless become more available [as] up-to-the-minute information and imagery about the body's deepest workings and its most complicated biosocial functions … now enter and become interwoven into the biomedical readability of the self' (1996, pp. 67–8). Then, software can be used to question familiar Euro-American notions of representation. After all, in certain senses 'we are moving into an information environment in which there is to be no representation at all. How we represent ourselves and form subjectivity, in relation to the real world, will no longer be an issue, as simulated entry into parallel digital worlds comes to supersede this relationship' (1996, p. 52; see also Brooks, 1991). Too strong, perhaps, yet it is not difficult to see how many artists – and programmers – are using software to question conventional notions of representation in ways which are very close to Strathern's recasting of Euro-American perspectivism:

> Suppose, instead of a Renaissance imagination which at times tried to make the whole world the singular object of the viewer's vision, having a perspective were regarded as a capacity belonging to animate life. What the writer could 'see' would be other life forms. What would be finite here? Could it be the manner in which one's perspective was returned to one? That is, closure would lie in the fact that one simultaneously had one's own perspective and received the perspective of another. Or, rather, the point at which that viewer was conscious that he or she had a perspective on things would be the point at which he or she would meet (so to speak) the reciprocal perspectives of other life forms. (1999, p. 249)

Again, software, precisely because it is an imperfect medium, can produce all kinds of opportunities for what Deleuze (1994) called 'bad mimesis'. Many forms of software are procedures which contain 'flaws' which can be used to produce new and interesting potentialities: the culture of the not-quite copy (Schwartz, 1997). And, finally, it is worth remembering how much software innovation has itself found its momentum from a line of dissident programmers (Moody, 2001; Lohr 2001) in the tradition of Thomas Nelson and Douglas Engelbart, who not only stand as part-inventors of hypertext, the World Wide Web, and so on, but were clearly concerned with using software to boost human capacities, and equally concerned with redefining what was 'human'.

The rise of semi-artificial life

Our problem in thinking about the automatic production of space by, with and from software is by now, we hope, clear. That is, we are schooled to ignore this kind of mechanical writing. It is a part of the taken-for-granted background, to the extent that some have suggested that it constitutes a kind of virtual skin (or set of skins) around human bodies (Bailey, 1996; Lévy, 1998), one that will become an ever better fit as wearable systems become common.

So how can we summarize software's effectivity as a new means of populating space, and as a new means of reproducing intelligence? As we have written this chapter, so we have vacillated between two answers, exactly as the literature does. One answer is to see software as an epochal event. Software signals a fundamental reorganization of the environment, a vast system of distributed cognition through which the environment increasingly thinks for itself, an extra layer of thinking.

Seen in this way, software is a part of the extended organism of a new form of humanity, a kind of extended phenotype in which the environment we have made speaks back to us: 'organisms are integral with the world outside them' (Turner, 2000, p. 6). If it is the case that modern biology of the kind typified by developmental systems theory is no longer sure what organisms are, so we can no longer be sure what humanity consists of – where it stops and something else begins. In this sense, software is building using writing. Rather than bricks and concrete, though, we have words and strings of words. And, of course, increasingly buildings may well become as much words as bricks. Mitchell may exaggerate the possibilities (see Bolter and Grusin, 1999) but even so we can see that some

> buildings of the near future will function more and more like large computers, with multiple processors, distributed memory, various devices to control, and network connections to take care of. They will suck in information from their interiors and surroundings, and they will construct and maintain complex, dynamic information overlays delivered through inanimate devices worn or held by inhabitants, screens and spaces in the walls and ceilings, and projections onto enclosing surfaces. The software to manage all this will be a crucial design concern. The operating system for your house will become as essential as the roof, and certainly far more important than the operating system for your desktop PC.
> Consequently a growing proportion of a building's construction cost will go into high-value factory-made electronics-loaded software – programmed computers and subsystems; a correspondingly decreasing proportion will go into on-site construction of the structure and cladding. As they become denser with wiring and electronic devices, buildings will become more like large-scale printed circuit boards than dumb wallboard. (1999, p. 65)

What we see – and will see more of – in Euro-American societies, therefore, is a complex ecology of software, 'wideware' (Clark, 2000), which will increasingly inhabit every nook and cranny of human life. Software as a kind of thinking grass. Latour and Hernant's (1997) Paris, made up of a vast panorama of signs, directions and objects, will be paralleled in the virtual realm, producing a more effective (because polycentric, multivocal and heterogeneous) assemblage of control, whole species of normativity interacting in ways as yet to be determined. But maybe this answer is a bit too grand and we need to turn to another answer instead, one that is less sweeping, more mundane. After all, to begin with, there is plenty of evidence that software does not always work that well (for example in surveillance cameras) and that much of the writing that takes place in the world will continue to be paper-based, not electronically coded (Sellen and Harper, 2002). Then most software is still initially written by human hands (McCullough, 1998). It arises from the striking of keyboards, the clicking of the mouse, the shifting of notes around on a desktop and the consulting of manuals to find various standards and classifications (Bowker and Star, 1999, p. 39). Software still flows from the interface between body and object – even though that interface may be what Knorr-Cetina (2001) calls 'post-social', resting on the fact that 'individuals in some areas relate to "some" objects not only as "doers" and "accomplishers" of things within an agency framework but as experiencing, feeling, reflexive and remembering beings – as bearers of the sort of experiences we tend to reserve for the sphere of inter-subjective relationships'.

And, finally, software is often written with what can only be described as 'human' concerns in mind. In particular, it is one of the key moments of 'virtualism' (Carrier and Miller, 1998), the proliferation of theories about the world which prompt efforts to make the world conform, rather than vice versa. Examples of such virtual moments abound in code, from the mobilization of biological analogies discussed above, through various exchanges with complexity theory (Thrift, 1999b), through numerous philosophical theories – from Heidegger (Winograd and Flores, 1987) to Bakhtin (Sparacino et al., 2000), to the use of Kevin Lynch's (1966) model of the city as a means to imagine the internal coherence of software (Dieburger and Frank, 1998). And 'human' concerns echo through software in other ways too. So the production of software is increasingly bound up with and incorporates an ethnographic mode of enquiry, whether that be work on more social interfaces, on CSCW, or on the psychology of artificial social actors (Dryer et al., 1999). In other words, an ethnographic model of human encounters defines the horizon of certain forms of software.

So, maybe instead of understanding software as writing the next chapter in the evolution of humanity (Leroi-Gourhan, 1993; Lévy, 1998) we can see it as a more practical extension of human spaces, consisting of three different processes. The first is a simple extension of textuality. So, for example, modern western cities are effectively intertextual: from the myriad forms issued by bureaucracies, through the book, the newspaper and the webpage, through the checkout till roll and the credit card slip, to the letter, the e-mail and the text message, the city is one vast intertext. Cities are quite literally written and software is the latest expression of this cursive passion. Second, software is a part of the paraphernalia of everyday urban life revealed by the turn to the non-cognitive. It is one of those little but large technologies that are crucial to the bonding of urban time and space, technologies like the pencil (Petroski, 1992) and the screw (Rybczynski, 2000), which in their very ubiquity go largely unnoticed. We can think of software in this way – as a holding together accomplished through the medium of performative writing. Third, we can see software as a means of transport, as an intermediary passing information from one place to another so efficiently that the journey appears effortless, movement without friction (Latour, 1997) – as a running description of the present.

Whatever the answer (and our inclination is to choose both at once), it seems certain that we can no longer think of city spaces in the old, time-honoured ways. Software challenges us to think 'beyond living', 'to mime an absent origin, "life"' (Doyle, 1997, p. 132). Software challenges us to reinscribe what we comprehend as inscription. And, most importantly, software challenges us to understand new forms of technological politics and new practices of political invention, legibility and intervention that we are only just beginning to comprehend as political at all: politics of standards, classifications, metrics, and readings (Barry, 2001). These orderings – written down as software – are becoming one of the chief ways of animating space. They should not be allowed to take us unaware. One of the more pressing contemporary political tasks must therefore be to design friendlier 'information ecologies' (Nardi and O'Day, 1999) which, because of their diversity of outcome, will allow us to shape overlapping spatial mosaics in which effective participation is still possible and still necessary. Automatic can be for the people.

9

Closer to the Machine? Intelligent Environments, New Forms of Possession and the Rise of the Supertoy

Introduction: the changing form of the commodity

In 2001, Steven Spielberg's new film *AI* finally appeared. The film is based on a short story by Brian Aldiss first published in 1969 – 'Supertoys last all summer long' – which he and Stanley Kubrick struggled unsuccessfully to make into a movie in the 1980s. It conjures up a world in which toys, powered by complex software, have all but come alive, creating all kinds of keen ethical dilemmas. The story was set well into the future. Yet perhaps – or so I will argue – that future is about to covertly arrive. For this chapter is concerned with the way in which commodities are coming 'alive' as we move towards greater technological performativity within the framework of 'everywhere' or 'ubiquitous' computing. And as these commodities begin to consider the world, so they are also posing questions for us about what it is to be 'human'.

Yet this change is still – even now – too often regarded as reducible to something else. So, for example, each of the four approaches to consumption which give commodities an active role in the world ultimately draw back from investing them with their own distinctive qualities. Whether commodities are repositories of cultural meaning, to be interpreted in some other way, or elements of actor networks engaged in the business of material semiotics, or sedimented biographies built up from a lifetime of exchange, or momentary presences in subliminal time and space, they are rarely, if ever, considered as having their own distinctive performative capabilities. Yet increasingly, as commodities are being loaded up with software, that is what is happening (Thrift and French, 2002). And what is interesting is how many of the most successful of these new 'live' commodities are proving to be toys.

For a long time, it has been a dream of the information technology industry to produce new kinds of heavily mechanized and highly performative space, 'intelligent environments' in which the boundaries of human and inhuman could be redescribed – and all kinds of new opportunities for profit could be grasped. In this chapter, I want to argue that the first emissaries of these kinds of space are now starting to be produced but, because they come in the mundane form of toys, their importance has not been recognized. In turn, I also want to argue that these toys also presage new means of configuring the user, to use Woolgar's (1991) by now famous phrase, so that they will fit into a world in which intelligent environments are the norm. Children who play with these toys will become adults who are practised in these new environments (Nadesan, 2002; John, 1999). In time, then, we might well have to ask 'Who is playing with whom?' as these toys begin to configure their users as appropriate subjects to deal with the new spatial order.

In order to address the issues that arise from such developments, this chapter makes an argument in three sections. The first section consists of an account of the gradual assembly of interlocking spaces of interactivity to the point where intelligent environments are becoming a probability rather than a possibility. Then, in the second section, I hope to show that the course of interactivity has nearly always been prefigured by the history of toys. And now toys have become one of the chief testbeds for the new ways of doing things. In turn, the problems that have been thrown up – how to emulate emotions, how to produce expressive effects like humour, how to produce contextual awareness, how to build character, how to synthesize perception, how to stimulate particular kinds of pleasure, how to become animal – have made toys not just into a profitable commodity in themselves but also into one of the means by which innovations arising from the communications, information technology and defence industries can get a first airing. In the third and concluding section, I will then suggest that the ethical outcomes of these developments are complex. It is easy to produce a condemnatory set of judgements, but these judgements need to be tempered by the knowledge that these new toys and the everyday economies that they represent may be able to exceed the parameters set for them.

1. The growth of intelligent environments

Once upon a time, interactivity with machines was a pipedream. It was part of either a deeply threatening future in which humans were taken over by machines or a transcendent future in which humanity disappeared into a shimmering web of thought. But now parts of that science fiction future are starting to come about as a result of the history of the intertwining of the communications, information technology and defence industries. Six closely linked developments are of particular note, each of which is directly operating on the fabric of space in order to produce environments that are full of machinic intelligence. First, the geography of computing is changing shape. From being centred and stable entities located at definite sites, through the greater use of wireless and various peer-to-peer set-ups, computing is now moving out to inhabit all parts of the environment. Accordingly, users are able to be much more mobile. Computing can then become a part of everyday environments since there are no longer any restrictions on where computing devices can be located. This is the advent of 'ubiquitous', 'pervasive' or 'everywhere' computing. Second, it follows that computing will become more and more context-dependent. This means that devices will, with the addition of small GPS transceivers or at least radiofrequency identifier tags (RFIDs), become more location-aware, knowing where they are in relation to users and other devices, and so able to interact and communicate with and adapt to users and other devices. In other words, computing – understood as a network of devices – will increasingly be able to be appropriate to the situation (Lieberman and Selker, 2000). Third, the time of computing is changing. Through open Internet access, the computing environment will be able to run continuously. It will always be on hand to interact with users and will not need to be turned on and opened up prior to use: 'being always on, the net will be woven with the fabric of our lives' (*New Scientist*, 21 October 2000, p. 34). Computing will become a constant 'cloud' of activity. Fourth, computing devices are changing. Through the advent of 'soft' computing based on algorithms that have a capacity to 'learn' and more user-friendly interfaces, computing is becoming adapted to and modulated by the user. It will increasingly second guess the user, becoming a part of how they decide to decide. Fifth, computing will be seen no longer as a primary task but as a subsidiary part of many different practices, just as many mundane tools are. Increasingly, the assumption is that the user will be doing something else at the same time as doing computing. In other words, the computing device is there to augment rather than monopolize attention, as in the case of wearables:

> Rather than attempting to emulate human intelligence in the computer, as is a common goal of research in artificial intelligence (AI), the goal of wearable computing is to produce a synergistic combination of human and machine, in which the human performs tasks that it is better at, while the computer performs tasks that it is better at. Over an extended period of time, the wearable computer begins to function as a true extension of the mind and body, and no longer feels as if it is a separate entity. In fact, the user will adapt to the apparatus in the same way that we adapt to shoes and clothing to such a degree that being without them most of us would feel extremely uncomfortable. (Mann, 1998, p. 7)

Sixth, computing is becoming more and more connective. The purpose of computing devices is increasingly to communicate not just with the user (through better interfaces like wearables) but with other devices. Thus computing becomes a communication system in which more and more of the communication will be interdevice.

The genesis of intelligent environments is being hastened by the production of third-generation wireless transceiver systems like Bluetooth which will allow detailed and fast interaction and by new interfaces using embodied conversational agents that are both richer and more specific in their operation. So users will increasingly be encapsulated in layer upon layer of more and more active computing power, able to mobilize their own 'personal area networks' via a 'roaming Internet'. Of course, such a move to ubiquitous computing is not without its problems, especially those of privacy and control. The result is that the balance of thinking in the field is now moving towards a notion of loosely networked 'local intelligence' – personal area networks that will allow human beings to choose particular levels of interactivity but still surround them with a kind of penumbra of computing power (Pentland, 2000; Thrift and French, 2002).

To summarize, computing is increasingly flowing out into the environment and, as a result, we are beginning to be able to see the advent of 'intelligent environments' in which the surfaces and textures of everyday life are boosted by all kinds of software-driven devices (Thrift and French, 2002). Projects like MIT Media Laboratory's 'Things That Think', Xerox PARC's 'Ubiquitous Computing', Motorola's 'Digital DNA' and MIT Artificial Intelligence Laboratory's 'Project Oxygen' have hastened a future in which spaces will become 'smart', 'embedding the means to solve problems in the things around us' (Gershenfeld, 1999, p. 13). And, in time, almost every object which makes up these increasingly performative spaces may well have some computing capability. For example, just so far, the new kind of computing capacity has been built not only into electric goods like televisions and fridges or platforms like automobiles but also into textiles (and so into clothing), into everyday domestic furniture like tables, couches and beds, into the ground in the shape of carpets and shoes, and so on (see any issue of journals like *Personal Technologies*).

Some of the luminaries in the field, such as Rodney Brooks (1991; 1999; 2002a; 2002b), are trying to go further than this and populate spaces with small autonomously acting 'robots' that will scurry around homes and offices and gardens carrying out basic, specialized tasks. For Brooks, 'machines are now becoming autonomous in the areas that bypassed them in the industrial revolution. Machines are starting to make the judgements that have kept people in the loop for the last two hundred years' (2002a, p. 11). Such vaulting ambitions are premised on the rise of behaviour-based and evolutionary robotics which use biological analogies to produce agents that interact adaptively with the environment, usually calling either on one of the variants of connectionism based on neural networks or on various forms of embodied cognition to produce more and more complex ethologies (see Holland and McFarland, 2001; Menzel and D'Aluisio, 2001; Nolfi and Floreano, 2002; Dautenhahn and Nehaniv, 2002; Dautenhahn et al., 2002).

What these developments presage is a considerable change in the nature of *space*. Spaces will be loaded up with more information, they will become more connected, they will be faster to react and they will be better able to read the concerns of their users. Spaces, in other words, will become much more performative, geared to make more of each encounter. In turn, these performative spaces will increasingly assume the presence of a certain kind of 'switched-on' user who comes equipped to interact. Users will be expected to develop new affordances – practical skill sets that incorporate expectations of how space turns up.

In the wake of these changes we can therefore expect to see some changes in current notions of distance, space and time, new presentifications and just-pasts which would not formerly have been possible, new textures and horizons occasioned by the presence of interactive spatial and temporal objects and events:

> If the computational system is invisible as well as extensive, it becomes hard to know what is controlling what, what is connected to what, where information is flowing, how it is being used, what is broken (vs. in action (including simply walking into a room)). (Weiser et al., 1999, p. 3)

Such changes can be interpreted as a bid to produce a new kind of phenomenality, a bid which bears some remarkable parallels with the attempts by the late Francisco Varela and other colleagues (see Petitot et al., 1999) to produce a realist interpretation of Husserlian transcendentalism. Varela wanted to naturalize Husserlian phenomenology, thereby producing a phenomenology 'made continuous with the properties admitted by the natural sciences' (Goffey, 2002). Such a project tries to show how:

> The morphologically emergent 'macro' level gets organised essentially around the singularities – qualitative discontinuities – of the underlying 'micro' processes, singularities which are phenomenologically dominant and structure the appearing. They therefore demonstrate that what Husserl called 'inexact morphological essences', essences foreign to fundamental classical physics, are indeed answerable to a physical account, provided that we rely upon the qualitative macrophysics of complex systems (and no longer upon the microphysics of elementary systems). (Roy et al., 1999, pp. 2, 55)

Central to this new kind of phenomenality is the redefinition of what counts as 'consciousness', as a result of the boosts given to 'human' communicative capacities, ability to memorize, and collaborative reach by the advent of intelligent environments. This redefinition simultaneously produces a change in the nature of what and how things are perceived. That is, the potentiality for appearing is fundamentally changed. A new 'informational ecology' (Nardi and O'Day, 1999) is produced based on a new set of key affordances which can be seen as a kind of evolutionary adaptation – and 'as a result of [this] evolutionary adaptation, the perception and action of a living organism are pretuned to the qualitative stature of its *Umwelt*: forms, qualities (colours, textures), and so on. These ... become for it intrinsically significant' (Roy et al., 1999, p. 69).

2. New per-forms of the commodity

What is striking is how many of the new textures and horizons that are now beginning to show up as a result of the possibilities offered by heightened interactivity are first appearing (other than as exotic one-off testbeds or very expensive high-end consumer goods) in the shape of toys. The centrality of toys should perhaps come as no surprise. Toys have a long history dating from much earlier than the 3000-year-old Egyptian tiger with hinged joints that could be pulled by a string (Fleming, 1996) or the toy animals found in graves from the Western Indian Harappa culture dated to 2800 BCE (Cross, 1997). However, in the West, modern toys came into existence in the period between 1550 and 1770 as a result of the concatenation of three processes.

One was the development of mass production which allowed toys to be constructed quickly and easily in bulk. The second was the growth of new notions of childhood and especially the growth of new child-rearing modes based upon solitariness. Increasingly children spent time by themselves in an enforced solitariness with their main companions being toys. 'Toys have always been primarily the models of that solitariness on which modern civilization relies. It needs people who can reliably go about relatively solitary tasks and pursue them to some successful end' (Sutton-Smith, 1986, p. 37). Then a third process has been toys' increasing involvement in a world of mechanism. Many toys became little machines, sometimes inseparable from automatons in their repetitive adroitness (Stafford, 1994; Stafford and Terpak, 2001). Indeed, in at least some senses 'the modern toy may be seen as a symbolic legatee of [the] first optimistic scientific view of the planned universe. In its smallness, the toy, along with other miniatures, represented a departure from the thousands of years in which the major "science" for the people of the world was the science of largeness, of the macrocosm, of astronomy' (Sutton-Smith, 1986, p. 59). Still, toys did not become a general feature of western childhood until the end of the nineteenth century. Before that time, most.

> children were obliged to work, helping parents with baby siblings and doing the housework that mothers had no time for. Children did have their special times of play, and made toys and dolls from rocks, sticks, straw and discarded crockery and cloth. But seldom did play involve a special space and time set aside for the free development of the child's imagination. And parents rarely gave specially made toys to their children. Showering children with play things on birthdays and Christmas is a recent custom. (Cross, 1997, p. 13)

However, since the end of the nineteenth century, three further processes have combined to produce the 'overstuffed toy box' (Cross, 1997) found in so many houses today. First, and most obviously, in the face of increasing affluence, toys have gone through a long history of sophisticated commodification, culminating in the bulk of their production being concentrated today in the hands of a few multinational corporations, and consisting of global commodity chains linking global toy corporations like Hasbro (founded in 1923) and Mattel (founded in 1945) with mass toy retailers like Toys 'R' Us (founded in 1957) through manufacturing bases which are now mainly concentrated in southern China (Thrift and Olds, 1996).

However, the chief expansion of commodified toys dates in particular from their association with the mass media. In the UK, this expansion dated from the 'Toytown' BBC radio series broadcast in the 1920s based around a series of small wooden toys from which a whole stylized town could be built up. The same link was made in the United States through the launch of a Shirley Temple doll in the 1930s which was an instant commercial success. But it was in the 1950s, with the institution of mass television advertising for children's toys, that the link between toys and mass media was finalized, so that 'today it seems impossible to conceive of the toy industry as being anything other than dependent on a popular culture which shapes and structures the meanings carried by toys' (Fleming, 1996, p. 40).

Second, toys have increasingly changed from solitary objects whose use was policed by adults to assemblages, linked elements of little fantasy worlds arising from media narrative and total marketing, in which adults have no place. Toys are now designed to invite re-enactment of identifiable complexes of characters and settings which can be sold as a package, either as a whole or through the joys of collecting. Most of their characters and settings are highly mediatized. From Star Wars figures to Transformers, from My Little Pony to Barbie, the worlds on offer are a series of micro-ontologies which children can link into. This kind of complex linkage between fantasy and practice was finally cemented by the appearance of the 'programme-length commercial' in the 1980s, the half-hour cartoon show that could be used to keep a product line constantly in front of children, and to develop new characters and settings on a continuous basis.

Then, third, toys have increasingly been conceived as existing within a realm of play. John Locke (1968/1693) is usually given credit for introducing the notion that toys were not merely baubles but should be given to children for didactic purposes. Now a whole realm of expertise has come into existence based around the cultural field of play: 'when children work on understanding the world around them it may be adults who see "play"' (Sutton-Smith, 1986, p. 11). This field of play has an uneasy relationship with commodification. For it is the case that toys are usually our first experience of learning about the commodity world. And as commodities – and toys – are made more technological, so this socialization experience of playing with them may well be becoming more crucial: toys are an early dip in the bath of commodified technology. At the same time, for many writers toys are supportive of a process of 'constructive elaboration' of the world, providing an opening on to otherness through processes of mimicry, vertigo (or giddiness), competition, and chance (Caillois, 1962). Toys are open to multiple usages, in part because of their association with play, and with other expressive orders. This is toys' paradoxical function: both as objects which matter to children and as consumerist things.

Whatever the case, what is striking is how many of the information technology innovations of contemporary capitalism and the military complex are being put into toys. But perhaps the centrality of toys should come as no surprise. To begin with, toys have become a kind of gateway to the interactive world:

> when the world of computers intersected with the world of toys, the concept of interactivity, of two-way communication between toy and child, opened up a new universe of possibilities. Now toys could listen to children, observing patiently as they worked at various spelling exercises or games, and read to them personally, like a watchful parent, constantly assessing performance, gently extending the boundaries of the child's knowledge. This reactive intelligence produces something greater than the sum of its parts: the child often feels more engaged and so works – or plays – harder. (Pesce, 2000, pp. 19–20)

Then, the toy-producing companies like Lego, Mattel, Hasbro, Kenner, Tomy and Bandai have become huge multinational corporations with profits to invest in new and ever more desperately imaginative products. And, finally, there is the massive growth in the buying power of many children, as well as some parents (Gunter and Furnham, 1998). Children of all ages have become a source of purchasing power in their own right. For example, one marketing consultancy reckoned that there had been a 38 per cent rise in pocket money for children aged 5 to 16 between 1993 and 1998 in both the US and the UK (Russell and Tyler, 2002).

In what follows, I will consider a number of the interactive toys that these corporations have produced in the last few years. These toys have varied both in complexity and in the age of the children they have appealed to, but they all have one thing in common: the ability to physically interact in a reactive fashion, rather than simply producing 'mechanical' responses, so that they may be regarded as *adaptive* in at least certain registers. This decision necessarily debars certain kinds of toy. It debars talking dolls, for example, like SCAMP (Self Contained Automotive Mobile with Personality), a 16 inch high furry puppy first produced in the 1980s which came complete with 300 different whines, bleeps and grunts and was programmed to have 12 different 'moods'. SCAMP, one of the first in a long line of small electronic dolls, was not interactive, since it had no learning capacity but simply worked to a series of probable behaviours. Similarly, for the moment at least, it debars the interactive entertainment robots that have started to appear on the market, like Sony's AIBO dog which was released in 1999 (and both upgraded and brought down in price in 2000) or the SDR biped series (a 60 centimetre tall robot which can dance and sing and which is expected to be in commercial production by the end of 2002). These robots are not really toys, given their cost and complexity. Rather, they are something between a personal organizer, an adult companion and a status symbol. (For example, AIBO now comes with personality enhancement software called 'life', memory software which tracks how the robot has 'matured', as well as the ability to read out e-mails, connect to computers, and so on; while the new SDR-4X adds to AIBO technology facial recognition, continuous speech recognition and short- and long-term memory. But, significantly, the costs of these robots are expected to fall, and Sony apparently has plans to market a budget version of AIBO retailing at $200–300 which will be targeted at children and teenagers, perhaps stimulated by the release of a similar but much cheaper AIBO-like product by Hasbro in 2002 called I-Cybie.) It debars purely web-based toys like the extraordinarily successful Neopets which have only very limited physical presence (although, interestingly, physical doubles of these toys are now being produced). And, last of all, it debars hand-held games systems like Nintendo's Game Boy which since its release in 1989 has sold 110 million units worldwide, because they tend to work to set scripts and so have little adaptive capacity.

One objection that can be made to the choice of adaptive toys I make below is that they are in some sense playthings of the child elite, selling to just a few well-off households. Some of these toys are undoubtedly expensive (and in the case of My Real Baby conceivably too expensive to become a commercial success), but it is important to point out that other toys that I will consider are not. Many of the expensive toys (for example, Lego Mindstorms) have sold well, whilst other cheaper toys (for example, Furby and Micropets) have been mass market successes.

Toys of tomorrow?

It is generally agreed that the first commercially successful interactive toy was the Tamagotchi, developed by the Japanese company Bandai in the mid 1990s. A virtual pet in cheap wristwatch form, consisting of a small LCD screen and three buttons, its most important feature was that as it 'grew up' it changed its behaviour patterns. In other words, it was a primitive reactive intelligence which required feeding and nurturing, accomplished by pressing the right buttons. The Tamagotchi was developed into a line of similar kinds of toys like Giga Pets.

But the true breakthrough was to be the Furby, a virtual electronic pet aimed at children of four and up developed in 1998 by Tiger Toys, now a division of Hasbro, which consisted of a body, a motor, various sensors and a large amount of software. The Furby could react to its environment. It could detect light and dark. It could hear. It could detect pressure and tilt. It could talk using a stripped-down syntax redolent of a child. It had an expressive face. And it had needs – to be fed, in particular. Further, the Furby could learn – through a basic memory of its interactions, through the use of a wider vocabulary, and by communicating with other Furbies through an infrared transceiver. Thus the Furby could interact with its owner. In turn, Furbies seem to have occupied a new category location in children's minds – conscious but not 'alive' – as Sherry Turkle's long-standing research on computers and children (e.g. Turkle, 1996) shows:

> a page on Turkle's website at MIT issues a call for children who own virtual pets. Turkle is collecting stories from them, gathering their experiences, and what she is learning is as startling as anything she's discovered before. These children are creating a third answer to the question 'is it animate or inanimate?' It seems that the distinction between living and not living, which used to be so very clear, has become muddy. And as these children learn and play within the world, this conclusion seems to persist. They don't want to class the Furby as an inanimate object, even though it is a machine, because it shows some of the qualities of fully animate beings. So rather than throw Furby into one category or another, these child-philosophers have opted for a novel approach: they're concocting a new definition for partially animate objects. Certainly not human, or even animalistic, but animate just the same. This is where Furby differs from all the toys that have preceded it. None of them forced a new definition of the categories we use to make sense of and give order to the world. The Furby is not one exception, but rather a new class of toy, which, by virtue of its capacity to mimic human relationships, has created a new standard by which we distinguish the living from the dead, human from machine. (Pesce, 2000, p. 68)

In other words, as Turkle puts it, children of the late 1990s were distinguished from the children of 10 years or so earlier in that:

> For today's children, the boundary between people and machines is intact. But what they see across the boundary has changed dramatically. Now children are comfortable with the idea that inanimate objects both think and have a personality. But they no longer worry if the machine is alive. They know it is not. The issue of aliveness has moved into the background as though it is settled. But the notion of the machine has been expanded to include having a psychology. (1996, p. 83)

Furby has been followed by a family of similar interactive toys, such as Tiger Toys' Poo-Chi, a robotic puppy, and an interactive Star Wars Yoda. Both of these toys incorporate several kinds of sensors and the ability to learn and display 'emotions'. Both of these toys can also interact with other such toys through infrared.

The third truly interactive supertoy consists of communities of small toys which can interact together in various ways, gradually adapting to both each other and the environment around them. The first of these kinds of toys seems to have been Chibibotto, a collection of six differently coloured toys manufactured by Tiger Toys and Bandai. But the most successful application has been Tomy's Micropets, a collection of 4 centimetre tall characters made for three-year-olds and up which first appeared in 2002. As well as being able to interact with each other, these toys also have voice recognition and can therefore follow simple commands. Each of the toys represents a particular character and is meant to have its own idiosyncrasies. They clearly meld together adaptivity with insertion into a narrative and are intended to be highly collectible.

The fourth truly interactive supertoy is the doll My Real Baby, launched in 2000 and aimed at children of age three and up. This 3.1 pounds doll was developed as a collaboration between Hasbro and a company called iRobot, which was founded in the 1990s by the already mentioned AI researcher Rodney Brooks, Director of the MIT Artificial Intelligence Laboratory, and two ex-MIT AI researchers, Colin Angle and Helen Greiner (Brooks, 1991). My Real Baby uses a combination of a web of sensors and a 'behaviour language system' to produce hundreds of facial expressions, numerous combinations of sounds and words, and the ability to react to touch, motion, and light. The doll is therefore highly expressive, able to develop behaviour over time, moving from a six-month-old's to a two-year-old's language capacity, and therefore able to participate in numerous play sequences. In effect, My Real Baby is a mass market robot, built on the non-representational principles for which Brooks has become famous, which stress learning through simple interaction with the environment rather than centralized cognition (see Brooks, 1991; 2002a; 2002b). But, though My Real Baby sold relatively well, it was probably too complex for the market:

> The television ads could not get across the excitement of the doll that everyone who bought one reported. There were too many new features, and the

advertisements were too busy with details, getting beat out by simpler dolls with only one trick up their sleeves. We sold more robot dolls than any other robot in existence, but it was not quite the megahit we had been hoping for. (Brooks, 2002a, p. 113)

However, the principles of My Real Baby are informing a whole generation of similar dolls now coming to market, such as a new walking dinosaur planned to launch in mid 2002.

The fifth truly interactive supertoy is a generative biomechanical robot called the BIO Bug (BIO: biomechanical integrated organisms), based on biomechanical machines designed by Mark Tilden of the Los Alamos National Laboratory. Introduced in late 2001 by Hasbro, the BIO Bug's interactivity is based on a neurogenic or neuromorphic chip which is, unusually, a low-power analogue chip built on biological principles. It is able, because of recent technological advances in biomechanics, to be much more responsive to its environment than a similar digital chip. At the heart of the BIO Bug is a central pattern generator, a kind of flexible pacemaker that allows continuous feedback between the movements of the bug and its environment (and other BIO Bugs). Each of the four colour-coded bugs is loaded with specific characteristics, for example greater ability to operate over rough terrain or quicker movement over smooth surfaces. The bugs can also be controlled by a wrist transmitter which acts as a homing beacon and as a 'feeding station'. A toy like the BIO Bug symbolizes an entirely different approach to interactivity which

may be the only way of achieving the goal that has eluded engineers trying to build efficient 'adaptive intelligent' control systems for years. Neuromorphic chips are going to have enormous implications, especially in applications where compactness and power consumption are at a premium – as, say, for replacement parts within the human body. This is slowly being recognised ... After genomics, perhaps the next stock market buzz will be neuromorphics. (*The Economist*, 6 January 2001, p. 6)

The sixth truly important interactive toy has been Lego Mindstorms, launched in 1998. Mindstorms is an interactive development of Lego produced in collaboration with a group of researchers at MIT for children of eight years old upwards. A bestseller even at a comparatively high price, Lego Mindstorms is essentially programmable Lego. It uses a simple programming language, Logo, to build Lego robots. A program from the computer is downloaded into the Lego robot that has been created. In turn, it is possible to learn by playful exploration, for three reasons. First, the system is continually adding capacity. For example, new sensors are constantly being added (e.g. touch, vision, temperature, rotation) and new software developer kits are constantly being offered. Thus, the most recent addition to Mindstorms has been a small 30 frames per second video camera which allows robots to be programmed to react to changes in light, motion and colour, to record videos, and to act as an intruder alarm. In other words this toy, like the other interactive toys and many other machinic products, is designed to be unfinished. It is more of a process than a product (Bolter and Grusin, 1999). Second, different lines are constantly being developed (e.g. robots with distinctive interchangeable personalities). Third, there is a series of websites around the world (now called the Lego community) at which new hardware and software options are being developed by consumers, rather like open-source software, often through competitive leagues.

The seventh interactive toy was unveiled by the Japanese toymaker Takara in 2002. It is called Bowlingual and, as its name implies, it is a dog translator. It consists of a wireless microphone which is attached to the dog's collar and a small terminal which matches the dog's various barks to a range of expressions: boredom, happiness, frustration, sadness, and so on. It can also be used to produce a record of the dog's 'emotional' day, so that owners can tell how their dog has been whilst they have been away. What is fascinating about this toy is not that it genuinely translates what a dog's expressive state is but that it adds into the world another informational apprehension of dogs, another canine texture.

What is clear is that these are just the beginning of a range of possibilities for interactive 'smarter' and more open toys. New kinds of sensor, affective computing, and greater opportunities to produce expression will lead towards a generation of 'supertoys'. MIT Media Lab's 'Toys of Tomorrow' project, set up in 1998, shows the likely direction of some of these new toys. They may include new kinds of musical toys; storytelling toys that will 'ask how a child's day has gone, listen to a child's story, attentively, ask questions, or tell an older child the stories from her younger years'; toys that will interact with one another, allowing the construction of not only 'structures and mechanisms, but also behaviours and communities'; toys that will function at a distance, for example, teddy bears that can send a hug from a parent who is away from home; toys that will interact with the media, for example, 'the digital sources of cartoons will be extruded into toys'; outdoor toys, for example, 'shoes that may know more about you every day than the doctor knows once in a blue moon', that 'may teach you how to dance', that 'may nag you to take a walk', that 'may link you to your doctor, or find friends to jog with'. In other words, these toys are meant to be used to produce new kinds of play (e.g. new kinds of outdoor games), new ranges of affect (e.g. the hug of the teddy bear), new modes of learning (e.g. through new means of making music), and new toy agencies (e.g. 'toys smart enough to tell the FedEx courier where to take them. When the toy arrives, it may even tell the child the story of its journey').

In other words, toys are rapidly becoming something else: something between a lumpen object onto which all manner of fantasies and all kinds of play could be projected, and a kind of alternative life form, participating in the world on at least some terms of its own choosing. We may, in other words, be witness to a kind of evolution of the commodity which, in turn, is dependent upon an intensive reorganization of everyday spaces which will endow them with an interactive awareness.

Of course, not too much should be made of these developments: many of these toys already lie broken or neglected at the bottom of toyboxes, passed over for something new. But neither should we make too little of them, either. For they may well herald the first steps into new kinds of more performative spaces in which the play of encounter is much more highly mediated.

Conclusions: spaces that might exist

It is, of course, very easy to sound off the negatives at this point. And there quite clearly are some. First, these interactive toys can be interpreted as a new stage of commodification which will allow corporate interests to settle ever closer to our concerns, becoming a vital part of the ecology of everyday life in ways which the old ideas of hegemony simply never envisaged. The mundane actions (walking) and literatures (stories) of everyday life can become ever more closely intertwined with commercial imperatives. Further, these toys have the potential to become spies for corporations, reporting back children's preferences and inserting children into a vast auto-mated commercial feedback loop which is reproductive rather than virtual, based on spinning out new versions of the present which lead to controllable futures rather than an open present leading to unknown futures. Toys as new agents of possession.

Second, and relatedly, these toys can be interpreted as means of socializa-tion into commodification which have all kinds of malign potentials. For example, they may well increase parenting at a distance, allowing toys to take on many parenting functions and to surround children in a tailor-made but increasingly anonymous cocoon, devoid of risks. Third, such toys might cut down the ability to fantasize and play by offering preformed 'imaginative' solutions which occupy children's time to the extent that they rarely think outside the envelope of interaction and narrative that has been created. The creative accident of play is foreshortened. And, finally, as Harry Collins (e.g. Collins and Kusch, 1998) has frequently noted, we have tended to take on some machine-like characteristics: we mimic machines just as they must mimic us. It follows that if interactive toys are produced with certain machinic characteristics, children may become like them in ways which should certainly give us pause for thought. The user is configured as well as the machine.

These are all clearly risks and I do not want to minimize them: concerted political action on a series of levels will be needed to defend children from becoming computer drones whose childhood is simply stolen away (Giroux and Kline, 2002; Kline, 1993). Part of this politics must surely include invent-ing 'playthings that give children a connection to the past and a constructive, but also imaginative view of the future, and ... [encouraging] manufacturers to produce them' (Cross, 1997, p. 238). So, in this final section, I want to con-centrate on some of the more positive manifestations of the new interactive toys (and, I might add, of intelligent environments more generally). First, and most straightforwardly, these toys contain within them the potential to be reverse engineered and so changed to other uses (*The Economist*, 2 December 2000). For example, Furby and Poo-Chi have been 'retrained' by hackers, to carry out other functions from reading e-mail to scaring away burglars (one online store even sells a 'Furby upgrade kit'). Actimate's Barney (a toy dinosaur) has similarly been recoded to other uses. Instructions for performing 'vivisections' on BIO Bugs are already appearing on the web. And as more and more toys became, in effect, small multipurpose computers with a series of interesting peripherals, so this trend is likely to intensify, no matter how hard multinationals try to stop it. (Indeed, as was pointed out earlier, some corporations – like Lego with Lego Mindstorms – now effectively accommodate hackers by releasing the source code of the program, which in turn has enhanced the kit's possibilities, so driving up sales.) Second, toys can be a means of producing more, not less, expressive possibilities. Thus, the agenda of research that is going on at the MIT Media Lab and other such outlets is clearly an attempt to produce these possibilities, modelled on the many attempts to use computing in the arts and humanities. For example, take the use of computing in performance (Laurel, 1993; Sparacino et al., 2000). Expressive communication can clearly be heightened in several ways: by the design of new kinds of clothing, alive to body movement (as in the famous conductor's jacket or the new expressive footwear: Paradiso et al., 2000); by the design of new kinds of active space (as in MIT projects like dance space, designed to allow dancers to generate music and colour graphics; the networked digital circus, designed to produce new gestural languages; and the improvisational theatre space, designed to produce 'media acts' able to combine action and text in new ways); by the design of new kinds of music based on collective sound (as in projects based on fully utilizing musical instrument digital interfaces, MIDIs); and by the design of whole ensembles of activity such as attempts to grow wearable items (Sparacino et al., 2000), or more and more playfully interactive story environments (as in the MIT kids room: Pinhanez et al., 2000), or 'toys that enable children to create vast symphonies together across the globe' (Machover, 2000, p. 2) (as in the MIT toy symphony project). In each case, much more attention is being paid to affective possibilities, in line with the general growth in affective computing (Picard, 1997; 2000).

Then, third, these toys may encourage new 'thinking styles', those preferred ways of disclosing the abilities that each person has. Sternberg (1997) has considered the range of different thinking styles that people currently use to learn: monarchic, hierarchic, oligarchic, analytic and so on. It may well be that the new toys, and interactivity more generally, can both adapt to the styles of particular children in ways that mass socialization systems like education find so difficult, and even encourage new thinking styles and collective intelligences to emerge. After all, thinking is already carried out through a diverse informational ethology of devices (Nardi and O'Day, 1999) and, in certain senses, the new interactivity simply extends the range and complexity of these ethologies, both by adding in new devices and by linking up those that already exist (Papert, 2000).

And, finally, interactive toys can be used to produce new affordances. Thus, most of the interactive toys outlined in the previous section are not gender neutral. For example, while such a statement can clearly be over-drawn, a number of these toys tend to appeal to traditionally 'masculine' values like competition (Holloway and Valentine, 2000). But what is interesting is all the attempts currently being made to refigure toys like these: by producing software that appeals to modes of interaction like co-operation, contact and friendship (*New Scientist*, 25 May 2002, pp. 36–41); by in general trying to create a more inclusive computer culture through 'alternative models of software [that do not] conform to assumptions about gender that are created and reinforced by existing market pressures' (Cassell and Jenkins, 1999, p. 24); and by attempting to temper traditional male models of technological fantasy, which are overwhelmingly concerned with transcending physical limitations, through producing toys which are more flexible and interactive.

In other words, the present age – like all ages – is one which contains both threats and potentialities for how we exist. What seems certain is that we need to proliferate real but conditional choices that matter as opposed to the essentially vacuous unconditional choices that the consuming ethos continually puts in our way (Dreyfus, 1999; 2001). At this point in their development, the new interactive toys – and their accompanying spaces – can still go either way. The times are exciting, then, because at this point we can still choose quality over quantity and an ethics of emergence over a morality of control (Massumi, 2002; Thrift, 2004). We can create toys and spaces, both understood as social-relations-cum-technologies, that will provide children with the kinds of 'expressive language' (Resnick, 2000) that will allow them to play with the world in positive and creative ways – ways which are both *of* their society and also *beyond* it at the same time (Sutton-Smith, 1986). We can still convey the excitement – the force, the vitality, the pleasure – of toys by seizing the technological opportunities that are now unfolding in order to open up new spaces of play which will provide a broader range of experiences for children to coevolve.

10

Electric Animals: New Models of Everyday Life?

Introduction

Biological metaphors have circulated in society for so long now that they have gradually sunk into the undertow of conscious thought. In this chapter, I want to think about how these metaphors have taken root in the everyday life of an increasingly informational society, and how that process is currently producing new artificial ethologies in which the biological and informational feed off each other and create new hybrids which demonstrate a certain kind of 'animality'.

My interest in this area has been stimulated by three different but related impulses. One of these impulses is a general dissatisfaction with the literature on everyday life. My concern is that it does not take in recent technological developments in any meaningful way, and indeed in some senses actively resists them by concentrating on conventional structures and sites of communication. In particular, its emphasis on a kind of proto-authenticity – as found, for example, in the stress on 'evasive everydayness' (Morris, 1998), or the renewed attention to rhythm as a practice of feeling right with world, taken from the historically specific accounts of authors like Bachelard, de Certeau and Lefebvre – seems to me to express a yearning for a romantic holism that it has taken a long time to unlearn. The second impulse has been born out of a general interest in the effectivities of software (Thrift, 2003b; Thrift and French, 2002). I believe that software constitutes a new actor in the world: as a kind of mechanical writing it is gradually producing a whole new informational ecology that is forming a dense undergrowth of muted but potent cause and effect, which is present in the background of most events and which, because of its increasing extent and almost baroque complexity, is producing all kinds of large emergences and small hauntings, different densities and queer intensities, whose exact origins we can no longer trace. The third impulse is practical. I have been taken by the degree to which since the 1970s the writers of software have increasingly drawn on biological models more or less exactly based on biological metaphors – genetic algorithms, artificial ethologies, and other forms of biomimicry – which express solutions to problems only faintly perceived. In particular, I have been taken by the desire to build electric animals for reasons which do not seem clear to either their inventors or their users. In other words, biological metaphors, having become firmly entangled with computer programs and lines of code, are producing an afterlife of 'artificial organisms' which seem set fair to become companions to everyday practice in much the same way as pets now do.

This chapter is a first exploration of this terrain and it can therefore hardly claim to be definitive. But I hope that by its end I will have been able to achieve the following. First, I hope to have begun to show how software produces an intensely theoretical underlay to the practices of everyday life. Carrier and Miller (1998) have termed 'virtualism' the process whereby in contemporary Euro-American societies theories have gradually changed the world to fit to their image, and I agree with this prognosis. Second, I hope to show that the desire to build software-driven entities like electric animals is more than just a bit of fun but reflects the working out in practice of these essentially theoretical dilemmas about what it means to be human and non-human, living and non-living, cultural and natural, which have been a constant of writings on both animals and machines. Third, I hope to briefly demonstrate that such projects are at least an indication of new disciplinary models and the kind of everyday life that is therefore likely to arise in the future.

The layout of the chapter is in three main sections which correspond to these three hopes. Thus, the first section considers the way in which software is producing a new layer of causality in the world which by its very nature is modest in scale but adds up to something more. Then the second section is concerned with how software has allowed new kinds of artificial nature to be built, and especially electric 'animals'. The final section then considers some of the dilemmas that have arisen or will arise by reference to the world of pets. Some brief conclusions round the chapter off. Here, I begin to discuss how new kinds of disciplinarity are becoming possible.

A new underlay to everyday life

As a term in general use, 'software' dates only from the 1950s. Its genesis was, of course, bound up with the invention of the first electronic computers and, more particularly, the first use of these computers for business applications in the late 1950s, a development which, in turn, led to the growth of companies specializing in the supply of software (Hayles, 2002). At the time, it referred to just a few lines of code that acted as a bridge between input and output. But, over the last 20 years in particular, software has grown from a small thicket of mechanical writing to a forest covering much of the globe in a profusion of over 200 different languages which now run all manner of everyday devices, from electric toothbrushes to cars (Thrift and French, 2002).

Almost since its inception, the biological and the informational have been intertwined in software. Right at the birth of the modern computer, the new machines were framed in biological terms. For example, from the 1940s John von Neumann had been interested in the connections between computational logic and biology. The classic *First Report on the EDVAC* (von Neumann, 1945) likened electronic circuits to neurons and the input and output part of the design to organs (Ward, 1999). Since those early days, biological metaphors have, if anything, become more prevalent in the world of software and computation. In some senses, this prevalence should not be thought of as surprising. After all, many early cybernetic and systems theory metaphors were in part drawn from reductive notions of the workings of the biological domain, and one might argue, as has Sedgwick (2003, p. 105), that the problem was that the 'actual computational muscle' was not as yet available to operationalize them. And biology itself has seen a long-drawn-out war between those who believe that the biological domain can be reduced to a set of computations and those for whom the organism cannot be reduced to the sum of its parts. For the former group of biologists, at least, cybernetic models were simply a natural extension of machinic thinking which had clear and obvious antecedents in the nineteenth century (but might even be traced further back to the Cartesian separation of man from machine-like animals). This kind of thinking finds its latest incarnation in a 'predictive biology' which hopes to model the behaviour of individual cells (and then tissues, organs, and even organisms) in computers.

Thus, software writers' initial flirtations with the biological may be seen as nothing more than business as usual but with a slightly more exotic tinge. But, at the same time, these flirtations were also expressing a need for something more. As software became more complex, so reductive models became increasingly inappropriate. Software more and more resembled a kind of ecosystem in which thickets of new code surrounded stands of legacy code which often stayed unchanged through many versions of a package. And as the sheer length of code became a problem in its own right, so all kinds of unexpected interactions and hidden errors came into play. The constant tinkering of numerous programmers started to produce programs large enough and complex enough to make it possible to regard programs as forming their own ecologies, complete with various niches and evolutionary tendencies. The result was that programs have increasingly come to be framed as environments in their own right, motivated by quasi-biological principles. Interestingly, such descriptions are used both by those only interested in programs as manifestations of narrow technique and by those who argue that programs occupy the realm of something more. For example, in the latter camp Nardi and O'Day (1999) want to argue for the creation of healthy 'information ecologies' which will exhibit several biological principles: systemic interrelation, diversity, coevolution, keystone species and the importance of local habitation.

Added to this, new algorithms were introduced which were clearly modelled on biological lines. The longest-running tradition of this kind of work is to be found in the so-called genetic algorithm and the more general phenomenon of evolutionary computing (Mitchell, 1996). Though there were antecedents, it is generally agreed that genetic algorithms were invented by John Holland in the 1960s as a way of mixing natural and artificial systems (Holland, 1975). Holland introduced a population-based algorithm which ran on evolutionary lines and could therefore produce programs that were able to do massively parallel searches (in which many different possibilities are explored simultaneously), that were adaptive, and that sought out complex solutions. In evolutionary computation, the rules are typically based on an idea of natural selection with variations induced by crossover and/or mutation. 'The hoped-for emergent behaviour is the design of high-quality solutions to difficult problems and the ability to adapt these solutions in the face of a changing environment' (Mitchell, 1996, p. 4). However, evolution has not been the only biological metaphor used to motivate computer programs. Another metaphor has come from neuroscience. Connectionism, which includes such models as neural networks, consists of the writing of computer programs inspired by neural systems. In connectionism, 'the rules are typically simple "neural" thresholding, activation spreading, and strengthening or weakening of connections. The hoped-for emergent behaviour is sophisticated pattern recognition and learning' (1996, p. 4). It would be possible to go on but, hopefully, the point is made: in amongst the continual rustle of many computer programs, biological analogy now holds sway.

To summarize, on a whole series of levels, one of the most prevalent descriptions of programming environments is now a biological one. And this description operates at a number of levels: as a means of framing programs, as a means of framing wider technological systems and as a means of making assumptions about how the world turns up. Perhaps it is no surprise, then, that the next step should be made: to try to produce 'artificial life' and, in particular, artificial animality.

Electric animals

Lippitt (2000) points out that the first known usage of the term 'anthropomorphism' is dated by the *Oxford English Dictionary* to the second half of the nineteenth century. It is probably no coincidence that at much the same time the history of technology and animals begins to intertwine ever more intimately:

> As they disappeared, animals became increasingly the subjects of a nostalgic curiosity. When horse-drawn carriages gave way to steam engines, plaster horses were mounted on tramcar fronts in an effort to simulate continuity with the older animal-driven vehicles. Once considered a metonymy of nature, animals came to be seen as emblems of the new industrial environment. Animals appeared to merge with the new technological bodies replacing them. The idioms and histories of numerous technological innovations from the steam engine to quantum mechanics bear the traces of an incorporated animality. James Watt and later Henry Ford, Thomas Edison, Alexander Graham Bell, Walt Disney, and Erwin Schrödinger, among other key figures in the industrial and aesthetic shifts of the late nineteenth and early twentieth centuries, found uses for animal spirits in developing their respective machines, creating in the process a series of fantastic hybrids. Cinema, communication, transportation and electricity drew from the actual and fantastic resources of dead animals. In this manner, technology and ultimately the cinema came to determine a vast mausoleum for animal being. (2000, p. 187)

One might argue that Lippitt exaggerates in her desire to present a kind of techno-animal crypt – after all, early twenty-first century cities are still chock full of animals which are very much alive (Amin and Thrift, 2002) – but the point is still made: the cultural intersection between technology and animals has grown and continues to grow (Simondon, 1958/1989). But just as the materiality of technology has become an insistent force in the world of animals, so the materiality of animals has become an insistent force in the world of technology. There is constant traffic between the two realms to the point where technology and animality have become suspect terms, perhaps better replaced by a standard actor-network theoretic depiction of a number of hybrid networks and other forms of flow which are perennially involved in diplomatic experiments which as one outcome perennially redefine prevailing cultural definitions of 'technology' and 'animal' (Whatmore, 2002). Whatever the case, it is clear that a notion of animality is a motivating force in current information technology, as various teams of scientists and programmers vie to produce something closer to biological life than heretofore has been possible.

Perhaps the best way to attempt to begin to show this work of shuttle diplomacy is by attending to the numerous attempts to produce simulations of organic life in computers. The point I want to make here is that these programs are being used to work through what organic life might consist of. They are experiments in action which are unfortunately accompanied by a good deal of hyperbole about 'life', 'virtual organisms' and 'living, breeding software' (Ward, 1999, p. 279) which conceals their essentially primitive nature. Attempts to produce artificial life in the form of computer programs date from the 1980s when a series of biologists and programmers like Larry Ray began to produce artificial computer worlds like Tierra. These worlds were, in part, born out of a dissatisfaction with the predefined and therefore closed-system nature of genetic algorithms which meant that they had no independent ability to reproduce, so that what lives and what dies is decided externally: 'self-replication is critical to synthetic life because without it, the mechanisms of selection must also be pre-determined by the simulator. Such artificial selection can never be as creative as natural selection' (Ray, 1991, p. 372). Such worlds have undoubtedly been successful in that they exhibit certain evolutionary characteristics but they have also proved to have flaws, most notably that the organisms produced are all made up of fewer instructions than the original ancestor; the simple Tierran organisms have not been able to make themselves into larger creatures. Though there is still considerable optimism that such constraints can be overcome, other tacks seem just as productive.

Of these alternatives, the most obvious is to build artificial organisms which have genuine physical extension: artificial creatures, in other words. Currently, there are a number of interrelated approaches to this conundrum. The first of these is biomimetics. Biomimetics is a young discipline that studies models from nature and then imitates or takes inspiration from these designs and processes to solve various problems. It therefore potentially spans a vast range of different scientific areas and processes, only a few of which I will point to here: those which are most relevant to my argument. Though in the past biomimetics has tended to concentrate on areas like materials, more recently considerable effort has been invested in animal mechanics. Many animal organs would display obvious utility if they could be imitated, such as the sticking power of mussels' feet or the ability of spiders to spin immensely strong silk (Benyus, 1997). However, interest has also been shown in trying to produce programs which approximate animal brains and are therefore equipped to analyse patterns in ways which conventional programs find difficult or impossible, such as through the use of redundancy to handle or even generate side-effects, to ride unforeseeable as well as foreseeable forces. These programs may use 'tactilizing' processors which are effectively large biosensors, or optical protein processors which detect light absorption at any site and recognize a pattern from that pattern, amongst a host of similar technologies (Benyus, 1997). Biomimetic robots range widely, from robots containing sensors that mimic a particular animal body part (for example, an electric analogue of the fly's motion-sensitive compound eye or the ant's polarized light sun compass) to attempts to construct a series of rapid prototypes which allow some degree of coevolution (Holland and McFarland, 2001).

The second approach focuses on imitation. Over the last 10 years or so imitation has emerged as a topic of interest in disciplines as different as psychology, ethology, philosophy, linguistics, cognitive science, computer science, biology, anthropology and robotics (cf. Cypher, 1993; Dautenhahn and Nehaniv, 2002; Heyes and Galef, 1996; Nadel and Butterworth, 1999; Zentall, 2001; Zentall and Galef, 1988). It is no surprise that a series of attempts has therefore been made to program animal characteristics by imitation, both as a functional approach and as a topic that is interesting and valuable in its own right. Imitation has been found to be one of the principal means of social learning by animals (including human beings) and aspects of its study are clearly able to be transferred to the artificial domain, especially when this domain is thought of as more than just a simple mapping between perception and action, sending and receiving. In particular, much work now revolves around understanding imitation as a property of situated and embodied agents operating in a particular environment that includes other agents as well as other sources of dynamic change (Dourish, 2001). So far as the building of artificial animals is concerned, the impetus behind this work is clear: to be able to develop complex affective skills like facial expression.

The third approach is perhaps the most obvious: the construction of actual artificial creatures. Of course, the construction of artificial creatures is hardly a new ambition. It dates from at least the automata of the early eighteenth century. And electronic automata date from the 1940s. For example, in the 1940s and 1950s Walter (1950; 1953) built a series of artificial creatures ('simple animals') that were intended to display spontaneity, autonomy and self-regulation. Based on a combination of vacuum tubes, actuators and two sensors (light and bump) these creatures exhibited conditioned reflex learning and a wide variety of behaviours. Since that time, large numbers of attempts have been made to build such creatures by roboticists and others, culminating in the current vogue for creating artificial ethologies:

> Mobile robots have now existed for some fifty years. During that time, most robots were developed within the technical and conceptual horizons of contemporary engineering, computer science, and artificial intelligence and only a small number, for a variety of reasons, were specifically designed to resemble animals in one way or another. Now it happens to be the case that animals and mobile robots, whether animal-like or conventional, necessarily share so many features that, in many ways, all mobile robots resemble animals to some extent. On the other hand, all robots, whether animal-like or conventional, have things in common that set them apart from animals. (Holland and McFarland, 2001, p. 15)

Most particularly, animals grow and evolve and as a result have, to some degree, to be functionally adaptable. Thus, though simple mimicry may produce animal-like behaviour, behaviour which may well be impressive in its apparent faithfulness, this may simply be because the robot and animal have converged on solutions dictated by the same restricted domain. Whatever the case, it is fair to say that perhaps the largest breakthrough in building artificial creatures has been the result of taking the environment more seriously, in recognition of the fact that many animal cognitive tasks are offloaded onto the environment. The environment provides a host of peripheral devices that store, enhance, streamline and generally re-represent meaning (Dennett, 1997). This is the 'subsumption' approach favoured by Rodney Brooks (1999; 2002a; Arkin, 1998). In that approach, an intelligent system is composed of a series of behaviour-producing subsystems, each of which independently connects sensing with action to achieve some particular behavioural competence such as 'avoid', 'wander' or 'explore'. This series of very basic affects could be linked in various ways but were, above all, able to respond to many domains precisely and economically because they did not rely on internal representations but instead used the environment to do much of the 'thinking': in the by now famous phrase, 'the world is its own best model'. This behaviour-based approach has been extended in various directions, and chiefly by making each affect and the entire system subject to evolutionary selection (as represented by genetic algorithms, neural networks and the like), thus introducing a definite learning trajectory. This adaptive approach, usually known as 'evolutionary robotics', is becoming increasingly popular as a means of selecting out and reinforcing particular competencies over time and as a means of coevolving different kinds of robots (cf. Nolfi and Floreano, 2002). In turn, such developments are leading to an interest in 'collective robotics' in which populations of robots are coevolved and exhibit a distributed intelligence, rather like insect colonies (cf. Bonabeau et al., 1999).

The fourth approach is simply to graft a living part of an animal into a robot, thereby producing an organic–artificial hybrid or 'hybrot'. Given the profound difficulties of preserving function in an isolated animal body part, such hybrids remain rare. For example, the antennae from silkworm moths have been dissected out and mounted on a small robot as a means of tracking pheromones. Similarly, the nervous system of a sea lamprey has been dissected out and used to drive motors and register light sensitivity in a small robot (Holland and McFarland, 2001; Geary, 2002). More recently, a part mechanical, part biological robot has been created that operates on the basis of the neural activity of rat brain cells grown in a dish. This robot has actually gone on the market (through the Swiss robotics maker K-Team: Eisenberg, 2003). Such experiments, and others like them, might be seen as part of a more general tendency to mix the organic and the digital in ways which take advantage of animal senses that cannot as yet be engineered, or as a means of framing new 'bionic' senses, or simply as part of further enquiries into animality.

The ambition that underlies each of these kinds of approach is clear enough. Though it is always dangerous to take the writings of ideologues as typical, still their very extremity has its uses in pointing to the dreams and ambitions of those currently attempting to design electric animals. This is, I think, to design a machine nature driven by a 'biologic'. This machine nature would display at least the following characteristics: an open-ended evolution or at least emergence, a capacity for learning, and very large amounts of problem-solving power arising from large populations of agents. Why? Because

> technology keeps getting more and more complex, which means that our traditional methodologies run up against a wall much sooner than they did before: more and more often they are overstretched ... That's when we start considering the biological, which often permits us to make do with but a partial design – to be completed through evolution, learning, and other biologically-inspired techniques. (Sipper, 2002, p. 187)

Some authors want to go further, of course. For example, Brooks (2002a) envisages a world not far from now in which there is a burgeoning artificial ecology of machines. These 'machines to live with' will have a hodgepodge of capabilities and will continually scurry about, tending to human needs in all manner of ways:

> There are going to be more and more robots in our homes. Pretty soon we will stop bothering to count them. They will be a new class of entity, moving about under their own free will, doing their tasks as they decide they need to be done. The ecology of our homes will be visibly more complex than it is today. Just as our houses with their refrigerators, washing machines, dishwashers, stereos, televisions, and computers would look sort of like a house but with a whole lot of weird stuff littered about, so too will the houses a century from now look a little strange to us. (2002a, p. 126)

This may seem to be a perfect example of the kind of rampant technological hyperbole that typified the late 1990s. Except for these facts: primitive robot vacuum cleaners and lawnmowers are now on general sale in North America and Western Europe; in Japan new generations of consumer robots are becoming generally (if usually very expensively) available; a number of companies have viable plans for combining wireless sensor networks and mobile robots so that the robots will need less brain power because they will be able to share it (Butler, 2003); environmental activists are already trying to produce 'feral' packs of AIBOs and other robotic dogs which can participate in staged media events – or just play soccer (Feral Robots, 2003). In other words, wherever we look in modern Euro-American cultures we can see new surfaces and objects appearing, powered by the motivating force of software, and more and more of these surfaces and objects will be quite literally animated by software. Further, this kind of animality is becoming more and more prevalent (Lupton, 2002). It is no longer far-fetched to think that in 20 years or so small machines will scuttle about largely unremarked in Euro-American households and workplaces carrying out mundane, specialized tasks or offering all manner of solace. The question that occupies the next section of the chapter is what kind of cultural model will be drawn on to describe these new 'wild things'.

Pets and power

So how will the new machines sink into the background of everyday life? Nearly every writer seems to fall back on a quasi-biological analogy in that they agree that the sheer density of informational devices is beginning to create something like a digital ecology. But thereafter, the accounts diverge, apparently radically. One account is dystopian: consumers are drawn into a seamless world of electronic interconnectivity and speed which constitutes a kind of 'connective dementia'. Following on from the millenarian accounts of writers like Virilio and Harvey which foresee a further round of time–space compression in which the real-time instant rules, in which here-and-now becomes all there is, a new generation of dystopians have forecast the end of reflexivity, since time to ponder the alternatives to what presents itself will become increasingly scarce:

> This top-to-bottom, inside-and-out connectivity, uniquely in the history of technological development, has created its own ecology – an ecology based on interconnectivity that is becoming more pervasive. To live in the digital ecology is to live within a chronoscopic temporality of the constant present. This is creating its own form of tyranny, 'the tyranny of real time' (Purser, 2000, p. 5). Linear, narrative times, through which we gain a sense of past, present and possible futures, are becoming compressed into instantaneity. Those 'multitude[s] of times which interpenetrate and permeate our daily lives' (Adam, 1995, p. 12) are themselves interpenetrated and permeated by ICT interconnectivity, digitizing them onto a single, temporal plane. Psychological research into human–computer interaction suggests that we

are only able to perceive what we concentrate upon, and when we do not have time to concentrate on a particular thing we suffer from 'inattentional blindness' (Nardi and O'Day, 1999, p. 14). In an information ecology based upon real-time chronoscopic temporality, this poses serious problems. If we are effectively 'blind' to that to which we cannot devote a durational time-span, in 'the buzz of the flickering present' (Purser, 2000, p. 5), then major problems loom as interconnectivity spreads deeper and wider. (Hassan, 2003, p. 102)

The other account is utopian. A favourite of 1990s commentators, it sees the emerging digital ecology as a kind of playground for a new and calmer generation of technologies in which everyday life becomes everyday life plus, a playground of augmented association and incidental learning taking place through a new set of cohabitees (Dertouzos, 2001). Thus

the science of digital ecologies is just beginning. More than just simulations running in the mind of a computer, artificial life has worked its way into the real world, in a variety of robotic forms. From robotic 'insects' to intelligences with faux human bodies, these robots learn from their continuous interaction with the environment, defining goals and changing strategies as they encounter the world. These machines have crossed an imaginary line from procedural to unpredictable, which delights their creators … Encountering a quirky, nonhuman, but thoroughly real intelligence is thrilling to both children and adults. In some way, it is life, and we instinctively recognise it. (Pesce, 2000, pp. 8–9)

Somewhere in these utopian accounts' future, the artificial and the biological usually become as one. Digital implants will augment the body while computers will increasingly depend on biological substrates. There will be a 'marriage of silicon and steel with biological matter' and, as we move 'beyond cyborgs', the 'distinction between us and robots is going to disappear' (Brooks, 2002a, pp. 233, 232, 236).

But both of these accounts are actually rather similar to each other. In particular, they both rely on technological determinism (whether that technology is silicon or cellular) to see them through. Everyday life is a mirror of the qualities of the machines (whether silicon or cellular) that are present. The heterogeneous and often historically accidental archive of practices which take these machines in, rather than vice versa, is ignored or minimized.

But perhaps there is another way of framing the relationships between people and the new generation of biologically inclined machines, one that draws precisely on our relationship with a particular subset of animals, namely *companion animals* or *pets*. Certainly, it seems a crucial political move at this juncture to think about ways of inhabiting everyday life which can move beyond the dystopian and the utopian towards conceiving the biological and the artificial as not just us but more than just other. Further, companion animals are a key part of Euro-American everyday life which have been widely and oddly ignored. For all the raft of writings about the powers of mundane objects and even of 'wild things' (Attfield, 2000), here is a set of entities which have been comprehensively overlooked, even though it would be relatively easy to make a case that companion animals provide a good part of the practical and affective life of many, many households (Wolfe, 2003a; 2003b).

Certainly, the sensory worlds of animals, whether wild or domesticated, are very different from those that humans inhabit, a claim made by von Uexkull in the late nineteenth century and since substantiated by numerous scientific studies (cf. Budiansky, 1998). There is no reason why his *Umwelten* approach cannot be applied equally to machines, in that machines also consist of a set of particular affects bound to the world and offering a particular sensing of it. However, it is clear that electric animals are meant to turn up helpfully in a human world, able to at least partially sense its needs and priorities. Given this, perhaps they are best thought of as like domesticated animals and most particularly as something akin to pets. And in so far as these animals are meant to be pet-like rather than simply commensal (that is, symbiotic with their hosts), their chief function seems to be to produce some of the same affective relationships and satisfactions that are best summarized by the now standard term 'companion animals'.

Of course, animals have a very long history of being companions to the everyday lives of humans. For example, cats are thought to have been domesticated for about 6000 years, and though it might be that to begin with they were primarily used to keep down rats and mice in grain stores, it is also clear that from an early period they also formed affective relationships with human beings (Sunquist and Sunquist, 2002). For example, from early in the Egyptian period cats were given special respect, and by 1000 BC cats were commonly owned purely as pets, with their own appropriate rites of mourning – including the placing of the embalmed body in one of many vast cat cemeteries. Similarly, dogs can be found from a comparatively early period in human history. It is possible that dogs lived in villages some 12,000 years BP. By neolithic times there starts to be good evidence for the presence of dogs, but evidence for dogs as pets dates from rather later: 'By four thousand years ago, there were dogs in abundance, but little evidence of identifiable breeds. By Roman times, two thousand plus years ago, writers are describing both sheepdogs and hunting dogs, and what sound like village curs are described in the Bible and other works written less than a thousand years before Roman times' (Coppinger and Coppinger, 2001, p. 286). In other words, for most of recorded historical time, human beings have had pet-like relations with animals, and one of the key components of everyday life has been the rhythms and requirements of these animals. They have become a key element of human inhabiting, something more than passive context, with their own demands and needs adding a vital affective gloss to many people's everyday lives. So, for example, it has been estimated that there are over 50 million household dogs in the United States and a further 35 million in Europe (Coppinger and Coppinger, 2001), most of which are pets. In the United States it has been reckoned that half of all households have a dog or a cat or both (Tuan, 1984). So what are the reasons why pets have come into existence?

In recent years, the pleasures and rewards of pet ownership have been the subject of considerable research from a mixed collection of anthropologists, sociologists, biologists and veterinarians, with the result that it has become possible to state with some degree of certainty the exact motivations behind pet ownership. First, it is clear that many people gain substantive emotional benefits from pets, benefits which can be shown to exist physiologically (in, for example, lowered blood pressure, better sleep patterns, and increased longevity). Second, pets can provide enhanced means of social association, all the way from simply meeting fellow dog walkers to participating in clubs for enthusiasts. Third, pets can give people more confidence, for example by providing a sense of emotional or physical protection. Fourth, pets can act as style accessories or other indexes of social worth in that how they look can be important for bolstering a person's self-esteem. Finally, pets provide companionship. In societies where single-person households are on the increase and many therefore live alone, this motivation is probably growing.

Pets, therefore, can clearly give a positive gloss to being human. But they are also the subjects of great cruelty. Not only are they regularly shown affection but they are also the object of various forms of domination. So they are regularly culled: on one estimate the majority of North Americans keep their dogs for two years or less and then tire of them (Tuan, 1984). Breeding involves selection which may be quite ruthless. Again, making a pet may require harsh treatment. Dogs are often trained simply 'because power over another being is demonstrably firm when it is exercised for no particular purpose and when submission to it goes against the victim's own strong desires and nature' (1984, p. 107). There may even be what Garber (1996) calls an 'erotics of dominance' in which the human portrays herself as falling under the spell of a pet because it is deserving of the human's love, thus valorizing her own actions and giving the pet no space to make difference.

But, all this said, pets clearly can and do inspire affection in and for themselves. Whilst this reaction is clearly part of a developing discourse of sentimentality towards animals whose origins date from the seventeenth century, it cannot be entirely reduced to just this story (Ritvo, 1987). For example, writers like Grenier (2002) have taken up the threads of the sensual history of dogs and shown how it intersects with the history of humans, spinning out of that intersection a kind of respectful rapport which recognizes the full range of affective responses to dogs: sincerity, love, disdain, indifference, and so on. Most particularly, a certain kind of faithfulness tends to be celebrated. Yet, even here, at the apparent apotheosis of the human–dog relationship, we see an instrumental attitude of sorts, rather well expressed by Lorenz:

> The place which the human friend filled in your life remains for ever empty; that of your dog can be filled with a substitute. Dogs are indeed individuals, personalities in the truest sense of the word, and I should be the last to deny this fact, but they are much more like each other than are human beings ... In those deep instinctive feelings which are responsible for their special relationship with man, dogs resemble each other closely, and if on the death of one's dog one immediately adopts a puppy of the same

breed, one will generally find that he refills those spaces in one's heart and one's life which the departure of an old friend has left desolate. (1964, pp. 194–5)

Finally, there is, of course, the pet's point of view, a view which tends to be placed to one side because that would mean acknowledging that pets have their own *Umwelten* which may still be very far from those of humans.

> The French, perhaps even more than others, talk to their dogs and cats as if they were human. And they are totally surprised whenever their pet exhibits a sudden return to animality. When, for example, rediscovering its ancient instinct to camouflage itself for hunting, a dog rolls in shit. How could our favourite conversation partner – one whose wit, wisdom, and even (why not?) philosophy we so admire – go so far astray? Baudelaire takes up this theme in his prose poem 'The Dog and the Flask'. The creature described as the unworthy companion of Baudelaire's sorry existence resembles the reading public. Exasperated by delicate perfumes, it sniffs with delight at carefully selected garbage.
>   Henri Michaux, in *Passages*, remarks that you never see a dog stopping to smell a rose or a violet. 'They carry a goddam dossier around in their heads, constantly updated. Who understands the menu of stink better?' (Grenier, 2002, pp. 11–12)

Even so, given the rather jolly tone of these kinds of contributions, it might be thought that, for all their differences, the population of pets has been able to arrive at the best kind of commensalism, a generally well-serviced ecological niche. For example, 'ecologically speaking ... the domestic dog is an incredibly successful species' (Coppinger and Coppinger, 2001, p. 231), having reached an equilibrium environment which sustains the canine ability to find food, avoid hazards and reproduce. But, equally, pets can be seen as suffering from the worst kind of amensalism (a living together in which one species hurts another, sometimes unknowingly). They are captured animals: animals that we adopt, rather than vice versa. Their lives are manipulated for the human host's benefit with generally malign results. Take the example of the dog again: 'When I look at the benefits for the dog [of a] symbiotic relationship with humans, it looks well-nigh hopeless ... I believe the modern household dog is bred to satisfy human psychological needs, with little or no consideration for the consequences for the dog ... These dogs fill the court-jester model of pet ownership' (2001, pp. 251–2).

What the literature on pets shows us, therefore, is the wide variety of responses to companion animals that exist in everyday life: domination and cruelty combined with sugary sentiment, a matter-of-fact instrumentalism combined with an awareness of a lurking otherness, and general uncertainty about the costs and benefits of the relationship for either party. As machines are loaded up with software and gain more and more independent mobility, so the same kinds of ethical dilemmas are likely to occur. These dilemmas may become more severe as some machines are invested with a capacity for emotional response, conversational capability, and so on. They will surely begin to demand some of the same kinds of ethical responses as are found in the case of companion animals. But the case of companion animals should also give us pause: indeed, as we have seen, it would be possible to argue that the world of companion animals too often lacks any concerted ethical response. Surely, this underlines once again the case for an everyday ethics of the kind favoured by Varela (2000), but one which does not stop at the 'human' world but acknowledges other intelligibilities as well.

Conclusions

Deleuze and Guattari's (1987) disdain for a culture which is locked into individualistic, possessive concerns is clear, not least in their comments on pets: 'individuated animals, family pets, sentimental, Oedipal animals each with its own petty history, "my" cat, "my" dog. These animals invite us to regress and they are the only kind of animal psychoanalysis understands' (1987, p. 240). And in their rush to conjure up what is essentially a Spinozan world of prepersonal natural forces, they clearly throw down a challenge to make the comfortable world of everyday life uncomfortable by stripping it of some of its most reassuring denizens. They want to head out in the direction of a wilder animality which is both frightening – and creative. It is possible to have considerable sympathy with this approach whilst at the same time having considerable doubts about it, ranging from the empirical (being scratched by a cat on a fairly regular basis) through the anthropological (many cultures through history seem to have kept pets in circumstances which are difficult to equate with western possessive individualism) to the ethical (is it necessarily so awful for people with very little in the way of companionship to seek it out in animal form?).

These same tensions are to be found in the construction of electric animals. What kind of culture is to be assumed? A wild electric panorama bereft of human figures but traversed by various lines of affect? A scurrying ecology full to bursting with all manner of informational life? A consumer mall of companions waiting to be sold and played with and as easily discarded? Or a welfare system gently caring for the emotional needs of its charges?

What I have tried to show in this chapter is that the advent of software-driven entities modelled on biological assumptions is a significant event which has the potential to decisively change everyday life by adding in a new range of cohabitees. In particular, it offers a new set of ethical dilemmas which have clearly not been solved in the case of companion animals (Gaita, 2003).

But one might argue that, in certain senses, the issue of electric animals is more pressing because these entities have the potential to discipline conduct in more explicit and rigid ways (Lecourt, 2003). They are being socially engineered but, in turn, they can become part of a new means of social engineering, half way between the disciplinary and the pastoral and combining elements of each. For it is quite clear that these animals can be made more or less lively and more or less threatening by the lines of code that animate them – not just in their capacity for surveillance (which is substantial) but also in their capacity to pass on and inculcate behaviours which may be inimical (for example, all manner of corporate dictates). There is therefore a lively politics of interspecies ethics to be pursued which can ensure that new hybrid relationships brought into existence are not malign – or simply vapid (Plumwood, 2002) – and are able to produce resolution through alliance and mutual assistance rather than domination. For example, there is nothing to stop surfaces and entities being designed that can inculcate values and practices of critical responsiveness by retaining ambiguity, ambivalence and respect of the kind that is sometimes seen in human dealings with companion animals.

Such scenarios have been the bread and butter of science fiction for many years now, of course, but that does not necessarily make them invalid. Rather, because the future has a tendency to turn up not as some kind of gleaming and polished modernity but as overused and battered pieces of equipment, our critical senses are dulled and we do not recognize that there are any similarities. However, at this time, that might be a dangerous assumption to make.

11

Remembering the Technological Unconscious by Foregrounding Knowledges of Position

Introduction: engraining anticipation

This chapter is part of a more general attempt to provide an account of the *spaces of anticipation* that are found in contemporary everyday life, an account of how it is that environments of which we are a part gradually come to be accepted as the only way to be because, each and every day, they show up more or less as expected (Thrift, 2000c; 2003a). Such spaces depend upon the gradual construction of complex ethologies of bodies and objects which are repositories of the 'correct' *positionings* and *juxtaposition-ings* which allow things to arrive and become known (Siegert, 1999). These very basic sendings and receivings of socio-technical life – and the modest but constant hum of connection and interconnection that they make possi-ble – have often been neglected. But it seems clear to me that as we move into an era populated by more and more objects whose *raison d'être* is pre-cisely to hone such sendings and receivings, so the task of understanding becomes far more pressing.

Far more pressing too because much of what we call the cosmological order is achieved through the simple positionings and juxtapositionings of human and non-human actants – positionings and juxtapositionings which have to be repeated over and over as particular spaces which assume spe-cific competencies (Weiss, 1996). This powerful infrastructural logic which allows the world to show up as confident and in charge is rarely written about in and for itself (for an exception see Gell, 1992), and yet this 'empti-ness' lies at the root of our being, producing senses of the rightness and wrongness of the world so fundamental that we find it difficult to articulate them or to consider that these senses could have been otherwise. But it is possible to find clockfaces in the fourteenth century that circuited counter-clockwise (Glennie and Thrift, 2003); large parts of the world read from right to left (Goody, 1987); in the early days of the automobile, seats were not always arranged in a two in front, two behind formation; in Norway and Sweden, washing up to the left or right of the sink can produce instant eval-uations of worth (Linde-Larssen, 1996); and so on.

In other words, our conventions of *address*, of what will show up where, and what will show up next, are often arbitrary, and they rely on knowledges of position and juxtaposition – sometimes tacit, but increasingly system-atized – which lie at the base of Euro-American societies. When practice is established and runs smoothly without being perturbed by disruptive events, conventions of address sit there quietly in the background and 'the fictional nature of organizational knowledges does not surface easily. Everything – objects, settings, routes, people – seems to be real, that is the way things properly are, provided with a sort of existential fixedness and ontological correctness' (Lanzera and Patriotta, 2001, p. 965). It is, above all, this anonymous history of *knowledges* of position and juxtaposition which I want to search out, the familiar–unfamiliar knowledges of how human and non-human actants can be transported and aligned.

These knowledges do not belong to 'us' or to the environment. Rather, they have been coevolved, and so refuse a neat distinction between organic and inorganic life or person and environment. As Ingold nicely puts it in regard to notions of the environment.

> The environment of persons is no more reducible than is their organic exis-tence to pure molecular substance. It is not merely physical, and it is certainly not blank. For example, the ground I walk on is surely a part of my environ-ment, but in a physicalist description the ground, as such, does not exist; there are only packed molecules of carbon, nitrogen, silicon and so on. As Reed has eloquently put it, 'it is the earth on which we walk, and the soil in which we plant, that is relevant for us as perceiving and acting creatures; not the molecules discovered by scientists' … The environment, in short, is not the same as the physical world as it exists and takes on meaning in relation to the beings that inhabit it … As such, its formation has to be understood in the same way that we understand the growth of organisms and persons, in terms of the properties of dynamic self-organisation of relational fields. (2001, p. 265)

In what follows, I therefore want to try to outline some of the knowledges and competencies concerned with position and juxtaposition, but I also want to go further. I want to claim that they constitute a 'technological unconscious' (Clough, 2000) whose content is the bending of bodies with environments to a specific set of addresses without the benefit of any cog-nitive inputs, a prepersonal substrate of guaranteed correlations, assured encounters, and therefore unconsidered anticipations.

In certain senses, one might understand this project as Foucauldian, but I want to drop down a level from where Foucault did most (although not all) of his work. Using a distinction often employed in literary theory, my analysis will be of form rather than genre. Knowledges of form are usually not regarded as subjective (though just as clearly they have subject effects) because they have no strong interpretive content. They are repetitive, empirical, bereft of intention. 'For genre to exist as a norm it has first to cir-culate as a form, which has no ontology, but which is generated by repeti-tions that subjects learn to read as organised inevitability' (Berlant, 2001, p. 46). In turn these repetitions offer up intelligibility and compulsion. 'As the subject negotiates becoming orderly, the world promises that the subject's compliance will be valued and reflected in the social, such that a guiding law that seems to come from the subject can remain the general index of clar-ity where there is otherwise none' (2001, p. 50). They are, if you like, the equivalent to Genette's (1999) 'paratexts', or Lury's (1999) 'phatic imagery': means by which senses are synchronized (and synchorized) so that practice can take place.

Of course, knowledges of form require a vast apparatus in order to produce successful repetitions and consistent consistencies – drawings, text, numbers, symbols, prose, statistics, tables, charts, maps – which set out sequences and prime practice. Infrastructure has precisely to be *performative* if it is to become reliably repetitive. Repetition is an achievement – and a method of achievement.

To summarize, my main concern in this chapter is with the basic conditions of life, and especially the style of repetitions that pertains at any point in history, the animated automatisms (Gehlen, 1990) that provide the stable ground for practices. Because I use the word 'automatisms' it should not be thought that these repetitions are arbitrary. Neither are they spontaneous. Rather they have been set in motion, and their momentum, and a good deal of improvisation, keeps them stable. My argument is that we are currently seeing a shift in the basic conditions of life, a move of the 'social' 'atomic structure' from one model to another as a full-blown *standardization of space* takes hold, very similar in its ambitions and effects to the nineteenth century standardization of time. (Other writers have attempted to consider changes in these basic conditions of life, most notably Virilio and Derrida – in his later writings in particular – but, as I hope will become clear, I will be taking a slightly different tack.)

I therefore want to search out some of the key knowledges of position and juxtaposition that make up the 'technological unconscious' and how they are currently changing, producing a new sense of how the world shows up. To this end, the rest of the chapter is in three main sections. The first section provides a capsule history of how a very few templates of position and juxtaposition have been powered up into an 'atomic structure' producing a specific kind of technological unconscious with its own forms of compulsion and fascination. Such a history is necessarily very partial but hopefully it gives a sense of the vast agenda of research that is being opened up. In the second section, however, I want to argue that in recent decades the nature (or style) of these templates has been changing as new modes of hyper-coordinated address have been invented, so that a new kind of technological unconscious is now being born which we need to grasp and understand. In the concluding section, I will then argue that the influence of this unconscious shows itself particularly in modern social theory which now assumes an event horizon quite different from what has gone before, an event horizon which is still all too easily misrecognized as the same as what went before.

1. Addressing the world

In this section, I will provide some general notes towards a history of knowledges of position and juxtaposition that were increasingly constituted by that very knowledge. Such a selective approach is necessary, since the topic is potentially so vast. In order to narrow the orbit of this section even further I will consider only one of these knowledges (though arguably the most important), the knowledge of sequence in time, which in turn allows orderly and guaranteed *repetition*.

A large number of different institutions generated knowledges of sequence in time, the demands of one influencing the demands of the others. Of these institutions, arguably the most important was transport. The problems of supply of large cities like London and Paris led to the need to develop formal means of co-ordination of road transport such as the *timetable*. Full regular timing of travel dates from early on. Thus, in England, returns from Elizabethan postmasters noted the time that the mail was received and dispatched (Brayshay et al., 1998) and quasi-timetables resulted. Though earlier publications like I*The Carriers Cosmographie* (1637) and *The Present State of London* (1681) provided timetable information, the first national timetables seem to have been a later invention. For example, by 1715 the *Merchants and Traders Necessary Companion* provided a fully comprehensive directory of courier and coach services to and from London, listing over 600 services a week. These proto-national timetables were the precursors of the extensive train and bus timetables of the nineteenth century which spread knowledge of timetabling across all sections of society and, in the guise of commuting, made the city into one vast timetable.

In turn, these developments in transport generated other needs for sequential order, of which the most important was probably the expansion of the hospitality and retailing industry. Inns and taverns were built to clothe stagecoach routes, usually to a relatively standardized design, as a means of passing bodies on from point to point. By the end of the eighteenth century, hotels had begun to appear, for example the 60-bed Hôtel de Henri IV built in Nantes in 1788 at a total cost of £17,500, a tremendous sum of money at the time. In 1794 the first purpose-built hotel in North America was opened in New York, the City Hotel with 70 rooms. 'Several other, similar hotels were built in other cities in the next few years, but it was not until 1829 that the first first-class hotel, Boston's Tremont House, with 170 rooms, was built. The Tremont innovated such features as private rooms, with locks, soap and water for each room, bellboys and French cuisine' (Gray and Liguori, 1990, p. 5). The tourist expansion of the nineteenth and twentieth centuries saw a further massive expansion of hotels and motels, producing a whole set of new sequencing techniques – reservation books, sliding blackboards, rack slips. Subsequently, the computerization of the 1960s and 1970s allowed many of these systems to be automated.

Similar developments occurred in retailing. As shops and then department stores grew in number and complexity through the eighteenth and into the nineteenth and twentieth centuries (Glennie and Thrift, 1996), so they generated a need for all kinds of knowledge of – and tools of – sequence, from delivery schedules to formal order books, which still exist in automated form in the complex supply chains of today.

All these development were mirrored on a daily scale. Personal co-ordination increasingly depended upon timetables which in turn led to the development of various textual devices as early as the eighteenth century. For example, the *diary* was, in certain senses, a textual analogue of the watch, a means of gridding everyday life via a calibrated narrative with its imperative to fill each dated blank space with observations. At the same time, the diary heightened skills of observation of everyday life as sequence, since the complications of the event now could be routinely noted down (Amin and Thrift, 2002). The diary went hand in hand with other items of textual comprehension like memo books, the taking of 'minutes' by clerks, and the use of shorthand ('tachygraphy' or rapid writing) to produce a textual comprehension much closer to that of the present – which indeed begins to produce a different kind of present, both compressed and, through the new possibilities now offered, opened out.

Alongside these more general developments came other more specialized knowledges of position and juxtaposition. Though there are many of these knowledges, perhaps the most important and equally the most neglected have been those emanating from armies, navies and, latterly, air forces (Giedion, 1998). The word *logistics* is normally reckoned to date in its modern form from Jomini's (1836) *The Art of War*, which set down 'logistics' as one of the six branches of 'the military art'. Of course, logistics had existed long before then; armies could not exist just on foraging and had to collect provisions together, and many armies on the move stretched over miles. But it is also true that modern logistics was probably born after that date, in the crucible of the American Civil War, when the industrial revolution, large spaces of movement, mass technologies of movement (including the railroad), and heavy casualties dictated the construction of complex knowledges of sequence in order to supply basic items like water, let alone ammunition. There was even strict traffic control discipline. By the First World War, logistics had become a major enterprise. For example, the British Army shipped 5,253,538 tons of ammunition (include over 170 million shells) to France (and, it might be added, 5,438,602 tons of hay for animals) (Huston, 1966; Mackinsey, 1989; Thompson, 1991).

As in civilian life, so the everyday life of the military was affected by the need for exact position and juxtaposition, in particular through the evolution of drill and similar rigid positionings of the body which came to take up increasing amounts of time in most armies (Holmes, 2001). Some of the drills developed by Maurice of Orange from ancients like Aelianus and Vegetius, which became general in much of Europe as a result of example and a series of books, can lay claim to being the first time-and-motion studies in their exact and exacting attention to time:

> From Aelianus [the] key borrowing was the simple notion of training soldiers to move simultaneously in response to stylised 'words of command'. Aelianus had listed 22 different 'words of command' used by the Macedonians; but when Maurice's cousin and aide, Johann of Nassau, had analysed the motions required to handle a matchlock, he counted 42 distinct postures, and assigned

a fixed word of command to each of them. A simpler drill, far closer to Macedonian precedents, was also derived for pikemen, who were needed to protect the arquebusiers from cavalry attack during the rather lengthy process of reloading.

The practical importance of such pedantry was very great. In principle, and to a surprising degree also in practice, it became possible to get soldiers to move in unison while performing each of the actions needed to load, aim, and fire their guns. The resulting volleys came faster – and misfires were fewer when everyone acted in unison and kept time to shouted commands. Practice and more practice, repeated endlessly whenever spare time allowed, made the necessary motions almost automatic and less likely to be disrupted by the stress of battle. More lead projected at the enemy in less time was the result: a definite and obvious advantage when meeting troops not similarly trained. This was what Maurice and his drill masters had aimed for; and once their success became clear, the technique spread to other European armies with quite extraordinary rapidity. (McNeill, 1995, pp. 128–9)

Thus, by the time that William of Orange arrived in England in 1688, he found 'a small standing army which had considerable and varied experience of active service, which was well-enough armed and equipped, and which was trained to a system of drill and tactics as up to date as those practised elsewhere in Europe' (Houlding, 1981, p. 172). Helped by the circulation of a large military literature and especially drill books like Dundas's *Principles of Military Movements* and their accompanying crib cards, by the eighteenth century drill had become a carefully defined practice of bodily sequence right across Europe – and an essential element of battle (Holmes, 2001).

During the same period, the military also put increasing emphasis on using soldiers' time profitably in tasks like field fortification: digging trenches, raising embankments, building redoubts, constructing bridgeheads, and the like. The approach was practical, since it was realized that 'the elaborate mathematics and geometry of engineers were subjects too dry for everyone to relish; and indeed there was no need of handling the scale and compass of problems, nor tiresome calculations, in order to learn the art of putting all kinds of posts into a proper state of defence' (Houlding, 1981, p. 224). But the upshot was clear: directed bodies involved chiefly in what were coming to be known as logistical activities.

Idleness, in effect, was banished from military life. This was a great departure from earlier custom, since waiting for something to happen occupies almost all of a soldier's time, and when left to their own devices, troops had traditionally escaped boredom by indulging in drink and other sorts of disruption. Debauchery was not banished entirely under the regime Prince Maurice and his imitators established, but it was usually confined to off-duty leave time. (McNeill, 1995, pp. 129–30)

Though these are clearly only notes towards a more general history of knowledges of position and juxtaposition – what Gille (1986) calls the 'maceration and purification' of space through a culture of interval – what is clear is that the goal was to produce a general configuration based on exact and countable sequencing which could roll over seamlessly into the future (as if to prove the point, some hotels now reserve rooms as long as eight years into the future). Everything would be in the right place at the right time.

Nowhere is this maceration and purification clearer than in the development of the modern system of *address*. The history of address is a long one of which England's history is only one example. There, streets seem to have been named for as long as there have been towns. For example, there are dozens of known street names from Saxon London. Although large and imposing houses, churches, inns and the like were named in medieval times, it seems likely that other dwellings were located by street names, by prominent landmarks – and by asking the way. More organized address systems (especially numbering of houses) seem to have come about on the back of more organized delivery systems. This numbering seems to have been done by the Post Office and by compilers of town directories. For example, in Bristol in 1775 Sketchley's first directory did attempt to number all houses but, significantly, felt the need to explain how. Though we cannot be sure, it seems unlikely that most houses would have displayed numbers at this time: postal deliveries were still made to a named householder. Even by the turn of the nineteenth century, numbering was still rare and order (in militia lists, ward ratebooks, etc.) was achieved without explicit numbering. The mix of name, number, and so on persists for a surprisingly long time, buttressed by the tacit knowledge of routes and places held in the bodies of those delivering mail and parcels.

But, the increasing scale of mass mailing systems (and especially the massive increase in business mail which gradually assumed about 80 per cent of volume in most postal systems) gradually led to the introduction of mechanized sorting in the 1950s and to the introduction of postcodes and zip codes in the 1960s (Rhind, 1992). The example of the United States is the most obvious here. Zip (for 'zone improvement plan') codes were introduced by the US Postal Service in 1963. By July 1963 a five-digit code had been assigned to every address in the country which identified region (the first digit), further subdivisions (the subsequent two digits) and post office (the final two digits). Interestingly, and in contrast to the British postcode, there seem to have been no maps of zip codes: they were a purely categorical device. Then in 1983, following the introduction of optical character readers able to read barcodes (see below), a further four digits were introduced (the zip + 4 code), allowing the pinpointing of the address to a 'delivery sector' scale (such as the floor of an office block). Nowadays, of course, such addresses have become, through mass systems of marketing, their own rapidly burgeoning industry, intimately connected to geodemographic categorizations of the population which announce new forms of commercial countability which are becoming as important as those of the state (Rhind, 1999).

It would be possible to portray the foregoing account – and what follows – as one based on a kind of Whiggish technological determinism, but this would be wrong. Rather the recurrent play of knowledges of sequence should be seen as a set (or, perhaps better, a series) of socio-technical mediations constantly in genesis that stabilize the collective so that sequence becomes possible (Simondon, 1992; Mackenzie, 2002). That said, it is important to point out that not everything works and not everything turns up on time, to put it but mildly. But such discrepancy can often be formative (Lowe and Schaffer, 2000). So, importantly, knowledge of error and delay has itself been built into knowledges of sequence. For example, modern forms of sequencing have classically included waiting in queues (and the development of associated technologies like taking tickets signalling position in an electronic queue) and, significantly, waiting itself has become the subject of a vast set of knowledges based on queuing theory and similar developments. Thus, delay can itself become a source of profit and other forms of advantage (Mackenzie, 2002).

Readdressing the world

In the world that has been developing since the 1960s, however, things have changed their character. What we can see is the evolution of new means of addressing the world based upon what is often called a *track and trace* model. This model assumes an underlying *standardization of space* which, at least in so far as it has become complex and extensive enough to take the variations of each milieu fully into account, is historically very recent. This new means of addressing the world can be said to have arisen from three different but related impulses which, taken together, provide a continuously updated, highly processed background which renders all sequences calculable. One is the general availability of a series of technologies which can continuously track position – lasers, various form of new information technology, wireless, geographical information systems, global positioning systems, and so on. The second is a series of formalized and integrative knowledges of sequences arising out of the general application of models drawn from logistics across a wide range of fields. As a formal field of study rather than a military 'art', logistics dates back to the 1940s and the applications of various operational research models to problems of inventory (storage) and distribution (flow), most especially in the context of the demands made by the Second World War. In the 1960s logistics became bound up with systems engineering and an associated array of technologies like flow charts, life-cycle analysis, network analysis, including scheduling approaches like PERT (programme evaluation and review technique) and CPM (critical path method), and so on. More recently, logistics has expanded again to become seen as an integral element of what production is, rather than as something subsequent to it (as 'distribution'). In turn, this has led to new means of production like distributive manufacturing. The third impulse is new means of countability which have provided new possibilities of calculation (Thrift and French, 2002). For example, spreadsheets have allowed all kinds of calculation to be made concerning future time periods which would have been difficult and time-consuming or just plain expensive before.

These three impulses have in turn had three closely related results. One, already referred to in previous chapters, has been a major change in the *geography of calculation*. Whereas 'computing' used to consist of centres of calculation located at definite sites, now, through the medium of wireless, it is changing its shape. Computing is moving into the environment as it becomes possible to connect up all kinds of computing activity (Dertouzos, 2001). From being centred and stable entities located at definite sites, computing is moving out to inhabit all parts of the environment and users are able to be mobile. Computing can then become a part of everyday environments since there are no longer any restrictions on where computing devices can be located: they will be located everywhere in constantly shifting and adapting peer-to-peer networks. This is the advent of 'ubiquitous', 'pervasive', or 'everywhere' computing. It follows that 'computing' will become more and more context-dependent. This means both that devices will become more location-aware, knowing where they are in relation to users and other devices, and that they will be able to interact and communicate with and adapt to users and other devices. In other words, computing – understood as a network of devices – will increasingly be able to be appropriate to the situation (Lieberman and Selker, 2000).

A second important result has been a change in the nature of the *address*. Increasingly, addresses are moving with human or non-human actants. Four different technological innovations that are both ubiquitous and all but unnoticed will serve to make the point.

The first of these is the humble barcode. The barcode is a crucial element in the history of the new way of the world, one which remains largely untold. Based on Morse code, the barcode was invented by Joseph Woodward and Bernard Silver in 1949 and patented in 1952. But it did not actually get used until the 1970s, in part because of the invention of laser scanners. In 1969, the Grocery Manufacturers of America and the National Association of Food Chains met to express the need for 'an inter-industry product code' and convened an *ad hoc* committee to jointly pursue a uniform 11-number grocery product code. In 1971 this *ad hoc* committee became the Uniform Product Code Council (UPCC), predecessor of today's Uniform Code Council (UCC). On 26 June 1974 at 8.01 a.m. in the Troy, Ohio, Marsh supermarket a 10-pack of Wrigley's Chewing Gum marked the world's first commercial barcode scanning. At first, use of barcodes was slow to take off. At the end of 1976 only 106 US stores were using barcodes. But this was soon to change. The addition of more and more stores, the expansion of barcodes out of the United States with the foundation of the European Article Numbering Association (EAN) in 1977 (changed to EAN International in 1992 to reflect its global reach), with its 13-number code which administers barcode usage outside North America, and the adoption of barcodes outside the grocery sector as a means of electronic data interchange allowing computer ordering and invoicing for the warehousing industry, all stimulated use (Hosoya and Schaefer, 2001). To signify this expanded role, the Uniform Product Code Council became simply the Uniform Code Council (UCC).

Today, it is estimated by UCC and EAN that barcodes are used by 900,000 companies worldwide in almost 100 countries and these codes are scanned 5 billion times a day. The codes are used in almost every kind of transaction. They are used by the shipping industry to track and deliver packages, the retail industry to track inventory and modulate pricing, and the medical industry to tag patients and encode their information. And they are used extensively by the armed forces. For example, since 1995 the US Department of Defense has used product codes in many logistics processes.

Indeed, demand is now so great that the barcode is being extended. New electronic commerce initiatives are in train. Attempts to standardize product codes worldwide by 2005 are being instituted, with US retailers expected to be able to scan 13 digits by that date, and with a general expansion to 14 digits being planned worldwide thereafter. New symbols are also being worked on worldwide which can fit space-constrained products.

But universal product codes are not universal. They actually only constitute about half of barcode usage in the US. There, large agencies like FedEx, UPS and the US Postal Services have constructed their own proprietary barcodes to move mail and parcels. Since 1982, for example, the US Postal Services has printed a barcode on every envelope that goes through its system, signifying the address.

Another important form of innovation which is worth commenting on might be thought of as the computer equivalent of the barcode, and that is the series of addresses that allow computers to communicate with each other. A good example is the .sig file. First invented *circa* 1980, probably on an online bulletin board like FidoNet, the .sig file is one of a number of network address systems, a short block of text that can be automatically attached to the end of e-mail messages, usually containing information like the sender, job title, company name, phone number, e-mail address and various other digital soundbites. Little used to begin with, the .sig file is now becoming a kind of electronic business card, including graphics. In turn, the .sig file was used to produce one of the most successful business strategies, Hotmail – free web-based e-mail which attracted more than 12 million users in its first 18 months of use. Now owned by Microsoft, Hotmail currently has some 60 million subscribers.

The third innovation is the SIM (subscriber information module) card, first used generally in the early 1990s and manufactured by a small group of companies like GEMPLUS. The SIM card is at the heart of the modern mobile phone industry. It is a small card which identifies the subscriber to the network, and contains a microprocessor which stores unique information about the subscriber including the phone number and security numbers, plus a number of other functions (for example, memory space for phone numbers and text messages). The SIM card functions as, in effect, a mobile address.

One more innovation, and perhaps in the end the one likely to prove the most powerful, is the RFID (radiofrequency identification) tag. Such tags consist of a microchip and an antenna, sandwiched in plastic. Invented in the 1990s, these recyclable tags can be used to mark any kind of object. Their advantage is that each object can be identified separately, and can be given a unique identity and history, making them very different from barcodes which can only identify relatively simple information on classes of object (e.g. box of Shredded Wheat, $3.95). Also unlike barcodes, RFIDs can be read remotely, out of sight of a reader. The new generation of RFIDs is small (often less than one millimetre in area and half a millimetre thick) and can be read from 1.5 metres from a passive array. Tags that signal actively can be read up to 6 metres away from a passive array. Currently, tags are too expensive at 20 to 30 cents a chip (compared with a price of 1 cent for a barcode) to achieve this kind of circulation, but this situation is changing. There seems every reason to believe that they will reshape the practical conduct of life in a way that the barcode has only partly achieved. Thus, it is generally agreed that RFIDs will reshape supply chains by allowing all objects to be tracked as they are produced (by tagging the whole inventory and assembly process), transported to the point of sale and even, in the future, tipped on to the landfill site (Ferguson, 2002; *Financial Times*, 2 October 2002). RFIDs are also being linked to all kinds of sensors so that they can give continuous updates on the condition of the objects that they are attached to. And, in time, it is hoped to make objects proactive: the possibilities are being worked out at this very moment but the clear intent is to make objects that are able to react creatively to the situation they find themselves in by reading all the other RFIDs broadcasting in their immediate area. As a result, a kind of continuous informational ethology is coming into being.

Thus, for example, it comes as no surprise to find that a number of currency printers and central banks (e.g. the European Central Bank) are now looking at the possibilities of RFIDs. Indeed, the ECB has a target of inserting RFIDs in all Euro notes by 2005. Of course, these tags have enormous potential to invade privacy, since almost anything will be able to be tagged (including illicit money and, no doubt, human beings: a Florida company has already developed a passive RFID chip compatible with human tissue). Indeed, given the possibilities of 'Little Angel' and other similar current surveillance schemes (see Katz and Aakhus, 2002) being powered up using RFIDs, the future is of considerable concern.

The third development is the growth of what is usually called in the mobile communication literature 'hyper-coordination' or 'micro-coordination' (e.g. Ling and Yttri, 2002). The developments in technology of the kind outlined above make it possible to continually track and trace human and non-human actants to produce levels of co-ordination that were previously unachievable. Hyper-coordination is distinguished by the quality of perpetual contact, whereby it is possible to be in continuous contact with actants, and the quality of perpetual revision, whereby it is possible to continually recalibrate agreements to meet or deliver at a specific time and place. In other words, it is possible to co-ordinate and re-coordinate at a distance on an all but continuous, and continually adjusted, basis. In turn, hyper-coordination offers up new possibilities for economic, social and cultural encounters, of which the most important is what is often called 'planful opportunism', a kind of just-in-time co-ordination (Perry et al., 2001). Encounters are able to be continually revised in a kind of intricate ballet of circumstances of the kind that used to have to be reserved for public meeting places like the street (Brown et al., 2002; Katz and Aakhus, 2002).

Courier companies like FedEx, which ships three million packages a day and uses some 3700 vans and trucks, 720 aeroplanes and 47,000 couriers, are built on hyper-coordination. Lastminute.com, which matches the last-minute supply of airline tickets, hotel rooms, package holidays and the like from 8500 suppliers to the demand from about 3.5 million subscriber users, could not exist without hyper-coordination, but neither could teenager mobile phone owners continually using their phones to meet their friends.

Thus what we see is a different kind of repetition which allows things to show up differently with different kinds of opportunities associated with them. Through the application of a set of technologies and knowledges (the two being impossible to separate), a style of repetition has been produced which is more controlled *and* also more open-ended, a new kind of roving empiricism which continually ties up and undoes itself in a search for the most efficient ways to use the space and time of each moment.

These developments are, I think, producing a new kind of embodied phenomenality of position and juxtaposition, one 'made continuous with the properties admitted by the natural sciences' (Petitot et al., 1999, p. 23), based on a background sense of highly complex systems simulating life. This is because in a self-fulfilling prophecy, as I have shown, highly complex systems (of communication, logistics, and so on) *do* structure life, and increasingly do so adaptively. This new phenomenality is beginning to structure what is human by disclosing 'embodied' capacities of communication, memory, and collaborative reach in particular ways that privilege a roving, engaged interaction as typical of 'human' cognition and feed that conception back into the informational devices and environments that increasingly surround us (Dourish, 2001; Goffey, 2002). In turn, we can perhaps begin to see the bare bones of this historically new kind of technological unconscious appearing now even in mundane activities like playing with highly complex games software that is increasingly opaque to rule-guided order and depends on a kind of sensitivity to – and sensibility of – emergence, a kind of planful opportunism incarnate:

> Take as an example one of the most successful titles from the Nintendo 64 platform, Shigeru Miyomoto's Zelda: Ocarina of Time. Zelda embodies the uneven development of the late-nineties interactive entertainment. The plot belongs squarely to the archaic world of fairy-tales – a young boy armed with magic spells sets off to rescue the princess. As a control system, though, Zelda is an incredibly complex structure, with hundreds of interrelated goals and puzzles dispersed throughout the game's massive virtual world. Moving your character around is simple enough, but figuring out what you're supposed to

do with him takes hours of exploration and trial and error. By traditional usability standards, Zelda is a complete mess: you need a hundred-page guidebook just to establish what the rules are. But if you see that opacity as part of the art then the whole experience changes: you're exploring the world of the game and the rules of the game at the same time.

Think about the ten-year-olds who willingly immerse themselves in Zelda's world. For them the struggle for mastery of the system doesn't feel like a struggle. They've been decoding the landscape on the screen – guessing at causal relations between actions and results, building working hypotheses about the system's underlying rules – since before they learned how to read. The conventional wisdom about these kids is that they're more nimble at puzzle solving and more manually dextrous than the TV generation, and while there's certainly some truth to that, I think we lose something important in stressing how talented this generation is with their joysticks. I think they have developed another skill, one that almost looks like patience; they are more tolerant at being out of control, more tolerant of that exploratory phase where the rules don't all make sense, and where few goals have been clearly defined. In other words, they are uniquely equipped to embrace the more oblique control system of emergent software. The hard work of tomorrow's interactive design will be exploring the tolerance – that suspension of control – in ways that enlighten us, in ways that move beyond the insulting residue of princesses and magic spells. (Johnson, 2001, pp. 176–7)

Conclusions: on topological complication

In this conclusion, I want to argue that these new conditionings of position and juxtaposition – and the new event horizon that results – go part way to explaining the emergence of social theory of a particular kind. Recently, writers like Turner and Rojek have argued for a 'robust political economy of social organization' which can combat some of what they see as the excesses of a more 'decorative' approach which focuses on 'aesthetic and technological revolutions' (2001, p. 199). But at least some of the work I think they want to excoriate on both theoretical and empirical levels strikes me, especially in its emphasis on a dynamic iterability, as exactly about trying to articulate the new technological unconscious of a world of performative infrastructures. If that is even partly the case – and I think that it is – then we can see many of the authors which the 'decorative' approach takes to task as actually attempting to describe a historically new situation and the skills and competencies that are needed to cope with it: a new kind of political economy of social organization, if you like, but operating at the molecular level.

Judith Butler is a good example. She is known for her notion of performance which problematizes the body as 'imaginary matter' (in which the body and unconscious fantasy, matter and the image, are indistinguishable). Butler 'relocates the matter of the unconscious to the interval between repetitions' (Clough, 2000, p. 120) so that, as Butler puts it:

If every performance repeats itself to institute the effect of identity, then every repetition requires an interval between the acts, as it were, in which risk and excess threaten to disrupt the identity being constituted. The uncon-scious is this excess that enables and contests every performance, and which never fully appears within the performance itself. (1991, p. 28)

Butler's notion of performance suggests that bodily matter is dynamic, more an event or a matter of temporality. Butler is drawing on Derrida here, and relating the unconscious repetition compulsion to a *différance* or pure repe-tition. Butler therefore argues that the unconscious should be located 'within a signifying chain as the instability of all interability'. The uncon-scious, therefore, 'is not "in" the body, but in the very signifying process through which that body comes to appear; it is the lapse in repetition as well as its compulsion, precisely what the performance seeks to deny, and that which compels it from the start' (1991, p. 28). Thus, as Clough puts it, 'by drawing the unconscious back to *différance*, Butler allows for a more general unconscious than the Freudian and Lacanian unconscious. But this rethink-ing of the unconscious presumes the deconstruction of the psychoanalytic configuration of the imaginary, the symbolic and the real' (2000, p. 120).

Deleuze (1990b) provides a similar kind of analysis of iteration in that repetition must, for him, pursue something open, even within a framework in which scenes may appear to move past as frozen and immured. Not everything is brought back:

> Exchange implies only resemblance, even if the resemblance is extreme. Exactness is its criterion, along with the equivalence of exchanged products. This is the false repetition which causes our illness. True repetition, on the other hand, appears as a singular behaviour that we display in relation to that which cannot be exchanged, replaced, or substituted – like a poem that is repeated on the condition that no word may be changed. It is no longer a matter of an equivalence between similar things, it is not even a matter of an identity of the Same. True repetition addresses something singular, unchange-able, and different, without 'identity'. Instead of exchanging the similar and identifying the Same, it authenticates the different. (1990b, pp. 287–8)

In each of these cases, and no doubt more (for example, some of Derrida's recent writings on the gift and on new forms of technological text like e-mail), what I think we can see is the attempt to *disclose and touch* (Marks, 2000) a world of planful opportunism, a world in which 'true repetition' occurs, but in part *because* exact exchange has been achieved. As a result, new senses of sense become possible built on the new frames of anticipation and forms of memory that can show up and be touched in and by events now. And perhaps this should come as no surprise. For example, Derrida's and Deleuze's models of thinking as an open system were heavily influenced by systems theory (see Johnson, 1993) and it would be possible to argue that the connected world we now live in, built upon the loops and whorls of systems theory, and their work share some common epistemic forebears.

Let me come to an end with a speculation concerning the vexed topic of resistance to, and subversion of, this generally unconscious order. For what seems clear is that resistance and subversion become a different matter. Take the example of the address. Through history materials and people have resisted the exigencies of the address in numerous ways, most often by seeking various forms of anonymity. But it seems to me that we need to think much more seriously about what might constitute resistance and subversion of the address under the new 'track and trace' model. One thing seems certain: old-style notions of 'getting lost' in space through random *dérives*, as in situationist texts, seem increasingly like an artefact of another age. Getting lost will increasingly become a challenging and difficult task, what with wearable computing, in-car navigation, and the like. Further, many actions will be tracked on a fairly continuous basis. It may be that this means we will have to get much better at harnessing the energy of moments by much greater attention to the minutiae of performativity (Thrift, 2000c). (Already, it seems as though the pure thrill experience of bungee jumping and the like has become a new way of getting lost.) On the other hand, modern complex systems are so overdetermined that in their interleavings all kinds of gaps are likely to be found in which new kinds of 'excursions' can be coaxed into existence. If things are showing up differently, we can do different things too, energetically opening up the new order of being. As the direction of attention changes, so perhaps we make a change in the direction of our attention, sensing possible emergences and new embodiments.

Bibliography

Aarseth, E.J. (1998) *Cybertext: Perspectives on Ergodic Literature*. Baltimore: Johns Hopkins University Press.

Abrahamson, E.J. (2004) *Change Without Pain: How Managers Can Overcome Initiative Overload, Organizational Chaos and Employee Burnout*. Boston: Harvard Business School Press.

Ackerman, M.S., Pipek, V. and Wulf, V. (eds) (2003) *Sharing Expertise: Beyond Knowledge Management*. Cambridge, MA: MIT Press.

Adam, B. (1990) *Time and Social Theory*. Cambridge: Polity.

Adam, B. (1995) *Timewatch: The Social Analysis of Time*. Cambridge: Polity.

Adams, S. (1996) *The Dilbert Principle: A Cubicle's Eye View of Bosses, Meetings, Management Fads and Other Workplace Afflictions*. New York: Harper Collins.

Aldiss, B. (2001) *Supertoys Last All Summer Long*. London: Orbit.

Alexander, C. (1995) *Fin-de-Siècle Social Theory: Relativism, Reduction and the Problem of Reason*. London: Verso.

Allsopp, S. and de Lahunta, S. (1999) On line. Special Issue of *Performance Research*, 4 (2).

Altvater, E. and Mahnkopf, B. (1997) The world market unbound. *Review of International Political Economy*, 4: 448–71.

Alvarez, J.L. (1996) The international popularisation of entreprenerial ideas. In S. Clegg and G. Palmer (eds) *The Politics of Management Knowledge*. London: Sage.

Amin, A. and Cohendet, P. (2003) *Architecture of Knowledge: Firms, Capabilities and Commodities*. Oxford: Oxford University Press.

Amin, A. and Thrift, N.J. (1995) Institutional issues for the European regions: from markets and plans to socioeconomics and powers of association. *Economy and Society*, 24: 41–66.

Amin, A. and Thrift, N.J. (2002) *Cities: Re-Imagining Urban Theory*. Cambridge: Polity.

Anders, G. (2001) Marc Andreessen, Act II. *Fast Company*, no. 43: 110–22.

Anderson, J.A. and Rosenfeld, E. (eds) (1999) *Talking Nets: An Oral History of Neural Networks*. Cambridge, MA: MIT Press.

Anderson, T. (2000) *Seizing the Opportunities of a New Economy: Challenges for the European Union*. Paris: OECD.

Ansell-Pearson, K. (ed.) (1997) *Deleuze and Philosophy: The Difference Engineer*. London: Routledge.

Appadurai, A. (2000) Grassroots globalisation and the research imagination. *Public Culture*, 12: 1–20.

Arbile, T. (1998) How to kill creativity. *Harvard Business Review*, September–October: 83–101.

Argyris, C. (1991) Teaching smart people how to learn. *Harvard Business Review*, May–June: 68–93.

Argyris, C. (2000) *Flawed Advice and the Management Trap*. New York: Oxford University Press.

Argyris, C. and Schon, D. (1974) *Theory in Practice*. New York: Wiley.

Argyris, C. and Schon, D. (1978) *Organizational Learning*. New York: Wiley.

Argyros, A.J. (1991) *A Blessed Rage for Order: Deconstruction, Evolution and Chaos*. Ann Arbor, MI: University of Michigan Press.

Arkin, R. (1998) *Behavior-Based Robotics*. Cambridge, MA: MIT Press.

Arnolfini (1997) *Arnolfini June/July 1997*. Bristol: Arnolfini Gallery.

Arthur, W.B. (1994) *Increasing Returns and Path Dependence in the Economy*. Ann Arbor, MI: University of Michigan Press.

Attfield, J. (2000) *Wild Things: The Material Culture of Everyday Life*. Oxford: Berg.

Audit Commission (1998) *A Stitch in Time: Facing the Challenge of the Year 2000 Date Change*. London: Audit Commission.

Bachelard, G. (1966) *The Poetics of Space*. Boston: Beacon.

Badaracco, J.L. (1991) *The Knowledge Link*. Cambridge, MA: Harvard Business School Press.

Bailey, C. (1996) Virtual skin: articulating race in cyberspace. In M.A. Moser and D. McLeod (eds) *Immersed in Technology: Art in Virtual Environments*. Cambridge, MA: MIT Press, 29–50.

Barabasi, A. (2002) *Linked: The New Science of Networks*. Cambridge, MA: Perseus.

Barlow, J.P. (1999) 'I'm the guy.' *Fast Company*, February–March: 84.

Barnet, R.J. and Cavanagh, J. (1995) *Global Dreams: Imperial Corporations and the New Order*. New York: Simon and Schuster.

Barnett, W.A., Kirman, A.P. and Salmon, M. (eds) (1996) *Nonlinear Dynamics and Economics*. Cambridge: Cambridge University Press.

Barry, A. (2001) *Political Machines*. London: Athlone.

Bass, T. (1997) *The Predictors*. New York: Harpers.

Batty, M. and Longley, P. (1995) *Fractal Cities*. London: Academic.

Bauman, Z. (1987) *Legislators and Interpreters*. Cambridge: Polity.

Bauman, Z. (1995) Searching for a centre that holds. In M. Featherstone, S. Lash and R. Robertson (eds) *Global Modernities*. London: Sage, 140–54.

Bauman, Z. (1998) *Globalization: The Human Consequences*. Cambridge: Polity.

Beck, U. (1992) *Risk Society: Towards a New Modernity*. London: Sage.

Beer, G. (1996) *Open Fields: Science in Cultural Encounter*. Oxford: Oxford University Press.

Beer, S. (1972) *Brain of the Firm: The Managerial Cybernetics of Organization*. London: Allen Lane.

Beer, S. (1975) *Platform for Change*. New York: Wiley.

Beinhocker, M. (1997) Strategy at the edge of chaos. *McKinsey Quarterly*, no. 1.

Belew, R.K. and Vose, M.D. (1997) *Foundations of Genetic Algorithms 4*. San Francisco: Morgan Kaufmann.

Benitez-Rojo, A. (1992) *The Repeating Island: The Caribbean and the Postmodern Perspective*. Durham, NC: Duke University Press.

Benjamin, A. (ed.) (1995) Complexity: architecture/art/philosophy. *Journal of Philosophy and the Visual Arts*, no. 6.

Bennett, J. (2001) *The Enchantment of Modern Life: Attachments, Crossings and Ethics*. Princeton, NJ: Princeton University Press.

Bentley, P. (2001) *Digital Life: A New Kind of Nature*. London: Headline.

Benyus, J.M. (1997) *Biomimicry: Imitation Inspired by Nature*. New York: Morrow.

Bergman, E. (ed.) (2000) *Information Appliances and Beyond*. San Diego, CA: Academic.

Berlant, L. (2001) Trauma and ineloquence. *Cultural Values*, 5: 41–58.

Bernstein, M.A. (1994) *Foregone Conclusions: Against Apocalyptic History*. Berkeley, CA: University of California Press.

Billinghusrt (n.d.) Quoted in 'Head to toe'. CNET.com at http://coverage.cnet.com/Content/Gadgets/FunToWear/ss03.html, accessed 29 December 2000.

Blanchard, G. and Bowles, M. (1998) *Gung Ho!* New York: Morrow.

Bloch, E. (1986) *The Principle of Hope*.Three volumes. Oxford: Blackwell.

Blumenberg, H. (1985) *The Legitimacy of the Modern Age*. Cambridge, MA: MIT Press.

Boden, D. (1994) *The Business of Talk*. Cambridge: Polity.

Boisot, M.H. (1995) *Information Space: A Framework of Learning in Organisations, Institutions and Culture*. London: Routledge.

Boltanski, L. and Chiapello E. (1999) *Le Nouvel Esprit du Capitalisme*. Paris: Gallimard.

Bolter, D. and Grusin R. (1999) Remediation: Understanding the New Media. Cambridge, MA: MIT Press.

Bonabeau, E., Dorigo, M. and Theraulez, G. (1999) *Swarm Intelligence: From Natural to Artificial Systems*. Oxford: Oxford University Press.

Bonissone, P.P. (1998) Soft computing and hybrid systems. In E. Ruspini, P.P. Bonissone and W. Pedrycz (eds) *The Handbook of Fuzzy Computation*. London: Institute of Physics Publishing.

Borgmann, A. (2000) Semi-artificial life. In M. Wrathall and J. Malpas (eds) *Heidegger, Coping and Cognitive Science: Essays in Honor of Herbert L. Dreyfus, vol. 2*. Cambridge, MA: MIT Press, 197–205.

Boruk, X. (1999) Chicago Business School picks Singapore: university to open permanent campus for executive MBA students. Asian *Wall Street Journal*, 25 January: 6.

Botwinick, A. (1996) *Participation and Tacit Knowledge in Plato, Machiavelli and Hobbes*. Lanham, MD: University Press of America.

Bourdieu, P. (1977) *Outline of a Theory of Practice*. Cambridge: Cambridge University Press.

Bourdieu, P. (1984) *Distinction*. London: Routledge and Kegan Paul.

Bourdieu, P. (2000) *Pascalian Meditations*. Cambridge: Polity.

Bowker, G.C. and Star, S.L. (1994) Knowledge and infrastructure in international information management. In L. Bud-Frierman (ed.) *Information Acumen: The Understanding and Use of Knowledge in Modern Business*. London: Routledge, 187–215.

Bowker, G.C. and Star, S.L. (1999) *Sorting Things Out: Classification and its Consequences*. Cambridge, MA: MIT Press.

Brandt, J. (1997) *Geopoetics: The Politics of Mimesis in Poststructuralist French Poetry and Theory*. Stanford, CA: Stanford University Press.

Brayshay, M., Harrison, P. and Chalkley, M. (1998) Knowledge, nationhood and governance: the speed of the royal post in early modern England. *Journal of Historical Geography*, 42: 263–88.

Brenner, R. (2003) Towards the precipice. *London Review of Books*, 6 February.

Bronson, P. (1999) *The Nudist on the Late Shift and Other Silicon Valley Stories*. London: Secker and Warburg.

Brooks, D. (2000) *Bobos in Paradise: The New Upper Class and How They Got There*. New York: Simon and Schuster.

Brooks, R. (1991) Intelligence without representation. *Artificial Intelligence Journal*, 47: 139–60.

Brooks, R. (1999) *Cambrian Intelligence: The Early History of the New AI*. Cambridge, MA: MIT Press.

Brooks, R. (2002a) *Robot: The Future of Flesh and Machines*. London: Allen Lane.

Brooks, R. (2002b) Lord of the robots. *Technology Review*, April: 78–82.

Brown, B., Green, N. and Harper, R. (eds) (2002) *Wireless World: Social and Interactional Aspects of the Mobile Age*. London: Springer.

Brown, M. (1997) *The Channelling Zone: American Spirituality in an Anxious Age*. Cambridge, MA: Harvard University Press.

Brown, S., Middleton, D. and Lightfoot, G. (2001) Performing the past in electronic archives: interdependence in the discursive and non-discursive ordering of remembering. *Culture and Psychology*, 7 (2): 123–44.

Bruno, G. (2002) *Atlas of Emotion: Journeys in Art, Architecture and Film*. London: Verso.

Bruns, S. (1997) *Managers' Lives*. Cambridge, MA: Harvard Business School Press.

Buchanan, M. (2002) *Nexus: Small Worlds and the Groundbreaking Science of Networks*. New York: Norton.

Buck-Morss, S. (1995) Envisioning capital: political economy on display. In L. Cooke and P. Wollen (eds) *Visual Display: Culture Beyond Appearances*. Seattle: Bay, 110–41.

Bud-Frierman, L. (ed.) (1994) *Information Acumen: The Understanding and Use of Knowledge in Modern Business*. London: Routledge.

Budiansky, S. (1998) *If a Lion Could Talk: Animal Intelligence and the Evolution of Consciousness*. New York: Free.

Bull, M. (ed.) (1995) *Apocalyse Theory and the Ends of the World*. Oxford: Blackwell.

Bunnell, T. (2002) (Re)positioning Malaysia: high-tech networks and the multicultural rescripting of national identity. *Political Geography*, 21: 105–24.

Burningbird (2002) The parable of the languages. At http://weblog.burningbird.net/archives/000581.php, accessed 30 December 2002.

Burton-Jones, A. (2000) *Knowledge Capitalism: Business, Work and Learning in the New Economy*. Oxford: Oxford University Press.

Butler, J. (1990) *Gender Trouble*. New York: Routledge.

Butler, J. (1991) Imitation and gender insubordination. In D. Fuss (ed.) *Lesbian Theories*. New York: Routledge, 23–38.

Butler, J. (1993) *Bodies That Matter*. New York: Routledge.

Butler, J. (2003) Mobile robots as gateways into wireless sensor networks. At http://www.linuxdevices.com/articles/AT2705574735.html.

Byrne, D. (1996) Chaotic cities or complex cities. In S. Westwood and J. Williams (eds) *Imagining Cities*. London: Routledge, 50–70.

Caillois, R. (1962) *Man, Play and Games*. Urbana, IL: University of Illinois Press.

Callon, M. (1987) Society in the making: the study of technology as a tool for sociological analysis. In W.E. Bijker, T.P. Hughes and T.J. Pinch (eds) *The Social Construction of Technical Systems*. Cambridge, MA: MIT Press, 83–103.

Callon, M. (ed.) (1998) *The Laws of the Market*. Oxford: Blackwell.

Campbell, J.A. (1990) Scientific discovery and rhetorical invention: the path to Darwin's Origin. In H.W. Simon (ed.) *The Rhetorical Turn: Invention and Permission in the Conduct of Inquiry*. Chicago: University of Chicago Press.

Campbell-Kelly, M. (2003) *From Airline Reservations to Sonic the Hedgehog: A History of the Software Industry*. Cambridge, MA: MIT Press.

Capra, F. (1996) *Web of Life*. London: Harper Collins.

Carrier, J.G. (ed.) (1995) *Occidentalism: Images of the West*. Oxford: Oxford University Press.

Carrier, J.G. (ed.) (1996) *Meanings of the Market*. Oxford: Berg.

Carrier, J.G. and Miller, D. (eds) (1998) *Virtualism: The New Political Economy*. Oxford: Berg.

Cassell, J. and Jenkins, H. (eds) (1999) *From Barbie to Mortal Kombat: Gender and Computer Games*. Cambridge, MA: MIT Press.

Cassell, J., Sullivan, J., Prevost, S. and Churchill, E. (eds) (2000) *Embodied Conversational Agents*. Cambridge, MA: MIT Press.

Cassidy, J. (2002) *Dot.Con: The Greatest Story Ever Sold*. London: Allen Lane.

Casti, J. (1991) *Searching for Certainty: What Scientists Can Know About the Future*. London: Scribners.

Casti, J. (1996) *Would-Be Worlds: How Simulation Is Changing the Frontiers of Science*. New York: Wiley.

Chan, C.B. (ed.) (2002) *Heart Work: Stories of How EDB Steered the Singapore Economy from 1961 into the 21st Century*. Singapore: EDB.

Chandler, A. (1962) *Strategy and Structure*. Cambridge, MA: MIT Press.

Chandler, A. (1977) *The Visible Hand*. Cambridge, MA: Belknap.

Chandler, A. and Cortado, J.W. (2000) A *Nation Transformed by Information*. New York: Oxford University Press.

Chanlat, J. (1996) From cultural imperialism to independence. In S. Clegg and J. Palmer (eds) *The Politics of Management Knowledge*. London: Sage, 121–40.

Chin-Ning Chun (1996) *White Face, Black Heart: The Asian Path to Winning and Succeeding*. London: Brealey.

Ciborra, C. (2002) *The Labyrinths of Information: Challenging the Wisdom of Systems*. Oxford: Oxford University Press.

Clark, G.L. (2000) *Pension Fund Capitalism*. Oxford: Oxford University Press.

Clark, J. (1995) *Managing Consultants: Consultancy as the Management of Impressions*. Buckingham: Open University Press.

Clark, T. (2001) *Critical Consulting*. Oxford: Blackwell.

Clarke, J. and Newman, J. (1993) The right to manage: a second managerial revolution? *Cultural Studies*, 7: 427–41.

Clegg, B. and Birch, P. (1999) *Imagination Engineering*. London: Financial Times.

Clegg, S. and Palmer, G. (eds) (1996) *The Politics of Management Knowledge*. London: Sage.

Clippinger, J. (ed.) (1999) *The Biology of Business*. San Francisco: Jossey Bass.

Clough, P. (2000) *Auto Affection: Unconscious Thought in the Age of Tele-Technology*. Minneapolis: University of Minnesota Press.

Coe, N. and Kelly, P. (2000) Distance and discourse in the local labour market: the case of Singapore. *Area*, 32 (4): 413–22.

Coe, N. and Kelly, P. (2002) Languages of labour: representational strategies in Singapore's labour control regime. *Political Geography*, 21: 341–71.

Collins, D. (2000) *Management Fads and Buzzwords: Critical-Practical Perspectives*. London: Routledge.

Collins, H. (1990) *Artificial Experts: Social Knowledge and Intelligent Machines*. Cambridge, MA: MIT Press.

Collins, H. and Kusch, M. (1998) *The Shape of Actions: What Humans and Machines Can Do*. Cambridge, MA: MIT Press.

Collins, J. (1995) *Architectures of Excess: Cultural Life in the Information Age*. London: Routledge.

Colvin, G. (2000) Managing in the Info Era. *Fortune*, 14 (5): F2–F5.

Conley, T. (1996) The wit of the letter: Holbein's Lacan. In T. Brennan and M. Jay (eds) *Vision in Context: Historical and Contemporary Perspectives on Sight*. London: Routledge, 45–62.

Connolly, W. (1999) *Why I Am Not A Secularist*. Minneapolis: University of Minnesota Press.

Connolly, W. (2002) *Neuropolitics*. Minneapolis: University of Minnesota Press.

Cooper, R.K. and Sawaf, A. (1997) *Executive EQ: Emotional Intelligence in Business*. London: Orion Business.

Coppinger, R. and Coppinger, L. (2001) *Dogs: A New Understanding of Canine Origin, Behaviour and Evolution*. Chicago: University of Chicago Press.

Coulson-Thomas, J. (ed.) 1997 *Business Process Re-Engineering*. London: Brealey.

Coveney, P. and Highfield, R. (1995) *Frontiers of Complexity: The Search for Order in a Chaotic World*. London: Faber and Faber.

Covey, S.R. (1989) *Seven Habits of Highly Effective People*. New York: Simon and Schuster.

Crainer, S. (ed.) (1995) *The Financial Times Handbook of Management*. London: Pitman.

Crainer, S. (1997a) *Corporate Man to Corporate Skunk: The Tom Peters Phenomenon*. London: Capstone.

Crainer, S. (1997b) Get me a writer! *Silver Kris*, December: 36–8.

Crainer, S. and Dearlove, D. (1998) *Gravy Training: Inside the Shadowy World of Business Schools*. London: Capstone.

Crang, P. (1999) Organisational geographies: surveillance, display and the spaces of power in business organisations. In J. Sharp, P. Routledge, C. Philo and R. Paddison (eds) *Entanglements of Power: Geographies of Domination/Resistance*. London: Routledge, 204–18.

Crary, J. (1999) *Suspensions of Perception: Attention, Spectacle and Modern Culture*. Cambridge, MA: MIT Press.

Crosby, T.W. (1996) *The Measure of Reality: Quantification and Western Society, 1250–1600*. Cambridge: Cambridge University Press.

Cross, G. (1997) *Kid's Stuff: Toys and the Changing World of American Childhood*. Cambridge, MA: Harvard University Press.

Crystal, D. (2001) *Language and the Internet*. Cambridge: Cambridge University Press.

Cubitt, S. (1998) *Digital Aesthetics*. London: Sage.

Cypher, A. (ed.) (1993) *Watch What I Do: Programming by Demonstration*. Cambridge, MA: MIT Press.

Dahle, C. (2000) Mind games. *Fast Company*, no. 31: 168–80.

Daly, C. (1993) The discursive construction of economic space. *Economy and Society*, 20: 79–102.

Dautenhahn, K. and Nehaniv, C. (eds) (2002) *Imitation in Animals and Artifacts*. Cambridge: MIT Press.

Dautenhahn, K., Bond, A.H., Canamero, L. and Edmonds, B. (eds) (2002) *Socially Intelligent Agents: Creating Relationships with Computers and Robots*. Dordrecht: Kluwer.

Davis, L. and Steenstrup, M. (1990) Genetic algorithms and simulated annealing: an overview. In L. Davis (ed.) *Genetic Algorithms and Simulated Annealing*. London: Pitman.

Davis, T.R.V. and Luthans, F. (1980) Managers in action: a new look at their behavior and operating modes. Organizational Dynamics, Summer: 64–80.

Dean, M. (1999) *Governmentality: Power and Rule in Modern Society*. London: Sage.

De Geuss, A. (1997) *The Living Company*. London: Brealey.

DeLanda, M. (1997) *A Thousand Years of Nonlinear History*. New York: Zone.

DeLanda, M. (2002) *Intensive Science and Virtual Philosophy*. London: Continuum.

Deleuze, G. (1986) *Foucault*. Paris: Éditions de Minuit.

Deleuze, G. (1990a) Postscript to Societies of Control. *October*, 31: 27–36.

Deleuze, G. (1990b) *The Logic of Sense*. New York: Columbia University Press.

Deleuze, G. (1994) *Difference and Repetition*. New York: Columbia University Press.

Deleuze, G. and Guattari, F. (1987) *A Thousand Plateaus: Capitalism and Schizophrenia*, trans. B. Massumi. Minneapolis: University of Minnesota Press.

Deleuze, G. and Parnet, C. (1987) *Dialogues*, trans. H. Tomlinson and B. Habberjam. New York: Columbia University Press.

De Lillo, D. (1990) *White Noise*. New York: Picador.

Dennett, D. (1997) *Kinds of Minds: Towards an Understanding of Consciousness*. London: Phoenix.

De Nora, T. (2000) *Music in Everyday Life*. Cambridge: Cambridge University Press.

Derrida, J. (1998) *Archive Fever*. Chicago: Chicago University Press.

Dertouzos, M. (2001) *The Unfinished Revolution: Human-Centred Computers and What They Can Do For Us*. New York: Harper Collins.

Dezalay, Y. and Garth, B. (2002a) *The Internationalization of Palace Wars: Lawyers, Economists, and the Contest to Transform Latin American States*. Chicago: University of Chicago Press.

Dezalay, Y. and Garth, B. (2002b) *Global Prescriptions: The Production, Exportation and Importation of a New Legal Orthodoxy*. Ann Arbor, MI: University of Michigan Press.

Diamond, C. (1991) *The Realistic Spirit*: Wittgenstein, Philosophy and the Mind. Cambridge, MA: MIT Press.

Dicken, P. (1998) *Global Shift: Transforming the World Economy*, 3rd edn. London: Chapman.

Dieburger, A. and Frank, A.U. (1998) A city metaphor for supporting navigation in complex information spaces. *Journal of Visual Languages and Computing*, 9: 597–622.

DiMaggio, P. (ed.) (2001) *The Twenty-First-Century Firm: Changing Economic Organization in International Perspective*. Princeton, NJ: Princeton University Press.

Doane, M.A. (2002) *The Emergence of Cinematic Time*. Cambridge, MA: Harvard University Press.

Dolven, B. (2000) Business class. *Far Eastern Economic Review*, 10 February: 48–9.

Dourish, P. (2001) *Where the Action Is: The Foundations of Embodied Interaction*. Cambridge, MA: MIT Press.

Downey, C.G. (1998) *The Machine in Me: The Anthropologist Sitting Among Computer Engineers*. Stanford, CA: Stanford University Press.

Downey, J. and McGuigan, J. (eds) (1999) *Technocities*. London: Sage.

Doyle, R. (1997) *On Beyond Living: Rhetorical Transformations of the Life Sciences*. Stanford, CA: Stanford University Press.

Dreyfus, H. (1999) Anonymity versus commitment: the dangers of education on the internet. *Ethics and Information Technology*, 1: 15–21.

Dreyfus, H. (2001) *On the Internet*. New York: Routledge.

Drucker, P. (1988) The coming of the new organization. *Harvard Business Review*, 88: 45–53.

Dryer, D.C., Eisbach, C. and Ark, W.S. (1999) At what cost pervasive? A social computing view of mobile computing systems. *IBM Systems Journal*, 38 (4).

Du Gay, P. (1996) *Consumption and Identity at Work*. London: Sage.

Duffy, F. (1997) *The New Office*. London: Conran Octopus.

Dumaine, B. (1997) Asia's wealth creators confront a new reality. *Fortune*, 8 December: 42–55.

Eagleton, T. (1995) Review of Derrida's Spectres of Marx. *Radical Philosophy*, 73: 35–7.

Eccles, R. and Nohria, N. (1990) The Post-Structuralist Organization. *Harvard Business School Working Paper* 92–003.

Economist Intelligence Unit (2000) Electronic Revolution in the Motor Industry. London: *The Economist*.

Edvinsson, L. and Malone, M. (1997) *Intellectual Capital: The Proven Way to Establish Your Company's True Value by Measuring its Hidden Brain Power*. London: Paitkus.

Egan, G. (1996) *Distress*. London: Gollancz.

Eisenberg, A. (2003) Wired to the brain of a rat, a robot takes on the world. *New York Times*, 15 May: 13–26.

Elkaim, M. (1997) *If You Love Me, Don't Love Me*. Northvale, NJ: Aronson.

Elliott, E. and Kiel, L.D. (eds) (1996) *Chaos Theory in the Social Sciences: Foundation and Application*. Ann Arbor, MI: University of Michigan Press.

Emery, F. (1969) *Systems Theory*. Harmondsworth: Penguin.

Engwall, L. (1992) *Mercury meets Minerva*. Oxford: Pergamon.

ERC (2002a) Report of the ERC Subcommittee on Services Industries: Part I. Singapore: ERC. At http://www.erc.gov.sg/frm_ERC_ErcReports.htm.

ERC (2002b) Developing Singapore's Education Industry. Singapore: ERC. At http://www.erc.gov.sg/frm_ERC_ErcReports.htm.

European Union (1997) *The Globalising Learning Economy: Implications for Innovation Policy*. DG XII, EUR 18307 EN. Brussels: EU.

Eve, R.A., Horsfall, S. and Lee, M.E. (eds) (1997) *Chaos, Complexity and Sociology: Myths, Models and Theories*. Beverly Hills, CA: Sage.

Ezzy, D. (2001) A simulacrum of workplace community: individualism and engineered culture. *Sociology*, 35: 631–50.

Feral Robots (2003) Feral robotics: dog report. At http://xdesign.eng.yale.edu/feralrobots.

Ferguson, G.T. (2002) Have your objects call my objects. *Harvard Business Review*, 80 (6): 138–44.

Ferguson, N. (ed.) (1997) *Virtual History: Alternatives and Counterfactuals*. London: Picador.

Ferry, G. (2003) *A Computer Called LEO: Lyons Tea Shops and the World's First Office Computer*. London: Fourth Estate.

Fine, C.H. (1998) *Clockspeed*. London: Orion.

Finn, C. (2001) *Artifacts: An Archaeologist's Year in Silicon Valley*. Cambridge, MA: MIT Press.

Fischer, S.R. (2001) *A History of Writing*. London: Reaktion.

Fleming, D. (1996) *Powerplay: Toys as Popular Culture*. Manchester: Manchester University Press.

Flores, F. (1998) Information technology and the institution of identity: reflections since Understanding Computers and Cognition. *Information Technology and People*, 7.

Flores, F. (2000) Heideggerian thinking and the transformation of business practice. In M. Wrathall and J. Malpas (eds) *Heidegger, Coping and Cognitive Science: Essays in Honour of Herbert L. Dreyfus, vol. 2*. Cambridge: MA: MIT Press, 271–91.

Flores, F. and Gray, J. (2000) *Entrepreneurship and the Wired Life: Work in the Wake of Careers*. London: Demos.

Foister, S., Roy, A. and Wyld, M. (1997) *Holbein's Ambassadors*. London: National Gallery.

Foucault, M. (1970) *The Order of Things: An Archaeology of the Human Sciences*. London: Tavistock.

Foucault, M. (1991) Governmentality. In G. Burchell, C. Gordon and P. Miller (eds) *The Foucault Effect*. Hemel Hempstead: Harvester Wheatsheaf.

Foucault, M. (1998) Interview with Didier Eribon, 1981. In L. Kritzman (ed.) *Foucault: Politics, Philosophy, Culture*. New York: Routledge.

Frank, A.W. (1997) *The Conquest of Cool: Business Culture, Counter-Culture and the Rise of Hip Consumerism*. Chicago: University of Chicago Press.

Frank, T. (2000) *One Market Under God: Extreme Capitalism, Market Populism and the End of Economic Democracy*. London: Secker and Warburg.

French, R. and Grey, C. (eds) (1996) *Rethinking Management Education*. London: Sage.

Froud, J., Haslan, C., Johal, S. and Williams, K. (2000) Shareholder value and financialization: consultancy promises, management moves. *Economy and Society*, 29: 80–110.

Frow, J. (1997) *Time and Commodity Culture: Essays in Cultural Theory and Postmodernity*. Oxford: Oxford University Press.

Fukuyama, F. (1992) *The End of History and the Last Man*. London: Hamish Hamilton.

Furusten, S. (1999) *Popular Management Books: How They Are Made and What They Mean for Organisations*. London: Routledge.

Gadrey, J. (2003) *New Economy, New Myth*. London: Routledge.

Gaita, R. (2003) *The Philosopher's Dog*. London: Routledge.

Gamble, K. and Kelly, J. (1996) The new politics of ownership. *New Left Review*, no. 220: 62–97.

Game, A. and Metcalfe, D. (1996) *Passionate Sociology*. London: Sage.

Garber, M. (1996) *Dog Love*. New York: Simon and Schuster.

Geary, J. (2002) *The Body Electric: An Anatomy of the New Bionic Senses*. London: Weidenfeld and Nicolson.

Geertz, C. (1993) *The Interpretation of Cultures: Selected Essays*. London: Fontana.

Gehlen, A. (1990) *Man in the Age of Technology*. New York: Columbia University Press.

Gell, A. (1992) *The Anthropology of Time*. Oxford: Berg.

Gell-Mann, M. (1994) *The Quark and the Jaguar: Adventures in the Simple and the Complex*. London: Little Brown.

Genette, G. (1999) *Paratexts: Thresholds of Interpretation*. Cambridge: Cambridge University Press.

Gershenfeld, N. (1999) *When Things Start to Think*. London: Coronet.

Ghoschal, S. and Bartlett, C.A. (1995) Changing the role of top management: beyond structure to process. *Harvard Business Review*, 73: 86–96.

Gibbons, M., Limoges, C., Nowotny, H., Schwartzman, S., Scott, P. and Trow, S. (1994) *The New Production of Knowledge: The Dynamics of Science and Research in Contemporary Societies*. London: Sage.

Gibson, A. (1996) *Towards a Postmodern Theory of Narrative*. Edinburgh: Edinburgh University Press.

Giddens, A. (1991) *Modernity and Self-Identity*. Cambridge: Polity.

Giedion, S. (1998) *Mechanization Takes Command: A Contribution to Anonymous History*. New York: Norton.

Gille, D. (1986) Maceration and purification. In M. Feher and S. Kwinter (eds) *Zone 1/2: The Contemporary City*. New York: Zone, 227–81.

Giroux, H.A. and Kline, S. (2002) *Out of the Garden: Toys and Children's Culture in the Age of TV Marketing*. London: Verso.

Gladwell, M. (2000) *The Tipping Point: How Little Things Can Make a Big Difference*. New York: Little Brown.

Gleick, J. (1999) *Faster: The Acceleration of Just About Everything*. London: Little Brown.

Gleick, J. and Porter, E. (1991) *Nature's Chaos*. London: Abacus.

Glennie, P. and Thrift, N.J. (1996) Consumers, identities and consumption spaces in early modern England. *Environment and Planning A*, 28: 25–46.

Glennie, P. and Thrift, N.J. (2005) *The Measured Heart: Episodes from the History of Clock Time*. Oxford: Oxford University Press.

Goffee, R. and Hunt, J.W. (1996) The end of management? Classroom versus boardroom. *Financial Times*, 22 March: 3–4.

Goffey, A. (2002) Naturalizing phenomenology: cognitive science and the bestowal of sense. Radical *Philosophy*, 114: 20–8.

Goldberg, D.E. (1989) *Genetic Algorithms in Search, Optimization and Machine Learning.* London: Addison-Wesley.

Goodwin, B.C. (1994) *How the Leopard Changed Its Spots.* London: Weidenfeld and Nicholson.

Goodwin, B.C. (1997) Community, creativity and society. *Soundings*, no. 5: 111–23.

Goody, J. (1971) *The Domestication of the Savage Mind.* Cambridge: Cambridge University Press.

Goody, J. (1987) *The Interface between the Written and the Oral.* Cambridge: Cambridge University Press.

Goody, J. (1996) *The East in the West.* Cambridge: Cambridge University Press.

Gordon, A.F. (1997) *Ghostly Matters: Haunting and the Sociological Imagination.* Minneapolis: University of Minnesota Press.

Grabher, G. (2000) Ecologies of creativity: the village, the group, and the heterarchic organisation of the British advertising industry. *Environment and Planning A*, 33: 351–74.

Graham, S. (1998) Spaces of surveillant simulation: new technologies, digital representations, and material geographies. *Environment and Planning D*: Society and Space, 16: 483–504.

Gray, J. (2002) *Straw Dogs: Thoughts on Humans and Other Animals.* London: Granta.

Gray, W.S. and Liguori, S. (1990) *Hotel and Motel Manager Operations*, 2nd edn. Englewood Cliffs, NJ: Prentice-Hall.

Gregory, C. (1997) *Savage Money.* Oxford: Berg.

Grenier, R. (2002) *The Difficulty of Being a Dog.* Chicago: University of Chicago Press.

Griffith, S. (2000) It's a man's new economy. *Financial Times*, 25 August: 12.

Griffith, V. (1996) Creating virtuality. *Financial Times*, 22 November: 14.

Grint, K. and Woolgar, S. (1997) *The Machine at Work: Technology, Work and Organisation.* Cambridge: Polity.

Gross, A.G. (1996) *The Rhetoric of Science*, 2nd edn. Cambridge, MA: Harvard University Press.

Guattari, F. (1996) *Chaosmosis: An Ethico-Aesthetic Paradigm.* Sydney: Power.

Gumbrecht, H.U. and Pfeiffer, K.L (eds) (1994) *Materialities of Communication.* Stanford, CA: Stanford University Press.

Gunter, B. and Furnham, A. (1998) *Children as Consumers.* London: Routledge.

Hague, D. (1994) *The Knowledge-Based Economy.* Oxford: Templeton College.

Hamel, G. and Prahalad, C.K. (1994) *Competing for the Future.* Boston: Harvard Business School Press.

Hamlin, K. (2002) Remaking Singapore. *Institutional Investor*, May.

Hammer, M. and Champy, J. (1993) *Re-Engineering the Corporation: A Manifesto for a Business Revolution.* London: Brealey.

Hampden-Turner, C. and Trompenaars, L. (1997) *Mastering the Infinite Game: How East Asian Values Are Transforming Business Practices.* London: Capstone.

Handy, C. (1989) *The Age of Unreason.* London: Arrow.

Hannerz, U. (1996) *Transnational Connections: Culture, People, Places.* London: Routledge.

Hansen, M. (2000) *Embodying Technesis: Technology beyond Writing.* Ann Arbor, MI: University of Michigan Press.

Harris, C. (ed.) (1999) *Art and Innovation: The Xerox PARC Artist-in-Residence Program.* Cambridge, MA: MIT Press.

Harrison, M.J. (2002) *Light.* London: Gollancz.

Harvey, D. (1989) *The Condition of Postmodernity.* Oxford: Blackwell.

Harvey, D. (2000) *Spaces of Hope.* Edinburgh: Edinburgh University Press.

Hassan, R. (2003) The MIT Media Lab: techno dream factory or alienation as a way of life. *Media, Culture and Society*, 25: 87–106.

Hatch, M.J. and Ehrlich, S.B. (1993) Spontaneous humour as an indicator of paradox and ambiguity in organisations. *Organisational Studies*, 14: 505–26.

Hawthorn, G. (1991) *Plausible Worlds*. Cambridge: Cambridge University Press.

Hayles, K. (1990) *Chaos Unbound: Orderly Disorder in Contemporary Literature and Science*. Ithaca, NY: Cornell University Press.

Hayles, K. (ed.) (1991) *Chaos and Order*. Chicago: University of Chicago Press.

Hayles, K. (1996) Narratives of artificial life. In G. Robertson, M. Mash, L. Tickner, J. Bird, B. Curtis and T. Putman (eds) *Future Natural: Nature, Science, Culture*. London: Routledge, 146–64.

Hayles, K. (1999) *How We Became Posthuman*. Chicago: University of Chicago Press.

Hayles, K. (2002) *Writing Machines*. Cambridge, MA: MIT Press.

Heckscher, C. and Donnellon, A. (eds) (1994) *The Post-Bureaucratic Organization*: New Perspectives on Organisational Change. Thousand Oaks, CA: Sage.

Heelas, P. (1991a) Cuts for capitalism; self-religions, magic and the enpowerment of business. In P. Gee and J. Fulton (eds) *Religion and Power: Decline and Growth*. London: British Sociological Association, 27–41.

Heelas, P. (1991b) Reforming the self: enterprise and the character of Thatcherism. In R. Keat and N. Abercombie (eds) *Enterprise Culture*. London: Routledge, 72–90.

Heelas, P. (1992) The sacralisation of the self and New Age capitalism. In N. Abercombie and A. Warde (eds) *Social Change in Contemporary Britain*. Cambridge: Polity, 139–66.

Heelas, P. (1996) *The New Age Movement: The Celebration of the Self and the Sacralisation of Modernity*. Oxford: Blackwell.

Heitkötter, J. and Beasley, D. (1999) The Hitch-Hiker's Guide to Evolutionary Computation. At http://www.cs.bham.ac.uk/Mirrors/ftp.de.uu.net/EC/clife/www/top.htm.

Helmreich, S. (1998) *Silicon Second Nature: Culturing Artificial Life in a Digital World*. Berkeley, CA: University of California Press.

Herzberg, F. (1965) *Work and the Nature of Man*. Cleveland, OH: World.

Hetherington, K. (1996) Identity formation, space and social centrality. *Theory Culture and Society*, 13: 33–52.

Heyes, C. and Galef, B. (1996) *Social Learning in Animals: The Roots of Culture*. San Diego, CA: Academic.

Hill, S. and Turpin, T. (1995) Cultures in collision: the emergence of a new localism in academic research. In M. Strathern (ed.) *Shifting Contexts: Transformations of Anthropological Knowledge*. London: Routledge, 131–52.

Hiscock, G. (1997a) Asia's next wealth club. *World Executive's Digest*, December: 19–22.

Hiscock, G. (1997b) *Asia's Wealth Clubs: Who's Really Who in Business: The Top 100 Billionaires in Asia*. London: Brealey.

Hobart, M.E. and Schiffman, Z.S. (1998) *Information Ages: Literacy, Numeracy and the Computer Revolution*. Baltimore: Johns Hopkins University Press.

Hofstede, G. (1991) *Cultures and Organisations*. New York: McGraw-Hill.

Holland, J.H. (1975) *Adaptation in Natural and Artificial Systems*. Cambridge, MA: MIT Press.

Holland, O. and McFarland, D. (2001) *Artificial Ethology*. Oxford: Oxford University Press.

Holloway, S. and Valentine, G. (eds) (2000) *Children's Geographies*. London: Routledge.

Holmberg, I., Salzer-Morling, M. and Strannegard, L. (eds) (2002) *Stuck in the Future? Tracing the 'New Economy'*. Stockholm: Bookhouse.

Holmes, R. (2001) *Redcoat: The British Soldier in the Age of Horse and Musket*. London: Harper Collins.

Horvath, R.J. (1974) Machine space. *The Geographical Review*, LXIV (2): 166–87.

Hosoya, H. and Schaefer, M. (2001) Bit structures. In C.J. Chung, J. Inaba, R. Koolhaas and S.T. Leong (eds) *Harvard Design School Guide to Shopping*. Cologne: Taschen, 156–62.

Houlding, D. (1981) *Fit for Service*. Oxford: Oxford University Press.

Huczynski, A. (1993) *Management Gurus: What Makes Them and How to Become One*. London: Routledge.

Hugh, J.W. (2000) We're 70! *Fortune*, 13 March: 7–9.

Huston, J.A. (1966) *The Sinews of War: Army Logistics 1775–1953*. Washington, DC: United States Army.

Illinitch, A.Y., Lewin, A.Y. and D'Aveni, R. (eds) (1998) *Managing in Times of Disorder: Hypercompetitive Organizational Responses*. Thousand Oaks, CA: Sage.

Ingold, T. (1990) An anthropologist looks at biology. *Man*, NS25: 208–29.

Ingold, T. (1995a) Building, dwelling, living: how animals and people make themselves at home in the world. In M. Strathern (ed.) *Shifting Contexts: Transformations in Anthropological Knowledge*. London: Routledge, 57–80.

Ingold, T. (1995b) Man: the story so far. *Times Higher Education Supplement*, 2 June: 16–17.

Ingold, T. (2001) From complementarity to obviation: on dissolving the boundaries between sociology and biological anthropology, archaeology, and psychology. In S. Oyama, P.E. Griffiths and R.D. Gray (eds) *Cycles of Contingency: Developmental Systems and Evolution*. Cambridge, MA: MIT Press, 255–79.

Isard, W. (1996) *Commonalities in Art, Science and Religion*. London: Avebury.

Jackson, K. (1999) *Invisible Forms: A Guide to Literary Curiosities*. New York: St Martin's.

Jackson, T. (1997) Not all rubbish. *Financial Times*, 24 December: 14.

Jacques, M. (1994) Caste down. *Sunday Times*, Culture Supplement, 12 June: 8–10.

Jencks, C. (1996) *The Architecture of the Jumping Universe. A Polemic: How Complexity Science is Changing Architecture and Culture*, rev. edn. London: Academy.

Jernier, J., Knights, D. and Nord, W. (eds) (1994) *Resistance and Power in Organisations*. London: Routledge.

John, D.R. (1999) Consumer socialization of children: a retrospective look at twenty-five years of research. *Journal of Consumer Research*, 26: 183–217.

Johnson, C. (1993) *System and Writing in the Philosophy of Jacques Derrida*. Cambridge: Cambridge University Press.

Johnson, C. (1999) Ambient technologies, meaning signs. *Oxford Literary Review* 21: 117–34.

Johnson, S. (1997) *Interface Culture*. New York: Basic.

Johnson, S. (2001) *Emergence*. London: Allen Lane.

Jones, S. (1994) Demonology: some thoughts towards a science of chaos in recent British theatre. *Contemporary Theatre Review*, 11: 49–59.

Journal of Management Inquiry (1994) Special Issue on Chaos and Complexity, 3 (4).

Jowitt, K. (1992) *New World Disorder: The Leninist Extinction*. Berkeley, CA: University of California Press.

Kanter, R.M. (1992) *When Giants Learn to Dance: Mastering the Challenges of Strategy Management and Careers in the 1990s*. London: Business Press.

Kao, J. (1997) *Jamming*. Boston: Harvard Business School Press.

Kaplan, R.S. and Norton, D.P. (1996) *The Balanced Scorecard: Translating Strategy into Action*. Boston: Harvard Business School Press.

Katz, J. and Aakhus, M. (eds) (2002) *Perpetual Contact: Mobile Communication, Private Talk, Public Performance*. Cambridge: Cambridge University Press.

Kauffman, S. (1995) *At Home in the Universe: The Search for Laws of Complexity*. Oxford: Oxford University Press.

Kay, J. (1993) *Foundations of Corporate Success*. Oxford: Oxford University Press.

Kay, J. (1995) The foundations of national competitive advantage. Fifth ESRC Annual Lecture. London.

Kay, L. (2000) *Who Wrote the Book of Life? A History of the Genetic Code*. Stanford, CA: Stanford University Press.

Keeble, D., Bryson, J. and Wood, P.A. (1994) *Pathfinders of Enterprise*. Milton Keynes: School of Management, Open University.

Kellaway, L. (2000) *Sense and Nonsense in the Office*. London: Financial Times Books.

Kemp, S. (2000) Trade in education services and the impacts of barriers to trade. In C. Findlay and T. Warren (eds) *Impediments to Trade in Services: Measurement and Policy Implications*. London: Routledge, 231–44.

Kenney, M. (ed.) (2000) *Understanding Silicon Valley: The Anatomy of an Entrepreneurial Region*. Stanford, CA: Stanford University Press.

Kerfoot, D. and Knights, D. (1996) 'The best is yet to come?' The quest for embodiment in managerial work. In D. Collinson and J. Hearn (eds) *Men as Managers, Managers as Men: Critical Perspectives on Men, Masculinity and Management*. London: Sage, 78–98.

Kestelholn, W. (1996) Toolboxes are out; thinking is in. *Financial Times*, 22 March: 7–8.

Khalil, E.L. and Boulding, K.E. (eds) (1996) *Evolution, Complexity and Order*. London: Routledge.

Khiang, Tam K., Khalid, M. and Yusuf, R. (1996) Intelligent traffic lights control by fuzzy logic. *Malaysian Journal of Computer Science*, 9 (2–3).

Kittler, F.A. (1997) *Literature, Media, Information Systems*. Amsterdam: OPA.

Klein, N. (1999) *No Logo*. London, Flamingo.

Kleiner, A. (1996) *The Age of Heretics: Heroes, Outlaws and the Forerunners of Corporate Change*. New York: Doubleday.

Kline, S. (1993) *Out of the Garden: Toys and Children's Culture in the Age of TV Marketing*. London: Verso.

Knath, D. (1997) *The Art of Computer Programming*, two vols. San Francisco: Addison-Wesley.

Knights, D. and Murray, F. (1994) *Managers Divided: Organisation, Politics and Information Technology Management*. Chichester: Wiley.

Knights, D. and Willmott, H. (1999) *Management Lives: Power and Identity in Work Organisations*. London: Sage.

Knorr-Cetina, K. (1997) Sociality with objects: social relations in postsocial knowledge societies. *Theory, Culture and Society*, 14: 1–30.

Knorr-Cetina, K. (2001) How are global markets global? The architecture of a flow world. Paper presented at the Conference on Economics at Large, New York.

Knorr-Cetina, K. (2003) *Handbook of Social Theory*. London: Sage.

Kogut, B. and Bowman, E.H. (1996) Redesigning for the 21st century. *Financial Times*, 22 March: 13–14.

Kohanski, D. (1998) *The Philosophical Programmer: Reflections on the Moth in the Machine*. New York: St Martins.

Komisar, R. (2000) *The Monk and the Riddle: The Education of a Silicon Valley Entrepreneur*. Boston: Harvard Business School Press.

Kurtz, H. (2000) *The Fortune Tellers*. New York: Free.

Lakoff, G. (1987) *Women, Fire and Dangerous Things*. Chicago: Chicago University Press.

Lamont, M. (1992) *Money, Morals and Manners: The Culture of the French and American Upper Middle Class*. Chicago: University of Chicago Press.

Lanzera, G.F. and Patriotta, G. (2001) Technology and the courtroom: an inquiry into knowledge making in organisations. *Journal of Management Studies*, 38 (7): 943–72.

Lapham, L.B. (1999) *The Agony of Mammon*. London: Verso.

Lash, S. and Urry, J. (1994) *Economies of Signs and Spaces*. London: Sage.

Latham, A. (2002) Retheorizing the scale of globalization: topologies, actor networks and cosmopolitanism. In A. Herod and M.W. Wright (eds) *Geographies of Power: Placing Scale*. Malden, MA: Blackwell, 115–44.

Latham, R. (1996) Globalisation, market boundaries and the return of the sovereign repressed. Paper presented to the SSRC Conference on Sovereignty, Modernity and Security, Notre Dame, April.

Latour, B. (1986) Visualisation and cognition. In H. Kuclick (ed.) *Sociology of Knowledge: Studies in the Sociology of Culture Past and Present*, 6: 1–40.

Latour, B. (1987a) The enlightenment without the critique: a word on Michel Serres' philosophy. In A.P. Griffiths (ed.) *Contemporary French Philosophy*. Cambridge: Cambridge University Press, 83–97.

Latour, B. (1987b) *Science in Action: How to Follow Scientists and Engineers through Society*. Cambridge, MA: Harvard University Press.

Latour, B. (1988a) Opening one eye while closing the other: a note on some religious paintings. In G. Fyfe and T. Law (eds) *Picturing Power: Visual Depiction and Social Relations*. London: Routledge, 15–38.

Latour, B. (1988b) The politics of explanation: an alternative. In S. Woolgar (ed.) *Knowledge and Reflexivity*. London: Sage, 155–77.

Latour, B. (1991) Technology is society made durable. In J. Law (ed.) *A Sociology of Monsters*. London: Routledge, 103–32.

Latour, B. (1993) *We Have Never Been Modern*. Brighton: Harvester Wheatsheaf.

Latour, B. (1995) The manager as network. *Organizational Studies*, 6: 13–24.

Latour, B. (1997) Trains of thought: Piaget, Formalism and the Fifth Dimension. *Common Knowledge*, 6: 170–91.

Latour, B. (2002) Gabriel Tarde and the end of the social. In P. Joyce (ed.) *The Social in Question: New Bearings in History and the Social Sciences*. London: Routledge, 117–32.

Latour, B. and Hernant, E. (1997) *Paris: Ville Invisible*. Paris: Institut Synthelabo.

Laurel, B. (1993) *Computers as Theatre*. Boston: Addison-Wesley.

Laurier, E. and Philo, C. (2001) Accomplishing the company region with a car, mobile phone, cardboard cut-out, some carbon paper and a few boxes. Paper presented at the Annual Meeting of the Association of American Geographers, February–March.

Law, A. (1999) *Creative Company: How St Luke's Became the Ad Agency to End all Ad Agencies*. New York: Wiley.

Law, J. (1994) *Organising Modernity*. Oxford: Blackwell.

Law, J. (1997) Traduction/trahison. *Sociology*, 56: 1–20.

Law, J. and Mol, A. (1995) Notes on materiality and sociality. *Sociological Review*, 28: 274–94.

Law, J. and Mol, A. (1996) Decisions. Paper presented to the Centre for Social Theory and Technology Seminar, November.

Lazonick, W. and O'Sullivan, M. (2000) Maximising shareholder value: a new ideology for corporate governance. *Economy and Society*, 1: 13–35.

Lechte, J. (1999) The who and what of writing in the electronic age. *Oxford Literary Review*, 21: 135–60.

Lecourt, D. (2003) *Humain, Posthumain: La Technique et la Vie*. Paris: Presses Universitaires de France.

Lee Kuan Yew (2002) An entrepreneurial culture for Singapore. Address by Senior Minister Lee Kuan Yew at the Ho Rih Hwa Leadership in Asia Public Lecture, 5 February, Singapore.

Legge, K. (1994) On knowledge, business consultants, and the selling of TQM. Unpublished paper.

Leonard, D. and Rayport, J.F. (1997) Spark innovation through emphatic design. *Harvard Business Review*, November–December: 163–75.

Leonard, D. and Strauss, S. (1997) Putting your company's whole brain to work. *Harvard Business Review*, July–August.

Leonard, D. and Swap, J. (1999) *When Sparks Fly: Igniting Creativity in Groups*. Boston: Harvard Business School Press.

Leonard-Barton, D. (1995) *Wellsprings of Knowledge: Building and Sustaining the Sources of Innovation*. New Canaan, CT: Harvard Business School Press.

Leroi-Gourhan, A. (1993) *Gesture and Speech*. Cambridge, MA: MIT Press.

Lessig, L. (1999) *Code and Other Laws of Cyberspace*. New York: Basic.

Lester, R., Piore, M.J. and Malek, K.M. (1998) Interpretative management: what general managers can learn from design. *Harvard Business Review*, March–April.

Lévy, P. (1998) *Becoming Virtual: Reality in the Digital Age*. New York: Plenum.

Lewin, K. (1951) *Field Theory in Social Science*. New York: Harper.

Lewin, R. (1993) *Complexity: Life on the Edge of Chaos*. London: Dent.

Lewin, R. and Regine, B. (1999) *The Soul at Work: Unleashing the Power of Complexity for Business Success*. London: Orion.

Lewis, D. (1973) Causation. *Journal of Philosophy*, 70: 556–67. Reprinted in *Philosophical Papers, vol. II*. Oxford: Oxford University Press, 1986.

Lewis, M. (1999) *The New, New Thing: A Silicon Valley Story*. London: Hodder and Stoughton.

Lewis, M. (2001) His so-called life of stock fraud. *New York Times Magazine*, 25 February: 26–33, 46, 59, 66–7, 73.

Leyshon, A. and Thrift, N.J. (1997) *Money/Space: Geographies of Monetary Transformation*. London: Routledge.

Lieberman, H. and Selker, T. (2000) Out of context: computer systems that adapt to, and learn from, context. *IBM Systems Journal*, 39 (3/4).

Linde-Larssen, A. (1996) Small differences, large issues: the making and remaking of a national border. *South Atlantic Quarterly*, 19: 1123–43.

Ling, R. and Yttri, B. (2002) Nobody sits at home and waits for the telephone to ring: micro- and hyper-coordination through the use of the mobile telephone. In J. Katz and M. Aakhus (eds) *Perpetual Contact: Mobile Communication, Private Talk, Public Performance*. Cambridge: Cambridge University Press.

Lippitt, A. (2000) *Electric Animal: Toward a Rhetoric of Wildlife*. Minneapolis: University of Minnesota Press.

Livingston, I. (1997) *Arrow of Chaos: Romanticism and Postmodernity*. Minneapolis: University of Minnesota Press.

Livingstone, D. (1992) *The Geographical Tradition*. Oxford: Blackwell.

Locke, J. (1968/1693) *Some Thoughts Concerning Education*. Cambridge: Cambridge University Press.

Lohr, J. (2001) *Go To: Software Superheros from Fortran to the Internet Age*. New World: Basic.

London, S. (2003a) When is a magazine not a magazine? When it's HBR. *Financial Times*, 9 June.

London, S. (2003b) Why are the fads fading away? *Financial Times*, 12 June.

Lorenz, C. (1989) The rise and fall of business fads. *Financial Times*, 24 June: 24.

Lorenz, K. (1964) *Man Meets Dog*. Harmondsworth: Penguin.

Low, L. (ed.) (1999) *Singapore: Towards a Developed Status*. Singapore: Oxford University Press.

Lowe, A. and Schaffer, S. (eds) (2000) *N01se*. Cambridge: Kettle's Yard.

Lundvall, B.A. (ed.) (1992) *National Systems of Innovation: Towards a Theory of Innovation and Interactive Learning*. London: Pinter.

Lunenfeld, P. (ed.) (1999) *The Digital Dialectic: New Essays on New Media*. Cambridge, MA: MIT Press.

Lupton, E. (2002) *Skin: Surface, Substance, Design*. Princeton, NJ: Princeton Architectural Press.

Lury, C. (1999) Marking time with Nike: the illusion of the durable. *Public Culture*, 11: 499–526..

Lynch, K. (1966) *The Image of the City*. Cambridge, MA: MIT Press.

Lyne, J. (1996) Quantum mechanics, consistency and the art of rhetoric: a response to Krips. *Cultural Studies*, 10: 115–32.

Maasen, S. and Weingart, P. (2000) *Metaphors and the Dynamics of Knowledge*. London: Routledge.

Machover, T. (2000) Future art: by and for whom, and for what? *IBM Systems Journal*, 39 (3/4).

Mackenzie, A. (2002) *Transductions: Bodies and Machines at Speed*. London: Continuum.

Mackenzie, D. (1996) *Knowing Machines: Essays on Technical Change*. Cambridge, MA: MIT Press.

Mackinsey, K. (1989) *For Want of a Nail: The Impact on War of Logistics and Communications*. London: Brusseg.

Maira, A. and Scott-Morgan, P. (1996) *Accelerating Organization*. New York: McGraw-Hill.

Mandel, M.J. (2000) *The Coming Internet Depression*. New York: Perseus.

Mann, M. (1997) Has globalisation ended the rise and rise of the nation-state? *Review of International Political Economy*, 4: 472–96.

Mann, S. (1998) Wearable computing as means of personal empowerment. At http://wearcam.org/icwc-keynote.htm.

Manovich, L. (2001) *The Language of New Media*. Cambridge, MA: MIT Press.

Marcus, G. (ed.) (1998) *Corporate Futures: The Diffusion of the Culturally Sensitive Corporate Form*. Chicago: University of Chicago Press.

Mark, J.P. (1987) *The Empire Builders: Power, Money and Ethics inside the Harvard Business School*. New York: Morrow.

Marks, L.U. (2000) *The Skin of the Film: Intercultural Cinema, Embodiment and the Senses*. Durham, NC: Duke University Press.

Martin, E. (1994) *Flexible Bodies: The Role of Immunity in American Culture from the Days of Polio to the Age of Aids*. Boston: Beacon.

Martin, R. and Turner, D. (2000) Demutualizations and the remapping of financial landscapes. *Transactions of the Institute of British Geographers*, NS 25: 221–42.

Maslow, A.H. (1954) *Motivation and Personality*. New York: Harper.

Massey, D. (1995) Masculinity, dualisms and high technology. Transactions of the Institute of British Geographers, NS 20: 487–99.

Massey, D. (1997) Spatial disruptions. In S. Golding (ed.) *Eight Technologies of Otherness*. London: Routledge.

Massumi, B. (2002) *Parables for the Virtual: Movement, Affect, Sensation*. Durham, NC: Duke University Press.

Maturana, H. and Varela, F. (1992) *The Tree of Knowledge*. New York: Shambhala.

Mayo, E. (1995) Small ideas which are changing our way of banking. *New Economics*, December: 6–8.

McCarthy, A. (2001) *Ambient Television: Visual Culture and Public Space*. Durham, NC: Duke University Press.

McCullough, M. (1998) *A Digital Craft: The Practised Digital Hand*. Cambridge, MA: MIT Press.

McGregor, D. (1960) *The Human Side of Enterprise*. New York: McGraw-Hill.

McKee, V. (1999) Dramatic challenge to art of team building. *The Times*, 6 February: 26–7.

McKelvey, M. (2000) The economic dynamics of software: comparing Microsoft, Netscape and Linux. Industrial and Corporate Change, 11: 23–42.

McKenna, R. (1997) *Real Time: Preparing for the Age of the Never Satisfied Customer*. Boston, MA: Harvard Business School Press.

McKenzie, J. (2001) *Perform – Or Else: From Discipline to Performance*. New York: Routledge.

McNay, L. (1999) Subject, psyche and agency: the work of Judith Butler. *Theory, Culture and Society*, 16: 175–94.

McNeill, J. (1995) *Keeping Order in Time*. New York: Norton.

Menzel, P. and D'Aluisio, F. (2001) *Robo Sapiens: Evolution of a New Species*. Cambridge, MA: MIT Press.

Micklethwait, J. and Wooldridge, A. (1996) *The Witch Doctors: Making Sense of the Management Gurus*. London: Times Books.

Mieszkowski, K. (1998) Barbara Waugh. *Fast Company*, December: 146–54.

Miller, D. (1996) *Capitalism: An Ethnographic Approach*. Oxford: Berg.

Miller, D. (1998) *Shopping, Place, and Identity*. London: Routledge.

Miller, D., Jackson, P., Thrift, N., Holbrook, B. and Rowlands, M. (1998) *Shopping, Place and Identity*. London: Routledge.

Miller, P. and Rose, N. (1997) Mobilising the consumer: assembling the subject of consumption. *Theory, Culture and Society*, 14: 1–36.

Mintzberg, H. (1973) *The Nature of Managerial Work*. New York: Harper and Row.

Mirowski, P. (1994) *Natural Images in Economic Thought*. Cambridge: Cambridge University Press.

Mirowski, P. (2002) *Machine Dreams: Economics Becomes a Cyborg Science*. Cambridge: Cambridge University Press.

Mitchell, M. (1996) *An Introduction to Genetic Algorithms*. Cambridge, MA: MIT Press.

Mitchell, T. (2002) *Rule of Experts: Egypt, Techno-Politics, Modernity*. Berkeley, CA: University of California Press.

Mitchell, W.T.J. (1999) *E-Topia*. Cambridge, MA: MIT Press.

Miyazaki, H. (2003) The temporalities of the market. *American Anthropologist*, 105 (2): 255–65.

Miyazaki, H. and Riles, A. (2004) Failure as an endpoint. In A. Ong and S. Collins (eds) *Global Assemblages:Technology, Politics, and Ethics as Anthropological Problems*. Oxford: Blackwell.

Mokyr, J. (2001) *The Gifts of Athena: Historical Origins of the Knowledge Economy*. Princeton, NJ: Princeton University Press.

Molotch, H. (2003) *Where Stuff Comes From*. New York: Routledge.

Moody, G. (2001) *Rebel Code*. London: Allen Lane.

Morgan, G. (1986) *Images of Organisation*. London: Sage.

Morgan, G. (1993) *Imaginisation: The Art of Creative Management*. London: Sage.

Morris, M. (1988) Banality in cultural studies. *Discourse X*, 10: 2–29.

Morris, M. (1998) *Too Soon Too Late: History in Popular Culture*. Bloomington, IN: Indiana University Press.

Morson, G.S. (1994) *Narrative and Freedom: The Shadows of Time*. New Haven, CT: Yale University Press.

Muoio, A. (2000) Idea summit. *Fast Company*, 31: 150–94.

Nadel, J. and Butterworth, G. (eds) (1999) *Imitation in Infancy*. Cambridge: Cambridge University Press.

Nadesan, M.H. (2002) Engineering the entrepreneurial infant: brain science, infant development toys and governmentality. *Cultural Studies*, 16: 401–32.

Naisbitt, J. and Aburdene, P. (1990) *Megatrends 2000*. London: Pan.

Nardi, B.A. (1995) *A Small Matter of Programming: Perspectives on End User Computing*. Cambridge, MA: MIT Press.

Nardi, B.A. and O'Day V.L. (1999) *Information Ecologies: Using Technology with Heart*. Cambridge, MA: MIT Press.

Newman, S. (1998) Here, there and nowhere at all: distribution, negotiation and virtuality in postmodern ethnography and engineering. *Knowledge and Society*, 11: 235–67.

Nohria, N. and Berkley, J.D. (1994) The virtual organisation: bureaucracy, technology and the implosion of control. In C. Hecksher and A. Donnellon (eds) *The Post-Bureaucratic Organization: New Perspectives on Organizational Change*. Thousand Oaks, CA: Sage, 108–28.

Nolan, J. (1998) *The Therapeutic State*. New York: New York University Press.

Nolfi, S. and Floreano, D. (2002) *Evolutionary Robotics: The Biology, Intelligence and Technology of Self-Organizing Machines*. Cambridge, MA: MIT Press.

Nonaka, I. and Takeuchi, H. (1995) *The Knowledge-Creating Company: How Japanese Companies Create the Dynamics of Innovation*. Oxford: Oxford University Press.

Norman, D.A. (1998) *The Invisible Computer*. Cambridge, MA: MIT Press.

Norman, D.A. (2000) Making technology visible: a conversation with Don Norman. In D. Bergman (ed.) *Information Appliances and Beyond: Interaction Design for Consumer Products*. San Francisco: Morgan Kaufman, 9–26.

Norris, C. (1995) Versions of apocalypse: Kant, Derrida, Foucault. In M. Bull (ed.) *Apocalypse Theory and the Ends of the World*. Oxford: Blackwell, 227–49.

Norris, P. (2002) *Democratic Phoenix: Reinventing Political Activism*. Cambridge: Cambridge University Press.

Nowotny, H. (1994) *Time: The Modern and Postmodern Experience*. Cambridge: Polity.

O'Shea, J. and Madigan, C. (1997) *Dangerous Company: The Consulting Powerhouses and the Businesses they Save and Ruin*. London: Brealey.

Olds, K. (2001) *Globalization and Urban Change: Capital, Culture and Pacific Rim Mega-Projects*. Oxford: Oxford University Press.

Omojola, O., Post, E.R., Hancher, M.D., Maguire, Y., Pappu, R., Schoner, B., Russo, P.R., Fletcher, R. and Gershenfeld, N. (2000) An installation of interactive furniture. *IBM Systems Journal*, 39 (3/4).

O'Riain, S. (2000) Net-working for a living: Irish software developers in the global workplace. In M. Burawoy et al. (eds) *Global Ethnography: Forces, Connections and Imaginations in a Postmodern World*. Berkeley, CA: University of California Press, 175–202.

Orr, J.E. (1996) *Talking About Machines: An Ethnography of a Modern Job*. Ithaca, NY: Cornell University Press.

Osborne, P. (1995) *The Politics of Time*. London: Verso.

Osborne, T. (2003) Creativity: a philistine rant. *Economy and Society*, 32.

Osborne, T. and Rose, N. (1997) In the name of society, or three theses on the history of social thought. *History of the Human Sciences*, 10: 87–104.

Owen, J.J. (1996) Chaos theory, Marxism and literature. *New Formations*, 29: 84–112.

Oyama, S. (2001) *The Ontogeny of Information*, 2nd edn. Princeton, NJ: Princeton University Press.

Pahl, R. (1995) *After Success: Fin-de-Siècle Identity and Anxiety*. Cambridge: Polity.

Papert, S. (2000) What's the big idea? Toward a pedagogy of idea power. *IBM Systems Journal*, 39 (3/4).

Paradiso, J.A., Hsiao, K., Benbasat, A.Y. and Teegarden, Z. (2000) Design and implementation of expressive footwear. *IBM Systems Journal*, 30 (3/4).

Parry, G. (1995) *The Trophies of Time*. Oxford: Oxford University Press.

Pascale, T. (1991) *Managing on the Edge*. Harmondsworth: Penguin.

Peat, D. (1994) *Blackfoot Physics*. London: Fourth Estate.

Pellegram, A. (1997) The message in paper. In D. Miller (ed.) *Material Cultures: Why Some Things Matter*. London: UCL Press, 103–20.

Pentland, A. (2000) It's alive. *IBM Systems Journal*, 39 (3/4).

Perez, C. (1985) Microelectronics, long waves, and world structural change. *World Development*, 13: 441–63.

Perlow, L.A. (1997) *Finding Time*. Ithaca, NY: Cornell University Press.

Perniola, M. (1995) *Enigmas: The Egyptian Movement in Society and Art*. London: Verso.

Perry, M., O'Hara, K., Sellen, A., Brown, B. and Harper, R. (2001) Dealing with mobility: understanding access anytime, anywhere. ACM Transactions in Human–Computer Interaction, 8 (4): 323–47.

Pesce, M. (2000) *The Playful World: How Technology is Transforming our Imagination*. New York: Ballatine.

Peters, T. (2001) True confessions. *Fast Company*, no. 53: 78.

Peters, T. and Waterman, R. (1982) *In Search of Excellence*. New York: Warner.

Petitot, J., Varela, F.J., Pachoud, B. and Roy, J. (ed.) (1999) *Naturalizing Phenomenology: Issues in Contemporary Phenomenology and Cognitive Science*. Stanford, CA: Stanford University Press.

Petroski, H. (1992) *The Pencil*. New York: Knopf.

Pettigrew, A. and Fenton, E.M. (eds) (2000) *The Innovating Organization*. London: Sage.

Pfeffer, J. (1992) *After Power*. New Canaan, CT: Harvard Business School Press.

Pfeffer, J. and Salancik, G.R. (1978) *The External Control of Organizations*. New York: Harper and Row.

Phelan, P. (1993) *Unmarked*. New York: Routledge.

Phillips, N. (1997) *Reality Hacking*. London: Heinemann.

Picard, R.W. (1997) *Affective Computing*. Cambridge, MA: MIT Press.

Picard, R.W. (2000) Towards computers that recognise and respond to user emotion. *IBM Systems Journal*, 39 (3/4).

Pine, B.J. and Gilmore, J.H. (1999) *The Experience Economy: Work Is Theatre and Every Business a Stage*. Boston: Harvard Business School Press.

Pinhanez, C.S., Davis, J.W., Intille, S., Johnson, M.P., Wilson, A.D., Bobick, A.F. and Blumberg, B. (2000) Physically interactive story environments. *IBM Systems Journal*, 39 (3/4).

Pink, P.H. (1999) What's your story? *Fast Company*, January: 32–4.

Plant, S. (1996) The virtual complexity of culture. In G. Robertson, M. Mash, L. Tickner, J. Bird, B. Curtis and T. Putman (eds) *Future Natural: Nature/Science/Culture*. London: Routledge, 203–17.

Plumwood, V. (2002) *Environmental Culture: The Ecological Crisis of Reason*. London: Routledge.

Plutowski, M. (2000) Emotional computing. At www.emotivate.com/Book/intro.html, accessed 1 February 2001.

Polanyi, M. (1958) *Personal Knowledge: Towards a Post Critical Philosophy*. London: Routledge and Kegan Paul.

Polanyi, M. (1967) *The Tacit Dimension*. London: Routledge and Kegan Paul.

Porter, T.M. (1995) *Trust in Numbers: The Pursuit of Objectivity in Science and Public Life*. Princeton, NJ: Princeton University Press.

Post, E.R., Orth, M., Russo, P.R. and Gershenfeld, N. (2000) E-broidery: design and fabrication of textile-based computing. *IBM Systems Journal*, 39 (3/4).

Power, M. (1997) *The Audit Society: Rituals of Verification*. Oxford: Oxford University Press.

Pratt, A. (2000) New media, the new economy and new spaces. *Geoforum*, 31: 425–36.

Purser, R. (2000) The coming crisis in real-time environments: a dromological analysis. At online.sfsu.edu/~rpurser/revised/pages/DROMOLOGY.htm.

Putnam, H. (1981) *Reason, Truth, and History*. Cambridge: Cambridge University Press.

Quah, D. (1997) The weightless economy. *Bank of England Quarterly Bulletin*, 37 (1): 49–56.

Rabinow, P. (1995) *Making PCR: A Story of Biotechnology*. Chicago: University of Chicago Press.

Rabinow, P. (1996) *Essays on the Anthropology of Reason*. Princeton, NJ: Princeton University Press.

Ramsay, H. (1996) Managing sceptically: a critique of organizational fashion. In S. Clegg and G. Palmer (eds) *The Politics of Management Knowledge*. London: Sage, 155–72.

Ranadive, V. (1999) *The Power of Now*. New York: McGraw-Hill.

Ransdell, E. (2000) The Nike story? Just tell it. *Fast Company*, no. 31: 44–52.

Rasch, W. and Wolfe, C. (eds) (2000) *Observing Complexity: Systems Theory and Postmodernity*. Minneapolis: University of Minnesota Press.

Rasiel, E.M. (1999) *The McKinsey Way*. New York: McGraw-Hill.

Ray, T. (1991) An approach to the synthesis of life. In C. Langton, C. Taylor, J. D. Farmer and S. Rasmussen (eds) *Artificial Life II: Santa Fe Studies in the Sciences of Complexity, vol. XI*. Redwood City, CA: Addison-Wesley, 371–408.

Readings, B. (1996) *The University of Ruins*. Cambridge, MA: Harvard University Press.

Redfield, J. (1994) *The Celestine Prophecy*. London: Bantam.

Reich, R. (2000) It's the year 2000 economy, stupid. *The American Prospect Online*, 29 November.

Remnick, D. (ed.) (2000) *The New Gilded Age*. New York: Random House.

Resnick, M. (2000) It's not just information. *IBM Systems Journal*, 39 (3/4).

Rheingold, H. (2002) *Smart Mobs: The Next Social Revolution*. Cambridge, MA: Perseus.

Rhind, D. (1992) *Postcode Geography*. London: Methuen.

Rhind, G. (1999) *Global Sourcebook of Address Data Management*. London: Gower.

Richardson, M. and Wildman, W.J. (eds) (1997) Religion and Science: History, Method and Dialogue. London: Routledge.

Rifkin, G. (1996) Finding meaning at work. *Strategy and Business*, 5.

Rifkin, J. (2000) *The Age of Access*. London: Tarcher/Putnam.

Ritvo, H. (1987) *The Animal Estate: The English and Other Creatures in the Victorian Age*. Cambridge, MA: Harvard University Press.

Roberts, R. (1994) Power and empowerment: New Age managers and the dialectics of modernity/postmodernity. *Religion Today*, 9: 3–13.

Roberts, S. (2002) Global strategic vision: managing the world. In R. Perry and B. Maurer (eds) *Globalization and Governmentalities*. Minneapolis: University of Minnesota Press.

Roberts, W. and Ross, B. (1995) *Make it So. Leadership Lessons from Star Trek: The Next Generation*. New York: Simon and Schuster.

Romer, P. (1990) Endogenous technological change. *Journal of Political Economy*, 98: S71–S102.

Roos, J. and von Krogh, G. (1995) *Organisational Epistemology*. London: Macmillan.

Roos, J. and von Krogh, G. (1996) *Managing Knowledge: Perspectives on Cooperation and Competition*. London: Sage.

Rose, N. (1996) *Inventing Our Selves: Psychology, Power and Personhood*. Cambridge: Cambridge University Press.

Rose, N. (1999) *Powers of Freedom: Reframing Political Thought*. Cambridge: Cambridge University Press.

Rothfels, N. (ed.) (2002) *Representing Animals*. Bloomington, IN: Indiana University Press.

Rowan, D. (2003) M&S faces righteous wrath over spy in a suit. *The Times*, 23 August: 5.

Roy, J., Petitot, J., Pachoud, B. and Varela, F.J. (1999) Beyond the gap: an introduction to natural-ising phenomenology. In J. Petitot et al. (eds) *Naturalising Phenomenology: Issues in Contemporary Phenomenology and Cognitive Science*. Stanford, CA: Stanford University Press, 1–82.

Rubin, H. (1999) The power of words. *Fast Company*, January: 142–51.

Rupert, G. (1992) Employing the New Age: training seminars. In J. Lewis and J.J.G. Melton (eds) *Perspectives on the New Age*. Albany, NY: State University of New York Press, 127–35.

Ruspini, E.H., Bonissone, P.P. and Pedrycz, W. (1998) (eds) *Handbook of Fuzzy Computation*. Bristol: Institute of Physics Publishing.

Russell, R. and Tyler, M. (2002) Thank heaven for little girls: Girl Heaven and the commercial context of feminine childhood. *Sociology*, 36: 619–37.

Rybczynski, W. (2000) *One Good Turn: A Natural History of the Screwdriver and the Screw*. New York: Simon and Schuster.

Sampson, A. (1995) *Company Man: The Rise and Fall of Corporate Life*. London: Harper Collins.

Santa Fe Center for Emergent Strategies (1997) Seminar announcement. At http://www.santa-strategy.com.

Sassen, S. (2001) *The Global City: New York, London, Tokyo*, 2nd edn. Princeton, NJ: Princeton University Press.

Scase, R. (1999) *Towards the Virtual Corporation and Beyond: Trends and Changes in Mobile Working*. Reading: Oracle.

Scase, R. and Goffee, R. (1989) *Reluctant Managers*. London: Unwin Hyman.

Schaffer, S. (1996) Babbage's dancer and the impressions of mechanism. In F. Spufford and J. Uglow (eds) *Cultural Babbage: Technology, Time and Invention*. London: Faber and Faber, 53–80.

Schien, E. (1996) *Strategic Pragmatism: The Culture of Singapore's Economic Development Board*. Cambridge, MA: MIT Press.

Schor, J. (1993) *The Overworked American*. New York: Basic.

Schrage, M. (2000) *Serious Play: How the World's Best Companies Stimulate to Innovate*. Boston: Harvard Business School Press.

Schulz, R., Hatch, M.J. and Larsen, M.H. (eds) (2000) *The Expressive Organization*. Oxford: Oxford University Press.

Schwartz, H. (1997) *The Culture of the Copy*. New York: Zone.

Sedgwick, E.K. (2003) *Touching Feeling: Affect, Pedagogy, Performativity*. Durham, NC: Duke University Press.

Seely Brown, J. (ed.) (1997) *Seeing Differently: Insights on Innovation*. New York: Harvard Business School Press.

Sellen, A.J. and Harper, R.H.R. (2002) *The Myth of the Paperless Office*. Cambridge, MA: MIT Press.

Senge, P. (1990) *The Fifth Discipline.* New York: Domesday.

Senge, P., Kleiner, A., Roberts, R., Roth, G. and Smith, B. (1999) *The Dance of Change: The Challenges of Sustaining Momentum in Learning Organizations.* London: Brealey.

Sennett, R. (1998) *The Corrosion of Character: The Personal Consequences of Work in the New Capitalism.* New York: Norton.

Serres, M. (1982) *Hermes: Literature, Science, Philosophy.* Baltimore, MD: Johns Hopkins University Press.

Serres, M. (1995a) *Genesis.* Ann Arbor, MI: University of Michigan Press.

Serres, M. (1995b) *Angels: A Modern Myth.* Paris: Flammarion.

Shapin, S. (1998) *Science Incarnate.* Chicago: University of Chicago Press.

Shapiro, E. (1995) *Fad Surfing in the Boardroom,* San Francisco: Addison-Wesley.

Shiller, R.J. (2000) *Irrational Exuberance.* Princeton, NJ: Princeton University Press.

Shneiderman, B. (2002) *Leonardo's Laptop: Human Needs and the New Computing Technologies.* Cambridge, MA: MIT Press.

Siegert, B. (1999) *Relays: Literature as an Epoch of the Postal System.* Stanford, CA: Stanford University Press.

Simon, H. (1981) *The Sciences of the Artificial,* rev. edn. Cambridge, MA: MIT Press.

Simondon, G. (1958/1989) *Du Mode d'Existence des Objets Techniques.* Paris: Aubier.

Simondon, G. (1992) The genesis of the individual. In J. Crary and S. Kwinter (eds) *Incorporations 6.* New York: Zone, 296–319.

Sipper, M. (2000) A Brief Introduction to Genetic Algorithms. At http://lslwww.epfl.ch/~moshes/ga_main.html.

Sipper, M. (2002) *Machine Nature: The Coming Age of Bio-Inspired Computing.* New York: McGraw-Hill.

Skapinker, R. (2000) Meet the new boss. *Financial Times,* 20 November: 23.

Sparacino, F., Davenport, G. and Pentland, A. (2000) Media in performance: interactive spaces for dance, theatre, circus, and museum exhibits. *IBM Systems Journal,* 39 (3/4).

Spinosa, C., Flores, F. and Dreyfus, H. (1997) *Disclosing New Worlds: Entrepreneurship, Democratic Action, and the Cultivation of Solidarity.* Cambridge, MA: MIT Press.

Spivak, G.C. (1993) *Outside in the Teaching Machine.* New York: Routledge.

Spufford, F. (1996) The difference engine and the difference engine. In F. Spufford and J. Uglow (eds) *Cultural Babbage: Technology, Time and Invention.* London: Faber and Faber, 266–90.

Spufford, F. and Uglow, J. (eds) (1996) *Cultural Babbage: Technology, Time and Invention.* London: Faber and Faber.

Stafford, B.M. (1992) *Body Criticism: Imagining the Unseen in Enlightenment Art and Medicine.* Cambridge, MA: MIT Press.

Stafford, B.M. (1994) *Artful Science: Enlightenment Entertainment and the Eclipse of Visual Education.* Cambridge, MA: MIT Press.

Stafford, B.M. (1996) *Good Looking: Essays on the Virtue of Images.* Cambridge, MA: MIT Press.

Stafford, B.M. and Terpak, B. (2001) *Devices of Wonder: From the World in a Box to Images on a Screen.* Los Angeles: Getty Research Institute.

Star, S.L. (1989) The structure of ill-structured solutions: boundary objects and heterogeneous distributed problem solving. In L. Gasser and N. Huhn (eds) *Distributed Artificial Intelligence.* New York: Morgan Kauffman, 37–54.

Steiner, M. and White, J. (2000) Training the ASDA way. *Sunday Times,* 16 March: B1–B2.

Stengers, I. (1997) *Power and Invention: Situating Science.* Minneapolis: University of Minnesota Press.

Sternberg, R.J. (1997) *Thinking Styles.* Cambridge: Cambridge University Press.

Stewart, N. (1976) *Contrasts in Management: A Study of Different Types of Manager.* London: McGraw-Hill.

Stewart, T.A. (1997) *Intellectual Capital: The New Wealth of Organisations.* London: Brealey.

Stiegler, B. (1998) *Technics and Time 1: The Fault of Epimetheus*. Stanford, CA: Stanford University Press.

Stiglitz, J.E. (1994) *Whither Socialism?* Cambridge, MA: MIT Press.

Stopford, J. (1996) Managing in turbulent times. *Financial Times*, 22 March: 5–6.

Strathern, M. (1995a) Foreword. In M. Strathern (ed.) *Shifting Contexts: Transformations in Anthropological Knowledge*. London: Routledge, 1–11.

Strathern, M. (1995b) Afterword. In M. Strathern (ed.) *Shifting Contexts: Transformations in Anthropological Knowledge*. London: Routledge, 177–85.

Strathern, M. (1996) The new modernities. In J. Wassman and V. Keck (eds) *Common Worlds and Single Lives: Constituting Knowledge in Pacific Societies*. Oxford: Berg.

Strathern, M. (1997) Cutting the network. *Journal of the Royal Anthropological Institute*, 2: 517–35.

Strathern, M. (1999) *Property, Substance and Effect*. London: Athlone.

Suchman, L. (1987) *Plans and Situated Actions: The Problem of Human–Machine Communications*. Cambridge: Cambridge University Press.

Suchman, L. (2001) Human/machine reconsidered. Department of Sociology, University of Lancaster. At http://www.comp.lancs.ac.uk/sociology/soc04015.htm.

Sunquist, M. and Sunquist, F. (2002) *Wild Cats of the World*. Chicago: University of Chicago Press.

Sutton-Smith, B. (1986) *Toys as Culture*. New York: Gardner.

Taylor, M.C. (2001) *The Moment of Complexity: Emerging Network Culture*. Chicago: University of Chicago Press.

Temple, J. (2002) The assessment: the new economy. *Oxford Review of Economic Policy*, 18 (3): 241–64.

Ten Bos, R. (2000) *Fashion and Utopia in Management Thinking*. Amsterdam: Benjamins.

Tenhaaf, N. (1996) Mysteries of the bioapparatus. In M.A. Moser and D. McLeod (eds) *Immersed in Technology: Art in Virtual Environments*. Cambridge, MA: MIT Press, 51–71.

Thomas, P.J. (ed.) (1995) *The Social and Interactional Dimensions of Human–Computer Interfaces*. Cambridge: Cambridge University Press.

Thompson, J. (1991) *The Lifeblood of War: Logistics in Armed Conflict*. London: Brassey.

Thrift, N.J. (1985) Flies and germs: a geography of knowledge. In D. Gregory and J. Urry (eds) *Social Relations and Spatial Structures*. London: Macmillan.

Thrift, N.J. (1991) For a new regional geography 2. *Progress in Human Geography*, 15: 456–66.

Thrift, N.J. (1995) A hyperactive world? In R.J. Johnston, P. Taylor and M. Watts (eds) *Geographies of Global Change*. Oxford: Blackwell, 18–35.

Thrift, N.J. (1996a) *Spatial Formations*. London: Sage.

Thrift, N.J. (1996b) Shut up and dance, or, is the world economy knowable? In P.W. Daniels and W. Lever (eds) *The Global Economy in Transition*. London: Longman, 11–23.

Thrift, N.J. (1996c) New urban eras and old technological fears: reconfiguring the goodwill of electronic things. *Urban Studies*, 33: 1463–93.

Thrift, N.J. (1997a) The rise of soft capitalism. *Cultural Values*, 1: 29–57.

Thrift, N.J. (1997b) The rise of soft capitalism. In A. Herod, G. O Tuathail and S. Roberts (eds) *Unruly World: Globalisation, Governance and Geography*. London: Routledge, 25–71.

Thrift, N.J. (1999a) Virtual capitalism: some proposals. In J. Carrier and D. Miller (eds) *Virtualism: The New Political Economy*. Oxford: Berg, 161–86.

Thrift, N.J. (1999b) The place of complexity. *Theory, Culture and Society*, 16: 31–70.

Thrift, N.J. (2000a) Afterwords. *Environment and Planning D: Society and Space*, 18: 213–55.

Thrift, N.J. (2000b) Performing cultures in the new economy. *Annals of the Association of American Geographers*, 90: 674–92.

Thrift, N.J. (2000c) Still life in nearly present time: the object of nature. *Body and Society*, 6: 34–57.

Thrift, N.J. (2000d) Spaces of everyday life in the city. In G. Bridge and S. Watson (eds) *The Urban Companion*. Oxford: Blackwell.

Thrift, N.J. (2001a) Elsewhere. In N. Cummings and M. Lewandowska (eds) *Capital*. London: Tate Modern.

Thrift, N.J. (2001b) New per-forms of the commodity. Paper presented at the Annual Conference of the Association of American Geographers, New York, March.

Thrift, N.J. (2001c) 'It's the romance, not the finance, that makes the business worth pursuing': disclosing a new market culture. *Economy and Society*, 30 (November): 412–32.

Thrift, N.J. (2002) Think and act like revolutionaries: episodes from the global triumph of management discourse. *Critical Quarterly*, 44: 19–26.

Thrift, N.J. (2003a) Bare life. In H. Thomas and J. Ahmed (eds) *Cultural Bodies*. Oxford: Blackwell.

Thrift, N.J. (2003b) Closer to the machine? Intelligent environments, new forms of possession and the rise of the supertoy. *Cultural Geographies*, 10: 389–407.

Thrift, N.J. (2003c) Remembering the technological unconscious by foregrounding knowledges of position. *Environment and Planning D: Society and Space*, 22: 175–90.

Thrift, N.J. (2004) Investigating the field. In M. Pryke and S.J. Whatmore (eds) *Thinking Through Research*. London: Sage.

Thrift, N.J. and French, S. (2002) The automatic production of space. *Transactions of the Institute of British Geographers*, NS 27: 309–35.

Thrift, N.J. and Olds, K. (1996) Refiguring the economic in economic geography. *Progress in Human Geography*, 20 (3): 311–37.

Tomkins, R. (2000) A virtual investment. *Financial Times*, 5 December: 26.

Tort, P. (1989) *La Raison Classificatoire: Quinze Etudes*. Paris: Ambier.

Townsend, A. (2000) Life in the real-time city: mobile telephones and urban metabolism. *Journal of Urban Technology*, 7: 85–104.

Tuan, Yi-Fu (1984) *Dominance and Affection: The Making of Pets*. New Haven, CT: Yale University Press.

Turkle, S. (1991) Romantic reactions: paradoxical responses to the computer presence. In J.J. Sheehan and M. Sosna (eds) *Boundaries of Humanity: Humans, Animals, Machines*. Berkeley, CA: University of California Press.

Turkle, S. (1996) *Life on the Screen: Identity in the Age of the Internet*. London: Weidenfeld and Nicolson.

Turner, B. and Rojek, C. (2001) *Society and Culture*. London: Sage.

Turner, F. (1997) Chaos and social science. In R.A. Eve, S. Horsfall and M.E. Lee (eds) *Chaos, Complexity and Sociology: Myths, Models and Theories*. Thousand Oaks, CA: Sage, xi–xxxii.

Turner, J.S. (2000) *The Extended Organism: The Physiology of Animal-Built Structures*. Cambridge, MA: Harvard University Press.

Ullman, E. (1997) *Close to the Machine: Technophilia and Its Discontents*. San Francisco: City Lights.

Ulmer, G. (1989) *Teletheory*. London: Routledge.

Urry, J. (1994) Time, leisure and social identity. *Time and Society*, 3: 131–50.

Urry, J. (2003) *Global Complexity*. Cambridge: Polity.

Van der Pijl, K. (1994) The cadre class and public multilateralism. In Y. Sakamoto (ed.) *Global Transformation: Challenges to the State System*. Tokyo: United Nations University Press, 200–49.

Van de Vliet, A. (1997) The balanced scorecard. *Management Today*, September: 22–3.

Vann, K. and Bowker, G. (2001) Instrumentalizing the truth of practice. *Social Epistemology*, 15 (3): 247–62.

Varela, F. (2000) *Ethical Know-How*. Stanford, CA: Stanford University Press.

Vidler, A. (2000) *Warped Space*. Cambridge, MA: MIT Press.

Von Krogh, G. and Roos, J. (1995) *Organizational Epistemology*. Basingstoke: Macmillan.

Von Krogh, G., Roos, J. and Kleine, D. (eds) (1998) *Knowing in Firms: Understanding, Managing and Measuring Knowledge*. London: Sage.

Von Neumann, J. (1945) First Draft of a Report on the EDVAC. Contract W-670-ORD-4926, US Army Ordnance Department and University of Pennsylvania. Moore School of Electrical Engineering, University of Pennsylvania, 30 June 1945.

Waddington, C.H. (1977) *Tools for Thought*. London: Allen Lane.

Wajcman, J. (1998) *Managing Like a Man*. Cambridge: Polity.

Waldrop, M.M. (1993) *Complexity*. New York: Viking.

Wall, L., Christiansen, T. and Orwent, J. (2000) *Programming Perl*. Sebastopol, CA: O'Reilly.

Walter, W. (1950) An imitation of artificial life. *Scientific American*.

Walter, W. (1953) *The Living Brain*. London: Penguin.

Ward, M. (1999) *Virtual Organisms: The Startling World of Artificial Life*. London: Pan.

Watts, D. (1999) *Small Worlds: The Dynamics of Order and Randomness*. Princeton, NJ: Princeton University Press.

Watts, D. (2003) *Six Degrees*. London: Heinemann.

Weick, K.E. (2001) *Making Sense of the Organization*. Oxford: Blackwell.

Weiser, M., Gold, R. and Brown, J.S. (1999) The origins of ubiquitous computing research at PARC in the late 1980s. *IBM Systems Journal*, 38 (4).

Weiss, B. (1996) *The Making and Unmaking of the Haya Lived World*. Durham, NC: Duke University Press.

Wells, P. (1998) *Understanding Animation*. London: Routledge.

Wenger, E. (1999) *Communities of Practice: Learning, Meaning and Identity*. Cambridge: Cambridge University Press.

Wenger, E., McDermott, R. and Snyder, P. (2002) *Cultivating Communities of Practice*. Boston: Harvard Business School Press.

Whatmore, S. (2002) *Hybrid Geographies*. London: Sage.

Wheatley, M.J. (1994) *Leadership and the New Science: Learning About Organization from an Ordinary Universe*. San Francisco: Berrett-Koehler.

Whyte, W.H. (1957) *The Organization Man*. New York: Doubleday Anchor.

Wilden, A. (1968) *The Language of the Self: The Function of Language in Psychoanalysis by Jacques Lacan. Trans. with notes and commentary by Anthony Wilden*. Baltimore: Johns Hopkins University Press.

Williams, K. (2000) From shareholder value to present-day capitalism. *Economy and Society*, 29: 1–12.

Williams, K. (2001) Trajectories of inequality. *Review of International Political Economy*, 8: 1–6.

Williams, R. (1978) *Marxism and Literature*. Oxford: Oxford University Press.

Williams, R. (1991) *Notes on the Underground*. Cambridge, MA: MIT Press.

Willman, J. (1999) Knowledge swap-shop. *Financial Times*, 22 January.

Wilson, A.G. (1994) *Modelling the City*. London: Routledge.

Winograd, T. and Flores, F. (1987) *Understanding Computers and Cognition: A New Foundation for Design*. Reading, MA: Addison-Wesley.

Winograd, T. (ed.) (1996) *Bringing Design to Software*. Reading, MA: Addison-Wesley.

Wittgenstein, L. (1978) *Remarks on the Philosophy of Mathematics*. Oxford: Oxford University Press.

Wolfe, C. (2003a) *Animal Rites: American Culture, the Discourse of Species and Posthumanism*. Chicago: Chicago University Press.

Wolfe, C. (2003b) *Zoontologies: The Question of the Animal*. Minneapolis: University of Minnesota Press.

Wood, J. (ed.) (1998) *The Virtual Embodied: Presence/Practice/Technology*. London: Routledge.

Wooldridge, A. (1995) Big is back: a survey of multinationals. *The Economist*, 24 June: 1–22.

Wooldridge, A. (1997) Trimming the fat: a survey of management consultancy. *The Economist*, 22 March.

Woolgar, S. (1991) Configuring the user: the case of usability trials. In J. Law (ed.) *A Sociology of Monsters: Essays on Power, Technology and Domination*. London: Routledge, 58–97.

Worthington, J. (ed.) (1996) *Reinventing the Work Place*. London: Butterworth Heinemann.

Wright, R. (1996) Art and science in chaos: contested readings of scientific visualisation. In G. Robertson, M. Mash, L. Tickner, J. Bird, B. Curtis and T. Putman (eds) *Future Natural: Nature, Science, Culture*. London: Routledge, 218–36.

Yates, J. (1994) Evolving information use in firms, 1850–1920: ideology and information techniques and technologies. In L. Bud-Frierman (ed.) *Information Acumen: The Understanding and Use of Knowledge in Modern Business*. London: Routledge, 26–50.

Yates, J. and Orlikowski, W.J. (1992) Genres of organisational communication. *Academy of Management Review*, 17: 299–326.

Zadeh, L.A. (1994) What is BISC? At http.cs.berkeley.edu/projects/Bisc/bisc.welcome.html.

Zentall, T. and Galef, B. (ed.) (1988) *Social Learning: Psychological and Biological Perspectives*. Hillsdale, NJ: Erlbaum.

Zentall, T. (2001) Imitation in animals: evidence, function and mechanisms. *Cybernetics and Systems*, 32: 53–96.

Zohar, D. (1990) *The Quantum Self*. London: Harper Collins.

Zohar, D. (1997) *Rewiring the Corporate Brain: Using the New Science to Rethink How We Structure and Lead Organizations*. San Francisco: Berret-Koehler.

Index